# PROPERTY RIGHTS

 THE INDEPENDENT INSTITUTE is a non-profit, non-partisan, scholarly research and educational organization that sponsors comprehensive studies in political economy. Our mission is to boldly advance peaceful, prosperous, and free societies, grounded in a commitment to human worth and dignity.

Politicized decision-making in society has confined public debate to a narrow reconsideration of existing policies. Given the prevailing influence of partisan interests, little social innovation has occurred. In order to understand both the nature of and possible solutions to major public issues, the Independent Institute adheres to the highest standards of independent inquiry, regardless of political or social biases and conventions. The resulting studies are widely distributed as books and other publications, and are debated in numerous conference and media programs. Through this uncommon depth and clarity, the Independent Institute is redefining public debate and fostering new and effective directions for government reform.

# PROPERTY RIGHTS

## EMINENT DOMAIN AND REGULATORY TAKINGS RE-EXAMINED

*Edited by*
*Bruce L. Benson*

Published in cooperation with The Independent Institute

Cover image: © iStockphoto.com/Kevin Russ; iStockphoto.com/Soubrette.
Front cover design by Christopher Chambers.

First published in 2010 by
PALGRAVE MACMILLAN®
in the United States—a division of St. Martin's Press LLC,
175 Fifth Avenue, New York, NY 10010.

Where this book is distributed in the UK, Europe and the rest of the world,
this is by Palgrave Macmillan, a division of Macmillan Publishers Limited,
registered in England, company number 785998, of Houndmills,
Basingstoke, Hampshire RG21 6XS.

Palgrave Macmillan is the global academic imprint of the above companies
and has companies and representatives throughout the world.

Palgrave® and Macmillan® are registered trademarks in the United States,
the United Kingdom, Europe and other countries.

ISBN: 978–0–230–10247–7

Library of Congress Cataloging-in-Publication Data

    Property rights : eminent domain and regulatory takings re-examined /
Bruce L. Benson.
      p. cm.
    Includes bibliographical references and index.
    ISBN 978–0–230–10246–0
      1. Eminent domain—United States. 2. Right of property—United
States. I. Benson, Bruce L.

KF5599.P76 2010
343.73'0252—dc22                                          2009040634

A catalogue record of the book is available from the British Library.

Design by Newgen Imaging Systems (P) Ltd., Chennai, India.

First edition: June 2010

10 9 8 7 6 5 4 3 2 1

Printed in the United States of America.

# CONTENTS

# Figures and Tables

## Figures

## Tables

# Acknowledgments

I am very grateful to the DeVoe L. Moore Center in the College of Social Science and Public Policy at Florida State University and the Center's director, Professor Keith Ihlanfeldt, for funding and sponsoring a conference at Florida State so the authors of the papers in this book could come together, present their papers, and receive comments and suggestions from each other as well as a number of discussants and attendees. I also thank the Program in Law, Economics, and Business, College of Law, Florida State University for hosting the conference, as well as the Independent Institute, especially David J. Theroux, President, and Alexander Tabarrok, Research Director, for agreeing to sponsor the book itself and to find a publisher for it. Judy Kirk did an excellent job in making all of the arrangements for the conference and making sure that everything ran smoothly, and Tom Mayock's assistance during the conference was also very helpful. The individuals who volunteered to serve as formal discussants of the papers at the conference have my gratitude, including contributing authors Richard Stroup, Perry Shapiro, Wallace Kaufman, Thomas Means, Christopher Coyne, Steven Eagle, Edward Stringham, and Sam Staley, as well as Florida State University faculty members Randy Holcombe (Economics), Ron Cheung (Economics), J.B. Ruhl (Law), and Charles Barrilleaux (Political Science). Finally, I thank the authors for an excellent set of papers.

Bruce L. Benson

# 1

## INTRODUCTION

## EMINENT DOMAIN, REGULATION, AND THE TAKINGS BACKLASH

### *Bruce L. Benson*

The first decade of the new century may prove to be a watershed in the evolution of both state powers and private property rights. The eminent domain powers of government for very broadly defined "public" purposes, including transfer to private developers, were reaffirmed in *Kelo v. City of New London* (545 U.S. 469 (2005)). While the decision was predictable, given precedents (e.g., *Berman v. Parker* 348 U.S. 26 (1954)), *Kelo* has served a dramatic political focal point, resulting in a widespread backlash against government use of eminent domain. This backlash has produced legislation in many states that at least appears to constrain takings powers. This *Kelo* backlash is actually part of a larger takings backlash, however. Regulatory takings through police power have also come under attack. This is exemplified by Oregon's Measure 7 passed by voters in 2000. This measure was intended to amend the Oregon Constitution by mandating compensation for takings through land-use regulation. It was declared unconstitutional by the Oregon Supreme Court (*League of Or. Cities v. Oregon*, 56 P.3d 892 (Or. 2002)), but Oregon voters responded by passing Measure 37 in 2004, this time requiring compensation by amending Oregon statute law.[1] This measure withstood court scrutiny. In 2006, Arizona passed a similar Measure. There has also been a revival of academic interest in the issues of eminent domain and regulatory takings, both among legal scholars and economists.

The papers in this volume were presented at an April 2007 symposium at Florida State University's Law School, which brought together a diverse group of scholars and practitioners in order to explore the uses and abuses of eminent domain and regulatory takings. The range of expertise is illustrated by a list of participants, including the attorney who represented Susette Kelo before the U.S. Supreme Court (Scott Bullock from the Institute of Justice), the legal scholar whose comprehensive treatise on *Regulatory Takings*, now in its third edition, is the leading resource on the relationship between government takings powers and private property rights (Steven Eagle), an expert on land value determination who has frequently served as an appraiser and expert witness in takings cases (Wallace Kaufman), an economist widely recognized as one of the leading experts on takings and compensation determination (Perry Shapiro), and a land-use policy expert who serves as Director of Urban and Land Use Policy at the Reason Foundation (Sam Staley). Other participants are recognized legal or economic exports on environmental regulation, regulatory policy, entrepreneurial activities, and economic behavior.

All of the chapters in this volume are critical of takings practices, although the degree of criticism varies. Views range from arguments that market failure justifies takings but that the current process is flawed and should be fixed, to arguments that government failure is inevitable and undermines any justification for government takings. The chapters address four categories of topics (note that several papers could be placed in more than one category).

First, two chapters offer solutions to what the authors see as abuses of or problems arising from eminent domain powers in light of the *Kelo* ruling. Steven Eagle from George Mason University' College of Law contends that eminent domain is desirable to overcome transactions costs in assembling large parcels of land for private development, but that it is also problematic because it can be inequitable (indeed, it can be used to intentionally transfer wealth in the face of rent seeking by developers). He notes that a more restrictive definition of "public use" might alleviate the potential abuses, but instead of making an extensive case for such a redefinition (an argument made by others), he proposes alternatives. Eagle contends that owners be provided with real opportunities for planning and equity participation in redevelopment, noting that his argument applies to both eminent domain and regulatory takings. In partial contrast, Sam Staley from the Reason Foundation argues that eminent domain is usually not necessary to promote redevelopment, but rather that it is used to achieve political expediency as private developers use it to avoid market transactions. Staley recommends a "checklist" for assessing whether eminent domain actually does generate public benefits for an urban redevelopment project: (1) it should only be used as a tool of last resort, (2) hold out problems should be demonstrated, (3) the project should have broad public benefits, (4) the process should be transparent, and (5) there should be true economic blight. Staley shows, in part by examining recent takings cases such as *Kelo*, that very few development projects would qualify for eminent domain takings if these criteria were applied.

The Eagle and Staley arguments recognize that part of the problem with eminent domain arises because individuals whose land is taken are unfairly compensated. Two chapters directly focus on this issue. Paul Niemann and Perry Shapiro, economists from the University of California, Santa Barbara, point out that pretakings "market value" basis for determining compensation in eminent domain takings is inefficient in that it creates a moral hazard problem and induces inefficient investments. They demonstrate that an equitable compensation rule wherein owners of condemned land are to be paid the value of the property had it not been taken also can induce efficient resource use. Thus, in theory at least, it appears that appropriate compensation could be paid. Wallace Kaufman, an expert on land value determination who has frequently testified in takings cases, takes us from theory to practice. He also emphasizes limitations of the "market value" definition used to determine compensation, but in addition, he stresses that the practical determination of compensation tends to be distorted and corrupted at many points in the appraisal process and legal proceedings in eminent domain cases. The result is that compensation is rarely what it "should be" from an equity or efficiency perspective. Furthermore, in contrast to conventional wisdom, compensation often is high rather than low. Therefore, Kaufman stresses the loss of liberty rather than the transfer of wealth, as the primary problem with eminent domain.

The next set of chapters examines the politics of eminent domain. Scott Bullock, Senior Attorney at the Institute for Justice, explains the inadequacy of the planning process as a substantive check on eminent domain, thus arguing against the Supreme Court's justification for allowing the *Kelo* takings. He emphasizes the tremendous private influence on public planning, using both theoretical public-choice analysis and the practical knowledge he has drawn from his experience litigating eminent domain cases and challenging eminent domain abuse. Ilya Somin from George Mason University's School of Law explores the political backlash against *Kelo*. He examines the state legislation produced by this political backlash, identifying those few states that have significantly constrained the use of eminent domain. He also explains why many of the new laws are ineffective, despite the existence of wide spread popular outrage at *Kelo* and "economic development" condemnations, including the political power of development interests that stand to benefit from condemnation (echoing Staley) as well as the rational political ignorance of most voters. Thus, he argues against the view that the legislative reaction to *Kelo* demonstrates that the political process can provide sufficient safeguards for property owners. Finally, economists Bruce L. Benson (Florida State University) and Matthew Brown (Florida State University and the Charles G. Koch Charitable Foundation) compare the likely market failure problems that would arise in the absence of eminent domain powers to assist private development (the hold-out problem that can prevent the assembly of large parcels of land, as suggested by Eagle) to the government failure problems arising with eminent domain (the rent-seeking and wealth transfer issues raised by Eagle, Staley, and Bullock, and the unlikely success of any judicial or legislative efforts to effectively constrain such activities, as suggested by Somin). The conclusion is that even if there is a potential market failure limiting the ability of private developers to assemble land (the authors agree with Staley that this problem is much less than is typically suggested), the high likelihood of government failure undermines the market-failure justification for an eminent domain solution. The paper concludes on a cautionary note, however, reminding us that takings also occur through the regulatory process (police powers) and that regulatory takings do not require compensation. Therefore, while limitations on eminent domain are justified when government failure is recognized, such limitations should be considered in the broader political context. If local governments' abilities to transfer wealth through eminent-domain condemnation and compensation are limited, these governments may substitute uncompensated regulatory takings for eminent domain (e.g., rather than condemnation in order provide low income housing, a local government can mandate that private developers provide low income housing as part of a development, land use regulation might be used rather than eminent domain to preserve environmentally sensitive or historical areas), and these regulatory takings have many undesirable consequences.

The final set of chapters turn to regulatory takings. They provide examples of the undesirable consequences of regulatory takings, whether the regulations are "justified" by alleged public benefits or are recognized as wealth transfer mechanisms. These consequences often arise because of the incentives that the regulations create. For example, economists Peter Boettke (George Mason University), Peter Leeson (George Mason University), and Christopher Coyne (West Virginia

University) explore the impact of takings on entrepreneurial activity, focusing on how takings change the rules of the game and therefore the opportunities that entrepreneurs face, thereby altering the entrepreneurial discovery process. Jonathan H. Adler, Case Western Reserve University School of Law, explains that failing to compensate private landowners for the costs of environmental regulations discourages voluntary conservation efforts, encourages the destruction of environmental resources, and means that land-use regulation is "underpriced" relative to other environmental protection measures so it is "overconsumed." Economists Matthew Brown (Florida State University, and the Charles G. Koch Charitable Foundation) and Richard Stroup (the Property and Environmental Research Center, and North Carolina State University) explain that the ability to use eminent domain and/or regulation to force historical preservation allows certain interest groups, including those with NIMBY (not-in-my-back-yard) or competitive concerns, to pursue their preferred outcome at low cost to themselves by shifting costs to taxpayers, landowners and to those who seek housing or other economic development. This leads to over-use of these solutions, altering incentives to landowners toward future potentially important discoveries, and to unintended incentives to hide or otherwise destroy the value of historic remnants. They explain that the professional codes of ethics published by professional archaeology societies, is an important factor in justifying such results, to the detriment of serious archaeology and its ability to generate both knowledge and the public's interest in that knowledge. Next, economists Tom Means from San Jose State University, Edward Stringham from Trinity College, and Edward López at San Jose State University, provide an empirical examination the consequence of inclusionary zoning (e.g., requiring a developer to set aside a certain percentage of his planned housing units to be sold at a below market rate price) on housing prices and availability, using data from California. They find that such city ordinances restrict the housing supply and raise overall housing prices. Indeed, they conclude that cities that adopt affordable housing mandates (mandates that some housing be made available at below market prices) drive up overall housing prices by an estimated 20 percent, and that they end up with 10 percent fewer housing units, relative to cities without such mandates. Thus, such mandates transfer wealth from all those who buy homes that are not part of the affordable housing mandate, from those who want to buy homes but cannot because prices are higher and quantity supplied is reduced, and from developers who must adjust prices and output in an effort to cover the costs imposed by the regulations.

The concluding chapter expands upon a number of points made in earlier chapters. For instance, Bullock criticizes the *Kelo* ruling, arguing against the Court's conclusion that an eminent-domain taking is justified if it is part of a government's development plan (and see Staley for complementary analysis). This argument is extended to encompass regulatory takings, by demonstrating that planning inevitably fails to do much of what its supporters claim it will do. In fact, planning, and subsequent efforts to implement plans through land-use regulations and eminent domain, inevitably is destabilizing as rules are constantly changing. It also is tremendously costly, but not just in terms of government expenditures. A more significant cost is the resources diverted into a never-ending competition to avoid and/or alter the plans and regulations, competition that plays out in markets, legislatures, bureaucracies, and courts. Many of the most significant costs are not even measurable, as regulation diverts the market's discovery process along a new evolutionary path that is likely to involve innovations driven by regulation avoidance incentives rather than by welfare enhancement, as explained by Boettke, Coyne, and Leeson. The uncertainty that characterizes a constantly changing regulatory environment also shortens time horizons, altering investment and resource-use decision in ways that reduce the long-run productive potential of resources, as illustrated by Brown and Stroup and Adler. Somin demonstrates that *Kelo* produced a dramatic political backlash as states across the country passed statutes and referenda which appeared to restrict eminent domain powers, while Benson and Brown explain that the backlash against the *Kelo* decision actually is another in a long chain of backlashes against government efforts to expand the scope and strength of the claim that the state is the actual property owner. The concluding chapter provides further evidence of both expanding government efforts to strengthen government-ownership claims and of citizen resistance by examining Oregon's tumultuous comprehensive planning and land-use regulation history.

Justice Stevens noted that imposing a fifth-amendment just-compensation requirement for regulatory takings "would undoubtedly require changes in numerous practices that have long been considered permissible exercises of the police power.... [and] would render routine government processes prohibitively expensive or encourage hasty decision-making" (*Tahoe-Sierra Pres. Council, Inc. v. Tahoe Reg'l Planning Agency*, 533 U.S. 302, 335 (2002)). But that is precisely the point of Oregon's Measure-37 and similar efforts in other states. Many citizens want to make impermissible those government practices that reduce the security of their property rights, even though they have been permissible. The process of taking wealth without compensation should not be "routine" for government. Furthermore, the *Kelo* backlash legislation indicates that requiring compensation is not enough for many citizens. They believe that the process of takings with compensation should not be routine either. Much more significant limitations on government's taking powers are widely desired. The chapters in this volume illustrate why by detailing many of the inefficient and inequitable consequences of government takings powers, whether through uncompensated regulatory takings, or compensated eminent-domain takings. Indeed, while some of the authors of chapters in this volume probably would not agree, the implication of these chapters as a group seems quite clear to this editor: those who are advocating limitations on government's taking powers are correct—much more significant limitations on government takings power should be imposed.

## NOTE

1. Measure 37 was amended in 2007, weakening some of the constraints that 37 placed on governments in Oregon. See Benson (conclusion, this volume) for details.

# 2

# ASSEMBLING LAND FOR URBAN REDEVELOPMENT

## THE CASE FOR OWNER PARTICIPATION

*Steven J. Eagle*

## INTRODUCTION

In *Kelo v. City of New London* (2005), the U.S. Supreme Court held that the condemnation of unblighted residential neighborhoods for economic development by private entities did not violate the U.S. Constitution's requirement that condemnation be limited to public use.[1] While the text of the 5–4 majority's opinion stressed deference to past precedent, the subtext was a settled belief that state and local governments would use what the dissent termed "uncabined" powers with fairness and skill. These assumptions arose from a lingering Progressive Era faith in the role of trained professionals as guides to good public policy and from an implicit perception that the institution of property itself had lost much of its coherence (Grey 1980).

The public uproar following *Kelo*, and the ensuing wave of legislative proposals and statures aspiring to undo it, indicate that the public is fearful that government officials and powerful interests would conspire to deprive citizens of their homes and small businesses. As information about the increasing use of eminent domain for private economic development has spread, these fears have grown (Somin 2007).

This chapter sets forth alternatives to condemnation as a mechanism for urban redevelopment. It does not address the constitutional issues in *Kelo*, but is premised on skepticism about its practical effects. This point was articulated in a speech delivered by Justice John Paul Stevens soon after he handing down his *Kelo* majority opinion (Stevens 2005). Similarly, Justice Anthony Kennedy, who provided the fifth vote for the majority, also wrote a concurring opinion that did not comment directly on the efficacy of condemnation for private economic development, but which did agree with the four dissenters that at least some classes of condemnations merit heightened judicial scrutiny (*Kelo*, Kennedy concurring, 493).

Justice Kennedy's wariness is well justified from a public choice perspective, since legislators and government administrators tend to subordinate even the sound judgments of disinterested professionals to contrary demands by interest groups (Buchanan, Tollison and Tullock 1980). Indeed, even the formal wisdom of experts may lead to sterility, given the importance of serendipity in creating livable cities (Jacobs 1961, Wickersham 2001).

All of this suggests that condemnation for private economic redevelopment should be approached with caution, and that alternative approaches might be preferable. Such approaches should be designed to reduce uncompensated losses now suffered by condemnees, to reduce opportunistic exercises of eminent domain that are likely to redound primarily for private benefit, and to reduce rent seeking behavior by public officials and redevelopers.

This chapter asserts that increasing the opportunities for land redevelopment by existing private owners and others acting through markets can help achieve all of these goals. Among the approaches suggested here are the financial participation of existing owners in redevelopment entities, the substitution of foreclosure for condemnation as the preferred mechanism for eradicating urban blight, and the transfer of zoning authority over neighborhoods from municipalities to supermajorities of landowners in those neighborhoods.

## PROPERTY AND LIBERTY

### Contesting the Meaning of "Property"

The faith in condemnation for private economic development articulated in *Kelo* (2005) results from deference to legislators, faith in government expertise, and doubts about the solidity of property rights.

Implicit is the view that the democratic process promotes fairness and the adherence to the Constitution by government officials. Indeed, Justice Stevens took the very "public outcry" that greeted his *Kelo* opinion as evidence of the correctness of these points (Stevens 2005). However, "[t]his is a faith in the intrinsic rationality of man, something the Founders might say indulges a delusional conception of human nature. The town meetings merely facilitated a faction's ability to take what was not theirs and reallocate it" (Kmiec 2005, 46).

Justice Stevens acknowledged that the disposition of *Kelo* "turn[ed] on the question whether the City's development plan serve[d] a 'public purpose.'" "Without exception," he declared, "our cases have defined that concept broadly, reflecting our longstanding policy of deference to legislative judgments in this field" (Kelo 2005, 480). Professor Gideon Kanner, a leading proponent of private property rights, ruefully noted that earlier cases upholding condemnation for private development, in instances where that approach promised otherwise unobtainable regional economic benefits, constituted the "first step down the slippery slope" by which "'public use' became transmogrified into 'public benefit'" (Kanner 2006, 350).

While Justice O'Connor's principal dissent focused on what is deemed the broad view's inability to cabin the eminent domain power (Kelo 2005, 494), Justice Thomas' separate dissent analyzed the cases cited by the majority as involving instances where the transferee of the condemned property used it, in the nature of a common carrier, for the benefit of the public (Kelo 2005, Thomas, dissenting, 517).

In addition, several of the Justices raised at oral argument in *Kelo* the issue of whether it was fair to condemnees that the assembly value added by condemnation (i.e., the increase in the aggregate value of previously separate parcels created by their consolidation) goes exclusively to local governments and redevelopers. Justice O'Connor asked the landowner's counsel whether there was any scholarship "that indicates that when you have property being taken from one private person ultimately to go to another private person, that what we ought to do is to adjust the measure of compensation so that the owner—the condemnee—can receive some sort of a premium for the development" (*Kelo* Transcript 2005, 22). Likewise, Justice Kennedy asked "if there is any scholarship to indicate that maybe that compensation measure ought to be adjusted when *A* is losing property for the economic benefit of *B*" (Ibid., 23).

As recapitulated in *United States v. Miller* (1943), the measure of compensation required by the Constitution is "fair market value," which is "what a willing buyer would pay in cash to a willing seller." (Ibid., 374). This is modified by the "scope of the project" rule, under which a landowner is not entitled to a share of the increase in the value of his or her property resulting from the project for which the condemned land is to be utilized (Ibid., 376–77). *Miller* also added that an owner is not entitled to compensation for loss of the condemned land's "special adaptability to his own use," and that the land's "special value to the condemnor as distinguished from others who may or may not possess the power to condemn, must be excluded as an element of market value" (Ibid., 375–77).

As explained by Richard Posner, a leading law and economics scholar as well as a federal appellate judge, "[c]ompensation in the constitutional sense is therefore not full compensation, for market value is not the value that every owner of property attaches to his property but merely the value that the marginal owner attaches to his property.... The taking in effect confiscates the additional (call it "personal") value that they obtain from the property, but this limited confiscation is permitted provided the taking is for a public use." *(Coniston Corp. v. Village of Hoffman Estates,* 1988, 464). Thus, owners' idiosyncratic value is systematically destroyed, an outcome justified only by the impossibility of accurately measuring such value and the fact that the land is to be put to a public use.

Although the subjective value in their homes held by owners such as Mrs. Kelo are lost on condemnation for economic redevelopment, the "scope of the project" rule does not adequately explain their failure to receive some of the assembly value generated by condemnation. The assembly value was treated as if it were a positive externality, as might inure in land taken in connection with the construction of an adjoining public transportation station or handsome amenity. However, assembly value is inherent in the land itself, although its realization largely is precluded by transaction costs. In 2003, the Supreme Court also awarded the equivalent of gains from assembly to the condemnor, when it held that the fair market value of the interest generated by law clients' funds was zero. The lawyers were required to deposit these funds in accounts earning interest for legal services programs. These accounts were exempt from regulations precluding the payment of interest, funds deposited in the lawyers' own trust accounts would have been subject to those rules (*Brown v. Legal Foundation of Washington* 2003).

It is not clear if the assertions by landowners that it is unfair that condemnors and subsequent redevelopers reap all of the gains from condemnation will gain traction in the Supreme Court. However, such unfairness could be alleviated through the use of redevelopment techniques not employing condemnation, as outlined in this chapter.

## The Growing Use of Eminent Domain

The recent trend toward the extensive use of eminent domain to facilitate private economic revitalization harkens to an earlier period that began with the Progressive Era and reached its apogee in *Berman v. Parker* (1954), in which great faith was placed in government intervention in land use as a cure for urban ills.

While the Progressives were idealists who placed their faith in disinterested expertise, it is important to recall that they did have a definite political program. In the Progressive understanding, "the general welfare" elevates communitarian goods and subordinates individualistic values, such as free expression in the use of land (Claeys 2004, 735). Correspondingly, Progressives perceived "property" not as a "zone of noninterference" for its owner, but rather as a stake in the civic order. Zoning empowered local majorities to express their "communal visions of community, security, and aesthetics." Experts implemented this vision through detailed plans and by granting limited exceptions (Ibid.).

The history of urban redevelopment in the United States has been checkered (Bingham 1975; Boyer 1983, 213–79). Urban renewal was concerned principally with deteriorated areas of older cities. One of its primary goals was the elimination of slum neighborhoods, a process which utilized massive demolition (Anderson 1964). Another, and not unrelated, goal was the renovation of central business districts, largely through the elimination of nearby blight (Greer 1965, 180–84). Proponents articulated a desire to benefit low-income residents of substandard areas. For them, such programs may have been a "disaster," Tenants and homeowners in redeveloped neighborhoods often tended to fare poorly, while "various outsiders, such as the leaders of established downtown firms, influential area developers, and suburban commuters, reaped substantial gains" (Barron 2003, 707).

> [T]o many mayors and other local government officials, urban renewal was seen as a means of increasing the property tax base of their cities....Still other urban renewal goals, in relation to some projects, were attracting back more upper-income residents to central cities and also strengthening urban hospitals, universities, and cultural centers by providing them with expansion space or making their surrounding neighborhoods safer and more attractive....
>
> The typical urban renewal procedure was for a local government agency to acquire land in need of redevelopment, clear it, and then sell the vacant land to a private or public developer who would build on it in accord with a local government plan for reuse. The writedown between acquisition cost and resale price–the difference in value between the land acquired improved and sold cleared–plus some administrative costs, were known as net project costs, and paid for mostly by federal government grants. In the typical project, however, most of the total cost was paid for by a private developer who purchased and built on the property. The usual attraction of renewal sites to private developers was the availability of large tracts of central city land that the private sector, not having eminent domain rights, normally could not assemble at a fair price, if at all. And these tracts normally came as raw land, the developer not having to pay the value of the prior improvements or the cost of removing them. In addition, the renewal plan often resulted in an upgrading of the neighborhood that was beneficial to the developer's project (Johnstone 1994, 393).

Not much has changed about the nature of condemnation for retransfer for redevelopment since, except that "renewal" often is restyled "revitalization," with "many suburbanites who left the city decades ago now itching to return to the promise of safe, burgeoning city life. Private developers are interested in land once thought forgotten. City officials, too" (Foster 2006, 536).

However, it appears that redevelopment efforts sponsored by government have failed in most cities (Larson 1995). City "neighborhoods continue to deteriorate, city dwellers have been unable to secure quality employment, and city space has been increasingly restructured to meet the various interests of developers, tourists, and upper-income consumers" (Quinones 1994, 691). Perhaps for this reason, the Progressive Era legacy of land use regulation has achieved less acceptance than its other reforms and is criticized from all political quarters (Larson 1995, 179–80).

Given the increased doubt about the capacity of urban renewal to redeem society,[2] one might ask if condemnation for economic development also is predicated on increased doubt about the ability of individual property owners to use their lands most effectively. The answer likely is "yes," predicated on a paradigm shift from Adam Smith's "invisible hand," by which landowners seeking to do well for themselves will do good for the community (Smith 1776). The new paradigm, a land ownership variant of the "prisoners dilemma" game under which landowners seeking to do well individually thereby do poorly for themselves and their communities, collectively, is often associated with Michael Heller's "anticommons" (Heller 1998).

Heller targets for blame the scale of individual property holdings, such that small slivers of property rights retard efficient utilization of property. Rescaling property, in turn, has been deemed a job for Progressive expertise and the administrative state (Bamberger 2006; Pierce 2006; Markell 2006). Conveniently enough, doubts about the proper scale of property merge with doubts about the viability of "property" as a societal institution, given its purported "entropy" (Parisi 2002) and "disintegration" (Grey 1980).

## PROPERTY AND LIBERTY

The importance of private property rights in the American scheme of liberty has been a thread running throughout our history (McDonald 1985). The author of the Constitution's Takings Clause, James Madison, had a "concern about the security of private rights was rooted in a palpable fear that economic legislation was jeopardizing fundamental rights of property" (Rakove 1996, 314–15). "The great focus of the Framers was the security of basic rights, property in particular, not the implementation of political liberty" (Nedelsky 1990, 92). "Property must have a special nature to serve as a limit to the democratic claims of legislative power" (Ibid., 239).

These concerns have not abated over time, since "the only dependable foundation of personal liberty is the personal economic security of private property. . . . Men cannot be made free by laws unless they are in fact free because no man can buy and no man can coerce them" (Lippmann 1934, 100–102).

In considering "entropy" and the "anticommons," assumptions about appropriate baselines can be beguiling. The common law approached this problem in connection with land utilization primarily by discouraging novel interests in land, stating that "incidents of a novel kind" cannot "be devised and attached to property at the fancy or caprice of any owner," by standardizing permissible interests, as restated by Merrill and Smith (2000), and by preventing an unreasonable period of uncertainty about the identity of all of the rights holders in a particular parcel, such as through the Rule against Perpetuities (Dukeminier, Krier, Alexander, and Schill 2006).

If one defines the "relevant resource" as a large block of urban land, then owners in fee of the small parcels that conceptually comprise the "resource parcel" might be said to possess anticommons rights of exclusion. The only difference is that they own all of the rights in a fraction of the resource parcel rather than, in Heller's account, fractional rights in the whole of the parcel.

However, the situation in most condemnation for retransfer for economic development cases differs from the situation described by Heller in that the small residential and commercial landowners threatened with condemnation for retransfer did not obtain "incoherent" rights. Indeed, they long had been in possession of fully standard and constitutionally protected ownership interests—fee simple interests. These rights subsequently became "fragments" only in the context of asserted socioeconomic or technological change, or increase in the zeal of government and its development partners to redesign cities.

It might be that the "initial seemingly attractive choice turns out to be suboptimal in the end" (Parisi 2002, 613). On the other hand, who is to have the last word as to dating "the end," either in the broad sweep of history,[3] or in continual reappraisals in American law.[4] Many urban districts that we now consider architectural and historical gems, such as the historic districts of Boston and Savannah, were developed long before land use planning (Emerson 2006, 637–646).

## THE CONCEIT OF REVITALIZATION

Less than two months after handing down the Supreme Court's *Kelo* opinion, Justice Stevens asserted that the case represented good law, but unwise policy: "My own view is that the allocation of economic resources that result from the free play of market forces is more likely to produce acceptable results in the long run that the best-intentioned plans of public officials" (Stevens 2005, 10–11).

It is a fatal conceit for planners to think that they could reconfigure society through command and control (Hayek 1988). It is impossible for a central authority to marshal each person's local knowledge of the myriad of factors that shape his own situation, although the individual could summarize that knowledge succinctly through the price that he is willing to accept or pay for a given resource (Hayek 1945). Much relevant information, in any event, is in the form of tacit knowledge not readily transmissible to others (Polanyi 1969). The economic vitality of American cities might no more require condemnation than the physical and cultural vitality of cities requires the wrecking ball.

## PUBLIC VS. PRIVATE GAINS

Society must have a means to allocate resources between competing uses. The market serves this function using price as a proxy for the value of the resource to potential purchasers (Malloy 1987, 95–98). In governmental regulation of the market, government artificially controls the allocation of resources, "when market allocation is thought to be undesirable." Instead of following actual demand, the government allocates the resource after looking to the most politically desired uses of the resources, often established by the "most influential participants of the political process" (Ibid., 96).

Justice O'Connor's dissent in *Kelo* argued that the Court's distinction between takings for a public use, in which the primary benefit was to the public, and takings for private use, in which the public benefit was only incidental, was, in practice, a chimera. "The trouble with economic development takings is that private benefit and incidental public benefit are, by definition, merged and mutually reinforcing. In this case, for example, any boon for Pfizer or the plan's developer is difficult to disaggregate from the promised public gains in taxes and jobs" (Kelo 2005, O'Connor dissenting, 502).

## INCENTIVES FOR REDEVELOPMENT ASKEW

Condemnation for revitalization should be viewed within the context of competing governments offering very costly incentives to attract new businesses and developers (Garnett 2003, 934–58). These reduce the predicted revenue benefits from the ensuing projects. One explanation for this apparent anomaly is that project decisions are made by local government officials, but financing often comes from the state and federal governments (Garnett 2006, 101–41). In *Kelo,* for instance, the State of Connecticut issued bonds totaling $15.35 million to support the redevelopment of New London (Kelo 2005, 473). In *Poletown Neighborhood Council v. City of Detroit* (1981), it seems that the impetus behind the condemnation of a vibrant ethnic neighborhood for the construction of a General Motors assembly plant was not GM's desire to commandeer a neighborhood within the city, but rather that the city had received federal funds earmarked for redevelopment projects, and the GM plant provided a way to use those funds. "It is unlikely the city of Detroit would have undertaken the project if it was required to raise its own funds to finance it or if the money had been given to the city by the federal government to do with as it pleased" (Fischel 2004, 929–30).

Both practical experience and economic theory demonstrate why the government's ability to bypass the market, and therefore avoid holdouts and other land assembly problems, makes eminent domain an attractive "incentive" to offer to private companies. The potential beneficiaries have a substantial incentive to engage in rent seeking to secure the benefit of this bypass. . . . This incentive only increases if the government is willing to transfer title to a private beneficiary at below-market prices—or along with an attractive package of tax incentives. A basic lesson of public-choice theory is that governments respond to connected insiders' demands and discount the needs of unorganized individuals (Garnett 2003, 958).

## ENHANCING OWNER PARTICIPATION

### The Increased Use of Eminent Domain for Private Development

While urban renewal through the 1970s is associated with massive demolition and rebuilding of city neighborhoods, the more recent wave of urban revitalization has emphasized a high volume of private projects that individually possess much smaller footprints. These functionally stealth projects collectively attracted little attention until the late 1990s. A widely noted 1998 account in the *Wall Street Journal* served as a catalyst, pointing out that, although condemnation has been a "device used for centuries to smooth the way for public works such as roads, and later to ease urban blight," it recently "has become a marketing tool for governments seeking to lure bigger businesses" (Starkman 1991). A follow-up story declared:

> Desperate for tax revenue, cities and towns across the country now routinely take property from unwilling sellers to make way for big-box retailers. Condemnation cases aren't tracked nationally, but even retailers themselves acknowledge that the explosive growth in the formal in the 1990s and torrid competition for land has increasingly pushed them into increasingly problematic areas—including sites owned by other people (Starkman 2004).

Likewise, an account by a leading libertarian advocacy group, which represented Mrs. Kelo, asserted with concern that from 1998 through 2002 there were over 10,000 condemnations with ensuing use of the land by private parties in the United States (Berliner 2003).

Largely in response to *Kelo* (2005) scholars are reconsidering the importance of eminent domain and public use (Pritchett, 2003; Kanner, 2006).

> Because private actors can use eminent domain to acquire land costlessly for their own objectives, these actors have an incentive to engage in excessive takings. Second, potential private beneficiaries can exploit disparities in legal and financial resources to obtain the state's condemnation authority. Indeed, while the primary beneficiaries of private takings tend to be real estate developers and corporations, the primary victims of these takings tend to be the economically disadvantaged, the elderly, and racial and ethnic minorities (Kelly 2006).

The elimination of blight has long been the traditional justification for the use of eminent domain in takings for redevelopment (*Berman* 1954), ["Editor" *Berman* refers to the court case discussed above—*Berman v. Parker*] and remains heavily utilized. Undoubtedly takings for "blight" has its appeal in limiting unnecessary takings while, at the same time, permitting government to use eminent domain as "a tool for eliminating pockets of poverty" (Bell and Parchomovsky 2006, 1412–37). Over time, however, blight has become so broadly defined as to become indistinguishable from conditions that might benefit from some sort of improvement. Aside from definitional problems, however, is the more fundamental question of why the removal of blight, as such, justifies eminent domain, given the historical bifurcation whereby government uses its police power to regulate threats to the public health, safety, and welfare, and uses eminent domain to acquire for public use valuable resources owned by private parties (Eagle, 2007).

Aside from the constitutional problem of justifying eminent domain solely on the existence of blight, there is the mission creep of Progressive reform, whereby the definition of "blight" has grown from physical dangers to health and safety to encompass a wide variety of more-or-less plausible economic and social suboptimalities. A good illustration of the blurring of blight and economic redevelopment is *Concerned Citizens of Princeton, Inc. v. Mayor and Council of Borough of Princeton* (2004), where a New Jersey appellate court upheld the condemnation of a municipal parking lot in an affluent town by a borough, on the grounds that a consultant's report indicated that the lot "was in a state of obsolescence because it represented 'yesterday's solutions' in a municipality such as Princeton, where '[s]tructured parking is now the standard'" (*Concerned Citizens* 2004, 691). This "inhibited 'urban center uses'" (Ibid.).

The court noted that the state constitution provided that the clearance or redevelopment of "blighted areas" constituted a public use, but that it did not define "blighted areas" (*Concerned Citizens* 2004, 701). Subsequently, the state supreme court declared:

> Community redevelopment is a modern facet of municipal government. Soundly planned redevelopment can make the difference between continued stagnation and decline and a resurgence of healthy growth. It provides the means of removing the decadent effect of slums and blight on neighboring property values, of opening up new areas for residence and industry. In recent years, recognition has grown that governing bodies must either plan for the development or redevelopment of urban areas or permit them to become more congested, deteriorated, obsolescent, unhealthy, stagnant, inefficient and costly.[5]

Consistent with this view, the state legislature came to replace the statutory term "blight" with the term "in need of redevelopment." An area might be determined in need of redevelopment if any of a laundry list of statutory factors was determined to exist, ranging from buildings that are unsafe or unsanitary, to land where a multiplicity of titles or "other conditions" results in "stagnant or not fully productive condition" (*Concerned Citizens* 2004, 698–99). It might not be uncommon that determinations of "blight" are casually added to facilitate revitalization projects.

> The presence of new stadiums, convention centers, retail centers, and office towers created by federal and later local redevelopment efforts have been abject failures in revitalizing the economies of metropolitan central cities. They have not arrested blight; they have not refilled the city's coffers; they have not revitalized the local economy; and above all they have not improved the life chances of inner-city residents.

\*     \*     \*

The local and federal redevelopment efforts were generated, planned, and implemented by local elites. As might be expected, local elites produced projects that they perceived to be important. Unfortunately, these projects did not benefit the city as a whole and particularly did not benefit low-income residents of the city (Quinones 1994, 691–3).

One of the reactions to the *Kelo* decision and the general trend of broadening the acceptable reasons for takings in redevelopment, is to more narrowly define blight, and place blight requirements on takings for redevelopment. In California, the Legislature recently amended the "Existence of blighted area; declaration and description" section of the Code to "restrict the statutory definition of blight and to require better documentation of local officials' findings regarding the condemnations of blight."[6] Other states have also reformed their codes to tighten up blight definitions, including Kentucky and Utah.[7] The Florida Legislature has responded even more strongly by prohibiting the use of eminent domain in the "eliminat[ion of] nuisance, slum, or blight conditions."[8]

## STATE ATTEMPTS TO INCLUDE OWNERS IN REDEVELOPMENT PROJECTS

A few states have enacted legislation facilitating the involvement of condemnees in the redevelopment process. Under California law: "Every redevelopment plan shall provide for participation in the redevelopment of property in the project area by the owners of all or part of such property if the owners agree to participate in the redevelopment in conformity with the redevelopment plan adopted by the legislative body for the area."[9] Because the statute left property owners involvement ambiguous and optional, owners in California have not successfully been able to involve themselves in the redevelopment process.

The California courts have held repeatedly that the development decisions are at the sole discretion of the local redevelopment agency. The leading case is *In re Bunker Hill Urban Renewal Project 1B of Community Redevelopment Agency of City of Los Angeles* (1964), which declared that "there is no absolute right of owner participation in the redevelopment of each separately owned parcel of land within the project area" and that "the Community Redevelopment Law does not contemplate that every redevelopment plan shall be so designed as to accommodate a redevelopment of each separate parcel within the financial ability of the present owner (Ibid., 563–4)." Any owner that does desire to participate must first agree to do so in conformity with adopted redevelopment plan. Furthermore, "[b]ecause the final plan necessitates assembly of large plots to carry out the proposed uses in certain areas of the project and requires prospective owner-participants to qualify as financially responsible, and thus in some cases renders it impossible for small property owners, as such, to separately participate with the same status, does not in and of itself establish a violation." (Ibid., 563).

While requiring the redevelopment agencies to meet their "duty of reasonableness and good faith" and "act fairly and without discrimination," a California appellate court held, in *Felom v. Redevelopment Agency of City and County of San Francisco*, that in the redevelopment of a "blighted area" where the agency chose to allow the participation of owners of developed land but not allow the participation of undeveloped land it was within their discretion and was not unreasonable or discriminatory. The agency had denied participation to 97 percent of the owners of the undeveloped land, while granting participation to 75 percent of the owners of developed land.

Similarly, in *Sanguinetti v. City Council of Stockton*, a community plan that designated only three owners in a nine block area as eligible for owner participation did not deny equal protection. "The Community Redevelopment Law permits, but it did not require owner participation, and whether or not and in what instances owner participation may be permitted is necessarily confided to the sound judgment of the agency in the adoption of the plan" (Ibid.,, 275). The agency survey of the nine-block neighborhood listed 47 families living in the area, and only eight of them were owners. The area also had a large population of transient individuals, creating a difficulty for the agency in providing for their relocation in the redevelopment plan.

More recently, a California court of appeal required the objecting owners to show that the agency abused its discretion, and, as long as the redevelopment agency had substantial evidence to support the adopted redevelopment plan, its rejection of the alternative proposals of the property owners would not be overturned (*Duncan* 1983).

Under Nevada law, "[e]very redevelopment plan must provide for the partici-pation and assistance in the redevelopment of the property in the redevelopment area by the owners of all or part of that property if the owners agree to partici-pate in conformity with the redevelopment plan adopted by the legislative body for the area"[10] Actions questioning the validity of a redevelopment plan must be brought within 90 days of the adoption or amendment of the plan, or of legislative or administrative findings in connection with it.[11]

The Supreme Court of Nevada interpreted this provision to grant any citizen standing to challenge redevelopment agency findings in *Hantages v. Henderson* (2005). However, the court rejected the challenge, filed one year after the rede-velopment plan was adopted, on the grounds that agency's approval of the owner participation agreement (OPA) was not a formal amendment, nor did it materially alter or deviate from the original plan, and therefore the 90-day challenge period did not restart. So while the plaintiff had the right to challenge the plan, the OPA was an integral part of the plan, not an amendment to the plan that granted a new challenge period.

Overturning a district court decision in favor of the owners, the Supreme Court of Nevada held, in *City of Las Vegas Downtown Redevelopment Agency v. Pappas,* that a redevelopment agency was not required to accept the owners' proposed par-ticipation through ground lease of the property. It found that the district court had substituted its own decision making process for that of the agency, and that the agency's finding that the financing of the garage would be unfavorable if it accepted the owners' ground rent proposal, was within it's power (Ibid., 16). The police power of the state was delegated to the agency, and it therefore had discretion in the process (Ibid.).

## WHAT FORM SHOULD OWNER PARTICIPATION TAKE?

### Private Assembly Often Is Achievable

While the fear of hold out problems has long been used as a justification for emi-nent domain, private developers have been successful in assembling redevelopment tracts by using secret agents (Kelly 2006, 20–33). Harvard University, Walt Disney, and other developers have been able to assemble parcels of up to 3,000 acres, in urban and rural areas, over periods ranging from 9 months to over a decade (Kelly 2006). By inserting an agent into the assembly process, the owner does not learn of the assembly plan, nor the identity of the assembler. As an extra precaution, the agent is often unaware of the assemblers' plan to develop the land. Both shields provide the opportunity to discover the best use of the land. In *County of Wayne v. Hathcock* (2004), the Michigan Supreme Court repudiated its earlier decision upholding as a "public use" the condemnation of an entire ethnic neighborhood in Detroit for transfer to General Motors in *Poletown Neighborhood Council v. City of Detroit* (1981). The court noted:

> The [subject] business and technology park is certainly not an enterprise "whose very *existence* depends on the use of land that can be assembled only by the coordination central government alone is capable of achieving." To the contrary, the landscape of our country is flecked with shopping centers, office parks, clusters of hotels, and cen-ters of entertainment and commerce. We do not believe, and plaintiff does not contend,

that these constellations required the exercise of eminent domain or any other form of collective public action for their formation (Hathcock 2004, 783–784).

In many instances, a case could be made that private assembly is not feasible because, as Professor Thomas Merrill put it, potential sellers would be able to capture for themselves a large share of what otherwise would be the value of the project to the public through holding out for economic rents (Merrill 1986). However, Merrill sees a lack of justification for condemnation where there are many potential sellers in "thick markets," so that rent seeking is not a significant concern (Merrill 1986, 76).

## Unitization

Through compulsory pooling, the United States petroleum industry provides a significant example of private solutions to the perceived problem of economic fractionalization.

"Unitization," the process of combining for integrated management and exploitation the separately owned portions of a producing oilfield (Williams & Meyers, 2003), is a solution to the ineffective exploitation of resources in oil fields (Kiew 2005) Once the courts applied the rule of capture, whereby oil or gas, treated as a fugitive resource akin to wild animals was not owned until it was released from the ground and captured. This caused landowners to haphazardly drill to try to capture as much of the oil or gas flowing under their land as quickly as they could. Unitization brings surface owners together to not only drill, but to plan the extraction process, and divide the proceeds. Since controlled drilling results in greater total extraction and lower expenses, there is substantial net benefit.

Most petroleum producing states, excluding Texas, have enacted compulsory unitization acts. These typically require the voluntary agreement of a significant percentage of owners prior to issuance of a compulsory unitization order. Some unitization acts also require a showing that unitization is necessary to allow for specific operations that require a coordinated effort, such as enhanced recovery or pressure maintenance operations (Anderson & Smith).

## Allocation of Fractional Rights in Lumpy Resources

Like oilfield unitization, fractional allocations in lumpy resources (Benkler 2004) assumes that the owners of lands also own pro rata shares in resources associated with those lands that cannot feasibly be assigned to the individual parcels. In the oilfield situation, unitization overcame the problem of many claimants wastefully seeking to exploit a common pool.[12] Fractional allocation, on the other hand, is a way to overcome the lumpy nature of certain property rights.

In its underappreciated decision in *Barancik v. County of Marin* (1989), the U.S. Court of Appeals for the Ninth Circuit provided an imaginative example of the division of ownership entitlements where the resource could be developed on only a few of the potentially eligible parcels. The county provided for "Transfer of Development Rights" in the Nicasio Valley, a rugged and beautiful area that still was sparsely developed. The plan treated what the court later termed the "homogeneous community of Nicasio Valley," as "complete land forum, one large property to be sensitively planned." Because development would only be permitted in few of the parcels in the county, the right to develop was divided into fractional shares among all the ranch owners. Ranchers in the valley were permitted to sell to other property owners in the valley the right to develop within the regulations of the community. A purchaser could accumulate more than one development right, in order to accumulate the necessary amount to redevelop their specific parcel (Ibid., 835).

Fractional allocations have been used in connection with "transferable development rights" (TDRs) given landowners in ostensible "mitigation" of the effects of stringent regulations that might otherwise constitute regulatory takings.[13] In *Suitum v. Tahoe Regional Planning Agency* (1997), the purchaser of a lot on which building subsequently was prohibited was given fractional development rights, when, accumulated with other such rights in sufficient numbers, would permit development in distant areas. The Court in *Suitum* held that TDRs constituted final agency decisions, thus ripening the matter for suit in federal court, but did not discuss the substantive merits of TDRs themselves. Justice Scalia's concurring and dissenting opinion "suggest[ed]...that the relevance of TDRs is limited to the compensation side of the takings analysis, and that taking them into account in determining whether a taking has occurred will render much of our regulatory takings jurisprudence a nullity" (*Suitum* 1997, Scalia, Concurring and Dissenting, 750).

The issue will grow in importance as it becomes clearer that residents in a receptor district could share in the gains to be derived from the few higher-density projects that might be permitted in the area. Governmental decisions to award this density to distant developers in the form of TDRs that "mitigate" what otherwise might constitute takings will then be perceived accurately as depriving some of actual property in order to create regulatory property for others.

## From Condemnation to Foreclosure

While "blight" often has been used to mean nothing more than suboptimal land utilization, it is blackletter law that conditions presenting serious threats to public health and safety justify condemnation. *Kelo* 1980, 485, *County of Wayne v. Hathcock* 2004. However, this usage varies from the traditional distinction between harms to the public, which are abated by nuisance and other forms of police power regulation, and goods that government entities seek to acquire for public use, for which eminent domain is employed.

If owners were served with orders promptly to abate nuisances instead of with complaints in condemnation actions, they would have limited times for remediation. If they do not comply, government agencies could do the necessary abatements, and charge the costs to owners in the form of betterment assessments. If the owners fail to pay, the betterment liens upon their property, akin to other taxes, could be foreclosed upon.

As I elaborate elsewhere, government or its selected redevelopers might acquire the property at the foreclosure sale, and operate as before. However, owners might remediate to prevent foreclosure, or they, their neighbors, or their mortgagees might purchase at the foreclosure sale. The foreclosure device opens the political process of condemnation for redevelopment into a market process in which private actors might engage in fixing up buildings and neighborhoods in less grandiose (and therefore probably more efficacious) ways than officials and their selected redevelopers would (Eagle 2007).

## From Zoning to Neighborhood Development as "Collective Property"

According to Professor Robert Nelson, the merchants and affluent suburbanites who agitated for the institution of zoning early in the past century regarded its ostensible police power justification as a "necessary camouflage" for a widespread distribution of property rights in land use controls to individual neighborhoods (Nelson 1999, 827–41). He asserted that, in practice, "grand land use planning" was "utopian" and never developed on a scientific basis.

> Instead, land development occurred opportunistically, as housing or other facilities were proposed for particular locations....Approval of new development was not achieved by verifying consistency with an existing comprehensive plan, as legal theory prescribed. Rather, the municipality typically amended the zoning ordinance, granting specific approval for individual development. The process resembled a business negotiation between the municipality and the developer. The parties made or did not make a deal regarding a particular proposed development project according to the specific benefits to each party (Ibid., 838).

Nelson noted a national commission study observing that zoning regulations were most efficacious when protecting uniformly developed residential neighborhoods, as first intended. "It is in the 'nice' neighborhoods, where the regulatory job is easiest, that regulations do their best job." (Ibid., 839).

Zoning created a collective property right because it gave the entire neighborhood, exercising its political influence over the municipal administrators of zoning, the collective power to exclude unwanted uses.

*   *   *

If the practical consequence of zoning was to provide a collective private property right, why not simply provide this property right directly through private means (Ibid., 839–40)?

Other land use scholars also observed early that, as a practical matter, zoning constituted a redistribution of property from the individual to the neighborhood.

Under Nelson's scheme, "[t]he provisions of RCAs [Residential Community Associations] could be extended to the private governance of existing neighborhoods that consist now of individually owned properties. Using an RCA model, the concept would be to establish the private neighborhood as a building block for metropolitan political and economic organization" (Tarlock 1972, 176).

Nelson's scheme requires a 60 percent majority of individual property owners within a neighborhood to apply to the state legislature for the creation of a RCA. They must define and defend their choice of boundaries of the neighborhood, as cherry picking the most desirable lots in an area occurs. Once approved, the state would authorize a neighborhood committee to negotiate a service transfer agreement with the appropriate municipal government" that would specify the ownership of community amenities such as parks, side walks and streets, assign the responsibility for public services such as police, fire, and trash, and specify the "future tax arrangements" (Nelson 1999, 834). Before final implementation, however, a super majority affirmative vote representing at least ninety percent of the total value of the neighborhood, and seventy-five percent of the "total value of the proposed neighborhood" (Ibid.). If the supermajority vote was achieved, the RCA would be binding upon all individual landowners, but as a body they would have control of future zoning decisions in the neighborhood, including redevelopment rights.

In the past, the present author objected to Nelson's neighborhood privatization scheme on the basis that it arrogated to a supermajority of neighbors the right to sell parcels that by right reposed in their individual owners (Eagle 1999). However, the coercive effect of compulsory privatization is much milder than that of condemnation for retransfer for economic development as countenanced by the U.S. Supreme Court in *Kelo* (2005).

A variant of Nelson's proffered substitute for eminent domain is the "land assembly district" (LAD) (Heller and Hills, 2004). LADs would provide a substitute for the use of eminent domain in all "blighted areas," or areas of fragmentations, but would not replace eminent domain where there is a unique site needed for serving a public infrastructure use. Under an LAD model, owners would take the responsibility of assembling the parcels, and negotiating as a whole with the developer. The governance should be democratic, and focused on protecting the rights of the individuals as well as the group as a whole, and in not harming the community. By taking the steps necessary for the parcel assembly, the owners would be entitled to higher compensation for the increased value in the land, providing more of an incentive to the owners to negotiate with each other. The owners would be empowered to negotiate as a body with the developer, protect the owners from the developers low balling, rent seeking efforts, and the market price designation of an expert that failed to consider the true worth and subjective value the property holds for the owner. While the security of an LAD would likely encourage an owner to be more likely to reveal his minimal acceptable price, where an owner refused to participate, or no compromise that was acceptable to an individual owner could be reached, and the problem of hold out arose, they would still be granted just compensation through condemnation.

When property ownership is held through a cooperative, the sale of a neighborhood can make the already assembled parcel more desirable to developers. In turn, the owners can seek a higher price for the assembled value. Recently Briny Breezes, a large ocean front Florida mobile home community with ownership of the parcel held in shares, attracted the attention of developers (Skoloff 2007). The development company Ocean Land Investments offered $510 million dollars, to be divided among the owners of the 488 mobile homes based on shares held. After the board of directors approved the sale, it must now be ratified by at least a two-thirds majority to sell (Skoloff 2007). Another suggestion is that in redevelopment projects, instead of paying fair market value for the individual property, a community premium should be added; and when and entire community is being dissolved, then the government should provide a place for them to relocate if the individual members so choose (Parchomovsky and Siegelman 2004).

Yet another recent vehicle that might assist in maintaining owner control of revitalization is the Modern Community Development Corporations (CDC) (Grogan 2000). CDCs were originally formed after residents became frustrated with the governmental channels established to address their problems. They seek to change things on their own through: "developing or renovating properties, building on assets, and generally drawing power and capital *in* to the community, rather than scaring it away" (Ibid.).

Traditionally, CDCs were anti redevelopment, fearing gentrification and loss of community. Now, the CDCs use the markets to their benefits, buying and developing property themselves, encouraging compatible private investment, and forming good relationship with businesses and local government (Grogan 2000, 70). They are a large supplier of affordable housing, by 1988 the supplied 20,000 units per year, and between 1994 and 1997 they supplied 247,000 new and rehabbed units (Ibid.).

The CDCs are not everywhere, however, and low income inner city residents are still often taken advantage of without the power the CDCs can garner. The concern is still justified that the process of redevelopment causes the costs of relocation and loss of community are born by the underprivileged, while the benefits of the development are given to the elite (Bezdek 2006).

Two additional devices that might assist landowners working to revitalize their own parcels and neighborhoods are the business improvement district (BID) and tax increment financing (TIF). BIDs are granted powers of taxation in order to provide specialized services on a customized basis (Ellickson 1998). BIDs have become a widespread practice in urban areas where business property owners were ready to accept responsibility for their district from the government. TIFs involves the issuance of bonds by the local government, to be repaid by the incremental real estate and other tax revenues generated by the project itself, with the proceeds directed to provide financing to the developers (London 2001, 778). One drawback is that, even if the project is successful, the short term advantage accruing to the local economy (and current political officials) is offset by the diversion of the ensuing tax revenues long after the decision makers are out of office (London 2001, 781). Similarly, industrial development bonds (IDBs) have tax exempt status, and permit localities to offer low-cost financing for revitalization projects (Malloy 1987).

## CONCLUSION

There are several feasible methods of involving property owners in the redevelopment process. Two of these, the preference for foreclosure instead of condemnation in cases of blight, and avoidance of condemnation where normal assembly is possible, may avoid eminent domain in the first instance. A fractional share alternative to the deprivation of development rights, exemplified by *Barancik v. County of Marin* (1989), would permit existing owners to capitalize on the development profits now retained by localities or transferred to outsiders. Owner involvement through mandatory participation in redevelopment after condemnation shows promise, although, as the California Supreme Court's decision in *Bunker Hill* illustrates, deriving statutory formulae providing owners with an effective means of participation under objective criteria would not be easy. Some type of standardized limited partnership might be appropriate. Robert Nelson's neighborhood privatization approach (Nelson 2005), where a super majority in a self-designated neighborhood could engage in redevelopment or approve a sale, with the proceeds divided between the neighbors, offers considerable promise, although it deprives individual owners of autonomy.

All of these methods provide ways of revitalizing community infrastructure within the framework of the owner and community involvement. They permit existing owners to capture some benefit from revitalization of their parcels. To that extent, they all discourage rent seeking by developers and public officials resulting in opportunistic condemnation. For these reasons, these devices also supplement the process-based assurances of fair treatment contained in Justice Stevens' majority opinion in *Kelo v. City of New London* and in Justice Kennedy's concurring opinion.

## NOTES

The author wishes to thank for Law and Economics Center at GMUSL for its financial support and Julia Ovando, GMUSL Class of 2008, for her very helpful research assistance.

1. U.S. CONST. Amend. V ("[N]or shall private property be taken for public use, without just compensation.").
2. Notably, *Kelo* was free of the rhapsodic language that marked Justice William O. Douglas' opinion in *Berman v. Parker*, 545 U.S. 469 (2005). "Miserable and disreputable housing conditions may do more than spread disease and crime and immorality. They may also suffocate the spirit by reducing the people who live there to the status of cattle. They may indeed make living an almost insufferable burden. They may also be an ugly sore, a blight on the community which robs it of charm, which makes it a place from which men turn. The misery of housing may despoil a community as an open sewer may ruin a river." Id. at 32–33.
3. A classic illustration occurred during a conversation between Henry Kissinger and Chinese Premier Zhou En-Lai, when Kissinger asked, "What is the historical significance of the French Revolution?" Zhou responded, "It is yet too early to tell." *See* Stephan Kux, *Confederalism and Stability in the Commonwealth of Independent States*, 1 NEW EUR. L. REV. 387, 395 (Spring 1993).
4. *See, e.g., Florida Rock Indus. v. United States*, 18 F.3d 1650, 1566 (Fed. Cir. 1994) (observing that "yesterday's Everglades swamp to be drained as a mosquito haven is today's wetland to be preserved for wildlife and aquifer recharge; who knows what tomorrow's view of public policy will bring, or how the market will respond to it....").
5. *Id.* (quoting Wilson v. City of Long Branch, 142 A.2d 837, 842 (N.J. 1958)).
6. CAL. HEALTH AND SAFETY CODE § 33030(1)(e) (2007).
7. *See* KY. REV. STAT. ANN. § 99.720 (2007),and UTAH CODE ANN. § 17C-2–301 (2006).
8. 2006 Fla. Sess. Law Serv. Ch. 2006–11 (H.B. 1567) (WEST), FL ST §73.014.
9. West's Ann. Cal. Health & Safety Code § 33339 (requiring that redevelopment agency plans provide for owner participation but not rely on that participation, adopt and publish owner participation rules; give preference to business owners to reenter that same redevelopment area, possess alternative plans in the case that the owners do not participate, and act in good faith to allow owner participation).
10. West's NRSA §279.566 (1).
11. West's NRSA §279.609.
12. *See* Charlotte Hess & Elinor Ostrom, *Ideas, Artifacts, and Facilities: Information as a Common-Pool Resource*, 66 Spg. LAW & CONTEMP. PROBS. 111, 114–123 (2003) (analyzing differences between open access and commons regimes).
13. *Penn Central Transportation Co. v. City of New York*, 438 U.S. 104, 137 (1978) ("While these rights may well not have constituted 'just compensation' if a 'taking' had occurred, the rights nevertheless undoubtedly mitigate whatever financial burdens the law has imposed on appellants and, for that reason, are to be taken into account in considering the impact of regulation.")

## REFERENCES

Anderson, Martin. 1964. *The Federal Bulldozer, a Critical Analysis of Urban Renewal, 1949–1962*. Cambridge, MA: MIT Press.

Anderson, Owen L. and Ernest E. Smith. 2004. Exploratory Unitization under the 2004 Model Oil and Gas Conservation Act: Leveling the Playing Field. *Journal of Land Resources & Environmental Law* 24 (2): 277–291.

*Barancik v. County of Marin*, 872 F.2d 834 (9th Cir. 1989).

Barron, David J. 2003. The Community Economic Development Movement: A Metropolitan Perspective. *Stanford Law Review* 56 (701).

Bell, Abraham and Gideon Parchomovsky. 2006. The Uselessness of Public Use. *Columbia Law Review* 106: 1412–1437.

Benkler, Yochai. 2004. Sharing Nicely: On Shareable Goods and the Emergence of Sharing As a Modality of Economic Production. *Yale Law Journal* 114 (2): 273–358.

Bezdek, Barbara L. 2006. To Attain "The Just Rewards of So Much Struggle": Local-Resident Equity Participation in Urban Revitalization. *Hofstra Law Review* 35 (1): 37–114.

Bingham, Richard D. 1975. *Public Housing and Urban Renewal, an Analysis of Federal-Local Relations.* New York: Praeger.

Boyer, Christine M. 1983. *Dreaming the Rational City: The Myth of American City Planning.* Cambridge, MA: MIT Press.

*Brown v. Legal Foundation of Washington*, 538 U.S. 216 (2003).

Buchanan, James M. and Gordon Tullock. 1962. *The Calculus of Consent, Logical Foundations of Constitutional Democracy.* Ann Arbor: University of Michigan Press.

Buchanan, James M., Robert D. Tollison, and Gordon Tullock, eds. 1980. *Toward A Theory of The Rent-Seeking Society.* College Station: Texas A&M University.

Bunker Hill Urban Renewal Project 1B of Community Redevelopment Agency of City of Los Angeles, 389 P.2d 538 (Cal. 1964).

*City of Las Vegas Downtown Redevelopment Agency v. Pappas*, 76 P.3d 1 (Nev. 2003).

Claeys, Eric R. 2006. Euclid Lives? The Uneasy Legacy of Progressivism in Zoning. *Fordham Law Review* 73 (2): 731–735.

*Concerned Citizens of Princeton, Inc. v. Mayor and Council of Borough of Princeton*, 851 A.2d 685 (N.J. Super. 2004).

*Coniston Corp. v. Village of Hoffman Estates*, 844 F.2d 461 (7th Cir. 1988).

*County of Wayne v. Hathcock*, 684 N.W.2d 765 (Mich. 2004).

Dukeminier, Jesse, James E. Krier, Gregory S. Alexander, and Michael H. Schill. 2006. *Property* (6th ed.). New York: Aspen, 262–274.

Eagle, Steven J. 1999. Devolutionary Proposals and Contractarian Principles, Ed. F.H. Buckley, *The Fall and Rise of Freedom of Contract*. 184–191. Durham, NC: Duke University Press.

———. 2007. Does Blight Really Justify Condemnation? *Urban Lawyer* 39 (4): 833–858.

Ellickson, Robert C. 1973. Alternatives to Zoning: Covenants, Nuisance Rules and Fines as Land Use Controls. *University of Chicago Law Review* 40 (4): 681–781.

———. 1998. New Institutions for Old Neighborhoods. *Duke Law Journal* 48 (1): 75–110.

Emerson, Chad D. 2006. Making Main Street Legal Again: The Smartcode Solution to Sprawl. *Missouri Law Review* 71 (3): 637–646.

*Felom v. Redevelopment Agency of City and County of San Francisco*, 320 P.2d 884 (Cal. Dist. Ct. 1958).

Fischel, William A. 2004. The Political Economy of Public Use in Poletown: How Federal Grants Encourage Excessive Use Of Eminent Domain. *Michigan State Law Review* (4): 929–930.

*Florida Rock Indus. v. United States*, 18 F.3d 1650, 1566 (Fed. Cir. 1994)

Foster, Sheila R. 2006. The City as an Ecological Space: Social Capital and Urban Land Use. *Notre Dame Law Review* 82 (2): 527–582.

Garnett, Nicole Stelle. 2003. The Public-Use Question as a Takings Problem. *George Washington Law Review* 71 (6): 934–958.

Greer, Scott. 1965. *Urban Renewal and American Cities, the Dilemma of Democratic Intervention.* Indianapolis: Bobbs-Merrill.

Grey, Thomas. 1980. The Disintegration of Property, in Property. J. Roland Pennock and John W. Chapman, eds. *NOMOS Monograph* 22.

Grogan, Paul. 2001. *Comeback Cities: A Blueprint for Urban Neighborhood Revival.* Boulder: Westview Press.

*Hantages v. Henderson*, 113 P.3d 848 (Nev. 2005).

Hayek, Friedrich A. 1945. The Use of Knowledge in Society, *American Economic Review* 35: 519–530.

———. 1988. *The Fatal Conceit: The Errors of Socialism.* Chicago: University of Chicago Press.

Hellegers, Adam P. 2001. Eminent Domain as an Economic Development Tool: A Proposal to Reform HUD Displacement Policy 2001. *Law Review Michigan State University Detroit College of Law* (3): 901–963.

Heller, Michael A. 1998. Tragedy of the Anticommons, Property in the Transition from Marx to Markets. *Harvard Law Review* 111 (3): 621.

Heller, Michael and Roderick M. Hills, Jr. 2008. The Art of Land Assembly Districts. *Harvard Law Review* 121 (6): 1465–1527.

Hess, Charlotte and Elinor Ostrom. 2003. Ideas, Artifacts, and Facilities: Information as a Common-Pool Resource. *Law and Contemporary Problems* 66 (1&2): 111–145.

Huntington Park Redevelopment Agency v. Duncan, 190 Cal.Rptr.744 (Cal. Ct. App. 2 Dist. 1983).

Jacobs, Jane. 1961. *The Death and Life of Great American Cities*. New York: Random House.

Johnstone, Quintin. 1994. Government Control of Urban Land Use: A Comparative Major Program Analysis. *New York Law School Law Review* 39 (3): 373–393.

Kanner, Gideon. 2006. The Public Use Clause: Constitutional Mandate or "Hortatory Fluff?" *Pepperdine Law Review* 33 (2): 335–350.

Kelly, Daniel B. 2006. The "Public Use" Requirement in Eminent Domain Law: A Rationale Based on Secret Purchases and Private Influence. *Cornell Law Review* 92 (1): 1.

*Kelo v. City of New London*, 545 U.S. at 502 (2005).

*Kelo v. City of New London*, 545 U.S. February 22, 2005. Transcript of Oral Argument: 22.

Kiew, Chiawen C. 2005. Contracts, Combinations, Conspiracies, and Conservation: Antitrust in Oil Unitization and the Intertemporal Problem. *Northwestern University Law Review* 99 (2): 931–970.

Kmiec, Douglas W. 2005. The Human Nature of Freedom and Identity—We Hold More Than Random Thoughts. *Harvard Journal of Law & Public Policy* 29 (1): 33–46.

Krueger, Anne O. 1974. The Political Economy of the Rent-Seeking Society. *American Economic Review* 64 (3): 291–303.

Larson, Jane E. 1995. Free Markets Deep in the Heart of Texas. *Georgetown Law Journal* 84 (2): 179–180.

Lippmann, Walter. 1934. *The Method of Freedom*. New York: Macmillian.

London, Frank S. 2001. The Use of Tax Increment Financing to Attract Private Investment and Generate Redevelopment in Virginia. *Virginia Tax Review* 20 (4): 777–778.

Malloy, Robin Paul. 1987. The Political Economy of Co-Financing America's Urban Renaissance. *Vanderbilt Law Review* 40 (67): 95–98.

McDonald, Forrest. 1985. *Novus Ordo Seclorum: The Intellectual Origins of the Constitution*. Lawrence: University Press of Kansas.

Merrill, Thomas W. 1986. The Economics of Public Use. *Cornell Law Review* 72 (61): 75–76.

Nedelsky, Jennifer. 1990. *Private Property and the Limits of American Constitutionalism: The Madisonian Framework and Its Legacy*. Chicago: University of Chicago Press.

Nelson, Robert H. 1999. Privatizing the Neighborhood: A Proposal to Replace Zoning with Private Collective Property Rights to Existing Neighborhoods. *George Mason Law Review* 7 (4): 827–841.

———. 2005. *Private Neighborhoods and the Transformation of Local Government*. Washington, DC: Urban Institute Press.

Parchomovsky, Gideon and Peter Siegelman. 2004. Selling Mayberry: Communities and Individuals in Law and Economics. *California Law Review* 92 (1): 75–146.

Parisi, Francesco. 2002. Entropy in Property. *American Journal of Comparative Law* 50 (3): 595–596.

Polanyi, Michael. 1969. *Knowing and Being: Essays*. Ed. Marjorie Grene. London: Routledge & K. Paul.

*Poletown Neighborhood Council v. City of Detroit*, 304 N.W.2d 455 (Mich. 1981).

Pritchett, Wendell E. 2003. The "Public Menace" of Blight: Urban Renewal and the Private Uses of Eminent Domain, *Yale Law & Policy Review* 21 (1): 1–52.

Quinones, Benjamin B. 1994. Redevelopment Redefined: Revitalizing the Central City with Resident Control. *University of Michigan Journal of Law Reform* 27 (3&4): 689–691.

Rakove, Jack N. 1996. *Original Meanings: Politics and Ideas in the Making of the Constitution*. New York: Knopf.

Skoloff, Brian.2007. In Florida, Upwardly Mobile Homes. *Washington Post* January 7: D3.

Smith, Adam. 1998. *An Inquiry into the Nature and Causes of the Wealth of Nations.* Ed. Kathryn Sutherland. London: Oxford University Press.

Somin, Ilya. 2007. The Limits of Backlash: Assessing the Political Response to Kelo. *George Mason Law & Economics Research Paper* 07–14. Available at SSRN: *http://ssrn.com/abstract=976298/.*

Starkman, Dean. 1998. Condemnation Is Used to Hand One Business Property of Another. *Wall Street Journal* December 2: A1.

———. 2004. Cities Use Eminent Domain to Clear Lots for Big-Box Stores. *Wall Street Journal* December 8: B1.

Stevens, John Paul. "Judicial Predilections," Address to the Clark County (Nevada) Bar Association, August 18, 2005.

*Suitum v. Tahoe Regional Planning Agency*, 520 U.S. 725 (1997).

Tarlock, Dan. 1972. Toward a Revised Theory of Zoning. Ed. Frank S. Bangs, Jr. *Land Use Controls Annual.* Chicago: American Society of Planning Officials, 141–152.

Tullock, Gordon.1967. The Welfare Costs of Tariffs, Monopolies, and Theft. *Western Economics Journal* 5: 224.

Wickersham, Jay. 2001. Jane Jacobs's Critique of Zoning: From Euclid to Portland and Beyond. *Boston College Environmental Affairs Law Review* 28 (4): 547–552.

Williams & Meyers Manual of Oil and Gas Terms 1206 (12th ed., 2003).

*Wilson v. City of Long Branch*, 142 A.2d 837, 842 (N.J. 1958).

# 3

# The Proper Uses of Eminent Domain for Urban Redevelopment

## Is Eminent Domain Necessary?

### Samuel R. Staley

## Introduction and Scope

The U.S. Supreme Court nullified substantive limits on the use of eminent domain for economic development purposes in *Kelo v. City of New London*. While planners, private developers, and local economic development officials praised the decision because it protected their discretion, the practical effect has been to make rights to private land development and improvements discretionary and subject to the desires of majoritarian interests within a city or state. As long as cities, states, and other government agencies follow the letter of the law and formal procedures, property can be condemned and transferred to the public sector or other private parties.

This decision has placed many communities and local governments in a procedural and policy bind. Despite the willingness of the U.S. Supreme Court to dismiss the importance of substantive review of government actions regarding "takings," many citizens and leaders still believe that the protection of private property rights should remain a core value of public policy. Dozens of state legislatures are considering legislation that places new constraints on takings for economic development purposes. The question, in a post-*Kelo* policy world, is how property rights can be protected now that the legal framework for protecting them has been abandoned.[1]

This paper is not intended to dismiss the potential for pursing economic development goals and strategies without resorting to Eminent Domain. Indeed, most land development in the U.S. does not involve "Takings" of private property. Moreover, the case of Anaheim, California described in Pringle (2007) provides a compelling case study of how an established urban area can successfully pursue revitalization goals with an explicit policy of not using Eminent Domain. Unfortunately, however, Anaheim is the exception, not the rule. Most U.S. cities pursue comprehensive redevelopment programs and strategies that allow the use of Eminent Domain consistent with judicial interpretations of the Fifth Amendment to the U.S. Constitution and state law.

Thus, this paper explores the implications of the *Kelo* decision and eminent domain within the context of mainstream urban economic development policy, and outlines a set of principles that can be used by public officials that respects private property rights. The next section discusses several cases where Eminent Domain has been used to further the public policy goals of local economic development or revitalization. These cases illustrate the types of projects that typically trigger the use of Eminent Domain for economic development purposes in an urban environment. They also provide the political and economic context for developing a policy framework more consistent with protecting property rights while still meeting the spirit underlying the public use exception in the Fifth Amendment.

This paper is not intended to evaluate other issues more common to eminent domain controversies, including the role private interests play in the development process, the legal definition, and interpretation of "public use" or what constitutes a public use, or the proper definition of urban blight. While these issues are important and relevant to this debate, they are beyond the scope of this paper. As a matter of federal law, economic development is now clearly considered within the scope of public use for Fifth Amendment takings and, by implication, constraints on government actions have been reduced to procedural concerns. The U.S. Supreme Court also has made it clear that that using eminent domain in a way that substantially (or even primarily) benefits another private party does not disqualify its use. These issues are now matters for state legislative debate that may be informed by this analysis but is not a driver of it.[2] Thus, the analysis does not start from the presumption that eminent domain should never be used for economic development purposes.[3]

The paper instead explores this issue by examining specific cases where eminent domain is used for economic development purposes (section 2). The third section then outlines specific criteria that can be used as a filter for determining when or if Eminent Domain is considered for economic development purposes. These criteria can form a checklist for local government officials when they are evaluating strategies and methods for approaching urban redevelopment projects. Section four applies these property rights friendly criteria to the four cases. Section five concludes with a brief summary and discussion of policy implications.

## EMINENT DOMAIN AND ECONOMIC DEVELOPMENT: THREE CASES

This section of the paper presents three brief case studies where eminent domain has been used to promote economic development and revitalization. Each case represents an illustration of the types of development that are common in contemporary economic development initiatives, the neighborhoods and areas that tend to be targeted for redevelopment projects that use eminent domain, and the types of proposals that are often involved in contemporary redevelopment projects. These cases were chosen because information about the local land market, details about the proposed development projects, and data on the targeted neighborhood were available, providing an avenue for examining market trends and the potential impacts of the proposed initiatives.

Because the primary focus of this paper is on eminent domain's use in urban economic development, these cases were not chosen for their legal implications, although each has been subject to substantial litigation and controversy (table 3.1).[4] They are, however, representative of the likely uses and applications in a *Kelo* policy environment—where economic development, broadly defined, is considered a public use and limits on eminent domain do not involve substantive issues.

Table 3.1   Key Characteristics of Case Study Cities

| Case Study Cities | Characteristics of Property | Proposed Use | Current Status |
| --- | --- | --- | --- |
| Mesa, Arizona | Commercial and residential properties | Contemporary retail commercial | Eminent demand action overturned by Arizona Court of Appeals in 2003 |
| Lakewood, Ohio | Older mixed-use neighborhoods, 1,700 homes | High-end commercial & residential with regional impact | Proposed development rejected at ballot box in 2003 and blight designation rescinded at ballot box in 2004 |
| Norwood, Ohio | Older residential area with neighborhood commercial and retail | Mixed commercial & residential with regional impact | Eminent domain action overturned by Ohio Supreme Court in 2005 |
| Long Branch, New Jersey | Older, bungalow-style residential neighborhood with beach access | High-end, luxury residential | Agreement reached with City of Long Branch to stop eminent domain proceedings in September 2009 |

## Mesa, Arizona

Mesa (Pop. 448,555) is a growing city immediately east of Phoenix with an aggressive development program. A key part of Mesa's economic development efforts focused on its downtown revitalization plans. In 1994, the city council adopted its Vision Plan for Downtown Mesa. The city actively assisted more than 14 redevelopment projects ranging from a major streetscape along Main Street to a $60 million resort. A key aesthetic component of the 20-year plan was creating visual "gateways" that would differentiate downtown from other parts of the city.

A cornerstone of Mesa's economic development efforts was using eminent domain to assemble property for new development (Staley & Blair 2005). Another key element was (and is) its reliance on the private sector to drive the redevelopment process. Private-sector interest in redevelopment became a formal part of city redevelopment policy in 1996. Like most states, Arizona cities are required to declare an area blighted before it can be condemned. The area must also be targeted for redevelopment through a formal planning process.

The city attempts to use the redevelopment and planning process as a way to accommodate private sector development. In some cases, this effort is explicit. City officials received numerous inquiries about redevelopment opportunities in Mesa in 1996, for example, but *all* the sites were outside the Town Center Redevelopment Area (Balmer 1996, emphasis in original). "In order to undertake any of these projects it will be necessary for us to first expand our Redevelopment Area," wrote Wayne Balmer, the city's community development director, in a 1996 memo to the city manager.

Few close followers of redevelopment in Mesa would have been surprised, then, when Mesa's downtown redevelopment area was amended in 1999 to add properties on the south and west sides of the city after private developers expressed interest in several parcels of land that came to be known as Site 24 (City of Mesa 1991). Site 24 consisted of several privately owned lots that included ongoing businesses, vacant land, and homes. The city then re-designated the entire one-square mile town center plus the additional properties a redevelopment area.

Private interest in using Mesa's power of eminent domain to acquire Site 24 was expressed as early as 1998. Lenhart's ACE Hardware was interested in expanding its retail store, but did not have sufficient space at its then current location in Mesa. The owner asked the city of Mesa to purchase ten separate lots on Site 24 and sell him the city-acquired property at $4 per square foot to facilitate his expansion.[5] The expansion would have allowed the hardware store to double the size of its business (Lenhart's ACE Hardware 2000). At the time, the full cash value for these properties averaged more than $8 per square foot according to the Maricopa County assessor's office.[6] The Mesa city council approved resolutions allowing the use of eminent domain to condemn private property on Site 24 not already owned by the private developers in March 1999.[7]

An analysis by the author of residential properties comparable to the ones that would be seized suggested the actual market value could be 25 percent to 30 percent higher than the value on file with the county tax assessor.[8] If a market adjustment were added to the full cash value, the development agreement would represent a significant direct subsidy to the owner of the ACE Hardware store and its development company, Redstone Investments, LLC.

A second developer joined Redstone after the city issued a Request for Proposals to develop the site, Palm Court Investments. Palm Court represented Mesa-based consumer electronics firm, Mesa Discount, that also wanted to expand. The two businesses would share parking and other physical facilities based on the joint development project.[9] Palm Court's subsidy would have exceeded $200,000 even without the market adjustment based on property values reported by the county tax assessor. Thus, the direct subsidy based on land acquisition for Site 24 could have ranged from $176,000 to $592,000.

The land proposed for condemnation by Lenhart, Site 24, anchored the immediate neighborhood and included several viable and thriving businesses. A fast-food restaurant on Country Club Drive, for example, generated a full cash value of $31.12 per square foot, almost three times the average for the entire site and almost five times more than the average for Lenhart's property. Bailey's Brake Service generated a full cash value of $9.73, about one third higher than the average for the properties already acquired by Lenhart. Overall, the full cash value of the independently owned properties subject to condemnation to make way for Lenhart's project is almost $9.00 per square feet, more than 25 percent higher than the property already acquired (Staley and Blair 2005).

Site 24 was also not blighted according to an objective assessment using the criteria in Arizona state statute. The businesses and properties were providing significant economic and social benefits to the city of Mesa. On average, the Site 24 properties increased in value by about 10 percent per year (table 3.2). Only three properties declined in value, and their change in value was likely the result of their reclassification on the assessor's tax records. While the properties owned by Redstone Development and Palm Court increased substantially, the independently owned properties increased as well. The full cash value of Bailey's Brake Service property increased 41 percent since 2000. Thus, the land and the businesses in Site 24 were not impairing economic or social progress in the community

**Table 3.2**   Change in Assessed Value in Site 24 by Ownership

|  | 2000 | 2002 | % Chg |
|---|---|---|---|
| All Site 24 Properties | $2,511,301 | $2,996,952 | 19.3 |
| Redstone & Palm Court | $1,134,556 | $1,540,932 | 35.8 |
| All Independent Properties | $1,376,743 | $1,456,020 | 5.8 |
| (Excluding parcels 73C, 83, 84A) | $1,175,739 | $1,389,520 | 18.2 |
| Redstone Develop. Properties | $2,445,559 | $313,410 | 28.2 |
| Independent (Redstone project) | $665,279 | $622,646 | −6.4 |
| (Excluding parcels 73C, 83, 84A) | $464,275 | $556,146 | 19.8 |
| Palm Court Investments | $890,000 | $1,227,522 | 37.9 |
| Independent (Palm Court project) | $711,464 | $833,374 | 17.1 |

*Note*: Five parcels were reclassified by the tax assessor, but only three reclassifications impacted the assessed value of the property. Parcels 73C, 83, and 84A were reclassified, resulting in a significant reduction in the assessed value of the property. Parcels 73C and 84A are vacant. Parcel 83 carries a designated land-use of commercial.

*Source*: Maricopa County Assessor, http://www.maricopa.gov.

or the local neighborhood and may have been providing a stabilizing force for the neighborhood.[10]

In the case of Mesa, land assembly through Eminent Domain was the primary (and perhaps only) redevelopment tool. The city took advantage of the broad discretion given to it by statute to condemn private property and transfer it to other private developers even though the evidence showed clearly:

- The properties being seized were viable and growing;
- Private investors relied on the city to acquire and negotiate the sale of land, and
- Direct subsidies to private developers could be substantial because the city agreed to sell the properties to developers at rates substantial below the market price.

## Lakewood, Ohio

The city of Lakewood, Ohio, a "first tier" lakefront suburb immediately west of Cleveland, provides another telling example of how eminent domain has become a cornerstone of city redevelopment initiatives.

Lakewood, like Mesa, is not a community mired in decline. On the contrary, the average home sells for $146,605, 15.9 percent higher than Cuyahoga County and almost on par with the average for all suburban Cleveland communities.[11] The city's assessed valuation increased by 15 percent between 1994 and 2000 according to the Cuyahoga County Auditor, significantly faster than the average for Cleveland's suburbs.[12] Despite being boxed in by surrounding communities, the city managed to issue 1,645 residential building permits between 1999 and 2000. By all significant indicators, Lakewood has a robust local economy.

Nevertheless, like most cities, not all neighborhoods fare equally well. The West End consists of 31 acres on the western edge of Lakewood. The area has substantial scenic value, looking over the Rocky River protected by the Cleveland park system. Almost 3,000 people lived in the neighborhood in 2000, living in more than 1,700 housing units according to the U.S. Bureau of the Census (table 3.3).[13]

Table 3.3   Comparison of West End Neighborhood to City of Lakewood

| | City of Lakewood | West End Neighborhood | |
| --- | --- | --- | --- |
| | | Census Tract 1607 | Census Tract 1608 |
| Population | 56,646 | 1,705 | 1,137 |
| Housing Units | 28,416 | 1,138 | 605 |
| Vacancy Rate | 6.1% | 8.0% | 4.6% |
| Mean Household Size (owners) | 2.5 | 2.6 | 2.7 |
| Mean Household Size (renters) | 1.7 | 1.5 | 1.5 |
| Median Household Income | $40,527 | $31,477 | $34,554 |
| % Families Below Poverty Level | 6.1% | 7.4% | 8.1% |
| Minority Population | 6.9% | 7.0% | 40% |

The West End neighborhood was developed primarily in the decades spanning the turn of the twentieth century. Almost all the non-apartment residential and commercial buildings were built between 1897 and 1925 (City of Lakewood 2002). Five large apartment buildings and three smaller, three-story apartment buildings were built during the 1960s and 1970s, replacing barns used to house streetcars.

During the summer of 2002, planning consultant D.B. Hartt and architectural consultant Square One, Inc. conducted surveys of the buildings in the West End. These surveys and city records led them to conclude that the West End neighborhood had "sufficient deficiencies…which together are detrimental to the public health, safety and welfare and which impeded the sound growth, planning and economic development of the City of Lakewood" and "that substantial portions of the" community development area met the definitions of blight as defined in the city's ordinances (City of Lakewood 2002). The consultants also believed that these conditions had deteriorated to the point where the city could use eminent domain to declare the area blighted.

Based on the consultants' findings, the city of Lakewood passed a resolution on December 16, 2002 approving a comprehensive development plan for the West End District that, in effect, required land acquisition through voluntary purchase or eminent domain. On June 16, 2003, it approved a development agreement between the city and Lakewood Shoppes, LLC, the private developer of the property.

The blight determination was based on weak evidence, taking advantage of the broad definitions for blight in Ohio statute and the general unwillingness of courts to closely scrutinize local government decisions on non-procedural issues. The city's consultants did not conduct a census of structures in the West End. Rather, they examined a sample of structures to make a determination for the entire area. The consultants, for example, examined the interior of 12 buildings to determine their condition and 13 buildings for fire code violations (City of Lakewood 2002), despite the fact the neighborhood included hundreds of residential and commercial structures. More troubling, perhaps, was that the consultants relied primarily on determinations of "economic" and "functional" obsolescence to support the city's blight determination. Homes with one bathroom, a one car garage, or a small kitchen could be considered "obsolete" since they were inconsistent with contemporary housing trends and characteristics.

In an era where increasing emphasis is placed on rehabilitation and renovation activities, many of the criteria used appear arbitrary and subjective. For example, the consultant's analysis notes that 62 percent of the parcels in the West End neighborhood have a real estate appraised value that is 40 percent less than the comparable value of *new* construction.

Another factor influencing the city's decision was the determination that 78 percent of the parcels did not conform to zoning regulations (City of Lakewood 2002). They were either a nonconforming use, lot sizes were smaller than code minimums (or prevented expansion), or did not have a sufficient number of parking spaces. These limitations, the consultants claimed (without support), "impairs the economic and residential growth of the community." (City of Lakewood 2002) In short, homes and buildings built in the early twentieth century did not conform to the city of Lakewood zoning code in 2002, and these discrepancies became evidence that the homes and businesses should be razed and redeveloped according to plans created by the city.[14]

In addition, home values in the city of Lakewood increased 61.1 percent between 1990 and 2000, rising to a median of $117,900 (figure 3.1). Home values were lower in the West End census tracts than for the city as a whole, but appreciation was significant. Median home values in tract 1607 (one of the two census tracts that comprise the West End) rose faster than for the city as a whole, increasing to $103,800 in 2000 (an increase of 70.4 percent over the previous decade). General inflation during this period was 31.8 percent, according to the Consumer Price Index for urban consumers, and housing price inflation was 32.4 percent (U.S. Census Bureau, 464). Thus, home values in parts of the West End were increasing at twice the inflation rate.

Vacancy rates are another common indicator of neighborhood deterioration. If vacancies grow because properties cannot be sold or rented at prevailing rates, they are at risk for deterioration as property owners attempt to maintain unsustainable rents and low revenues prevent maintenance and renovation. Occupancy and vacancy trends in the West End, however, mirror those for the city as a whole.

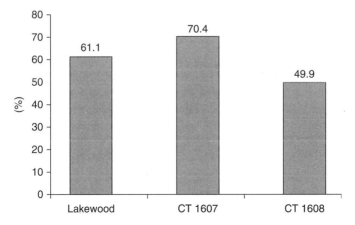

**Figure 3.1**   Change in Home Values in West End Census Tracts vs. Lakewood, 1990 to 2000
*Source*: U.S. Bureau of the Census.

**Table 3.4**  Vacancy Rates in Lakewood and West End Neighborhood

|                              | 1990  | 2000  | % Chg.   |
|------------------------------|-------|-------|----------|
| Lakewood                     |       |       |          |
| Owner-occupied               | 1.2%  | 0.9%  | −25.0%   |
| Renter-occupied              | 4.9%  | 6.4%  | 30.6%    |
| West End-Census Tract 1607   |       |       |          |
| Owner-occupied               | 1.1%  | 0.6%  | −45.5%   |
| Renter-occupied              | 5.7%  | 8.4%  | 47.4%    |
| West End-Census Tract 1608   |       |       |          |
| Owner-occupied               | 1.0%  | 0.5%  | −50.0%   |
| Renter-occupied              | 3.5%  | 5.5%  | 57.1%    |

*Note*: Vacancy rates for the city of Lakewood exclude the West End.

*Source*: U.S. Census Bureau.

While the vacancy rates for rented housing increased, vacancy rates for owner occupied housing fell dramatically (table 3.4). Owner-occupied housing vacancy rates actually fell twice as fast as for the city of Lakewood. This is consistent with home value trends—tight real estate markets put upward pressure on home values and allow vacant homes to be sold more quickly.

The similarities in vacancy rates between the West End census tracts and Lakewood are striking. While vacancy rates for renter-occupied units increase faster in the West End census tracts, the differences are probably not large enough to suggest that the West End neighborhood is significantly different from the rest of the city.

A third conventional indicator of neighborhood deterioration is the rate of homeownership. Neighborhoods with a large share of homeowners are typically more stable than those with high shares of renters (and thus transient populations). When owners leave the area and rent their housing units, physical standards may also drop. This finding applies to stand-alone units as well as to multi-family housing units.

The citywide rate of owner occupancy has remained steady although Lakewood seemed to experience a small decline in the overall rate (figure 3.2). Homeownership rates increased in the West End census tracts. Thus, increasing homeownership in the West End helped support and stabilize the citywide homeownership rate.

Thus, little objective evidence suggests that the West End neighborhood is in decline. In fact, the evidence from the Census Bureau suggests the neighborhood was experiencing a rebound—home values were increasing faster than for the city as a whole, vacancy rates were declining, homeownership was increasing, and rents were stable. Clearly, the West End neighborhood was not in imminent danger of "deteriorating into a blighted or deteriorated area. "Nevertheless, the key legal rationale for using eminent domain was to eliminate blight and prevent "the further development and spread of blight" (City of Lakewood 2003).

With an official finding of blight, the city was legally free to pursue whatever economic development strategy it felt was necessary to redevelop the property. In this case, the redevelopment plan called for a comprehensive approach and emphasized replacing the existing neighborhood with a mix of upscale apartments and

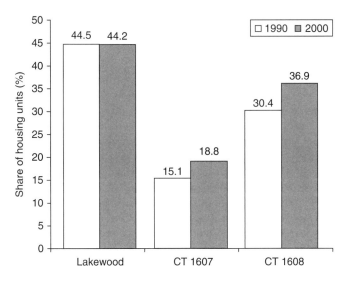

**Figure 3.2**  Changes in Homeownership Rates in Lakewood and West End Neighborhood
*Source*: U.S. Bureau of the Census.

commercial uses to be marketed as a "Lifestyle Center." According to the development agreement eventually signed by the city of Lakewood, the city would acquire all the necessary land (funded through public debt) and the developer would then purchase the land from the city. In fact, the city committed to acquiring all the remaining property within 90 days of signing the development agreement (City of Lakewood 2003). The city also capped the developer's exposure to land acquisition costs at $28.5 million (City of Lakewood 2003).

The agreement is instructive in that it lays out the content of the development and provides an important contrast to land uses in the current neighborhood. The West End currently consists of small homes on small yards with a scattering of neighborhood businesses and cheap office space. The city intended to develop the neighborhood as a commercial destination that would draw from throughout the region. Few of the businesses would target the everyday needs of the neighborhood. In fact, the agreement prevented neighborhood businesses such as inexpensive restaurants, conventional fast food, convenience stores, or discount pharmacies in order to protect the development's branding as a high-end destination. The agreement between the developer and city stipulates that the center will consist of: mid and upscale specialty stores; a book store as an anchor tenant; full-service sit down restaurants; high-end carryout restaurants such as a Starbucks; a multi-screen movie theater; home furnishing stores, and at least 25,000 square feet of general office space. The agreement explicitly prohibits convenience stores, "big box" tenants, or discount drug stores. In short, the city was fundamentally changing the character of the neighborhood, shifting it from an affordable residential neighborhood to an upscale commercial mixed-use area.

The fiscal benefits to the city of this expansion would be substantial. The value of all real estate in the current West End neighborhood amounts to $31.3 million (Hartt and Hopkins 2002). Significantly expanding the commercial mix of the land and replacing the existing affordable homes with upscale housing would increase the total value of real estate to between $79.8 million and $131.1 million dollars (figure 3.3). Redevelopment could boost city tax revenues from just $638,694 to as much as $1,657,733. Real-estate tax revenues would triple and income tax revenues would double. Importantly, no public evidence was presented that the proposed units would in fact generate the value. Moreover, the area was surrounded by physically larger homes selling for significantly less (about $80,000), which would likely dampen the market price for higher end condominiums.

The effects on the residential market would be substantial. Although the proposed redevelopment schemes would reduce the number of homes in the neighborhood by half, the average value of homes would increase dramatically (figure 3.4). Current homes average $41,727. The most intensive redevelopment proposal was expected to boost the average home value to almost $200,000. Thus, the neighborhood housing market would fundamentally shift from an affordable, mixed income community to an exclusive, high-end residential community.

Projected tax revenues were the only evidence presented that the Lakewood Community Action Plan would, according to the Ohio Revised Code (P719.01.1

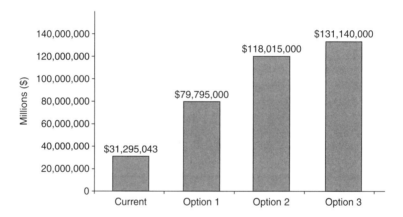

**Figure 3.3**  Real Estate Value of West End under Alternate Development Proposals

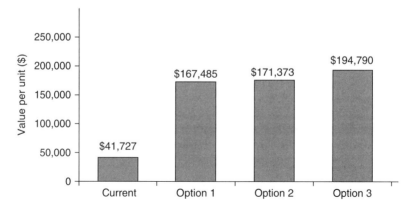

**Figure 3.4**  Value of West End Residential Real Estate per Housing Unit under Different Development Proposals

and 719.011), generate economic development "in order to create or preserve jobs and employment opportunities and to improve the economic welfare of the people of such impacted city, may appropriate, enter upon and hold real estate within its corporate limits." The benefits of assumed higher property values and assumed employment increases were valued according to their contribution to the fiscal health of the community.

Lakewood's approach was substantially different from Mesa's, but both cases reflect an increasingly common core objective of local government: The city, in effect, determines what the "highest and best" economic use for the land would be by first seizing private property, assembling the land, and then offering it to the private sector via a Request for Proposals (RFP) directed to large real estate developers. In Lakewood, the city determined that a higher and better use for the West End District was as a Lifestyle Center rather than a neighborhood dominated by older, affordable homes and businesses.

As a practical matter, Lakewood stretched the definition of blight to the point where it had little substantive meaning or content. Indeed, the objective data on trends showed clearly that the neighborhood could not be considered blighted or deteriorating. The standards for determining blight were sufficiently broad and subjective that the city would be able to condemn any property for its redevelopment purposes.

### Long Branch, New Jersey

In a more current case, the City of Long Branch, New Jersey attempted to condem a small residential area of the city to make way for a redevelopment project featuring luxury apartments and condominiums. The area is south of a public park, adjacent to the Atlantic Ocean, and called the Marine Terrace, Ocean Terrace and Seaview Avenue, or MTOTSA, neighborhood. The city condemned the MTOTSA properties after determining they were "blighted" under New Jersey's housing and redevelopment law and including the property in the Beach Front North Blight Zone. While they agreed to no longer pursue the homeowners property through eminent domain in September 2009, the case illustrates an important tactic used by cities to pursue economic development through eminent domain. Moreover, the agreement protecting the homeowners in the MTOTSA neighborhood are specific to the Long Branch case and do not represent statewide policy or a change in city policy beyond the MTOTSA development.

Like the previous cases, MTOTSA neighborhood represents the type of development projects cities are typically engaged in, and are facilitated by the reasoning under *Kelo*. The homeowners occupy modest homes, most of which are several decades old. The likelihood these families can purchase similarly situated homes—a block from an ocean front beach and publicly protected open space—is small. Indeed, the City of Long Branch admits as much since their goal, as explained in the master plan, is to redevelop these properties for luxury housing selling at $500,000 or more, far above what families with modest incomes can afford. Using conventional financing, a household income in excess of $125,000 per year would be necessary to support the mortgage on the cheapest condominium planned for this redevelopment project.[15]

The properties in *Long Branch* were targeted because of their desirable ocean-front location, not because they were blighted. Condemnation proceedings on the well-kept, modest homes of working-class families in the MTOTSA neighborhood began after the City of Long Branch decided to include the homes within the Beachfront North blight zone to satisfy the private developer's desire for more beachfront property. The MTOTSA area is part of Phase II of the Beachfront North redevelopment plan. The first phase included 290 townhome and condominium units while the second phase commits to building an additional 185 condominium units.[16]

The MTOTSA neighborhood was not originally considered blighted, and the city publicly said it would work with residents to preserve their neighborhood. The blight zone was created with the intention of turning the project over to private developers. Applied Companies was awarded the contract and eventually incorporated Beachfront North, L.L.C. to implement the agreement. Beachfront North, L.L.C. signed contracts in 2000 for the redevelopment of several sections of the city for upscale, oceanfront condominium and townhouse developments. These properties were targeted for their profit potential, not the negative impact of the neighborhoods on the community or local area.

This application of eminent domain for redevelopment of the MTOTSA neighborhood appears consistent with the intent of the use of eminent domain under New Jersey's redevelopment law. The New Jersey Local Redevelopment and Housing Law is clear that factors other than local government intentions or planning goals are important for determining whether an area is in need of redevelopment. In order for an area to qualify as "in need of redevelopment," the law specifically makes references to the descriptive characteristics of property in the targeted area. According to the state's redevelopment law, properties in the targeted neighborhood need to be substantially characterized as: substandard, unsafe, unsanitary, dilapidated, abandoned, untenable, in disrepair, remote, overcrowded, lack ventilation, cover excessive amounts of land, characterized by diversity of ownership, unwholesome in living or working conditions.

Few of these criteria apply in a meaningful way to the MTOTSA neighborhood. While the MTOTSA neighborhood includes a few vacant parcels, they are not too small to provide a viable redevelopment opportunity on a parcel by parcel basis. More importantly, the properties are not considered substandard, particularly for oceanfront homes in tourist areas.

New Jersey law establishes seven major criteria for determining whether an area can be designated as "in need of redevelopment" according to the New Jersey Local Redevelopment and Housing Law (Chapter 40A:12A-5), but no formal report or study applied these criteria to the MTOTSA neighborhood. The city did conduct a "windshield" survey of the area, but this technique is unscientific and generally used to generate an overall impression of a neighborhood. They are not useful as a foundational study for determining public policy.

Most of this information is easily available from the local planning department, local government agencies, or a regional planning agency. Census data provide block breakdowns of demographic information, county clerks keep records of real estate transactions and tax records, and local law enforcement should have data on crime rates and trends. Data on assessed valuations for properties in the proposed redevelopment areas are particularly noteworthy. An area in need of redevelopment would exhibit declining property values. The author is not aware of any systematic assessment of the targeted properties and neighborhoods undertaken by the

City of Long Branch. Based on information from the Monmouth County, New Jersey Clerk's Office (available online), the properties on Ocean Terrace are valued at $330,200 (LaRosa), $204,900 (Hoagland), and $190,700 (Vendetti). Rose LaRosa's building alone (excluding land) is valued at $170,200.

## PROPERTY RIGHTS AND EMINENT DOMAIN IN A POST-*KELO* ERA

The urban neighborhoods described in the previous section have several common characteristics that made them vulnerable to takings through eminent domain for economic development purposes.

- The neighborhoods were older, with housing or businesses that were either fully depreciated or represented development styles inconsistent with contemporary trends or the zoning code;
- The neighborhoods were not blighted in the conventional sense since the land was in productive economic use and, in two cases, the neighborhoods were clearly economically and socially stable;
- Ownership and land were fragmented, representing dozens (and in Lakewood hundreds) of individual interests and a wide range of concerns;
- The neighborhoods were located at strategic points that increased the economic value of their properties, either as a gateway to the downtown, a central regional location, or immediate access to a significant amenity such as a beach;
- Private sector interests had recognized the potential economic value of development in the areas, particularly if land was assembled by the local government;
- Older infrastructure contributed to the fragmented and factionalized nature of development, suggesting substantial upgrades in public infrastructure would be necessary to realize the proposed redevelopment projects.

The proposed projects were generally large and comprehensive in nature, investing in entire blocks or neighborhoods rather than parcel by parcel development.

In principle, these cases would be ideal candidates for public intervention to promote redevelopment and revitalization. Indeed, many economic development professionals support the use of eminent domain in these cases because it is a tool that can address many of these concerns and lay the groundwork for new investment. The need to invest in new infrastructure to support larger, more comprehensive investments in development suggests that current economic development projects have what economists call "public good" properties; they have widespread or broad based community benefits that require government action to supersede individual interests. Implicit in the concept of a public good is an unwillingness of the private sector to provide a good or service. The private sector may be unwilling to provide the good or service, in this case develop the property, because it cannot capture sufficient revenues to cover the costs (or make a reasonable profit), it may not have the capacity to provide sufficient resources to develop a project, it may not recognize the demand for the product, or the transaction costs associated with executing the project are sufficiently high the project is unprofitable.

The last justification for public intervention is the most prevalent for economic development projects involving Eminent Domain. Redevelopment specialists argue that land is so fragmented in older urban neighborhoods that the costs of assembling land are too high for the private sector to do on its own. Combined with the higher costs of demolition, private investors need the assistance of public officials to identify the owners of each parcel of land and negotiate a price. Land acquisition is presented as if it were a service provided by local governments to facilitate redevelopment.

## The Special Characteristics of Eminent Domain

Administrative efficiency, however, is not the only, nor perhaps the most important, criterion for selecting a tool or strategy that can potentially promote redevelopment or revitalization. This is where Eminent Domain differs from other tools such as tax abatements, building permit streamlining, grants, or loans. Most redevelopment programs do not directly limit or compromise the liberties of other citizens or property owners.[17] In fact, several redevelopment strategies can achieve the public policy goal of urban redevelopment by increasing individual liberty and economic opportunity, such as deregulating the land market through reform of local zoning laws, or streamlining the permitting or development approval process (Pringle 2007).

Eminent Domain is a particularly aggressive redevelopment too because, at its core, it employs the coercive force of the government to disenfranchise its citizens. Property (real and tangible) is physically taken by the government and redirected for a purpose that explicitly contradicts the intended use of the current property owner. Moreover, in the cases discussed in the previous section, the pre-development uses were not measurably contributing to the further decline of the neighborhoods or city.

The aggressive and potentially abusive nature of Eminent Domain was explicitly recognized by the framers of the U.S. Constitution and the states when they adopted the Fifth Amendment. Private property could only be taken for a "public use" and required "just compensation" be given to the current property owner. Thus, despite the reasoning of the majority in *Kelo,* and following the reasoning of Justice O'Conner in her dissent in *Kelo* and the majority decision by the Ohio Supreme Court in *Norwood,* Eminent Domain deserves a higher level of scrutiny before being used as a tool for urban development.

Unfortunately, little attention has been given to what those criteria would be. The remaining part of this section attempts to flesh out criteria that citizens and government officials can use to determine a legitimate threshold for using Eminent Domain to economic development uses within a mainstream economic development context. The next section will apply these criteria to the three cases discussed in the previous section. Importantly, all of these principles presuppose the validity of private property rights as a legal entitlement, a core principle consistent with the original intent of the U.S. Constitution. In short, the presumption is in favor of protecting property rights. Seizing property must be justified on substantive grounds, not simply procedural ones.

### *Principle #1: Eminent Domain Should Be*
### *a Tool of Last Resort*

Eminent Domain is a particularly aggressive tool that should be used sparingly if at all. By definition, Eminent Domain requires the compulsive transfer of property from one property owner to another. Thus, if local governments value individual liberties and freedoms, as liberal democracies such as the U.S. do, Eminent Domain

THE PROPER USES OF EMINENT DOMAIN

should be used sparingly and bear the burden of a higher threshold of justification before it is used. Ironically, even proponents of the aggressive use eminent domain qualify their support based on the belief it is used as a tool of last resort (Staley 2001). Urban policy makers and economic development professionals have a wide range of policy tools at their disposal before they can resort to eminent domain. Among the more obvious and common tools are:

- Offering market premia for property in the area targeted for economic development;
- Using grant, loan, and tax incentive programs to encourage existing property owners to reinvest, renovate, or upgrade their property;
- Streamlining regulatory permitting process to allow easy conversion of land and buildings to more profitable uses;

An example of how these alternative strategies can be used to foster urban revitalization can be found in the experiences of Anaheim under Mayor Curt Pringle (2007).
    Other, less obvious strategies can include:

- Inclusion of property owners in the targeted redevelopment areas early in the redevelopment approval process;
- Phasing development projects to accommodate existing property owners reluctant to sell or transfer their property

In short, policymakers should ensure that all reasonable paths for the voluntary transfer or property or incentives to promote reinvestment have been explored and attempted before resorting to the use of Eminent Domain.

### Principle #2: True Hold-Outs Prevent a Project from Moving Forward

A related but independent principle addresses the so-called "hold out" problem— the stubborn and "unreasonable" resistance of a one, two, or a few property owners to sell their property and prevents a project with significant public benefits from moving forward. Importantly, the hold- out problem is not simply an unwillingness to sell. The decision not to sell must have the practical and tangible effect of preventing the project from moving forward. Thus, this case is not simply a case where developers (or the government) have failed to negotiate a sales price or conditions of a purchase. The effect must be a true roadblock: Attempts to redesign a project, phase its implementation, grandfather in the property as a nonconforming use (that would expire once the owners sold the property or transferred title), or otherwise accommodate the property owners have been tried and failed, and without that specific parcel of property the project cannot be completed. Thus, determining a hold out is not simply a matter of failing to negotiate; developer negotiation costs are not the primary trigger determining when Eminent Domain will be used.

    By implication, this adds a further restriction on the use of Eminent Domain. While the first principle requires government to make affirmative efforts to satisfy property owners concerns before forcing the transfer of their property, the second principle stipulates that the strategic and practical importance of the parcel of property is critically important to the success of project, and it could not move forward or be implemented without it.

Notably, cases where hold outs prevent projects from going forward are rare. More importantly, the "hold out" argument is often used as a bargaining tactic for invoking Eminent Domain rather than the result of a true assessment of the strategic importance of the parcel of property. For example, the hold out problem was invoked in the *Hathcock v. Wayne Co.*, to justify Eminent Domain, yet the project moved forward immediately after the Michigan Supreme Court ruled against the county's use of Eminent Domain. Similarly, the state of Mississippi attempted to seize private property to assemble land for an automobile assembly plant, justifying the seizure in part on the strategic importance of the properties in the development plan. But, the investment went forward even without the disputed property after the property owners successfully litigated in defense of their property rights.

Large scale urban redevelopment projects that are subject to hold-out problems tend to be more complex and nuanced, and can often be tailored to fit into a complex neighborhood and urban fabric by using mixed commercial and residential uses, pedestrian friendly environments, and "human scale" urban landscapes. The likelihood individual properties present significant barriers to development is small. A sports stadium cannot be built if a home is located in a major portion of the proposed structure. But, stadiums can be re-sited. More often, developments can use techniques such as phasing to address hold-out concerns directly. Large scale development projects often take ten years or more to fully implement, allowing time to become and project evolution to accommodate individual property owner concerns. All three projects examined in the previous section were potentially "scalable" in this way, and they will be discussed further in the following section.

Moreover, while land assembly is a critical element of any major development project, policymakers should not assume the convention or standard practice is the benchmark for using tactics such as Eminent Domain. Because of its coercive nature, Eminent Domain should be subjected to a higher threshold for use and level of scrutiny than, say, using a municipal development corporation to assist in the negotiating the sale and transfer of property voluntarily, or land banking in anticipation of future development. Thus, standard practice is not a sufficient threshold for seizing land for another purpose.

### Principle #3: Tangible and Measurable Communitywide Benefits Must Be Identifiable, Achievable, and Likely

The public use qualification for Eminent Domain was intended to be a substantive limit on government seizure of private property. Only in the mid- twentieth century did the definition of public use expand so significantly that any substantive limit could be abandoned under *Kelo*. Despite the broad reasoning in *Kelo*, the majority believed that economic development was a legitimate public use because they presumed that the local government had performed the due diligence to ensure that redevelopment project met basic thresholds to qualify and ensure substantial public benefits. In other words, the benefit was still not narrowly or solely private.

The third principle extends this reasoning to suggest that any project where Eminent Domain is used should be a bona-fide public purpose. In broad terms, this principle implies that the project has communitywide benefits that cannot be provided independently through the private sector. Similarly, the benefits of the project should be widely received throughout the community.

Notably, this principle goes beyond the mere economic viability of the project. Virtually all development projects have the potential to be economically viable. Successful land development is a common and routine feature of a market economy. Public policies using Eminent Domain are an intervention in the market economy, not a mirror of it. Thus, projects involving Eminent Domain must have characteristics that exceed the normal market outcomes—they must have unique, communitywide benefits that could not be captured without public intervention.

Local policymakers and public officials must perform the due diligence to ensure the benefits are not primarily or principally private in nature or character. This principle, if applied, ensures that Eminent Domain is not simply a mechanism for private land owners, developers, and other parties to use the state or local government as a substitute for normal, voluntary, market-based real-estate transactions.

The days of the defining public use in a traditional sense—a jail, city hall, or other public project—are effectively gone. This principle reflects this reality but also recognizes that safeguarding property rights to prevent de facto private to private transfers means adding a constraint that Eminent Domain be used only for projects that have substantial communitywide or regional benefits that will accrue broadly.

### Principle #4: All Subsidies and Burdens Are Transparent

As a matter of sound public finance, the fourth principle stipulates that the fiscal implications for citizens and the private parties should be transparent and publicly available. Development agreements should be public and accessible (e.g., posted on web sites), and all fiscal and in-kind transfers should be transparent to ensure local developments minimize subsidies to private parties. The principle, like the previous one, helps ensure that Eminent Domain does not become a substitute for using the voluntary real-estate market to acquire properties for development projects.

Transparency, however, implies another characteristic often missed in policy discussions and debate. For a project to be fully transparent, the outcomes and results should flow clearly and logically, so that ends and means are connected. In economic development, this is problematic. The hypothetical connection between investment and outcome is clear enough—an investment of X number of dollars should be able to create a building of X square feet. While this engineering and construction relationship may exist, the ends-means relationship is much more indirect when the economic potential of a site is in question. The mere fact plans have been made does not imply that the plan will be fulfilled. Indeed, plan fulfillment, particularly in the original concept and design, is rare in the private and public sector. In the case of the forced taking of private property to fulfill an economic development purpose, projects should be tangibly tied to realistic probabilities of success. Thus, there should be transparency in results, not simply intent.

Operationally, this element of transparency can be tied into economic development practice by stipulating that economic development projects should have a substantial likelihood of success. Many development planners might balk at the constraint of "substantial" likelihood. Given the aggressive nature of Eminent Domain, and the risk to civil society of its systematic abuse, this constraint raises the stakes on economic development projects to meet a heightened scrutiny threshold implied in the *Kelo* dissent (and more recently the unanimous Ohio Supreme Court decision in *Norwood*).

### Principle #5: Continued Existing Ownership Has a Measurable Negative Impact on Other Property Owners

Finally, Eminent Domain should be used where continued private ownership exerts a measurable and tangible *negative* impact on surrounding properties. This principle draws heavily on the reasoning underlying *Berman v. Parker* where the U.S. Supreme Court upheld the use of Eminent Domain to offset the effects of urban blight. Unfortunately, in too many cases, state legislatures have allowed blight designations to be so broadly interpreted that virtually any property over a certain age could be considered blighted.

Yet, blight and negative impacts on surrounding properties can be measured and evaluated effectively using well accepted criteria as the previous section demonstrated (Staley and Blair 2005). Crimes rates, property values, persistent poverty, and other criteria can be used to determine whether a neighborhood or redevelopment area is in a persistent state of decline and whether those areas have negative impacts on developing surrounding areas. In other words, the "externalities" or spillover impacts of persistent poverty and underdevelopment can be measured and compared, and these should be a crucial element in policy decisions over whether Eminent Domain should be used for redevelopment purposes. Notably, the elastic nature of blight criteria in the Ohio Constitution and their application for redevelopment purposes were crucial elements of the decision by the Ohio Supreme Court to overturn Norwood's use of eminent domain.

## Summary

Each of these principles is designed to provide the underpinnings of a larger framework for anchoring the use of Eminent Domain for economic development purposes. Importantly, these criteria should be applied in a comprehensive way; they all should be applied to a project where Eminent Domain is used to promote economic development. Each principle presents a substantive reason why Eminent Domain should not be used or applied in a specific case.

Notably, these principles act as a substantive limit on government action, but they operate in two fundamentally different ways. The first two—the last resort and hold-out principles—impose an affirmative mandate on government to explore alternatives to using Eminent Domain and defer to voluntary, market transactions. The other three place explicit limits on government action by establishing minimum threshold and performance criteria before Eminent Domain can be used. How these principles can be applied in the real world is the subject of the next section of this paper, drawing on the background provided in the case studies of Mesa, Lakewood, and Long Branch.

## APPLICATIONS

The three case studies described in the second section of this paper provide a useful lens through which these principles can be tested and evaluated. This section uses the data from each of the case studies to illustrate the ways in which these principles

**Table 3.5** Application of Property Rights Principles to the Cases of Mesa, Lakewood, and Long Branch

| Principle | Mesa | Lakewood | Long Branch |
|---|---|---|---|
| #1 Last resort | NO | NO | NO |
| #2 Hold out | NO | NO | NO |
| #3 Communitywide benefits | NO | YES | NO |
| #4 Transparency | YES | YES | YES |
| #5 True blight | NO | NO | NO |

could be applied to actual cases where Eminent Domain was used to further economic development purposes. Notably, each case exists in a state where economic development was a recognized public use based on state statute. A summary of the analysis for each case is provided in table 3.5.

### Mesa, Arizona

The case of Site 24 in Mesa violated most of the principles outlined in the previous section. Indeed, it may be close to a "textbook" case for when Eminent Domain should *not* be used. In Mesa, Eminent Domain was not subjected to *any* level of higher scrutiny. The city became a pass-through for private parties to use eminent domain to satisfy their own need to expand and become more profitable in a competitive market.

Bailey's Brake Service had been operating as a family-owned and operated business on Site 24 for decades. Bailey remained the principal tenant (and landowner) even after Redstone Investments began purchasing the businesses and land around him. As other buildings were purchased by Redstone, they were left vacant and continued to deteriorate, substantially undermining the economic viability of Bailey's business and property. Nevertheless, Bailey kept his business open and thriving at the location. His business thrived based on references, reputation, and an intergenerational client base. Redstone did not even approach Bailey about purchasing the property. In fact, Bailey approached Redstone to discuss the possibility of incorporating his business into the redevelopment plan, but the development company spurned his queries. Instead, Redstone referred Bailey to the city of Mesa, which was acquiring property for the redevelopment project.

The memorandum of understanding (MOU) for Lenhart's ACE Hardware stipulated that the city of Mesa would acquire twelve lots constituting about two-thirds of the proposed site. In the case of Palm Court, the city's MOU called for acquiring nine lots. Of the 26 lots in Site 24, the city was using eminent domain to acquire 21.

The total assessed value of Site 24 was almost $3 million in 2002 (table 3.6). Together, Palm Court and Redstone acquired only about half of the assessed value of the property. While Redstone Investments acquired six parcels in its proposed project area, or about 41 percent of the proposed project area, these properties comprised only about one-third of the total value of the property. Thus, Redstone was using the city of Mesa to forcibly acquire property worth two-thirds the value of land needed for its portion of the project.

So, economic development policy violated the first two principles for a market-based approach to Eminent Domain: It was a tool of first resort and its use was not restricted to hold outs.

**Table 3.6**  Assessed Value for Site 24 in Mesa, Arizona

|  | 2000 | 2001 | 2002 |
|---|---|---|---|
| Total Assessed Value (Site 24) | $2,511,302 | $2,517,733 | $2,996,952 |
| Total Value Redstone Project | $909,838 | $794,178 | $936,056 |
| Redstone Owned | $244,559 | $244,612 | $313,410 |
| Independently Owned | $665,279 | $549,566 | $622,646 |
| Share Independently Owned | 73.1% | 69.2% | 65.5% |
| Assessed Value—Redstone & Palm Court | $1,134,559 | $1,209,252 | $1,540,932 |
| Independently Owned (Total Site 24) | $1,276,743 | $1,308,481 | $1,456,0202 |
| Share Independently Owned | 54.8% | 52.0% | 48.6% |

*Source*: Maricopa County Assessor's Office, www.maricopa.gov.

The Mesa case also violated principle three. Eminent domain was used explicitly to add the expansion of a specific private business, and the city acted as the agent for acquiring the property on behalf of the private party (Redstone and Palm Court). Both businesses would likely have found alternate locations within the city (although outside the immediate downtown area), allowing the city to capture the sales tax revenues even without the redevelopment of Site 24. Moreover, the proposed project did not have unique properties or communitywide benefits that would satisfy traditional public good criteria and trigger public intervention. The proposed project would be considered a "normal" market outcome, and Site 24 did not have unique characteristics critical to success of either the hardware or discount electronics store. The project's economic impact would not create unique benefits to the community, either.

The transactions were arguably transparent in that the development agreement was publicly available the details discussed in public meetings. Thus, the Mesa case does not violate Principle 4 on its face.

The city of Mesa's approach to redevelopment, however, precluded an adequate assessment of alternate locations for these investments, and the city did not even appear to explore alternative scenarios. As discussed earlier, the city was heavily subsidizing the investment in the new ACE hardware facility, ensuring that most of the benefits would be private rather than public or communitywide. Combined with the rising property values and thriving small businesses, little evidence suggested Site 24 was negatively impacting neighboring properties (violating principle #5).

Thus, a property rights and market-based framework for scrutinizing Eminent Domain would have recommended that Eminent Domain not be used in the case Site 24 in Mesa.

## Lakewood, Ohio

The case of Lakewood is substantially different from Mesa since it involved a large section of the city that included thousands of residents and dozens of businesses. In addition, the proposed development project was a large-scale, sophisticated mixed-use project focusing on a high-end retail Lifestyle Center. The redevelopment project entailed the comprehensive redevelopment of the West End and could potentially have transformed large swaths of he city. Indeed, the primary justification for the project was a substantial increase in revenues and property values as a result of the project. In the scope of the proposed project, the redevelopment would generate substantial community benefits. In theory, the scale of the impact suggests that the project would plausibly meet the criteria of the third principle.[18]

In addition, the development agreement and purpose of the local government was transparent. In fact, this transparency contributed to the political fall out that eventually led to the project's defeat at the ballot box. Thus, this case would meet the basic threshold for Principle Four.

Notably, the future value of both the new development as well as the evolution of existing land uses are highly speculative and malleable. The Lakewood Shoppes represented a relatively new "community center" model at the time for retail development. Whether the development would actually be able to generate the consumer spending in the stores envisioned to sufficiently support the projected value of those shops was problematic, particularly when one considers that the revenue streams are valued over a 30-year period. Different assumptions about how much revenue will be generated over different time periods can significantly influence the outcomes. And the basis for selecting one assumption over another is unknown. The Community Development Plan used in the Lakewood case provided no data on likely spending, consumer preferences, regional buying power or comparable shopping sites to support the value (and hence the tax revenue) of the proposed center.

The Lakewood project fails when the other three principles are applied. In this case, the entire neighborhood was condemned without consider alternative strategies for promoting economic development. Although grass roots resistance eventually ended the project at the ballot box, properties were not acquired for the development since the city intended to condemn the entire neighborhood to assemble the property for the project. Thus, the values, wishes and concerns of the minority were not even seriously considered. No assessment was done concerning how the project could be phased to accommodate individual property owners, or which parcels were essential for the development to be successful, violating Principle Two. Finally, although the city determined the neighborhood was blighted, the designation required the use of criteria so broad and vague that almost any older neighborhood could have fit the description. The West End was not a blighted neighborhood in the conventional sense of urban decline: property values were increasing, homeownership rates were increasing, and property values were increasing.

## Long Branch, New Jersey

Long Branch provides the third case study for these principles. While a few families continued to resist the proposals to sell to the city to make way for the development in the MTOTSA neighborhood, the remaining families were not hold outs in the sense defined in this analysis. The proposed beachfront development of high-end condominiums would not necessarily be prevented from moving forward if the homeowners failed to sell their properties at the time the proposal was developed. In fact, the nature of the development suggests that the interests of the existing property owners could be accommodated or even incorporated into the development plan. The developers, for example, have indicated their willingness to reserve units in the proposed development for current MTOTSA residents at a discount.

Proceeding in a phased development might increase the project costs to the developer, but these costs are unlikely to be sufficiently high to stop the development. The proposed development project calls for 185 luxury condominiums on the properties, some of which are currently vacant. The layout and phasing of the project might have to be redesigned, but most of the units can be built on the existing properties. Higher costs to a private developer should not be misconstrued as a public externality. Rather, these would be normal production costs for developers with projects in other, less favored neighborhoods.

Thus, while these families are "hold outs" in the procedural sense—they turned down the city's proposed offer to buy their properties—they are not hold outs in the traditional sense of the term where the failure to sell the parcel would prevent the private developer from proceeding with his plans.

The Long Branch project is also unlikely to have substantial communitywide benefits. The proposed project is part of an incremental development of ocean front properties in Long Branch, and the failure to develop the MTOTSA neighborhood would have minimal impact on long-term economic development and revitalization trends. Indeed, the MTOTSA neighborhood does not have any unique properties other than those that make the properties more valuable in the real estate market—ocean and park access in a revitalizing section of the city. Since the condominium development is part of an ongoing regeneration process along the shore, the direct benefits will accrue almost exclusively to the new property owners and the developers. Increases in property values, benefits from access to the Ocean and beach amenities, and relatively secluded neighborhood will not provide spillover benefits to the community in excess of what would normally occur through the unsubsidized market process.

Finally, the properties in the MOTOTSA neighborhood are clearly not blighted. They are older homes, but their property values are appreciating substantially, and the city itself has admitted that the neighborhood is not blighted.

## New London and Norwood

Applying this property rights framework for Eminent Domain use to two other controversial cases might help further explore the different ways in which these criteria can be used and applied in a contemporary economic development context. In *Kelo,* the U.S. Supreme Court upheld the use of Eminent Domain in New London, Connecticut. The city condemned the Fort Trumbull neighborhood as part of its effort to comprehensively redevelop the property for luxury and high-valued residential, commercial, and office development. Like the neighborhoods in Lakewood and Long Branch, the homes and businesses were not blighted in the traditional sense. Indeed, Susette Kelo and other families had reinvested in their properties. Small businesses had existed profitably in the neighborhood for generations.

The Fort Trumbull neighborhood was condemned by the city based on the city's *intent* to redevelop the property. While a redevelopment plan had been adopted by the city, little tangible evidence of private sector interest, or public-sector commitment to redevelop the properties according to the plan existed. The scope of the plan suggested that the interests of the remaining property owners could have been accommodated given the complex, phased nature of the intended redevelopment plan. The redevelopment plan called for a series of smaller developments that could have been phased in over time, or reconfigured to meet new requirements. Notably, the city

**Table 3.7** Property Rights Principles Applied to the Cases of Norwood and New London

| Principle | New London | Norwood |
|---|---|---|
| #1 Last resort | NO | YES |
| #2 Hold out | YES | YES |
| #3 Communitywide benefits | YES | YES |
| #4 Transparency | NO | YES |
| #5 True blight | NO | NO |

decided to keep a historic building that was the site of a wealth social club rather than tear it down, an indicator of the kind of flexibility creative planners and developers can adopt when they are required to for economic or political reasons (table 3.7).

Applying the issue matrix to the Fort Trumbull neighborhood, the Eminent Domain action would fail on several of these tests. Eminent Domain was not used as a tool of last resort. Rather, it was an integrated part of the redevelopment process. The property owners were not hold outs in the sense their unwillingness to sell would have hindered the redevelopment of the area.

The comprehensive redevelopment of the Fort Trumbell neighborhood, however, would have likely created significant communitywide benefits that would have spillover to the city more broadly. But, keeping the discussion of transparency in context, the city had drawn plans and little tangible evidence existed that the plans could be brought to fruition.

Ironically, the case of Norwood comes closest to passing the property rights test even though this may be the precedent setting state case that counters the reasoning in *Kelo*. In Norwood, Ohio, Rookwood Partners planned to invest in a contemporary mixed residential and commercial use property, displacing several businesses and homes. The developer approached the property owners and acquired the majority of properties voluntarily. The city, in fact, required the developers to approach the property owners several times before it relented to beginning Eminent Domain proceedings. The city conducted a blight study, commissioning professional consultants, and the developer underwrote the costs of the study. However, the blight determination hinged on the finding that the neighborhood was not currently blighted, but was in danger of becoming blighted (a key element of the Ohio Supreme Court's decision to declare Ohio's Eminent Domain statutes unconstitutional). The proposed development was substantial enough that the positive impact could be regional in scope, allowing unproductive land to be brought into more productive use and providing a framework for improving transportation access to regional retail, office, and residential development. Thus, the proposed project would likely have passed the transparency and communitywide benefit tests.

The only criteria that would likely have kept the Norwood case from moving forward as an Eminent Domain application was the blight criteria.

## CONCLUSION

This analysis has attempted to delve more fully into the policy implications of Eminent Domain's use to promote economic development in the wake of *Kelo v.*

*City of New London.* In *Kelo,* the U.S. Supreme Court effectively validated state efforts to remove substantive legal protections for property owners by upholding economic development as a valid public use under the Fifth Amendment. This decision, however, is controversial, and ignited a firestorm of legislative activity with state and a few cities enacting laws and statutes limiting Eminent Domain's use for these purposes. Thus, as a matter of urban policy, the issue is far from settled, and a new wave of debate may just be starting.

The five principles outlined in this chapter place two types of burdens on government before it uses Eminent Domain. The first burden places an affirmative duty on the government to explore as many alternatives as possible to promote a voluntary exchange and transaction in the real estate market by requiring Eminent Domain be used as a last resort (Principle #1) and conducting due diligence to ensure the property is critical to the success or failure of the project if the property owner refuses to sell (Principle #2). The other three criteria impose substantive limits on governments by specifying minimum thresholds and performance standards below which a project would not qualify for assistance through Eminent Domain. These principles limit government intervention to cases where communitywide benefits and impacts are measurable and tangible (Principle #3), all subsidies and burdens connected to the project are transparent (Principle #4), and continued private ownership has measurable negative impacts on other property owners (Principle #5).

Because of the inherently coercive nature of Eminent Domain, government has a responsibility to conduct due diligence and evaluate the substantive rationale and justification for proposed economic development projects. This paper has attempted to outline an approach that can be used by policymakers on the state and local level that still respects property rights and individual liberties. The framework starts from with a foundation that acknowledges the U.S. Constitution recognizes that in certain circumstances, private property rights can be violated. This paper has attempted to flesh out a tangible and practical set of criteria that can be used as a filter for local officials concerned about the property rights and civil liberties implications of unfettered use of Eminent Domain to seize homes and businesses under the broad *Kelo* criteria.

## NOTES

1. Takings issues have always been contentious and controversial because the Fifth Amendment (and similar state level limits) explicitly recognizes a public interest in seizing private property under certain circumstances. Private property rights have never been constitutionally inviolable or sacrosanct. *Kelo,* however, represented the first time at the federal level that public purpose was determined to be so broad as to include virtually any government action as long as the government agency made a procedurally legitimate claim to the public value of the action.
2. Similarly, the issue of urban blight, while contentious, is an ongoing controversy that will be settled on a state-by-state level.
3. While strong legal and philosophical arguments can be made for excluding economic development from the range of public uses allowed through state and the U.S. Constitution (see Pringle 2007), the U.S. Supreme Court and most state courts have not embraced such a restrictive application. In a potentially precedent setting state case, the Ohio Supreme Court recognized economic development as a valid public use in *Norwood v. Horney.* In *Norwood,* the Ohio Court restricted eminent domain's use by requiring that economic development could not be the sole reason for its application and that more rigorous standards be applied to ensure that decisions to condemn private property are not arbitrary (Staley 2006; Owsiany 2006).
4. Each of these cases was the subject of litigation the included the Institute for Justice, a public interest law firm supporting property owners and private property rights based in Arlington,

Virginia. The author has provided expert testimony on behalf of the Institute for Justice in the Mesa case, and co-authored amicus briefs on behalf of Reason Foundation in the Norwood and Long Branch cases.

5. Correspondence from Ken Lenhart, Lenhart's ACE Hardware to Wayne Brown, Mayor, and Deborah Duvall, Chair, Downtown Development Committee, February 20, 1998. See also the correspondence from Ken Lenhart to Greg Marek, Redevelopment Director, City of Mesa, September 1, 1998.

6. In 2000, the last year data for these properties were listed, the assessed values for the parcels not owned by Redstone Development, the development company representing Lenhart's redevelopment project, averaged $8.93 per square foot according to the Maricopa County Assessor's office. Actual market value for these properties is likely much higher.

7. Resolutions 7336 and 7337. Minutes, city council of the city of Mesa, March 15, 1999. According to the Memorandum of Understanding between the City of Mesa and Lenart's ACE Hardware, Lenhart agreed to purchase the land from the city of Mesa for $11.74 per square foot, a slight premium over the full-cash value reported by the Maricopa County Assessor. On the surface, this suggests that Lenhart was subsidizing the city of Mesa. However, Lenhart's agreement allowed him to swap his existing store and property for the newly acquired property instead of pay cash. In addition, the full cash value of the property did not reflect actual market values.

8. Comparable sales price data were found for twelve properties via the Maricopa County Assessor. On average, the actual sales price exceeded the full cash value price by 31.2 percent.

9. Palm Court Investments LLC, Response to Mesa's Redevelopment Project Site #24, January 24, 2000.

10. In an interesting twist, the jobs in the proposed redevelopment project would likely be low-wage retail jobs, or high-end jobs that were simply redistributed from other parts of the city. Lenhart's ACE Hardware expected to add 31 new jobs because of its expansion. These jobs were likely to be part-time and relatively low wage, suggesting that the overall benefit was likely to be smaller than anticipated. Jobs provided by firms such as Bailey's Brake Service earned 40 percent to 100 percent more than retail establishment's because of their skilled and semi-skilled nature.

11. The Urban Center, Maxine Goodman Levin College of Urban Affairs, Cleveland State University, cited on the city of Lakewood's Web site, http://ci.lakewood.oh.us/soc local. html, accessed 1/12/05.

12. City of Lakewood Web site, http://ci.lakewood.oh.us/soc local.html, accessed 01/12/05.

13. Data for the West End neighborhood refer to Census data for census tracts 1607 and 1608. Unfortunately, precise neighborhood data were not available from the Census Bureau.

14. Importantly, the consultants' report did not provide evidence on whether the majority of structures in the West End neighborhood meet the criteria for blight. The conclusions rest on inferences from small samples of buildings and a fundamental belief that older buildings are inherently inferior to new, comprehensive development. The comprehensive development plan discusses area-wide concerns without linking those concerns to properties in general, let alone to a majority of properties.

In fact, there is virtually no evidence presented by the consultants regarding ill health, transmission of disease, infant mortality, and juvenile delinquency, or moral hazard in the West End. Almost all the evidence presented highlights features of buildings and sites typical of neighborhoods eighty years old outside the primary growth path of a region. While crime appears to be higher in the West End, the data were not adjusted for the mix of land uses (commercial areas normally have more crime) or for population densities (higher density areas typically have more crime per acre).

Indeed, significant differences appear to exist in different areas of the West End. These differences would be expected where some areas are characterized by very high densities, and others by lower densities. Moreover, this kind of diversity is part of the natural evolution of neighborhoods. With regard to safety due to fire, the CDP showed that there were higher rates of fires responses per acre (nearly twice) for the West End compared to Lakewood as a whole. Again, the analysis would be more convincing if the fire calls were expressed on a per capita basis rather than a per acre basis because fire calls are related to population (among other things). The bulk of the evidence the city relies on to justify the comprehensive rede-velopment of the West End points out truisms of older urban neighborhoods: they are demo-graphically diverse.; they have older housing stock and commercial buildings; they have older infrastructure. They have the attendant social problems associated with older, more diverse neighborhoods with mixed incomes and land uses.

15. Any compensation provided the current families would be pegged to existing market rates, not the future value of their property, or the psychological benefits of owning a family home at the beach. This is acknowledged in the most recent amendment to the redevelopment agreement signed by the City of Long Branch and Beachfront North, L.L.C. (the city desig-nated developer). According to Exhibit B, current owners and occupants would be paid "fair market value" and allowed, at the developer's discretion, to purchase new condominiums at a 10 percent discount. Even at this discount, many of the property owners in this neighborhood would be unable to purchase the unit. Purchasing a new unit would add a significant financial burden that families with modest incomes or fixed retirement incomes cannot reasonably bear. If current owners do not purchase a new unit, the developer would provide relocation benefits equal to $2,000 per month for up to 36 months.Thus, the redevelopment plan of the Beach Front North area of Long Branch effectively forecloses the possibility of replacing their homes, while developers benefit from the value they created through their long-term invest-ments in the MTOTSA neighborhood.

16. Second Amended and Restated Agreement Between the City of Long Branch and Beachfront North, L.L.C. for the Redevelopment Area Designated as Beachfront North, sec. 3.1; Amendment to Redeveloper's Agreement for Beachfront North Phase II, Sec. 4(A).

17. To the extent the programs involve taxation, public programs and interventions may limit liberty, but these limits are indirect. Moreover, to the extent tax revenues support legitimate public goods and services, taxes do not unambiguously reduce liberty.

18. Although this should not be confused with a public good—a product or service that would be publicly provided because it the private sector would or could not. State and federal courts have explicitly ruled that public use is defined much more broadly than public goods in this sense.

## REFERENCES

Balmer, W. 1996. Memorandum from Community Development Manager, City of Mesa to Charles Luster, City Manager, City of Mesa, July 24, 1996.

Hartt, D.B. and K. Hopkins. 2002. Revisions for Consideration—Community Development Plan for the West End District, Memorandum to Frank Pietravoia, December 16, 2002.

Lakewood, City of. 2002. *Community Development Plan for the West End District: Volume I Determination and Actions,* prepared for the city of Lakewood by D.B. Hartt, Inc. and Square One, Inc., July 25, 2002.

———. 2003. Development Agreement with Lakewood Shoppes LLC, adopted June 16, 2003.

Institute for Justice. Putting the Brakes on Eminent Domain Abuse in Mesa, Arizona, Litigation Backgrounder, http://www.ij.org/private_property/arizona/background.html/.

———. Ohio's City of Homes Faces Wrecking Ball of Eminent Domain Abuse, Litigation Backgrounder, http://www.ij.org/private_property/lakewood/backgrounder.html/.

Lenhart's ACE Hardware. 2000. Proposal for City of Mesa, Site 24 Redevelopment Project, January 24.

López, Edward J. and Sasha M. Totah. 2007. *Kelo* and Its Discontents, *The Independent Review* 11 (3): 397–416, http://independent.org/pdf/tir/tir_11_03_04_lopez.pdf/.

Mesa, City of. 1999a. Minutes, Downtown Development Committee Meeting, January 21, 1999.

———. 1999b. Minutes. City Council, March 15, 1999.

Owsiany, D. 2006. Ohio Court Restores Balance to Eminent Domain, *Akron Beacon Journal,* August 1, 2006, http://www.reason.org/commentaries/owsiany_20060801.shtml/.

Pringle, C. 2007. *Development Without Eminent Domain.* Washington, DC: Institute for Justice, http://www.castlecoalition.org/pdf/publications/Perspectives-Pringle.pdf/.

Reason Foundation. *Amicus Curiae* brief, *City of Long Branch v. Gregory P. Brower, et al.,* Superior Court of New Jersey Appellate Division, n.d.

———. *Amicus Curiae* brief, *City of Norwood v. Horney,* Ohio Supreme Court, n.d.

Staley, S.R. 2003. Wrecking Property Rights, *Reason,* February.

———. 2006. Property Owners Score Major Victory in Ohio, *Reason.org,* July 27, 2006, http://www.reason.org/commentaries/staley_20060727.shtml/.

Staley, S.R. and J.P. Blair. 2005. *Eminent Domain, Private Property, and Redevelopment: An Economic Analysis,* Policy Study No. 331. Los Angeles: Reason Foundation, February, http://www.reason.org/ps331.pdf/.

Turnbull, G.K. and R. Salvino. 2006. *Kelo v. Leviathan:* The Public Purpose Doctrine and Government Size, Working Paper No. 06–02, Urban and Regional Analysis Group, School of Policy Studies, Georgia State University, July.

U.S. Census Bureau, *Statistical Abstract of the United States: 2004–2005.* Washington, DC: U.S. Government Printing Office.

# 4

# COMPENSATION FOR TAKING WHEN BOTH EQUITY AND EFFICIENCY MATTER

## *Paul Niemann and Perry Shapiro*

## THE CASTLE

Darryl Kerrigan is the master of a modest house at 3 Highview Crescent, Cooloroo, on the edge of the Melbourne International Airport. In *The Castle*, an Australian movie made in the early 1990s, Darryl receives an official notice that his property is to be condemned to make way for an airport expansion. The house with its many unique modifications, including a kennel for his racing greyhounds, is Darryl's "Castle." Because it is not just a house it is a "home" he is determined to remain and employs his friend, the solicitor Dennis Denuto, to challenge the condemnation. Denuto, a small time solicitor whose legal experience stretches to doing real estate conveyances, is well out of his depth with this case. Dennis knows Darryl is fighting the "big boys" on an issue that is clearly a constitutional challenge. Nonetheless, Denuto, as an act of friendship, agrees to represent Darryl. In response to a question put by the judge in the first court appearance, Denuto raises a constitutional challenge to the condemnation. Asked directly about the constitutional point, Denuto responds, "It's the vibe of it [the Australian Constitution]." The judge is puzzled since she cannot recall any part of the Australian constitution that deals with the vibe. Naturally enough, Darryl-Denuto loses the first round. The movie continues to a victorious conclusion for Darryl, when a distinguished QC takes up the case. In the High Court, bewigged judges and all, Darryl's attorney argues that Section 51 of the Australian Constitution which states "The Parliament shall...have the power to make laws for...the government of the Commonwealth with respect to:....(xxxii) The acquisition of property on just terms...." is the vibe. It is clear to the QC, as he argues before the high court justices, that it cannot be just to force a family out of the home it loves and cherishes. As in all good stories, Darryl wins the day.

Not withstanding the elegance of the QC, it is unlikely that Darryl would have prevailed in most courts. Nonetheless, the appeal to the "vibe" certainly has a contemporary ring to it. The public outcry over the U.S. Supreme Court decision in the case of *Kelo v. City of New London*[1] is foreshadowed in the movie. Darryl emerges from the High Court to the cheers from a sympathetic public. The plaintiffs in *Kelo* were unsuccessful in their attempt to block the condemnation of their property, but the public sympathy was similarly passionate. While the majority of the Supreme Court justices chose to uphold the City of New London's right to take the property in its redevelopment effort (affirming a long-standing rule that public use is anything the legitimately constituted public authority says it is), the dissent of Justice O'Connor focuses on an aspect of the case that is reminiscent of Darryl's dilemma. Justice O'Connor was clearly bothered by the injustice of the forced removal of a family from its castle. In her dissent she focuses on the plight of "[p]etitioner Wilhelmina Dery...[who] lives in a house on Walbach Street that has been in her family for over 100 years. She was born in the house in 1918; her husband, petitioner Charles Dery, moved into the house when they were married in 1946. Their son lives next door with his family in the house he received as a wedding gift...."

The sense of outrage that followed *Kelo* likely will change the way taking for public purpose is applied. While the highest courts have decided that as long as the taking choices are not made in favor of a particular party and not prejudicial against others, legally constituted public authorities can decide what is public use. It is up to the elected legislature to deal with the popular outcry and set limits on public condemnation of private property.

It is not unusual to learn from the media of outrageous and heavy-handed application of the public exercise of the power of eminent domain. Stories of widows driven from their ancestral homes make good copy. However there is often a compelling public interest in converting land use through public condemnation. The issue is not whether government should be allowed to take private property, but how it should be constrained.

The US constitution requires "just" payment for property acquired. The public appetite for private property is constrained by the need to make payment. In practice, the amount of compensation given is the market value of the property at the time of the taking. From an economist's perspective there are problems with market value compensation in that it encourages over-investment in land that may be acquired for public use in the future. In other words there is a real efficiency cost to market value compensation. From the public perspective, as witnessed in the reaction to *Kelo*, there is, perhaps, a more serious cost: that of forcing private citizens off of property that they value more than does the market.

The problem is complicated and we do not deal with every aspect of it. Perhaps the most difficult issue—the evaluation of subjective value—is resolved here only in cases where there are potential market manifestations of that value. Personal attachment to a place is beyond our reach. However, there are examples of takings, characterized by the road model in the following pages, for which there are observable indicators of personal value. A landowner can suffer from a condemnation because, unlike his luckier neighbors who enjoy project-induced capital gains, he is forced to surrender his land for a market value that does not incorporate project benefits.

We propose a compensation rule with which a landowner does not regret condemnation and is immune from the efficiency loss induced by current market value rules. The scheme is equitable in the sense that among equivalent landowners there are not those who gain and those who lose by the public decision—rather the welfare of all landowners are enhanced equally by the public choices. We cannot solve all equity issues: the results are limited to an important class of public projects, namely, those whose benefits are captured fully in land values.

Our proposal is that compensation is market value based, but rather than current value—the value at the time of condemnation—the public project enhanced amount is paid for the condemned land. We will argue both the efficiency and equity of the plan, even though we recognize the quixotic nature of the proposal in view of the case law. The Supreme Court decision in the case of *United States v. Reynolds*[2] addresses this very issue: "The Court early recognized that the 'market value' of property condemned can be affected, adversely or favorably, by the imminence of the very project that makes the condemnation necessary. And it was perceived that to permit compensation to be either reduced or increased because of an alteration in market value attributable to the project itself would not lead to the 'just compensation' that the Constitution requires."[3] In spite of the weight of precedent, perhaps the argument put forward in this paper will prompt a consideration of what constitutes compensation justice.

The analysis of compensation rules encompasses two distinct issues. The first is that the rules themselves affect the decisions of both government and landowners. The government's appetite for private property is limited by the acquisition costs. The landowners' investment in property improvements depends on the level of compensation if the land is taken. The second is that the perceived fairness (equity) of the outcome depends on the compensation. The importance of a equitable outcome is highlighted in the Supreme Court's 1960 decision in *Armstrong v. United States*: "[t]he Fifth Amendment's guarantee . . . [is] designed to bar Government from forcing some people alone to bear the public burdens which, in all fairness and justice, should be borne by the public as a whole."[4]

The economic literature has concentrated on the efficiency aspects of compensation with little written about the "just" part. An early work by Johnson (1977) focuses on the governmentally induced distortion of a bureaucracy faced with unreasonably low prices for land taken. Without prices, regulatory planning is inefficient—the need to pay compensation constrains an avaricious government. In Blume, Rubinfeld, and Shapiro (1984) another line of inquiry was launched: full compensation induces inefficiently high investments in property improvements. Fischel and Shapiro (1988, 1989) pursue a similar line of inquiry from a constitutional perspective that concentrates on efficiency consequences only. Miceli and Segerson (1994, 1996) suggest that if there is enlightened judicial intervention, full compensation does not distort private land investment choices. They were among the first economists to raise concerns about fairness as well as efficiency. Innes (1997, 2000) notes that compensation can affect the timing of investment as well: the threat of small, or no, compensation induces landowners to invest inefficiently early to discourage condemnation. In a paper which influenced our thinking, Nosal (2001) proposes compensation based on the average market value of all property rather than the market value of the condemned property alone. Landowners, unable to significantly influence their own potential compensation choose efficient levels of property improvements. The most notable attempt to incorporate perceived equity into the analysis is found in Michelman (1967). The paper suggests quantifying (putting a dollar value on) the demoralization of citizens because they perceive a threat to the integrity of their own property rights and empathize with others so threatened.

It is our intention to find compensation rules that are both efficient and equitable. Whether or not there is such a rule depends on the motives of the participants (the government and the landowners) and the process by which the taking and property improvement decisions are made.

As a beginning we propose the following criteria for judging the efficiency/equity of a compensation.

1. A compensation rule is *efficient* if the resulting amount of land taken and the investment on the land are such that it is impossible to increase the net output of a community by changing the amount of land taken and/or the level of land-improving investment.
2. A compensation rule is *equitable:*
   a. Ex post if the post-taking income is the same for those whose land is taken and those whose land is not taken. This stringent equity standard is equivalent to that proposed by Epstein: "…the ideal solution is to leave the individual owner in a position of indifference between the taking by government and retention of the property;"[5] and,
   b. Ex ante if all landowners, prior to the taking decision have the same expected net income.

## THE GAME AND THE PLAYERS

We attempt to get a grip on the taking efficiency-equity problem by modeling it as a game. We focus the analysis by limiting it to two types of player, the government (more accurately, the bureaucracy that makes the taking choice) and the landowners. But even this partition is insufficient. It is further specified that there are many landowners and that they have no market power and cannot collude. Each landowner has the power to affect only his own parcel of land—one that constitutes a trivial part of the whole.

For many public projects the benefits are difficult to quantify. For instance a winning sport team is a source of civic pride and the public finance of facilities for the team is justified even though enhanced citizen utility has no market manifestation. The analysis of this paper cannot be applied to public spending of this sort. The following analysis is limited to public projects whose benefits are captured fully as increased income for the non-taken landowners.

We find that what is feasible depends on who knows what and when. Many papers on taking rules, those that claim to have discovered ones that promote efficient choices, have compensation rules based on foreknowl-edge of what amount of private investment is optimal. If the efficient choices are known, it seems superfluous to use compensation rules to achieve them. The efficient options only need to be mandated. What we will be looking for are compensation rules—rules that apply to the government as well as the landowners—that do not rely on the socially efficient choices.

It is a feature of all models that players' objectives must be specified. While these objectives might be very complicated, we intend to analyze a world in which they are quite simple. The landowners only seek to make their annual incomes as high as possible (they are risk neutral). The government behaves in the manner of the bureaucracy modeled by Niskanen (1994): it seeks to maximize its total budget.

It is well understood what is meant by efficiency, but equity is another matter. A sensible notion of equity is that like individuals are treated equally. The application of this easily stated concept is more difficult. First, how do we know when two people are alike? In what follows, landowners are indistinguishable from one-another. Second, what is meant by equal treatment? A reasonable equal treatment criterion is that no matter the final outcome, likes are treated similarly if their expected outcomes are the same. Another, more stringent, requirement is that their realized rewards are the same ex post. Economists tend to favor the first while public policy (certainly the popular reaction to public policies) is often guided by the second.

## MODEL

### The Farmers and the Road

We will develop a formal model with results that apply with considerable generality. Before launching the general specification a simple tangible example can clarify what is to follow. Think about a simple featureless plane on which wheat can be grown. Without loss of generality, let the total land area be 1 (one acre, one square mile, one-hundred square miles). A fraction $q$ $(0 \leq q \leq 1)$ of the total will be assembled by a public bureau for a road as illustrated in figure 4.1. The remaining $1-q$ of the land will be used to grow wheat.

The per acre yield (bushels per acre) of the land is related to the investment on it (the intensity of cultivation, the extent and quality of the irrigation system and any other investment that is lost if the land is taken). This relationship is expressed as the concave function $Y = \sqrt{x}$, where $Y$ is the per acre yield and $x$ is the capital investment per acre. The wheat, in order to be economically relevant must be transported to market, where its market price is assumed to be $1 per bushel (the price is chosen for computational convenience and not for market realism). Transport costs are a declining function of the road size—the larger the road, the more efficiently the product can be moved to market. Let the relationship between transport cost (dollars per bushel) and road size be $T = 1 - q^{0.1}$. The function implies that when there is no road, $q = 0$, the transport cost per bushel equals the market price—it is clearly uneconomic to produce wheat on the plain when there is no road on which to take it to market. If the road occupies the entire area, transport costs are zero, an unrealistically small price, but there will be no land left for wheat.

Wheat must be transported to market to achieve its full value. The stalks in the field are not the same commodity as the grains at market. For this example, a bushel

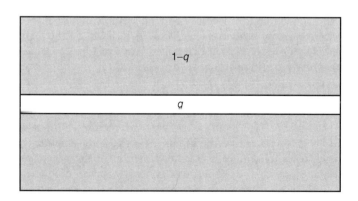

**Figure 4.1**  The Proposed Road and Surrounding Environs

of wheat transported to the market is the output we are considering. The production function that relates the size of the public project and the level of investment to the yield per acre of market-delivered wheat is computed in the following way. Let $\Upsilon$ be the bushels per acre yield and $T$ be the transport cost per bushel. The per acre transport cost is $\Upsilon T$. The yield per acre of market wheat is $y = \Upsilon - \Upsilon T = f(x,q)$. The production function is[6]

$$y = f(x,q) = q^{0.1} \sqrt{x}.$$

The general case focuses on the taking of land for a public project, as in the road example above, whose full benefits are captured in the market value of the surviving property. While there are many such projects, road building is a common example. The particular aspects of a road is that land is consumed in its completion, surviving land benefits from increased accessibility to markets and improved access leads to higher values for the uncondemned property.

Takings involve two distinct actors, each with their own objectives and each with distinct strategic options. There are the landowners, who choose the level of capital improvements in order to maximize annual income. There is also the government who chooses which and how much land to condemn in order to maximize its objective. Since the decision of one participant affects the choices of the others the process is modeled as a game between landowners and bureaucrats.[7] In order to model the game we first specify its components: the first is the environment in which the game is played; the second is the technology of production; the third is the landowner's objectives and strategies and the fourth is the bureaucracy's objectives and strategies.

For the analysis all costs are stated in annual flows. The rate of interest is known and fixed in perpetuity at $r$. The government's total condemnation cost is $qC$ for which it sells consols (interest only bonds) with an annual debt service of $c = rqC$. Rather than writing the financial transactions in this way, we simply state the annual payment to the condemnees as $c$.[8] The only source of revenue for debt service is an ad valorem property tax at a fixed rate $\tau$. The tax rate is set as the result of a complex political process to address a multitude of issues. Consequently, the probability that $\tau$ is set equal to any particular value is equal to zero. Most important for the analysis to follow, the tax rate is determined independently of the taking decision. If the bureau decides the tax rate as well as the condemnations, our conclusions would change.

Prior to the condemnation decision all land is indistinguishable—one parcel is exactly the same as any other irrespective of its location on the plain. However once the condemnation policy is in place there are two types of land—the taken and the untaken. We distinguish between these two types with the subscripts of $t$ and $-t$ respectively. If a property is taken it produces no output. The rate at which output is produced (yield per acre) on the untaken land is $f(x_{-t}, q)$ and zero on the taken property. The function $f(\ )$ is strictly quasi-concave in both arguments and the marginal product of each input is strictly positive and each input is 'essential': $f(0,q) = f(x,0) = 0$. Furthermore the inputs are strict complements: the marginal product of each is a monotonically positive function of the other ($f_x(x_{-t}, q) > 0$, $f_q(x_{-t}, q) > 0$ and $f_{xq}(x_{-t}, q) > 0$). The quasi-concavity of the production function implies that both second derivatives are negative and that the Hessian matrix is negative semi-definite.

The analyses and conclusions of this paper depend in important ways on an individual landowner's inability to manipulate the land prices. For this reason it is assumed that there are many landowners, enough so that no single one of them has significant market power. Whether or not there is a continuum of landowners or simply many makes no difference here. Naturally, landowners will have discrete parcels, but the taken amount does not necessarily conform to an individual's entire holding. For our analysis, if a fraction of a landholding is condemned, the owner pursues two separate interests, those of the taken and those of the not-taken, independent of each other. In effect, fractional condemnation creates two separate landowners. We assume that the landowners are unable to form coalitions.

The lucky landowners, those whose land escapes condemnation, will have an annual income equal to the land product, less annual costs. In order to simplify the stock-flow accounting we assume that all quantities are annual flows. Capital is financed with bonds that are serviced for $rx_{-t}$ per annum. In addition to the capital service, the landowners must pay an annual ad valorem property tax of $\tau V_{-t}$, where $V$ is the property market value and $\tau$ is the property tax rate that is set and unchanged by the contemplated public project. If the market price of land is the discounted value of its annual income, with a market rate of interest of $r$, the net income of the non-taken landowner is

$$y_{-t} = \frac{r}{r+\tau}[f(x_{-t}, q) - rx_{-t}].$$

The flow of income to the condemned landowner is the amount of compensation paid for the taking less the annual capital debt service

$$y_t = c - rx_t.$$

As is common in the economics literature on takings, the landowners are motivated to maximize their annual income. There is, however, no such standard treatment of government motivations. We choose to think of the government represented by its agency, the bureaucracy. There is a widely recognized model of bureaucracy—the one proposed by Niskanen (1994). For Niskanen the bureau seeks to be as large as possible by making its budget as large as possible.

We embed the bureaucracy in an environment common to many public projects in the United States. The bureau will receive all of the property tax revenue from the condemnation area. What we have in mind is similar to tax increment financing, commonly used for redevelopment projects.[9]

The bureau's objective is to maximize its tax collections with its condemnation choice. It does this constrained in two ways. The first is that the property tax rate is fixed and not subject to change (by either the bureau or the landowner).[10] The second is that the tax revenues collected must be sufficient to cover the annual debts service, $qc$, for the public project. The bureau's welfare is

$$b(q,x) = \begin{cases} \tau(1-q)V_{-t} & \text{if } \tau(1-q)V_{-t} \geq qc \\ 0 & \text{otherwise} \end{cases}$$

The outcome of the game between the landowners and the bureaucrats is evaluated against certain criteria. One of the most important is the efficiency of the outcome: what is the community income when the game is in equilibrium and how does it compare with the maximum possible? The usual comparison is how well the game does compared to what an omniscient and benevolent planner would do. The comparison outcome is the equilibrium income compared with the maximum community income. Aggregate income, after the public project is in place is

$$(1-q)[f(x_{-t},q)-rx_{-t}]-qrx_{-t}.$$

If the production function is quasi-concave, as assumed, maximization of community income (and thus, efficiency) requires that the amount of land taken satisfies the first order condition

$$(1-q)f_q(x_{-t},q)-[f(x_{-t},q)-rx_{-t}]-rx_t = 0.$$

This has a straight-forward interpretation: the sum of the marginal benefit from expanding the size of the taking, $(1 - q) f_q(x_{-t}, q)$, must equal the marginal cost, that is the loss of net income from taking the marginal parcel instead of leaving to benefit from the project, $[f(x_{-t}, q) - rx_{-t}]$, plus the cost of the capital lost, $rx_t$.

## COMPENSATION

We propose that there are four distinct desiderata for a compensation rule. The first is that it should not induce inefficient use of resources. The inducement of compensation should not promote resource expenditures to augment compensation if land is taken or to affect taking choices by other resource using means such as political lobbying. The second is that the rule should be equitable: similar individuals should have similar outcomes. There is little dispute about this definition, but its implementation is problematic. It is reasonable to label as equitable a public policy that gives no individual a better chance at a good outcome than anyone else, even though realizations are widely disparate. However, it is likely that treating the outcome of a public choice process as a simple gamble does not coincide with the popular notion of distributive justice. For instance, it may be "just" if one person wins a fortune while another looses the farm at the same horse race, but the same distributive outcome from a political process is judged to be wildly unfair. An outcome in which identical people end up with similar outcomes is more consistent with commonly held notions of equity and thus more policy relevant than is an ex ante equal chance.

The features of ideal compensation can be summed up as follows:

[E] Efficiency: the amount of land taken and the level of investment are jointly community income maximizing. The efficient outcome, $(x_{-t}^*, x_t^*, q^*)$ is

$$(x_{-t}^*, x_t^*, q^*) \in \arg\max(1-q)(f(x_{-t},q)-rx_{-t})-qrx_t \ .$$

[Q] Equity: like individuals have like outcomes
$Q_P$ Ex Post: Income is the same for all landowners whether or not their land is condemned

$Q_A$ Ex Ante: Every landowner has the same expected income.
[B] Balance Budget: The amount collected in taxes must be at least as much as the compensation paid, $\tau (1-q)V_{-t} \geq qc$.
[K] Reasonable Knowledge: The compensation rule cannot be based on fore-knowledge of the efficient choice, namely, $c$ is not a function of $(x^*_{-t}, x^*_t, q^*)$.

## Ideal Compensation

We propose that compensation be awarded for condemned land at the market price of the remaining land after the public project is completed. Using the previ-ous-ly defined symbols annual compensation is

$$c = \frac{r}{r+\tau}[f(x_{-t}, q) - rx_{-t}].$$

This rule is undeniably equitable, both ex ante and ex post. Because the wealth of all landowners is the same, no matter the taking choice, there is no question of unfairness. It also satisfies condition [K] in that its implementation does not require foreknowl-edge of the efficient level of capital improvements. The bureau makes the taking choice, $q$, that generates the most tax revenue, conditional on the existing level of investment, $x$. Simultaneously, landowners, make investment decision, $x$, based on the bureau-determined project size, $q$. In this way, condition [K]—Reasonable Knowledge—is satisfied: the landowner knows only how the choice of investment affects his profits and the bureaucrat knows only the tax revenue effect of the project size. In this "Reasonable Knowledge" environment, the bureaucrat and landowners must calculate what is best for their own objective, given what the other has done.

The balanced budget condition [B] will be met because of the tax increment financing—the agency whose job it is to condemn land must collect sufficient tax revenues to service the debt incurred by the public project. Note that the compensation scheme does not depend on the value of investment in the land to be taken. Whether or not the compensation rule induces efficient choices for both sets of actors—the landowners and the bureaucrats—is to be examined.

Consider the case in which the bureau has chosen a project size $q'$ that is less than the optimal $q^*$ and start with the landowners decision calculus with the pro-posed compensation for taking. Those landowners outside the project area will choose the level of investment, $x'_{-t}$, that maximizes their net income: it is the value that equates the marginal product of capital with its price $f_x(x_{-t}, q') = r$. The result is that it is the level that produces an income of $y_{-t} = f(x'_{-t}, q') - rx'_{-t}$. The net income for those landowners within the project area is what they receive as compensation less what they spend on capital improvements $(y_t = y_{-t} - rx'_t)$. It is clear that a condemnee's best choice is no capital expenditure, $x'_t = 0$. It is important to point out that the optimal level of investment for the out-of-project land is smaller, when $q'$ is less than $q^*$ than it would be when the efficient project size is chosen. This conclusion follows from the assumption that fixed capital investment and proj-ect size are strict complements: the larger is $q$ the larger is the marginal product of capital, for a fixed $x$.

Consider now the implication for the government of private investment $x' = (x'_{-t}, x'_t) < x^*$. The bureau does its own calculation to choose a revenue–maximizing project size conditional on a fixed $x = x'$. Its calculus for deciding whether or not to marginally increase the projects from $q'$ is straightforward. If an additional amount of land is condemned, the loss of tax revenue from that marginal parcel is $\frac{\tau}{\tau + r}(f(x',q') - rx')$. The bureau's benefit from a marginal expansion is the increased revenue from the (approximately) $1-q'$ remaining properties. That amount is the increased tax revenue attributable to the larger public project $\frac{\tau}{\tau + r}(1 - q)f_q(x',q') \cdot$ As long as the marginal increase in the tax revenue from the non-taken land exceed the revenue loss from the last property taken, the government will continue to expand the project size. The bureau expands until $(1- q)f_q(x,q)$ is equal to $f(x,q)—r$.

The implication is that there is at least one project size, say $q^*$, that induces landowners to invest $x^*$ and conditional on this level of investment the bureau will choose $q^*$ as the project size. In other words $(x^*,q^*)$ is a Nash equilibrium in the game between the government and landowners and the equilibrium choices maximize the aggregate value of all land. In addition there is no investment on the condemned land, thus no wasted capital resources; the level of capital expenditures on the remaining land equates its marginal product with the price of capital, $r$ and, $q^*$ is the project size that maximizes the total land values conditional on the choice $x^*$. Thus, the compensation scheme induces an efficient equilibrium of the simultaneous move landowner-bureau taking game. The conclusion is formalized as Theorem 1.

**Theorem 1:**  The strategy profile $(x_t^*,x_{-t},q^*)$ (the efficient levels of investment and land taken) is the unique Nash Equilibrium for the game in which the landowners and the government move simultaneously.

The formal proof of this theorem is in the appendix. It should be noted that the theorem states a result much stronger than the one suggested by the wheat farmer road example that precedes Theorem 1. Not only is the efficient outcome an equilibrium of the game it is the *only* Nash equilibrium. The proof of uniqueness relies on the concavity of the production function. Due to the technical nature of the proof, we are unable to construct a simple example like the one above. However, a return to the farmer-road example demonstrates the nature of the equilibrium.

Wheat, at market, is the output. The production of this commodity depends on both $x$ and $q$ in the following way[11]

$$f(x,q) = q^{0.1}\sqrt{x}.$$

With this production function, the Nash equilibrium is $q^* = 0.17$

$$\text{and } x^* = \begin{cases} x_t = 0 \\ x_{-t} = \dfrac{(0.17)^2}{4r^2} \end{cases}.$$

These values are the ones that maximize the community net surplus and, thus, are efficient. Suppose that the area under consideration is one square mile. In equilibrium, with the proposed compensation rule, the road occupies 0.17 square miles.[12] If, for instance the price of capital is $r = 0.5$, the capital intensity of wheat production, on the untaken land, is 0.015 per acre.

In light of Theorem 1 we can see that if those whose land is condemned are compensated at the value of the land had it enjoyed the benefit of the public project, all of the criteria of ideal compensation are fulfilled. The outcome is [E]fficient. It is ex post $E[Q_p]$uitable since both the taken and untaken landowners share equally in the benefits of the public project. The [B]alanced budget condition is forced on the solution with the constraint that the bureau's expenditures must be covered by its tax collections. Compensation is purely market based and is independent of the efficient outcome. In this way the [K]nowledge requirement is fulfilled, however, there is even a more subtle way in which the spirit of [K] is met as well. Each player makes a choice conditional on the choices of all other players. None need know the objective of all others to make a conditionally best decision.

This is a most optimistic conclusion: there is a compensation rule that meets all the ideal criteria. Unfortunately, the conclusion is based on assumptions that are rightly challenged. For instance it is held that the property tax rate is independent of the taking choices. This means that the bureau producing the public project cannot influence the tax rate. However, while there are many factors that influence the tax rate, it is unrealistic to presume that a large public project is not one of those factors. The motivation of the bureau is at least as important as the determination of the tax rate. The size-maximizing bureau is the first Niskanen model, but there is a second. Niskanen has published a reconsideration of his original assertion and now believes that the bureau's objective is to maximize its tax revenues less its expenditures (its surplus).[13] If project size influences the tax rate and/or the bureaus behave as Niskanen's second version, the conclusion is not so optimistic.

The reason for this is pretty clear. With revenue maximization and a fixed tax rate, the bureau's objective is a scalar multiple[14] of aggregate land values. The necessary conditions for maximizing the bureau's objective are the same as those for overall efficiency, namely $(1-q)f_q(x_{-t},q)-[f(x_{-t},q)-rx_{-t}]-rx_t = 0$, the marginal contribution of the last property taken equals the income produced by that property if it is not taken. When it is possible for the bureau to influence the tax rate and the bureau seeks to maximize its surplus, its objective is $\frac{1}{\tau+r}[\tau(1-q)-rq][f(x_{-t},q)-rx_{-t}]$. In this case the optimum for the bureau depends on the elasticity of the tax rate with respect to its taking decision and its total outlays. Even if the tax rate influence is ignored, i.e., if the elasticity of the tax rate with respect to $q$ is zero, the bureau's necessary condition, $(-\tau-r)[f(x,q)-rx_{-t}]+[\tau(1-q)-rq][f_q(x,q)] = 0.$, does not coincide with that necessary for efficiency. This discouraging conclusion is summarized in Theorem 2. It is, by the way, curious that if the bureau maximizes its surplus, rather than revenue, it will choose a $q$ smaller than what is efficient.

**Theorem 2:** In the simultaneous move game in which the government maximizes net revenues (its surplus) the strategies $(x^*_t, x^*_{-t}, q^*)$ are not a Nash Equilibrium.[15]

There is another issue that relates to implementation. Our very favorable conclusion in Theorem 1 concerns the equilibrium of a simultaneous move game. While such an equilibrium is a compelling outcome prediction, it is legitimate to question whether or not there is a dynamic process from which the equilibrium can be expected. It is impossible to examine all possible dynamics, but a reasonable one to study is a stage game in which one of the participants announces a first choice and the other responds based on the commitment of the opponent. Subgame perfection is the natural equilibrium choice for such games.

Since ex post compensation fails to induce efficient equilibria choices when the bureau aims to maximize its surplus, it is not surprising that the sequential game results are not more optimistic. For that reason the bureau as a revenue maximizer is the maintained assumption for all that follows.

First suppose the bureau is the first mover and can anticipate the reaction of the landowners to a choice of $q$.[16] From a deduction similar to the one presented for the simultaneous version of the game, the bureau knows that the landowners will choose the efficient level of investment conditional on the choice of $q$. Since the bureau wants land values, and consequently its tax revenues, to be as large as possible, it will choose the efficient project size $q^*$. In response, the landowners choose $x^*$.

Consider what choices are made if the landowner makes the first choice, with the knowledge of the bureau's response. The compensation equivalent to the value of a parcel of non-taken land increases as $q$ increase. Suppose the bureau has chosen $q^*$. There are owners whose land is just outside, on the boundary of the project. If the boundary owners invest $x^*$ their income is $f(x^*,q^*) - rx^*$. However, if these same boundary owners invest nothing they know that the land will be taken. The result is that the income from all remaining land is larger. A boundary landowner's income is highest if nothing is invested and the land is taken. Extending this logic, the only equilibrium is one in which the balanced budget requirement restrains further public acquisition. Formally this is

**Theorem 3:**   If compensation is the ex post equitable compensation scheme, there is no unreasonable knowledge of the efficient strategies the government's objective is to maximize tax revenues, and the budget is balanced then the subgame perfect equilibrium of the two stage dynamic game in which the landowners move first is efficient only if $\tau = q^* / (1-q^*)$ .

The proof of this proposition is in the appendix.

## MARKET IMPLEMENTATION: THE LEHAVI-LICHT PROPOSAL

The sequential game framework is instructive and it is encouraging that there is a setting in which the efficient outcome can be achieved. The unfortunate aspect of the dynamic setting and the search for a subgame perfect equilibrium requires that the leader, whether it is the bureau or the landowner, needs to know the reaction function of the followers. This is a large supposition. We might inquire whether or not there is a market-like mechanism which achieves the same desirable end.

The conclusion of the compensation methodology which pays the post-project value is that all landowners, whether their land survives condemnation or not, benefit equally from the public project. The compensation scheme, financed with an ad valorem property tax, works because all project benefits are incorporated in property values. What about the New London redevelopment and those with similar attributes? That project, and its famous *Kelo* decision fallout, condemns land and gives it (long-term lease at one dollar per year) to private developers. In New London, the condemned space was to be used for office, residential and hotel development. The city is to benefit from a revitalized economy, now depressed from its loss of its historically prominent shipbuilding industry. Nationwide there are many examples of cities employing redevelopment projects in similar ways: public condemnation for private development. These redevelopment efforts may, or may not increase the value of surrounding land, but the major beneficiaries are the private developers. While this may generate headlines about the fattening up of the already fat cats at the expense of the aged, disabled and widowed, the prospect of a good return is essential to induce the risk-taking inherent in development.

At the beginning of a land development project there are a multitude of uncertainties. Developers assume considerable risk at the inception and the outcome is often not known for many years. In all work to date, including that on the previous pages, it is assumed that there is no risk. Production and profits are generated automatically from the choice of inputs. This, of course, is a fiction, convenient for modeling simplicity. But the reality is that there is considerable risk and uncertainty in any large capital project. These are rarely computed as part of public benefit/cost studies—ranges of values are sometimes given, but most are given as point predictions. These predictions are the ones on which public decisions are taken. The high frequency of cost overruns indicates how unrealistic this is. There is no mechanism within the public sector decision process to accommodate uncertainty, except the prospect of defeat in forthcoming elections if the project goes sour. The market, however, is adept at accounting for risk and uncertainty. The market value of a project, what someone is willing to pay for it, reflects the most current consensus of the likelihood and extent of its success.

The preceding discussion is focused on public projects whose total value is reflected perfectly in land values. These are reflections of the market's evaluation of the project value. In this case, it is valid to point out that if the project-induced increase in land values does not exceed the project cost, the project should not be undertaken. Similarly, this market test is valid for a taking for private development: if the market value of the project, from the time of its inception to the time construction bids are accepted, does not exceed the value of the taken property, it is inefficient and should not be undertaken. This insight suggests an alternative compensation, one that induces efficient choices and is fair ex post.

When seeking an ideal compensation plan the recent paper by Lahavi and Licht (2007) (referred to as LL henceforth) offers much to be admired. A condemnee is offered a chance to participate in the value of assemblage.

One of the often used justifications for employing eminent domain rather than private market alternatives is the excessive cost of assembling large parcels from previ ously fragmented ones. Presumably, the assembled land has greater market value than the sum of the fragmented values (super-additivity). There are many parts to the LL proposal, but the overriding idea is to offer condemnees the current market value of their property or a share in the value of the assembled parcel. LL envision the application of eminent domain for acquisition and then a public auction to sell the acquired land as a whole. The proceeds from the auction are to be distributed to the condemnee-shareholders.[17]

This is a proposal with considerable merit, particularly in the light of the compensation rule given in this paper. In the early, formal presentation we restricted the domain of our proposal to projects whose total benefits accrue to non-taken land. If appraisals are accurate, there is an objective measure for the project-enhanced value compensation. For many, if not most, public assemblages, most value is captured by the large parcel. It is common for public authorities to use the land so acquired as a subsidy to private developers. There is, in that case, no way to measure the value we propose. LL will put the land to public auction and, if markets function perfectly, the winning bid is the measure of the compensable value we desire. LL design a detailed structure in which many of the potential problems, such as those referred to as agency issues, are given real-world solutions. LL write about a body of corporate and securities law that safeguards against many potential abuses. However, one aspect bothers us.

The condemnees are not likely to be sophisticated security traders. For this reason many are not able to evaluate the securities offered. Their naïveté leaves them vulnerable to exploitation. In addition, they may not be willing to endure the risk inherent with a security and choose to take a lower valued current market price. For this reason we offer a small modification of the LL proposal.

We suggest that it is better (and fairer to the potentially risk-averse) to give to each condemnee a tradable option to choose between the market value of their property or an LL security. The option is time dated, namely, within a specified amount of (e.g., six months) the holder of the option must decide between the house value or the share of the assemblage. In order to understand how the modified LL compensation satisfies all the criteria for an ideal compensation methodology one must think about the market for the options.

The minimum value of the option held by each condemnee must be the current market value of the house, for the value is a certain reward. If the market evaluates the option value at an amount greater than the current market value, the potential project returns must be larger than the value of the property to be converted into project use. If the options sell for more than the existing property value, the project benefits outweigh the costs. If, however, the options are valued only at the condemned property value, it is doubtful that the project evaluation can survive a true benefit/cost test—it should be abandoned and the property returned to the original owners. Notice that all aspects of an ideal compensation methodology are met.

The compensation is equitable in that those whose property is condemned benefit as much from the project as the receivers of the land. A landowner does not need to exercise the option, but can sell it anytime its market value is sufficient. An owner does not necessarily need to bear the risk of uncertain assemblage profits and can sell his option to someone willing to assume the risk.

Option-based compensation induces efficient choices for the landowner as well as the project developer. Increased investment does not increase the landowners' compensation since, if the project is efficiently chosen, the value of his option is independent of his investment choice. Personal investment choices affect compensation only if the project is inefficient, the case in which the option values do not exceed the property values. Project managers are motivated to maximize profit, and consequently, the return to those holding shares in the project.

There are certainly no unreasonable knowledge assumptions which motivate this conclusion. Landowners need not know the plans of the potential bidders, the market for the options is all the information they will have. Of course, if they contemplate exercising the option for a share in the project, they may be inclined to find out details about the project plans and management. LL remind us that all will be provided, as is required by laws governing publicly traded securities.

## CONCLUSION

Whether or not a person whose house is condemned considers a share of the benefits, rather than the house's market value, adequate compensation, the benefit share rule passes the efficiency/equity test proposed. It induces both the landowners and the government to make efficient choices. Landowners do not benefit from overinvestment and government's appetite for private property is controlled by the price it must pay. Since all landowners, whether their land is condemned or not, benefit equally from the public project, the outcome is equitable. These are very optimistic results, however, our optimism must be tempered by examining the conditions under which the conclusions hold.

The first is that the bureau that represents the government seeks to maximize its revenues. If revenues are generated by an ad valorem property tax, the government's objective is coincident with that of the public. However, if the bureau has another aim, perhaps to maximize its net revenues, the coincidence of the public interest and that of the bureau is broken and the result is an equilibrium in which, both the amount of public takings and the private investment are inefficient.

The second is that the optimality of the implementation, modeled as a sequential game, depends on the order of play. If the government is the leader in the game, the sub-game perfect equilibrium is efficient. However, if the landowners move first, the outcome is not optimal.

A hopeful possibility is implementation through the private market. Following from a pioneering work of Lehavi and Lichts (2007), we suggest that giving the condemned landowners options, with a fixed exercise date, will lead to an efficient outcome. The success of the option scheme depends on how well the asset market works for small-scale projects.

## APPENDIX

**Theorem 1:** The strategy profile $(x_t^*, x_{-t}^*, q^*)$ (the efficient levels of investment and land taken) is the unique Nash Equilibrium for the game in which all landowners and the government move simultaneously.

**Proof of Theorem 1:** Consider first the landowners whose land lies outside of $q^*$, that is, those landowners whose land is not to be taken. The landowners will act to maximize the payoff from their land, equivalent to solving

$$\max_{x>0} \frac{r}{\tau+r}[f(x,q^*)-rx].$$

The first order condition yields

$$f_x(x_{-t}, q^*) = r.$$

The non-taken landowner has no reason to deviate from the efficient strategy.

Consider the landowners that own land that is taken. These landowners will receive a compensation that is independent of their investment. Any investment in their land is lost. Thus there is no reason to invest and $x_t = 0$.

Next consider the government. It is bound by the need to collect at least as much tax revenue as it spends. To achieve this, the project size can be no larger than $\tau/(\tau+r)$. Thus the government's best response solves

$$\max_{q \in \left[0, \frac{\tau}{\tau+r}\right]} \frac{\tau}{\tau+r}(1-q)[f(x_{-t}^*, q) - rx_{-t}^*].$$

Let's first consider the case where the balanced budget constraint is not binding, that is where $q^* < \tau/(\tau+r)$. For an interior solution the first order condition is

$$(1-q)f_q(x^*_{-t},q) = f(x^*_{-t},q) - rx^*_{-t}.$$

The government chooses the efficient level of taking—or more accurately has no incentive to deviate from the efficient level of taking and the efficient outcome is a result of a Nash equilibrium in the simultaneous move game.

Consider now the case in which the balanced budget constraint is binding for some $q' < q^*$.

$$q' = \frac{\tau}{\tau+r} < q^* .$$

Let $x' = x(q')$. By the envelope theorem $dx(q)/dq = -f_{xq}/f_{xx}$ and since, by assumption $f_{xq} > 0$, then $dx(q)/dq > 0$. Therefore the derivative of the bureau's objective $b(x, q)$ with respect to $q$ is positive for all $q < q^*$. It follows that the budget constrained equilibrium is $(q', x')$. It is efficient conditional on the tax rate constrained balanced budget condition.

We will now prove the uniqueness of the Nash Equilibrium. The strict quasiconcavity of $f(\cdot)$ ensures that there is a unique optimal $x$ for every value of $q$ and $r$. Let the mapping from $q$ and $r$ to the optimal level of investment be denoted by $x_t(r, q)$ and $x_{-t}(r, q)$ for the taken and untaken property respectively. We have established that

$$x_t(r, q^*) = 0 \quad \text{and} \quad x_{-t}(r, q^*) = x^*_{-t}.$$

By way of contradiction suppose that there is a second equilibrium $q'' > q^*$ (the proof for $q'' < q^*$ is analogous). Then the government's first order condition is:

$$(1 - q'')f_q(x_{-t}(r, q''), q'') = f(x_{-t}(r, q''), q'') - rx_{-t}(r, q). \tag{1}$$

From the envelope theorem the derivative with respect to $q$ of the right hand side of this equation is equal to $f_q(x_{-t}(r, q''), q'') > 0$ for all values of $q$. Therefore

$$f(x_{-t}(r, q''), q'') - rx_{-t}(r, q'') > f(x_{-t}(r, q^*), q^*) - rx_{-t}(r, q^*).$$

The partial derivative with respect to $q$ of the left hand side of the government's optimizing equation (1) is

$$\frac{\partial}{\partial q}(1-q')f_q = (1-q'')\left(f_{qx}\frac{\partial x_{-t}}{\partial q} + f_{qq}\right) - f_q.$$

From the envelope theorem we know that $\partial x_{-t}/\partial q = -f_{xq}/f_{xx}$ and thus:

$$\frac{\partial}{\partial q}(1-q'')f_q = (1-q'')\left(\frac{-f_{xq}^2 + f_{qq}f_{xx}}{f_{xx}}\right) - f_q < 0.$$

The inequality follows from the concavity of $f(\cdot)$. Therefore we can conclude that

$$(1 - q'')f_q(x_{-t}(r, q''), q'') < (1-q^*)f_q(x_{-t}(r, q^*), q^*).$$

Thus we have

$$(1 - q'')f_q(x_{-t}(r, q''), q'') < f(x_{-t}(r, q''), q'') - rx_{-t}(r, q''),$$

which contradicts equation 1. Therefore the efficient Nash equilibrium is unique.

## Computation of Nash Equilibrium—Example

The Nash Equilibrium is found as the solution of two simultaneous equations that represent the necessary conditions for each player's best response

Government:   $(1 - q)f_q = f - rx$

Landowners:

Taken $x = 0$

Non Taken $f_x = r$

With the proposed production function $f = q^{0.1}\sqrt{x}$ we know that

$$f = 2xf_x = 2rx$$

for the non taken land. We also know that the marginal product of q is

$$f_q = 0.1f / q = 0.2rx / q.$$

Putting this into the government foc

$$0.2(1-q)rx / q = rx$$

The solution for this is

$$q^* = 0.2/1.2 = 0.17.$$

The equilibrium value of $x = x^*$ is found as the solution to

$$f_x(x, q^*) = \frac{q^{*0.1}}{2\sqrt{x}} = r.$$

**Theorem 2:**   In the simultaneous move game in which the government maximizes net revenues, the strategies $(x_t^*, x_{-t}^*, q^*)$ are not a Nash Equilibrium.

**Proof of Theorem 2:**    The argument follows the same lines as for the other simultaneous game for the road model for the two types of landowners. The landowners'
strategies will be the efficient ones—namely those whose land is not taken will
invest to the point that $f_x = r$, while those landowners whose land is taken will
invest zero. That leaves us to check the government's strategy choice. Recall that
the government's payoff function from above is:[18]

$$\frac{1}{\tau+r}[\tau(1-q)-rq][f(x_{-t},q)-rx_{-t}].$$

The first order condition is:

$$(-\tau-r)[f(x,q)-rx_{-t}]+[\tau(1-q)-rq][f_q(x,q)]=0.$$

Rearranging gives us:

$$\left(\frac{\tau}{\tau+r}-q\right)f_q(x_{-t},q)=f(x_{-t},q)-rx_{-t}.$$

This does not match the efficiency first order condition with respect to $q$. Since
$\tau/(\tau+r)$ is less than 1 we are able to conclude that the taking will be less than the
efficient amount.

This only proves that there exists *a* Nash equilibrium that is not efficient. In
order to prove that the efficient strategies are not a Nash equilibrium we will prove
that the Nash equilibrium we found is unique.

Recall that there are two first order conditions: For the government:

$$(\tau(1-q)-rq)f_q(x_{-t},q)-(\tau+r)[f(x_{-t},q)-rx_{-t}]=0;$$

and for the landowner (for untaken land):

$$f_x(x_{-t},q)-r=0.$$

From the solution to the two equations comes the best response functions $q(x)$
and $x(q)$.

We take the derivative of both equations with respect to $x$ and insert the best
response functions in the appropriate places. First for the government:

$$-(\tau-r)\frac{dq}{dx}f_q+(\tau(1-q)-rq)f_{qx}+(\tau(1-q)-rq)f_{qq}\frac{dq}{dx}$$

$$-(\tau+r)f_x-(\tau+r)f_q\frac{dq}{dx}+(\tau+r)r=0$$

Notice that $f_x = r$. Solving for the slope of the government's reaction function we
find that:

$$\frac{dq}{dx}=\frac{(\tau(1-q)-rq)f_{qx}}{2(\tau+r)f_q-(\tau(1-q)-rq)f_{qq}}.$$

By virtue of the fact that $f_{qx} > 0$ and $f_{qq} < 0$ then we know that $dq/dx > 0$. Now, for the landowner:

$$f_{xx}\frac{dx}{dq} + f_{xq} - r\frac{dx}{dq} = 0.$$

The slope of the landowner's reaction function is:

$$\frac{dx}{dq} = \frac{f_{xq}}{r - f_{xx}} > 0.$$

We no determine whether the slope of the landowners' reaction function is larger, equal to, or smaller than the slope of the government's reaction function as

$$\frac{f_{xq}}{r - f_{xx}} \gtreqless \frac{2(\tau + r)f_q - (\tau(1-q) - rq)f_{qq}}{(\tau(1-q) - rq)f_{qx}}.$$

Notice that the numerator and denominators of both sides of the inequality are positive and thus we can cross multiply without changing the direction of the inequalities;

$$(\tau(1-q) - rq)[f_{qx}^2 - f_{qq}f_{xx}] \gtreqless 2(\tau + r)rf_q - 2(\tau + r)f_q f_{xx}.$$

By virtue of the strict quasiconcavity of $f(\cdot)$ in both $x$ and $q$, the right hand side of the inequality is positive and the left hand side is negative (Hessian with alternating sign).[19] Thus we can conclude that:

$$\left.\frac{dx}{dq}\right|_{Landowner} < \left.\frac{dx}{dq}\right|_{Government}.$$

Thus the reaction functions will intersect at most once. Therefore, if there exists a Nash equilibrium, it must be unique.

We have shown that there both exists an inefficient Nash equilibrium and that such equilibrium is unique.

**Theorem 3:**   If compensation is the ex post equitable compensation scheme, there is no unreasonable knowledge of the efficient strategies, the government's objective is to maximize tax revenues, and the budget is balanced then the subgame perfect equilibrium of the two stage dynamic game in which the landowners move first is efficient only if $\tau = q^*/(1-q^*)$ .

**Proof of Theorem 3:**   By way of backward induction we consider the reaction of the Government first. The government wishes to maximize tax revenues. Define $\bar{q}$ such that

$$\bar{q} \in \arg\max \frac{\tau}{\tau + r}(1 - q)[f(x_{-t}, q) - rx_{-t}].$$

Let 1 be the amount of land that has zero investment. The government, as the second mover in this game will be faced with some fraction $1 \in [0, 1]$ of empty land. If $1 < \bar{q}$ then the government will take $\bar{q}$ because doing so will maximize its tax revenue by the definition of $\bar{q}$. Now suppose that $1 > \bar{q}$. In this case the value of the land with zero investment is zero, which means that the tax revenue from this land is zero. The best the government can do is to take the land with zero investment in order to boost $q$ and subsequently boost the value of the remaining land thereby increasing the tax revenue. This is the case since $f_q(x, q) > 0$. Thus the government will take $\max\{1, \bar{q}\}$. Note that since the project is worth undertaking $\bar{q} > 0$.

Now let us consider the landowners. Let us start with the primary landowner; that is, consider the landowner whose land is right in the center of the land which is proposed for the road. Given that $\bar{q} > 0$, this landowner knows that her land will be taken, thus in order to maximize utility she will invest nothing in the land since all investment will be forfeit. Similar logic holds for all of the people whose land lie within $\bar{q}$. Now consider the marginal landowner whose land is on the periphery of $\bar{q}$. This landowner has to choose between keeping her land and investing $x_i$. Keeping the land will give a payoff of:

$$\frac{r}{\tau + r}[f(x_i, q(0, x_i, x_{-t})) - rx_i] \tag{2}$$

The marginal landowner can also invest nothing and, knowing the government will take the land, be paid compensation. The compensation paid will give a payoff of:

$$\frac{r}{\tau + r}[f(\bar{x}_{-t}, q(0, 0, \bar{x}_{-t})) - r\bar{x}_{-t}]. \tag{3}$$

Note that $q(0, x_i, x_{-t}) < q(0, 0, \bar{x}_{-t})$ by the previous argument regarding the government's strategy. Since $f_q(x, q) > 0$ it must be that equation 3 is greater than 2. It is easy to see that this is the case. As $q$ increases the value of the payoff increases.[20] Now consider the case of the next landowner. She will face the same decision and for the same reasons come to the same conclusion—invest nothing, let the government take the land and receive the compensation. In fact, every marginal landowner will invest nothing in favor of the compensation. This will continue until the balanced budget condition is reached. Specifically until $q = \tau/(1+\tau)$. This is efficient only if the tax rate happens to be set so that $\tau/(1+\tau) = q^*$.

## NOTES

1. *Kelo v. New London*, 545 U.S. (2005)
2. *United States v. Reynolds*, 397 U.S. 14 (1970)
3. Ibid, citing e.g., *Shoemaker v. United States*, 147 (1893)
4. *Armstrong v. United States*, 364 U.S. 40 (1960)
5. Epstein (1985, 182).
6. Later in the paper we formulate production as a strictly quasi-concave function of the size of the public project, $q$, and the level of investment, $x$. This is a specific example of such a function.
7. This perspective is not unique and original to this paper. The idea was first suggested to us in a paper by Ed Nosal (2001). Robert Innes (1997, 2000) applies the game analogy to the taking problem with great success as well.

8. This is equivalent to making the landowners the holder of the government debt.
9. See Brueckner (2001).
10. If the bureau's actions affect the tax rate, the bureau's desire to maximize its tax collections would depend on the change in the tax rate as well as the change in aggregate property values.
11. It should be noted that the production function has all of the assumed properties of the general function: $f_x = 0.5 \frac{1}{\sqrt{x}} q^{0.1} > 0;$

$$f_q = 0.1 \frac{\sqrt{x}}{q^{0.9}} > 0;$$

$$f_{xq} = 0.05 \frac{1}{q^{0.9} \sqrt{x}} > 0; \quad \text{and,}$$

the function is strictly concave.
12. The computation of the equilibrium values is in the appendix.
13. Niskanen (1994).
14. The scalar is $\tau$, the fixed tax rate.
15. The proof is in the appendix.
16. The bureau is a Stackelberg leader.
17. We give only the most bare-bones description of the LL proposal. The authors have thought through many of the potential problems associated with the scheme and have proposed structural solutions for them. Our stark description is intended to indicate how the post project compensation we suggest has a market-like implementation.
18. Note that the annual tax collected is

$$\tau(1-q) \frac{[f(x_{-t}, q) - rx]}{\tau + r}$$

and the annual payments are

$$\frac{rq[f(x_{-t}, q) - rx]}{\tau + r}.$$

19. The term in the square brackets is the negative of the Hessian.
20. This is the case no matter how $x$ changes since the value would be higher with no change in $x$ and any change in $x$ made by the landowners would only increase their payoff.

## REFERENCES

Blume, Lawrence, Daniel L. Rubinfeld, and Perry Shapiro. 1984. The Taking Of Land: When Should Compensation Be Paid? *The Quarterly Journal of Economics* 99 (1): 71–92.

Brueckner, Jan K. 2001. Tax Increment Financing: A Theoretical Inquiry. *Journal of Public Economics* 81: 321–343.

Epstein, Richard A. 1985. *Takings: Private Property and the Power of Eminent Domain.* Cambridge, MA: Harvard University Press.

Fischel, William A. and Perry Shapiro. 1988. Takings, Insurance and Michelman: Comments On Economic Interpretations Of Just Compensation: Law. *The Journal of Legal Studies* 17 (2): 269–293.

———. 1989. A Constitutional Choice Model of Compensation for Takings. *International Review of Law and Economics* 9: 115–128.

Innes, Robert. 1997. Taking, Compensation and Equal Treatment for Owners of Developed and Undeveloped Property. *Journal of Law and Economics* 40 (2): 403–432.

———. 2000. The Economics of Takings and Compensation When Land and Its Public Use Value Are in Private Hands. *Land Economics* 76 (2): 195–212.

Johnson, M. Bruce. 1977. Planning Without Prices: A Discussion of Land Use Regulation without Compensation in Bernard H. Siegan, ed. *Planning Without Prices: The Taking Clause as It Relates to Land Use Regulation Without Compensation.* Washington, DC: Heath, 63–111.

Lehavi, Amnon and Amir N. Licht. 2007. Eminent Domain Inc. *Columbia Law Review* 107: 1704–1748.

Miceli, Thomas J. and Kathleen Segerson. 1994. Regulatory Takings: When Should Compensation Be Paid? *The Journal of Legal Studies* 23 (2): 749–776.

———. 1996. *Compensation for Regulatory Takings: An Economic Analysis with Application.* Greenwich, CT: JAI Press.

Michelman, Frank I. 1967. Property, Utility and Fairness: Comments on the Ethical Foundations of Just Compensation Law. *Harvard La Review* 80 (6): 1165–1258.

Niskanen, William A. 1994. *Bureaucracy and Public Economics.* Cheltenham, UK: Edward Elgar.

Nosal, Ed. 2001. The Taking of Land: Market Value Compensation Should Be Paid. *Journal of Public Economics* 82: 431–443.

# 5

# How Fair Is Market Value?
## An Appraiser's Report of
## Temptations, Deficiencies, and
## Distortions in the Condemnation
## Process

*Wallace Kaufman*

## Introduction

Eminent domain and its legal procedures have been part of government for at least two thousand years. Taking the power away from government is no more possible than doing away with government itself. Government's *dominium eminens,* supreme lordship, shall always be with us, like the poor. We have the first recorded instance about 870 BC when Jezebel uses Phoenician law to acquire Naboth's vineyard for Ahab (1 Kings 21). Eminent domain's excuse for being will always be making us, as a community, richer. The accompanying requirement to pay just compensation to the dispossessed is supposed to prevent anyone who must surrender property to enlarge the public domain from becoming poorer.

Prevailing wisdom, however, perceives that when the lord exercises his power to take, the citizen whose property is taken becomes poorer. My intent is to dispute this conventional wisdom that the dispossessed always suffer an economic injustice, but at the same time I will confirm that eminent domain makes our store of political liberties poorer.

If we cannot or do not want to liberate ourselves from this government power, then the only reason for discussing it is to understand how it works and how it might be made to work better. Several areas of improvement come to mind

- How can it be a lighter burden on our liberties?
- How can it be less demanding on the fruits of our labors?
- How can it be fairer and thus create greater confidence in our laws and those who use them?

I cannot answer these questions as a scholar steeped in economic theory and practice or jurisprudence. I will address these issues from some thirty years practice in real estate appraisal. I offer as an apology for getting personal what Thoreau offered at the beginning of Walden: "I should not talk so much about myself if there were anybody else whom I knew as well. Unfortunately, I am confined to this theme by the narrowness of my experience."

My experience is narrow because it is limited to the eminent domain procedures that call for real estate appraisal. You might consider the other papers in this symposium to be the legal and economic theory and consider me as a field test. My practice as an appraiser, however, may be wide enough to be of some use in explaining why eminent domain, especially that mutation of it made possible by *Kelo*, widens the possibility of unfair outcomes, who is most likely to be injured, how, and why.

I began appraising as an expert witness in eminent domain proceedings for the B. Everett Jordan Dam and Lake in North Carolina in 1973. That practice expanded to include many kinds of taking cases, including airport expansion and noise damages, community redevelopment, mining, power line and gas line rights of way, highways, landfills, and down zoning. In 1991 I began to work in the former Soviet Union and Eastern Europe. In Kazakhstan I served as the resident advisor for housing and land reform while also teaching property valuation for the World Bank in Central Asia. Finally, as an appraiser in eminent domain proceedings I have not looked at my subjects through the narrow focus of an iron pipe, but with a wide angle, fish-eye lens, taking in the entire ocean I swam in. Herewith I offer you an appraisal, not of the properties, but of the procedures by which government takes them, and of the human temptations those procedures bring into play.

## RELEVANT LEGAL MECHANICS

On paper, most states and the federal government have what seem to be reasonable laws, regulations, and manuals of procedure for the conduct of a takings process by eminent domain. The questions of justice begin with the very first step—what qualifies the government in the name of "public purpose" to take property from a private citizen. I pretend no great expertise in that matter. I do know enough, however, to believe that a close look at the nuts and bolts of the litigation process that begins after a public purpose is established, both deepens our appreciation of the dangerous forces set in motion and of the very real likelihood that a takings process, once set in motion, will lead to great injustice.

For any particular property the appraiser first enters the taking process when the government decides that it needs the particular property of John or Jane Doe. Although the process from declaration of public purpose to the definition and payment of just compensation is familiar to many, let me list those actions most relevant to my propositions. Let us assume a city has decided to acquire several blocks of homes. The typical steps are as follows:

Step one. *Preliminary appraisal.* The city does at least informal appraisals of the properties.

Step two. *The Negotiation Probe.* The city sends out a negotiator to present the government's estimate of value and to make an offer.

Step three. *Offers and counter offers.* The city and private owner negotiate. (Or sometimes the owner refuses to negotiate.)

Step four. *Take it or leave it.* The city makes a final offer.

Step five. *Condemnation.* The city files condemnation papers, puts on deposit a sum equal to its formal offer.

Step six. *Cry uncle or go to trial.* The owner can cry "uncle" and take the offer, or challenge the justice of the offer in court.

Step seven. *The trial.* A judge, commission or jury hears the evidence and decides how much money is just compensation.

Obviously I have left out many activities, including the appeal that sometimes comes after the trial. I have listed only the steps that are the most common milestones in a takings process and the ones where I have seen the goal of just compensation ambushed by participating rent seekers.

## How Well Do These Prescriptions Work To Provide Just Compensation?

Each of these seven steps is often corrupted by chance or on purpose. My experience convinces me that the process never did work very well—for any party—and that *Kelo* expands government power in ways that put ever greater burdens of economic risk on those least able to survive them.

Property owners, however, are not the only ones put at risk. The other principal party to a takings case is not, as many people presume, the government. It is the taxpayer. The government may be the recipient of the title, but it pays for that title with taxpayer funds, and it acquires, holds or conveys that title in the name of the taxpayers. What *Kelo* confirms is that the government may now openly act as the taxpayers' real estate agent, acquiring property with no intention of holding it, but buying land from one party on behalf of another private party: all for the taxpayers' ultimate benefit, of course. That's why the process can proceed under the legal cover of "public purpose."

In theory, the government, like any real estate agency, has a fiduciary duty to its client. Herein lies the first distorting vector in the process of rendering just compensation. By the time the taxpayer's fiduciary has begun the taking, that fiduciary has created a special interest of its own. That interest seldom serves either taxpayer or the property owner well. Like a stock broker buying for his client's portfolio, government agents must also watch out for their own interests, and those may conflict with the interests of both of the other parties. The government planners and the politicians who enable their vision of community investment are locked into their definition of public purpose and the numbers for costs and benefits.

The second distorting vector arises because government officials and politicians do not want to be seen as paying too much, while on the other hand, they cannot be seen as bullying or cheating innocent citizens. In other words, they must be seen as reasonable and nice. Ideally this would lead to a dispassionate consideration, a just price, a golden mean or, shall we say, "market value?" Sometimes it does. More often it does not because the goal is not market value but the appearance of wisdom and fairness and career tenure. Career tenure is a proxy for a secure flow of rents known as salary and benefits. In other words, the interest of the bureaucrat is best served not by achieving just compensation, but by pleasing the party or parties most likely to protect job tenure. Since the parties to a takings procedure want to maximize their gain and are seldom equal in their political influence, government's actors skew their efforts toward the participants most likely to reinforce their career tenure. We will see this in action soon. Neither taxpayers nor property owners, however, are entirely helpless, and property owners in particular have options for active defense and offense to maximize their own gains.

## The Uncut Diamond

Finding a diamond in a rough stone is one of the most common landowner tactics. We all know that the cut diamond looks entirely different and has much greater value than an uncut piece of milky stone. Rightly or wrongly, innocently or with guile, most landowners think a significant part of their property value is hidden even to the most experienced eye, no less to a government bureaucrat or to blind justice. They practice a variety of ways to make that value credible before the filing of condemnation fixes the taking date and the date of value. A Condemnation date, of course, freezes the date for just compensation.

One of the most common diamonds in the rough is the undeveloped subdivision. Courts have often addressed the "subdivision value" by rulings that say an undeveloped piece of land cannot be appraised on the basis of finished lots that lie in its imagined transformation into a housing subdivision (or any other unrealized use). Typically, appraisers follow court and appraisal guidelines that a highest and best use that is not the present use of the property, must be possible in the immediate future.[1] With that in mind, many owners take measures to show that they have begun to cut the rough diamond. They do soil tests, apply for subdivision permits, obtain septic approvals, get subdivision plans drawn up, and survey and stake lot lines. Some property owners go as far as making physical improvements and obtaining contingent contracts of sale. Once such things are done, the property owner is in a better position to ask an appraiser to estimate a present value for the future prices of the lots.

A much shadier way of revealing the diamond inside the rough stone is to inflate the prices recorded for comparable sales or to actually fake such sales. The owner of a property being taken for Interstate 85 once gave me the deeds and purchase agreements for several lots and homes sold on land adjacent to the land the Department of Transportation was taking from him. The buyers confirmed the prices. I used the sales for estimating value of the condemned property. Only when the federal attorney cross-examined the owner did anyone discover that the sales were to members of the owner's own church, to his good friends, and to partners in crime.

Any appraiser must be part investigative journalist and detective, and any good appraiser knows that public records alone are not sufficient documentation of market transactions. Professional standards, however, do not oblige an appraiser to be a criminal investigator.

## The Big Chill

Many opportunities to game the takings process, legal and illegal, arise because of a delay between the public announcement of a project and the actual date of taking. This window of opportunity may be open from several months to a decade or more. An agile property owner can take advantage of even a short lapse of time. The preferred tactics are those which allow the owner to undertake the activities that reveal the diamond in the rough. Under the law, property is considered marketable until condemned, the equivalent of innocent until proven guilty. The longer the window is open, however, the more likely that the government will benefit, whether it means to or not.

The announcement of a project that requires taking property casts over property values what we call the "chill of condemnation." It is also known as "condemnation blight" and in California as "Klopping damages."[2] While states differ on when the precise date of taking occurs—some using date of valuation, some trial date, others date of depositing funds, etc—all allow a long open window between the time the public knows property will be taken and the time it is considered taken. Only the most wily or zany speculators will deliberately buy a property that is certain to be condemned.

Congress first proposed North Carolina's 48,000-acre B. Everett Jordan Dam and Lake in the early 1960s. All the land was within 20 miles of booming Chapel Hill and the rapidly expanding University of North Carolina. Much of it lay within five miles. At least ten years passed between announcing the project and the first offer to buy a tract of land. Land and homes certain to be taken became less saleable as the project inched closer to reality. City and county governments passed laws making changes in land use more difficult. Near the very end, environmental lawsuits delayed the taking two or three years. Government appraisers and attorneys often claimed that the lack of sales and development supported their highest and best use designation—farmland or woodland—and its accompanying low value.

The moral of the story is that the longer the chill of condemnation lasts, the more heavily it burdens property values and the ability of property owners to prove what market value should be. Owners lose the ability to cite recent comparable sales of neighboring properties, the most reliable appraisal method. *Kelo*'s justification of taking blighted properties or any properties that pay low taxes puts all poor neighborhoods on an orange level takings alert and chills their value. Many owners of such properties will never know this, and if they did know it, they could not afford the cost of the statistical work to document it.

## Made As Instructed

One of the most prestigious designations for an appraiser is Member of the Appraisal Institute, or MAI. In the adversarial world of litigation, lawyers attacking an appraiser with this designation often quip that MAI stands for *Made As Instructed*. In step one of the taking procedure, the preliminary appraisal, the condemnor's appraiser often receives suggestions that amount to instructions. Because many appraisers want the well paid repeat business of appraising for government agencies and utilities, they are willing to make their appraisal as instructed or as they believe they are being instructed or even as they believe they might be instructed. We shall see this in action as we move through the description of later steps in the taking process. Suffice to say that the staff appraiser's job and promotions are on the line, and the independent fee appraiser, working for either government or a trial lawyer has a lucrative steady client to please. The client, of course, has a reputation to protect and perhaps political constituents to please.

The corollary of the instructed appraisal is the buyout of the threatening appraiser. When an expert witness gains the reputation of being a particularly effective witness, it behooves lawyers who might face this witness to hire him before the other side does, whether or not they intend to use his work product. This deprives the jury of his expertise unless the other side is astute enough to find out he has been financially abducted by the opponent and decides to subpoena his work product.

## CONTRACT CONDEMNATION

A slight variation on Made as Instructed is what I call "Contract Condemnation." Contract condemnation is the sibling of contract zoning. Driving through the countryside, we have been surprised often enough by a road that goes straight for miles, then suddenly makes a big curve and comes back onto the straight line. Other observers have cited the "highway churches" that seem to have a divine power to make roads go around their land, passing by but not through sacred ground.

In the takings process it also happens that a landowner uses political influence to get part of his property condemned for a use that will significantly raise the value of his remaining property. Having a highway interchange take a fraction of a large landlocked property, for instance, can create a highest and best use windfall, the equivalent of upzoning. Partial takings for water and sewer lines, lakes, and reservoirs can create the same effect. Very few landowners would be unhappy to have a small portion of their land taken for a lake if the large remainder ends up sitting before a beautiful water view that typically raises its value a minimum of 50 percent and often over 100 percent.

Alternatively, or additionally, a property owner might want condemnation because he is confident of receiving a highly inflated appraised value. Every now and then an enterprising investigative reporter is astute enough to catch these political payoffs that provide a condemnation dowry to a political concubine and victimize the taxpayers. Another term for this phenomenon might be "Beam Me Up Action."

## SHOCK AND AWE

The result of the preliminary appraisal is often "shock and awe" in the second step of the taking process—the negotiator's approach to the landowner. This kind of "Shock and Awe," does not involve artillery and bombs, but the most susceptible victim will be the least battle-hardened owner. To use a piece of the standard market value definition, this is usually an owner who is not well informed.

The government negotiator, not unlike the buyer at a used car lot, makes a first offer that is either well below-market value or at least at the low end of the government's appraisal reports. It may come accompanied by frightening descriptions of government powers, court proceedings, or insinuations that if this offer is not accepted, it will be withdrawn and a judge, commission, or jury might award less. The shocked and awed and poorly informed owner accepts a low offer.

The less educated, sophisticated, or experienced an owner is, the more he will be shocked and awed by the power of government, and the less likely that he will feel ready to negotiate, not to mention gird for battle in the courts. Within 20 miles of North Carolina's booming Research Triangle Park and three major universities, I saw government negotiators offer farmers owning 20 to 100 acres of good development land the price that a farmer deep in the boondocks might find attractive. Some who had farmed all their lives, a few totally illiterate, could not imagine land values beyond farming. With the stick of government power behind them and an apparently juicy carrot in front, they took the government's offer. They often felt the government was nice to add some moving money.

The opposite of shock and awe is what I call the "Mouse and Elephant Syndrome." Often the little landowner who threatens to make the government take his property scares the government into paying a higher price to avoid the large expense of legal proceedings and the big risk of a jury biased for the landowner and/or against the government. A Nevada study showed that local government paid 17 percent more than market value for lands taken for public projects, perhaps to avoid administrative and legal costs.[3]

## Vexation Factor

In step three, as the government and the owner negotiate, we often see another distorting vector gather strength. I call this the Vexation Factor. Often the very process of negotiation destroys the conditions for a market transaction. Both parties are, if not unwilling, at least under duress. The definition of market value requires that "neither party be under duress." Duress is sure to cause emotion to enter the negotiating process. It arises because the owner often asks an inflated price based on misinformation, opportunism, or vengeance. The government negotiators often react by deciding they must teach the troublesome owner a lesson and set an example to deter others from outrageous demands. Owners under the cloud of condemnation are often neighbors and neighbors tend to talk to each other, especially in time of crisis.

For instance, the state legislature says the Parks Department must buy an unusually high hill in the flat coastal plain for a nature preserve. The state executive then becomes a buyer who may be willing but who also has no choice. The seller of the 100 plus acres informs the state that his beloved father, an accomplished amateur geologist, acquired the mountain because it was the only significant deposit of molybdenum ore east of the Mississippi. Drilling and assay has proven the deposit. The owner offers to sell the surface rights, to do shaft mining, to abide by environmental restrictions, and to leave the shaft in such condition it can be used as a geological exhibit. The parks people are afraid of mining and demand they get all and leave the landowner nothing. Condemnation proceedings begin. The civil but angry owner then hires an appraiser and a geologist and an economist to demonstrate for a jury the present value of the ore. The state—meaning taxpayers—ends up paying for minerals it will never use and foregoing the opportunity for an interesting exhibit that might have enhanced the park.

In theory negotiations should mimic the market, but in fact, they often mimic the emotional run up to a war.

## The False Benchmark

Given the stakes and the emotions, it is no wonder that steps four and five, the final offer, take it or leave it, and the condemnation documents filed as the basis of the legal proceedings, set a false benchmark. Government officials understand that a jury often compromises between the government's formal offer and the property owner's estimate of market value. The "market value" that the government places on deposit as it files condemnation documents is often far below the final offer made in negotiation. Government may or may not have had the foresight or slight of hand to have an appraisal that backs up this minimal estimate of market value.

The most common way to justify a market value far below a property owner's claim is to specify a highest and best use that is not nearly as profitable as others, but one that seems logical or harmonious with existing uses. Thus, the farmland taken for the B. Everett Jordan Lake in North Carolina's Research Triangle area was often appraised on the assumption that its highest and best use was farming.

I once appraised a group of lots and ramshackle rental cottages in what was called the Red Row district of Rocky Mount, NC. The city rightly described the buildings and lots as slum property and capitalized the minimal rents into minimal values. They wrongly described the highest and best use as slum rental although the word slum was absent. All the properties were zoned B-2 for industrial and commercial use. They were the only B-2 land in the city not used for industry or commerce. Many of them abutted the railroad with its nearby rail yard. Given that almost all the owners lived in other parts of town and held the properties for investment, the highest and best use was clearly for assemblage as an industrial-commercial property. (I suppose one might have considered a highest and best use of historical monument since Red Row in 1917 had become the birthplace of jazz musician Thelonius Monk.) *Kelo*, of course, raises a very similar issue. If a group of modest properties are suited for a much more profitable use through assemblage, shouldn't they be valued and owners compensated on the basis of that use? After all, government's own planners have decided that it is an immediately feasible use.

False benchmarks in dollars are very often backed up by faulty assumptions of highest and best use. We often have a well-wrought appraisal based on a bad assumption. Appraisers, of course, are supposed to research and prove highest and best use, but in practice they often assume what they are told to assume, or they assume what seems obvious. A slum is a slum is a slum. A farm surrounded by other farms is farmland. Government sometimes uses this tactic effectively if the property owners are unaware of demographic trends, zoning, pending infrastructure development, and land use planning—all strong shapers of highest and best use. This is another case of market value being negated by one party not being "fully informed."

The opposite side of the coin is the owner and owner's appraiser who propose an unlikely and unsupportable highest and best use. It's not uncommon for a jury to be convinced that almost any highway intersection is a commercial gold mine, every forest a subdivision.

## THE DISECONOMY OF SCALE

A typical challenge to condemnation means that the landowner will pay his attorney's firm about a third of any compensation that is over and above the money the government has put on deposit as its estimate of market value. Obviously the attorney stands to gain more from 33 percent of a $500,000 increase than 33 percent of a $5,000 increase. This economy of scale for the lawyer is almost always a diseconomy of scale for the owner of a modest property. If the owners of Rocky Mount's Red Row rental shacks had not lucked onto a homegrown, star class trial attorney with an interest in civil rights, they would have been hard pressed to find any attorney willing to fight individual cases speculating on increases of a few hundred dollars here and there.

Occasionally a civil rights group, a firm donating pro bono services, or a public interest law firm will take up the case of the small property owner, but even if the owner finds such representation, it is not likely to be a firm or attorney specializing in eminent domain. Perhaps one of the stronger arguments against the *Kelo* decision is that by affirming perceived blight and low tax revenues as a justification for eminent domain, it specially enabled government to take property from the poor.

Some observers have said that the wealthy have a much better chance than the poor to be justly compensated for property taking. My own experience is that it is not how wealthy the client is that determines the odds for justice, but how wealthy the case might make the lawyer.

## The Br'er Rabbit Maneuver

In step six where the property owner must cry "uncle" or go to trial, we often see the "Br'er Rabbit Maneuver," where the landowner is the rabbit and the briar patch is the trial to determine just compensation. In many instances an owner and/or his astute lawyer bets that inside the briar patch will be 12 sympathetic and/or gullible men and women of a jury. It is no coincidence that many of the same trial lawyers who have risen from humble backgrounds on the "wings of justice" suing doctors and hospitals also show up on the winning side of property condemnation proceedings. Studies that show property owners win some 41 percent of their cases show that going to trial is a reasonable risk (Cohen, 2004),[4] And such averages say nothing about individual attorneys. I have known attorneys who have a 90 percent or better success rate.

Almost every condemnation trial is at least as much a contest of professional skills as it is a contest of evidence. The professional skills include both the attorneys and the expert witnesses. The witnesses are almost always the landowner and his or her appraiser. In the 1980s Bill Thorpe of Rocky Mount, NC was perhaps the state's most successful trial lawyer before the rise of John Edwards. His down-home manner and self-deprecating wit and noblesse oblige toward the opposition created a strong predisposition for any jury to want to believe his case. He was also a very careful case builder, and I count it a compliment that I was often the lead appraiser in his group of expert witnesses. I also count it a personal honor that on a few occasions he dismissed me before trial because my findings did not provide the numbers he wanted.

## Appraiser Shopping

This raises yet another practice that influences the quality of just compensation that a court awards—"appraiser shopping." For the same reasons many addicts go "doctor shopping" condemnors and condemnees go appraiser shopping—to find a professional who will agree with their diagnosis and give them the prescription they crave. Appraisers themselves are not immune to the addiction, and if an appraiser can satisfy the addiction while representing the "little guy" against government, there's also a satisfying feeling of an emotional and moral high. An appraiser, of course, should never 'represent' anyone, but I have seen several appraisers on the witness stand respond to the question "Whom do you represent, Mr. Appraiser?" with the name of their client. Too often the answer, "I represent myself and my research," is not the honest answer.

## THE MEDIUM IS THE MASSAGE

I have already noted that the trial itself can be a Br'er Rabbit's briar patch for the property owner, and that once both sides are committed to trial, the outcome may depend as much or more on the skill of the lawyers and witnesses as on the quality of the evidence. In my experience most trials have been contests between relatively well-matched teams of witnesses and experts, but I would also maintain that a significant number of exceptions exist. Many lawyers are adept at turning a courtroom into a theater. The story is almost inevitably the struggle of the little guy against the callous or even evil forces of government power. When government is taking land to confer on other private citizens, an adept lawyer-dramatist can imply dark conspiracies. When the story is played out most successfully, the winner is likely to get not only just compensation but a bonus for being an innocent victim. This bonus, of course, victimizes the taxpayers.

## BLINDERED JUSTICE

By far the larger question about the trial rules is the justice of the definition of just compensation. Legal history has effectively narrowed the definition of just compensation to market value. Quickly stated, market value is as *the most probable price a property would bring if placed on the open market for a reasonable length of time, neither buyer nor seller being under duress and each being informed of the relevant facts.* With various versions of this definition, the legal system has censored and gagged landowners and put blinders on judges, commissioners, and juries. The most common grievance for most property owners is that they cannot receive a dime's worth of compensation for the many very real values inherent in their properties (e.g., *United States v. Miller, 317 U.S. 369, 375 (1942)*). Consider just a few excluded values: historical value, aesthetic value, psychological value, environmental value, hobby value, religious value, and family value. Before we consider the possibility of compensation for any of these values, let's remember that the law does compensate for such values in other kinds of cases. Let an incompetent doctor's practice kill my wife or son, and my monetary losses are just part of the compensation I would receive for these people who, if they will pardon my saying so, have no market value right now. In libel cases a plaintiff also may be compensated for non-economic damages.

The narrow definition of just compensation in takings cases appears to put property owners in an inferior legal class. It certainly makes a mockery out of legal pronouncements about "making the property owner whole again." For many property owners this is a bit like being considered whole again after being paid for a mandatory brain transplant or castration. Perhaps good reasons explain why, in the taking of property, juries should wear blinders, but such reasons are not obvious or air tight.

## CONCLUSION

Having listed the many distortions in the eminent domain playing field from beginning to end, I admit that I have lacked the means to discover with reasonable accuracy how prevalent these distortions are. I have not discovered with statistical certainty what distance they have put between even the market value definition of just compensation and the actual awards. I have not subjected these distortions to the kinds of research that would determine the two most important parameters:

- how frequent they are?
- are they strong enough factors to merit the expense and risk of changing the process?

I cannot even say with certainty which party—taxpayer or property owner—is most often the victim of injustice. (We should realize, of course, that even if on average market value is paid, this is like saying no more than sometimes owners are victimized, sometimes taxpayers.) In the end the most important message for a consideration of the justice of just compensation is that the key actions of the takings process are open to distortion and corruption. Have I suggested improvements? I admit that I have not. I do maintain that understanding the problem is the foundation of any solution. Legal scholars and economists have provided the cornerstones of this foundation, and I hope that I have provided at least some useful bricks and mortar.

## NOTES

1. *Accord, Thorton v. Birmingham,* 35 So. 2d 545 (Sup. Ct. Ala. 1948); *State of Utah v. Tedesco,* 291 P. 2d 1028, 1029 (Sup. Ct. Utah 1956); *Santa Clara County Flood Control etc. District v. Freitas,* 117 Cal. App. 2d 264, 267, (1960); 172 F. wd 990 (4th Cir. 1949); cert. denied 337 U.S. 931 (1949).
2. *Klopping v. City of Whittier* (1972) 8 Cal.3d 39.
3. Clauretie, Terrence M., William Kuhn, and R. Keith Schwer. Residential Properties Taken Under Eminent Domain: Do Government Appraisers Track Market Values? *Journal of Real Estate Research,* July–September 2004.
4. Cohen, Thomas H. and Steven K. Smith, Civil Trial Cases and Verdicts in Large Counties, 2001. *Bureau of Justice Statistics Bulletin,* April 2004, available at http://www.ojp.usdoj.gov/bjs/pub/pdf/ctcvlc01.pdf.

## REFERENCES

Cohen, Thomas H. and Steven K. Smith. 2001. Civil Trial Cases and Verdicts in Large Counties. *Bureau of Justice Statistics Bulletin,* April 2004. Available at http://www.ojp.usdoj.gov/bjs/pub/pdf/ctcvlc01.pdf/.

Guidry, Krisandra and A. Quang Do. 1999. Eminent Domain and Just Compensation for Single-Family Homes Transactions of Single-Family Homes from a Large Metropolitan Area during the Construction of a State Highway Between April 1991 and October 1991, 207. Available at http://207.208.196.137/webpac-bin/pdf/SingleFamilyHomes.pdf/.

Munch, Patricia. An Economic Analysis of Eminent Domain. 1976. *The Journal of Political Economy,* 84(3, June): 473–498.

Walter, William. 1995. Appraisal Methods and Regulatory Takings: New Directions for Appraisers, Judges and Economists. *The Appraisal Journal* (July): 331–349.

6

# The Inadequacy of the Planning Process for Protecting Property Owners from the Abuse of Eminent Domain for Private Development

*Scott G. Bullock*

## Introduction

In its now infamous opinion in *Kelo v. City of New London*,[1] Justice Stevens and the majority focused on the supposedly vital role of planning in remaking the Fort Trumbull neighborhood where Susette Kelo and her neighbors lived. Justice Stevens declared the takings of the homes were legitimate because the "City has carefully formulated an economic development plan that it believes will provide appreciable benefits to the community, including…new jobs and increased tax revenue.…Given the comprehensive character of the plan, the thorough delibera- tion that preceded its adoption, and the limited scope of our review, it is appropriate for us, as it was in Berman, to resolve the challenges of the individual owners, not on a piecemeal basis, but rather in light of the entire plan."[2]

It is clear that the majority opinion in *Kelo* was very impressed by the planning process that the City of New London went through in devising the Fort Trumbull Municipal Development Plan. The Court noted that the City of New London had public hearings in which members of the public testified. It produced a plan that was several inches thick. The City received the necessary approvals for the plan from various planning bodies and agencies at the state and local level. Indeed, the American Planning Association, one of the primary supporters of the use of eminent domain for private development, proudly noted that there were more than 30 references to "plan," "planning," and "planner" in the majority's opinion (Lucero 2005). The majority clearly viewed this planning process as a check upon eminent domain abuse.[3]

The Court's emphasis on the planning process and the existence of redevelop- ment plans as a check on eminent domain abuse suffers from two major defects, both addressed below. First, the Court ignores the fact that the planning process and even the plans themselves are often reflective of the interest groups with the most to gain from the use of eminent domain for private development projects. Second, the Court ignores the fact that a vast majority of cases where eminent domain is used for private development occur within the context of redevelopment or municipal development plans.

## The Conflation of Public and Private Interests within the Planning Process

The *Kelo* majority seemed to take an extremely benign view of the planning process undertaken by the City of New London. The Court was impressed that the process contained several public hearings and that all parties, including Susette Kelo and the Pfizer Corporation, whose new headquarters were right next door to the Fort Trumbull neighborhood, were able to participate in the public hearings. The Court seemed to believe that all opinions were weighed equally and then the New London City Council made its decision based upon "public" interests rather than the interests of any particular private party.

The Court's approach ignores the powerful public choice factors at work in a process similar to the one engaged in by New London. In their seminal work on public choice, James Buchanan and Gordon Tullock noted that "it is the opportunity to secure differential benefits from collective activity that attracts the political 'profit-seeking' group (1965, 277)." They also noted that "[m]any collective projects are undertaken in whole or in part primarily because they do provide benefits to one group of the people at the expense of the other groups (Buchanan and Tullock 1965, 279)."

The process used by the City of New London illustrates these public choice insights. Susette Kelo and a small band of committed community activists pleaded with the City to save a portion of their neighborhood from demolition. Pfizer stated that it wished to have certain "requirements" within the project plan area, including a five star luxury hotel, upscale condominiums for its short-term employees, and private office space for its subcontractors. Influential members of the community, including Pfizer CEO George Milne and then-Connecticut governor John Rowland, pushed for the retention of the Italian Dramatic Club, a private, social club popular with political figures and others in the state. Most members of the community, because it did not affect their interests directly, did not participate in the planning process nor did they testify at the public hearings.

After New London conducted its hearings and received the necessary approvals from the various agencies at the state and local levels, the municipal development plan contained a five-star luxury hotel, private upscale condominiums, and private office space, exactly what Pfizer wanted in the municipal development plan.[4] Also, the Italian Dramatic Club was preserved, but the voices of Susette Kelo and her supporters were ignored: all of the homes in Fort Trumbull were slated for acquisition and demolition.

Clearly, Pfizer and the eventual private developers in Fort Trumbull were to gain highly concentrated benefits in the form of higher profits and amenities for their staff and subcontractors while the costs of the project were widely diffused among Connecticut citizens. (Virtually the entire project was funded by the State of Connecticut.) Likewise, city officials stood to gain from the possible extra tax revenue generated by the new projects and the political support that could come from improving the local economic climate. The individuals who paid the highest costs—Mrs. Kelo and her neighbors—were small in numbers. The remainder of the New London community, apart from dedicated community activists largely made of local preservationists, were "rationally ignorant" of the process since it did not directly affect their homes or lives.

While the Supreme Court completely ignored the public choice dynamics at work in the Fort Trumbull plan, it did have a response to what it recognized as potential abuses of the eminent domain power. The Court noted that there was no specific evidence in the *Kelo* case that the City put together the municipal development plan simply to benefit a particular private party, whether it was Pfizer or some other unknown future private developer.[5] There are two fundamental problems with this notion, however. First, it is very difficult to know what motivates government officials for their actions. Unless you have a smoking gun email or a breakdown on the stand (which happens more in Hollywood movies than in a real-world courtroom), how do you really know someone's true motivations for doing something? Moreover, even the privately motivated action could be easily dressed up in the language of public-spirited projects. But even more importantly, if one concludes, as the Court did in *Kelo*, that the trickle-down benefits of private economic development in the form of higher taxes and more jobs are now public uses under the Fifth Amendment, it is virtually impossible to separate out public and private benefits.

It is true that there was no evidence in *Kelo* that New London approved the municipal development plan and the condemnations pursuant to it because they were Pfizer stockholders or because they received direct personal gains from the implementation of the plan or that the City only wanted to benefit Pfizer or some other private party. But the City's attitude can be fairly characterized as: "what is good for Pfizer is good for the City of New London." Indeed, the only way that the "public" can benefit in the form of higher tax revenue and more job growth is if the private business is successful. Accordingly, it makes sense for the City to want to give as many benefits as possible to a private business such as Pfizer. That is why, as Justice O'Connor noted in her dissent, that recognizing private economic development as a public use really demolishes the distinction between public and private use.[6] A city gives benefits to private companies because it wants to gain the so-called public benefits. The disproportionate influence of wealthier and more powerful private interests in the planning process only compounds that synergy. As a result, the planning process does little good in ferreting out supposedly private condemnations.

## EMINENT DOMAIN FOR PRIVATE DEVELOPMENT OCCURS RARELY, IF EVER, OUTSIDE THE CONTEXT OF A REDEVELOPMENT PLAN

There is another major problem with *Kelo*'s emphasis on the planning process. The *Kelo* majority seemed to assume that abusive condemnations will take place only outside of a redevelopment plan. The Court explained that the *Kelo* facts did not present "a one-to-one transfer of property, executed outside the confines of an integrated development plan." It then commented that "such an unusual exercise of government power would certainly raise a suspicion that a private purpose was afoot" and that "[c]ourts have viewed such aberrations with a skeptical eye."[7]

What the Court overlooked, however, is that nearly all condemnations for transfer to private parties occur pursuant to development plans and within designated redevelopment areas. State reporters are replete with cases involving private-to-private transfers only within the context of a larger plan.[8] In fact, most states authorize municipalities to condemn property within the context of redevelopment plans or designated redevelopment zones.[9] It is important to note, too, that redevelopment area plans authorize the use of eminent domain against multiple properties often within large areas.

The *Kelo* majority cites *99 Cents Only Stores v. Lancaster Redevelopment Agency*,[10] as an example of an improper private taking because it constituted a one-to-one transfer of property "outside the confines of an integrated development plan."[11] However, *99 Cents* is actually an example of a taking *within* the context of a redevelopment plan.[12]

Indeed, the Court's failure to recognize that a vast majority of eminent domain cases for private development occur pursuant to redevelopment or economic development plans demonstrates the majority's disconnect from how these cases actually play out in the real world. On a personal level, I was not only co-counsel in the *Kelo* case, but I have been involved in scores of eminent domain cases and controversies throughout the country. And I can state from personal experience that, even in cases where some defenders of eminent domain for private development admitted that the takings could be abusive, there was *always* some type of planning process and actual plan in each of these cases. The existence of these plans, however, provided no effective check upon eminent domain abuse whatsoever.

*Kelo* seems to strongly imply that once a redevelopment designation has been established and a plan is in place, there can be no judicial review of takings within the area, for as long as the redevelopment designation and plan lasts. In addition to ignoring that virtually all private development takings occur in the context of a plan, the Court also ignores the fact that redevelopment designations and plans usually last for decades.[13] Even worse, in many states, redevelopment area designations *never* expire.[14] If *Kelo* precludes, as a matter of law, any and all private use takings claims within the borders of a redevelopment area and plan, then developers and local governments will have a free pass to use their power for private gain with impunity.

## Two Case Studies of Eminent Domain Abuse in the Context of a Redevelopment Plan

### National City, California

A prime example of the inadequacy of the planning process in curbing eminent domain abuse and the capture of that process by powerful interest groups is California's rampant manipulation of its "blight" laws in order to gain property for private development projects, as demonstrated in particular in a case playing out in National City just outside of San Diego. California enacted its first blight law in 1945.[15] The purpose of what is now known as the Community Redevelopment Law[16] was to remedy unsanitary urban slums that posed a genuine threat to the health and safety of the public. Like blight laws all over the country, the Community Redevelopment Law grants local governments the authority to use eminent domain to seize private property and transfer it to another private owner in the hope that the latter will cure the purported blight.[17]

Though blight eradication has been deemed a "public use" for which eminent domain may be employed, the first California case to consider the constitutionality of transferring "blighted" property to a different private owner warned that government planners should never apply the redevelopment power simply because they think they can make better use of a citizen's property than he or she can.[18] To do so, the court observed, would subordinate "fundamental rights" to whatever "currently attractive projects" had caught the fancy of government officials.[19] Despite this stark warning, redevelopment in California often has little to do with true blight. Instead, redevelopment evolved into a multi-billion dollar industry. The scope of the California redevelopment industry is enormous. There are 395 active redevelopment agencies in California (about 80 percent of municipalities have one) overseeing 759 blight zones (California Redevelopment Association 2005). In fiscal year 2005–2006, these redevelopment agencies owned $12.9 billion worth of property (a $1.5 billion dollar increase) and had $8.7 billion in revenues (up $1.5 billion over the previous year) (California Redevelopment Association 2005).

The engine driving the redevelopment machine is debt and taxes. Under California law, once a local government declares an area "blighted," its redevelopment agency gets a property tax windfall. In a scheme known as Tax Increment Financing, redevelopment agencies get 100 percent of the property tax revenue from a blight zone over and above the baseline amount of property taxes the area generated when it was first declared blighted. For example, suppose that an area produced $100 million in property taxes in 1990 when it was first declared blighted, but by 2007, because assessed property values have risen, was generating $250 million in property taxes. The county would still only be eligible for $100 million and the redevelopment agency would get $150 million, even if there is no evidence the redevelopment agency had anything to do with the increase in property values.

California's redevelopment agencies now siphon off most of the property taxes from the hundreds of blight zones across the state. In fiscal year 2005–2006, for example, the total assessed value of property in California's blight zones was $537 billion (California Redevelopment Association 2005). Because of Tax Increment Financing, however, redevelopment agencies received 100 percent of the property taxes on $381 billion of this total (California Redevelopment Association 2005). Overall, redevelopment agencies capture about 10 percent of all property taxes collected in California (Municipal Officials for Redevelopment Reform 2006, 6).

A redevelopment agency, however, is only entitled to its property tax windfall if it goes into debt to implement the redevelopment plan. By 2004, redevelopment agencies in California had a total debt of $61 billion, and historical trends show that agency debts double about every 10 years (Municipal Officials for Redevelopment Reform 2006, 12). In fiscal year 2003–2004, for example, the redevelopment agency of La Quinta, California (pop. 33,104) reported nearly $1.6 billion in debt (Municipal Officials for Redevelopment Reform 2006, 13). Overall, in fiscal year 2003–2004, about 45 cents on every dollar spent by a California redevelopment agency went to debt payments (California State Controller's Office 2005, 252).

The perverse financial incentives of California's redevelopment laws mean that redevelopment agencies: (1) want their blight zones to be as large as possible; (2) want their blight zones to last as long as possible; and (3) want to incur massive debt. Cities, for their part, have perverse incentives of their own. They always want to replace low-tax land uses like single-family homes and small businesses with tax-intensive uses such as high-rise condominiums and big box stores (Municipal Officials for Redevelopment Reform 2006, 18; describing a survey showing that city managers overwhelmingly prefer retail land uses and place residential land use at the bottom, down with heavy industry).

While redevelopment advocates and those in the planning community like to point out their new developments, there are a few things they do not like to talk about. First, studies repeatedly show that redevelopment projects are net economic losers once the true costs are tallied in terms of jobs and businesses destroyed, and tax breaks and other subsidies to big business.[20] They also do not talk about how the preference for sales tax-generating retail mega-stores creates no-skill service jobs and destroys small businesses that frequently require skilled labor. Redevelopment agencies also do not talk about the personal implications of taking away someone's cherished home or an entrepreneur's small business. Finally, the last thing redevelopment apologists discuss is the fact that redevelopment overwhelmingly targets the poor and minorities (Carpenter and Ross 2007).

National City, California is a predominately Hispanic, working-class city of 55,000 in southern San Diego County.[21] It is also in a state of continuous and never-ending redevelopment. Between 1969 and 1978, National City declared four distinct blight zones within its boundaries (Community Development Commission 1995, 3). In 1981, National City merged these into a single mega-blight zone encompassing everything between Interstates 5 and 805, about two-thirds of the city (Community Development Commission 1995). Then, following other intervening amendments, National City expanded its blight zone again in 1995 to capture everything to the west of Interstate 5 (Community Development Commission 1995).

In June 2007, almost forty years after its first blight declaration, National City was preparing once again to declare the same two-thirds of the city still "blighted." The particular purpose of this latest blight declaration is (1) to subject much of the commercial property in the city to another 12-year eminent domain threat, and (2) to perpetuate the municipal redevelopment agency's entitlement to Tax Increment Financing money.[22]

National City is re-blighting more than 1,000 homes, businesses, churches, public buildings and service organizations despite the fact that property values have soared. In 2001, the average National City home sold for $186,000. By 2006, the average price had climbed to $443,000. With respect to commercial properties, the average price in 2001 was $351,000, while in 2006 it was $1.2 million.[23]

The Community Youth Athletic Center (CYAC) is one of many National City property owners now threatened with eminent domain as a result of the City's planned extension of its blight and eminent domain authority. The CYAC is a non-profit, all-volunteer youth boxing and mentoring program serving at-risk kids. A few years ago, with the help of generous sponsors, the CYAC bought a little building in National City in the heart of its "blight" zone. Then, two years ago, National City promised the CYAC's property to an influential private developer who intends to build high-rise luxury condos for the wealthy. The upcoming re-declaration of blight is a prelude to the inevitable condemnation of the gym.[24]

The blight study is supposed to be an independent and objective evaluation of property conditions. Because a blight designation confers major redevelopment powers, including the authority to use eminent domain on behalf of private for-profit entities like big box stores, local governments like National City are required to take the blighting process seriously and not simply rationalize decisions that have been made in advance.[25]

Indeed, the problem of local governments finding "blight" anywhere and everywhere has led to such pervasive eminent domain abuse that in 2006 the California Legislature enacted statutory reforms designed to concentrate the attention of local lawmakers on their responsibility to review the evidence carefully and proceed with due caution for the fundamental property rights of citizens.[26]

It is obvious, however, the entire series of events leading up to the impending blight declaration and re-authorization of eminent domain in National City has been a deliberate fraud in which the finding of blight under the plan was a foregone conclusion. According to an internal Community Development Commission (CDC) management plan, the CDC blight consultant, Rosenow Spevacek Group (RSG), was on March 30, 2007 to "[b]egin research *to substantiate blight* and fold in to Report to Council[.]"[27] RSG was not, on other words to analyze the proposed eminent domain area objectively, but instead simply to go out and "substantiate" blight.

The CDC schedule then lays out what actions the CDC, the City Council, and RSG must do between March 30 and July to ensure that a blight designation is enacted. The document in fact states that RSG will spend a week preparing a response if a citizen presents written objections at the joint public hearing (apparently no one at RSG or in the city government thinks that oral objections require any response). Every scenario contemplated by the CDC's management plan results in an official blight declaration. The plan does not even contemplate that RSG will fail to find blight or that the CDC or the City Council will fail to ratify RSG's findings.

RSG employees working on the blight plan obviously understood that their job was not to perform an objective analysis of property. Instead, RSG employees were simply on a mission to find whatever information they could to justify a preordained "blight" designation. For example, in an email, an RSG employee named Zach Mikelson wrote to a National City employee named Luis on April 24, 2007 asking for code violation data. Mikelson informed Luis that he needs this information because "[RSG] is trying to prove existing blight and [is] most concerned with code violations."[28] Setting out to "prove" blight, needless to say, is not the same thing as conducting an independent review from arm's length.

In addition, RSG prepared blight and related studies for National City in 1995, 2001, 2005, and produced the 2007 study under a $35,500 contract.[29] It is difficult to imagine that National City and RSG now understand their relationship as anything but cash for blight. The fact that the "blight" designation is a foregone conclusion is further evident in the City Council's dereliction of its statutory duty to independently review the CDC's proposed blight findings. Indeed, one major purpose of the joint public hearing is for the city to be able to consider all the evidence regarding the proposed findings of blight and the redevelopment plan, including objections.[30] Moreover, as discussed above, the California Legislature recently revised the Community Redevelopment Law to require more documentation and more review. The purpose of requiring all this documentation, in addition to public review, is to supposedly enable the city itself to carefully consider the evidence and decide if the area is blighted and meets all the other requirements of the statutes. Yet the City Council did not receive even the draft of the Report or any documentation supporting the finding of "blight" until two business days before the public hearing.[31] There is no way that the City Council can have had time to engage in the focused consideration and evaluation required by California Statutes.[32]

The blight designation was also obviously a foregone conclusion because the CDC has redevelopment contracts with a variety of private developers and businesses for projects that will necessitate the use of eminent domain. The CYAC requested copies of the CDC's redevelopment contracts with the various private developers for the eminent domain zone, but that request was ignored by the CDC and National City. The CYAC knows, however, that the CDC has a contract with developer Jim Beauchamp to erect luxury condos on the property where the gym sits.[33] The CDC budget for FY 2006–2007 indicates that a developer, presumably Beauchamp, deposited $3.4 million with the CDC for this project.[34] The CDC also has contracts with Home Depot.[35] Finally, the CDC budget documents indicate a variety of active projects involving millions of dollars within the eminent domain zone, each of which is of a scope that will likely require eminent domain.[36] The CDC will not be able to perform its obligations under these contracts if RSG does not produce a favorable blight study and the CDC and City Council do not ratify it.

The evidence documented even in the early stages of the National City litigation demonstrate clearly how the planning process is manipulated by special interests with the most to gain from the process and how difficult it is for small property owners to fight back. It is obvious that the purpose of the planning process undertaken by National City is simply to enable the CDC to proceed under pre-existing contracts with the transfer of land from one party to another for the latter's private economic benefit. But the CYAC is going to have to spend enormous time and resources and time to demonstrate that the planning process is a fraud.

## Port Chester, New York

A recent decision from the U.S. Court of Appeals for the Second Circuit in which the U.S. Supreme Court declined review also illustrates the problems of the Court's notion that having a plan and a planning process weeds out abusive takings. In this case, *Didden v. Village of Port Chester,* 173 Fed. Appx. 931, 933 (2d Cir. April 5, 2006), the property owners alleged that a private developer approached them and demanded a direct cash payment of $800,000 or a 50 percent equity interest in their business in exchange for not having their property taken by eminent domain.[37] The property owners refused, and condemnation papers were filed the following day. The owners further alleged that the condemning body, the Village of Port Chester, New York, knew about and approved of these actions by the private developer and that the condemnation was solely for the purpose of furthering the private financial goals of the developer. The property was located within a preexisting redevelopment plan.[38]

Petitioners brought an action under 42 U.S.C. § 1983, alleging that the condemnation of their property was for the purpose of satisfying the financial goals of a single private party and not for a public purpose. They also alleged that the attempted extortion and subsequent condemnation violated their rights to due process and equal protection. The Southern District of New York granted FRCP 12(b)(6) motions to dismiss the complaint.[39] The Second Circuit affirmed, relying on the Court's decision in *Kelo* to hold that a claim of a taking for "private use within a redevelopment district" did not state a cause of action on which relief could be granted.[40]

The Second Circuit interpreted the Court's holding in *Kelo* to mean that any use of eminent domain within a redevelopment district is constitutional, *as a matter of law.* That interpretation is extremely dangerous. In the Second Circuit's view, once a municipality has gone through its planning process and created a designated redevelopment area where eminent domain is authorized to implement the redevelopment plan, that area becomes, in effect, a constitution-free zone; any use of eminent domain will be deemed constitutional under *Kelo.* Thus, the court explained that "to the extent that [the property owners] assert that the Takings Clause prevents the State from condemning their property for a private use within a redevelopment district...the recent Supreme Court decision in *Kelo v. City of New London,* 125 S. Ct. 2655, 162 L. Ed. 2d 439 (2005), obliges us to conclude that they have articulated no basis on which relief can be granted."[41]

As noted, the *Kelo* court and the Second Circuit in *Didden* ignore the fact that pretextual and other highly questionable condemnations can and often do occur within a larger and generally valid development plan.[42] Yet, in the Second Circuit's view, *Kelo* has apparently turned redevelopment areas into free passes under the Takings Clause—any taking, however pretextual or illegal the public purpose, will pass muster as long as it occurs within a redevelopment area and pursuant to redevelopment plan.

The sole question presented to the Court in *Didden* was whether an owner alleging the use of eminent domain for attempted financial extortion and to assist the purely private financial goals of a single private party has stated a cause of action under the Constitution, even when the condemnation takes place within an "integrated development plan" area. By declining review, the Court has opened an avenue for governments, under the cover of the planning process and redevelopment plans, to abuse eminent domain authority for the benefit of private parties.

## CONCLUSION

The Court's decision in *Kelo* touched off a public firestorm of protests and reform efforts, resulting in over 40 states reforming their eminent domain laws. Moreover, two state supreme courts (in Ohio and Oklahoma) have rejected *Kelo* under their respective state constitutions (while five other supreme courts have cast doubt on the viability of *Kelo*). The majority in *Kelo* viewed the planning process as providing meaningful checks on abusive condemnations for private economic development. Unfortunately for home and small business owners, the existence of a plan and a planning process will do little, if anything, to curb the use of eminent domain to build big-box retail centers, "lifestyle centers," high-end condominiums, and other private development projects sought by cities to boost their tax revenue and improve the overall economic health of their communities. Until *Kelo* is either overturned or substantially modified, property owners must continue to look to state constitutions, new state laws, and grassroots activism to protect themselves from the misuse of one of the most awesome powers a government has at its disposal.

## NOTES

1. 125 S. Ct. 2655, 162 L. Ed. 2d 439 (2005).
2. *Id.* at 2665.
3. *Kelo,* 125 S. Ct. at 2665–68.
4. *Kelo,* 125 S. Ct. at 2659.
5. *Id.* at 2661–62.
6. *Id.* at 2671.

7. *Kelo,* 125 S. Ct. at 2667 and n.17.
8. See, e.g., *Birmingham v. Tutwiler Drug Co.,* 475 So. 2d 458, 460–61 (Ala. 1985); *Mar. Ventures, LLC v. City of Norwalk,* 894 A.2d 946, 952–53 (Conn. 2006); *State ex. rel. United States Steel v. Koehr,* 811 S.W.2d 385, 387 (Mo. 1991); *City of Las Vegas Downtown Redev. Agency,* 76 P.3d 1, 6–7 (Nev. 2003).
9. See, e.g., Ark. Code Ann. § 14–168–304(7)(a); 20 Ill. Comp. Stat. 620(9)(b); Va. Code Ann. § 36–27(A). See also Wendell E. Pritchett, *Beyond Kelo: Thinking about Urban Development in the 21st Century,* 22 Ga. St. L. Rev. 895, 912–14 (2006) (describing the use of development plans to transfer property to private developers).
10. 237 F. Supp. 2d 1123 (C.D. Cal. 2001), *appeal dismissed as moot,* 2003 U.S. App. LEXIS 4197 (9th Cir. Mar. 7, 2003)
11. *Kelo,* 125 S. Ct. at 2667 n.17.
12. See *99 Cents,* 237 F. Supp. 2d at 1125 ("In 1983...Lancaster enacted an ordinance establishing the Amargosa Redevelopment Project Area and adopted a Redevelopment Plan....").
13. See, e.g., *Redev. Agency v. Rados Bros.,* 115 Cal. Rptr. d 234, 237 (Cal. Ct. App. 2001) (redevelopment project originally adopted in 1974); *Aposperos v. Urban Redev. Comm'n,* 790 A.2d 1167, 1174 (Conn. 2002) (redevelopment plan originally adopted in 1963); *Mounts v. Evansville Redev. Comm'n,* 831 N.E.2d 784, 789 (Ind. Ct. App. 2005) (redevelopment plan originally adopted in 1984).
14. See, e.g., 315 Ill. Comp. Stat. 5/13; Nev. Rev. Stat. §§ 279.572, 589; N.J. Stat. §§ 40A: 12A-4, -5, -14; W. Va. Code § 16–18–5.
15. Cal. Stats. 1945 Ch. 1326, § 1.
16. Cal. Health & Safety Code § 33000, *et seq.*
17. *Id.* at § 33391.
18. *Redevelopment Agency of San Francisco v. Hayes,* 122 Cal. App.2d 777, 812 (1954).
19. *Id.*
20. E.g., (Public Policy Institute of California 1998; This study compared 114 redevelopment project areas to similar areas not in redevelopment zones. The study concluded that the redevelopment effort was not responsible for any economic development and was a net drain on public resources.). See also, (Municipal Officials for Redevelopment Reform 2006, 22–25), (Castle Coalition 2006).
21. http://www.ci.national-city.ca.us/about/2000%20Census%20Profiles%20-%20City%200f%20National%20City.htm
22. See Public Notice for joint public hearing, which is on file with the Institute for Justice.
23. Residential real estate prices were obtained through the Multiple Listing Service. Commercial real estate prices were based on information recorded with the San Diego County Recorder.
24. In July 2007, the Institute for Justice filed a lawsuit on behalf of the CYAC challenging the blight plan and the threatened use of eminent domain against the center.
25. See, e.g., *BAM, Inc. v. Board of Police Commissioners of the City of Los Angeles,* 7 Cal. App. 4th 1343, 1346 (1992) ("Findings are not supposed to be a post hoc rationalization for a decision already made. To the contrary, they are supposed to conduce the administrative body to draw legally relevant sub-conclusions supportive of [the] ultimate decision.") (internal citations omitted).
26. See Cal. Stats. 2006 ch. 495, § 1(e) (intent of legislature "to focus public officials' attention and extraordinary redevelopment powers on properties with physical and economic conditions that are so significantly degraded that they seriously harm the prospects for physical and economic development without the use of redevelopment").
27. CYAC Obj. Appx. Vol. III, Tab 18 CDC Schedule of Actions 2007 Eminent Domain Amendment (emphasis added).
28. CYAC Obj. Appx. Vol. III, Tab 19 April 24, 2007 email from Mikelson to Luis. There are likely other such documents that the CYAC would be able to obtain with further Public Records Act requests if there were more time.
29. CYAC Obj. Appx. Vol. III, Tab 20.
30. See Cal. Health & Safety Code § 33363.
31. CYAC Obj. Appx. Vol. I, Tab 2, Nunez Statement No. 2.

32. See Cal. Health & Safety Code §§ 33030, 33031, 33321, 33333, 33333.2, 33333.4, 33352, 33354.6, 33363, 33367, 33411; Cal. Stats. 2006 Ch. 495, § 1.
33. CYAC Obj. Appx. Vol. I, Tab 23; Vol. VI, Tab 2.
34. CYAC Obj. Appx. Vol. III, Tab 2.
35. CYAC Obj. Appx. Vol. VI, Tab 3.
36. CYAC Obj. Appx. Vol. I, Tab 23.
37. All facts are taken from the Amended Complaint in the case. The allegations of the Amended Complaint must be accepted as true on an appeal from a dismissal under FRCP 12(b)(6). See, e.g., *Sutton v. United Airlines*, 527 U.S. 471, 475 (1999).
38. *Id.* at 30.
39. *Didden v. Village of Port Chester*, 322 F. Supp. 2d 385, 391 (S.D.N.Y. 2004).
40. *Didden v. Village of Port Chester*, 173 Fed. Appx. 931, 933 (2d Cir. April 5, 2006).
41. 173 Fed. Appx. at 933.
42. *See, e.g., Cottonwood Christian Ctr. v. Cypress Redev. Agency*, 218 F. Supp. 2d 1203, 1210–11, 1229 (C.D. Cal. 2002); *99 Cents Only Stores*, 237 F. Supp. 2d at 1125 (C.D. Cal. 2001); *Casino Reinv. Dev. Auth. v. Banin*, 727 A.2d 102, 111 (N.J. Super. 1998) (hotel development plan generally valid but particular contract with private developer gave impermissible "blank check" to developer); *In re Condemnation of 110 Wash. St.*, 767 A.2d 1154, 1156 (Pa. Commw. Ct. 2001); *Redevelopment Auth. v. Owners*, 274 A.2d 244, 252 (Pa. Cmmwlth 1971) (property within urban renewal area taken to provide substitute property to another party whose other property was being condemned for a public project); *City of Dayton v. Keys*, 252 N.E.2d 655, 660–61 (Ohio Ct. Comm. Pleas 1969) (property within urban renewal plan area condemned in order to satisfy contractual obligation to single developer).

## References

Buchanan, James and Gordon Tullock. 1965. *The Calculus of Consent: Legal Foundations of Constitutional Democracy*. Ed. Charles K. Rowley. Indianapolis, IN: Liberty Fund, 2004.
California Redevelopment Association. 2005. Redevelopment Agency Fact Sheet for FY 05–06 of the California Redevelopment Association. Retrieved July 24, 2007, from http://www.calredevelop.org/AM/Template.cfm?Section=Facts_and_Reports1&TEMPLATE=/CM/ContentDisplay.cfm&CONTENTID=3109.
California State Controller's Office. 2005. *Community Redevelopment Agencies Annual Report, Fiscal Year 2003–2004*. Retrieved July 24, 2007, from http://www.sco.ca.gov/ard/local/locrep/redevelop/reports/0304redevelop.pdf.
Carpenter, Dick M., and Ross, John K. 2007. *Victimizing the Vulnerable: The Demographics of Eminent Domain Abuse*. Arlington, VA: Institute for Justice.
Castle Coalition. 2006. *Redevelopment Wrecks: 20 Failed Projects Involving Eminent Domain Abuse*. Retrieved July 24, 2007, from http://www.castlecoalition.org/publications/redevelopment-wrecks/index.html.
Community Development Commission. City of National City, CA. 1995. *Redevelopment Plan for the National City Redevelopment Project*. Retrieved July 24, 2007, from http://www.ci.national-city.ca.us/Departments/CDC1/pdf/RDPLAN70.pdf.
Lucero, Lora A. 2005. *Commentary—July 2005, Kelo v. City of New London*. Retrieved July 24, 2007, from http://www.planning.org/PEL/commentary/jul05kelo.htm.
Municipal Officials for Redevelopment Reform (MORR). 2006. *Redevelopment: The Unknown Government*, 8th ed. Fullerton, CA:MORR.
Pritchett, Wendell E. 2006. Beyond Kelo: Thinking about Urban Development in the 21st Century. *Georgia State Law Review* 22: 895.
Public Policy Institute of California. 1998. *Subsidizing Redevelopment in California*. California: Public Policy Institute of California.

# 7

# The Limits of Backlash

## Assessing the Political Response to *Kelo*

### *Ilya Somin*

## Introduction

The Supreme Court's decision in *Kelo v. City of New London* generated a massive political backlash from across the political spectrum (545 U.S. 469 [2005]). *Kelo's* holding that the Public Use Clause allows the taking of private property for transfer to new private owners for the purpose of promoting "economic development" was denounced by many on both the right and the left. Over forty states have enacted post-*Kelo* reform legislation to curb eminent domain.[1] The *Kelo* backlash probably resulted in more new state legislation than any other Supreme Court decision in history.[2]

Prominent scholars and jurists such as Judge Richard A. Posner and Chief Justice John Roberts (when questioned about *Kelo* at his Senate confirmation), have suggested that this political response demonstrates that legislative initiatives can protect property owners and that judicial intervention may be unnecessary.[3] Posner concluded that the political reaction to *Kelo* is "evidence of [the decision's] pragmatic soundness" (Posner 2005,98).

This paper challenges the validity of claims that the political backlash to *Kelo* will provide the same sort of protection for property owners as would a judicial ban on economic development takings. It provides a comprehensive analysis of the *Kelo* backlash through early 2008,[4] and finds that the majority of the newly enacted post-*Kelo* reform laws are likely to be ineffective.[5]

It also suggests a tentative explanation for the often ineffective nature of post-*Kelo* reform: widespread political ignorance that enables state and federal legislators to pass off primarily cosmetic laws as meaningful "reforms." I do not attempt to assess either the validity of the *Kelo* decision or the desirability of economic development takings as a policy matter.[6] Instead, I document the results of the *Kelo* backlash and provide a tentative explanation for the seeming paucity of effective reform laws.

Part I describes the *Kelo* decision and then documents widespread backlash that it generated. Both state-level and national surveys show overwhelming public opposition to "economic development" takings—a consensus that cuts across gender, racial, ethnic, and partisan lines. The decision was also condemned by politicians

and activists across the political spectrum ranging from Ralph Nader[7] on the left
to Rush Limbaugh on the right.[8] Traditional models of democratic politics predict that such a broad political consensus is likely to result in swift and effective
legislative action.[9]

Part II considers the state and federal political response to *Kelo*. Thirty-five state
legislatures have enacted post-*Kelo* reform laws. However, twenty-one of these are
largely symbolic in nature, providing little or no protection for property owners.
Several of the remainder were enacted by states that had little or no history of condemning property for economic development. Only seven states that had previously
engaged in significant numbers of economic development and blight condemnations have enacted post-*Kelo* legislative reforms with any real teeth. The limited
reforms enacted by the federal government are likely to be no more effective than
most of the state laws.

The major exceptions to the pattern of ineffective post-*Kelo* reforms are the
ten states that recently enacted reforms by popular referendum. Six or seven of
these provide meaningful new protection for property owners. Strikingly, citizen-
initiated referendum initiatives have led to the passage of much stronger laws than
those enacted through referenda initiated by state legislatures.

Part III advances a tentative explanation for the pattern of ineffective post-*Kelo*
reform. While there is overwhelming public support for measures banning economic
development takings, some thirty of fifty states, as well as the federal government,
have either enacted laws that are likely to be ineffective, or no reforms at all.[10]

However, I tentatively advance the theory that the ineffectiveness of much post-
*Kelo* reform is largely due to widespread political ignorance. Survey data collected
for this Article shows that the vast majority of citizens do not know whether their
states have passed post-*Kelo* reform legislation and even fewer know whether that
legislation is likely to be effective.

Most voters are "rationally ignorant" of public policy, having little incentive to
acquire any substantial knowledge about the details of government actions. Studies
have repeatedly shown that most citizens have very little knowledge of politics and
public policy.[11] Most are often ignorant even of many basic facts about the political
system (Somin 1998, 416–19). Such ignorance is a rational response to the insignificance of any one vote to electoral outcomes; if a voter's only reason to become
informed is to ensure that she votes for the "best" candidate in order to ensure that
individual's election to office, this turns out to be almost no incentive at all because
the likelihood that any one vote will be decisive is infinitesimally small.[12]

The publicity surrounding *Kelo* made much of the public at least somewhat aware
of the problem of economic development takings. But it probably did not lead voters to closely scrutinize the details of proposed reform legislation. Few citizens have
the time or inclination to delve into such matters and many are often ignorant of
the very existence of even the most important legislative items. In Part III, I present survey data showing that the vast majority of Americans were indeed ignorant
of the content of post-*Kelo* reform legislation in their states. In an August 2007
Saint Index survey, only 21 percent of respondents could correctly answer whether
or not their state had passed eminent domain reform legislation since *Kelo*, and
only 13 percent both knew whether their state had passed legislation and correctly
indicated whether that legislation was likely to be effective.[13]

The political ignorance hypothesis cannot definitively explain the outcomes
of the *Kelo* backlash. However, it correctly predicts three important events: the

sudden emergence of the backlash after *Kelo,* in spite of the fact that economic development takings were already permitted under existing precedent; the passage of "position-taking" laws by both state and federal legislators; and the fact that that post-*Kelo* laws enacted by popular referendum tended to be much stronger than those enacted by state legislatures. No other theory can easily account for all three of these seeming anomalies.

## *KELO* AND ITS BACKLASH

### The *Kelo* Decision[14]

The *Kelo* case arose from the condemnation of ten residences and five other properties as part of a 2000 "development plan" in New London, Connecticut, that sought to transfer the property to private developers for the stated purpose of promoting economic growth in the area (545 U.S. 469, 474–77 [2005]). Unlike in leading 1954 case *Berman v. Parker* (348 U.S. 26 [1954]), none of the properties in question were alleged to be "blighted or otherwise in poor condition" (*Kelo,* 545 U.S. 469, 475 [2005]). The condemnations were initiated pursuant to a plan prepared by the New London Development Corporation (NLDC), a "private nonprofit entity established...to assist the City in planning economic development" (at 474).

In a close 5–4 decision, the Supreme Court endorsed the New London takings, upheld the "economic development" rationale for condemnation, and advocated broad judicial deference to government decision making on public use issues (at 478–85). Justice Stevens' majority opinion endorsed a "policy of deference to legislative judgment in this field" (at 480). The Court rejected the property owners' argument that the transfer of their property to private developers rather than to a public body required any heightened degree of judicial scrutiny (at 480–81). It also refused to require the City to provide any evidence that the takings were likely to actually achieve the claimed economic benefits that provided their justification in the first place (at 487–88). On all these points, the *Kelo* majority emphasized that courts should not "second-guess the City's considered judgments about the efficacy of the development plan" (at 488).

Despite this result, *Kelo* may have represented a slight tightening of judicial scrutiny of public use issues relative to the earlier case of *Hawaii Housing Authority v. Midkiff,* which held that the public use requirement is satisfied so long as "the exercise of the eminent domain power is rationally related to a conceivable public purpose" (467 U.S. 229, 241 [1984]). Moreover, it is important to recognize that four justices not only dissented but actually concluded that the economic development rationale should be categorically forbidden shows that the judicial landscape on public use has changed (*Kelo,* 545 U.S. 469, 499–504 [2005] [O'Connor, J., dissenting]; at 518–23 [Thomas, J., dissenting]). A fifth, Justice Kennedy, signed on to the majority opinion, but also wrote a concurrence emphasizing that heightened scrutiny of eminent domain decisions should be applied in cases where there is evidence that a condemnation was undertaken as a result of "impermissible favoritism" toward a private party (at 492 [Kennedy, J., dissenting]). The fact that four (and possibly five) justices had serious misgivings about the Court's ultra-deferential approach to public use issues is a major change from the unanimous endorsement of that very position in *Midkiff.* Although a major defeat for property owners, *Kelo* also represented a small doctrinal step forward for them.

## The Public Reaction

Although *Kelo* was consistent with existing precedent, the decision was greeted with widespread outrage that cut across partisan, ideological, racial, and gender lines. The U.S. House of Representatives immediately passed a resolution denouncing *Kelo* by a lopsided 365–33 vote (H.R. 340 2005).[15] In addition to expected denunciations from conservatives and libertarians,[16] *Kelo* was condemned by numerous liberal political leaders including former President Bill Clinton,[17] Democratic National Committee Chair Howard Dean (who blamed the decision on a "Republican-appointed Supreme Court"),[18] and prominent African-American politician and California Representative Maxine Waters.[19] The NAACP, the American Association of Retired Persons, and the liberal Southern Christian Leadership Conference had filed a joint amicus brief in *Kelo* urging the Court to rule in favor of the property owners (*Kelo* Amicus Brief of NAACP, AARP, & SCLC 2004). So too had the generally conservative Becket Fund for Religious Liberty (*Kelo* Amicus Brief of Becket Fund for Religious Liberty 2004).

Public opinion mirrored the widespread condemnation of *Kelo* by political elites and activists. In two national surveys conducted in the fall of 2005, 81 percent and 95 percent of respondents were opposed to *Kelo*.[20] As table 7.1 demonstrates,

**Table 7.1**  National Public Opinion on *Kelo*

|  |  | Zogby Survey[a] | | Saint Index Survey 2005[b] | |
|---|---|---|---|---|---|
|  |  | Percentage | | | |
|  |  | Agree | Disagree | Agree | Disagree |
|  | Total | 2 | 95 | 18 | 81 |
| Gender | Male | 2 | 94 | 22 | 77 |
|  | Female | 2 | 95 | 14 | 84 |
| Racial/Ethnic Group[c] | White | 2 | 94 | 17 | 82 |
|  | African American | 0 | 97 | 28 | 72 |
|  | Asian | 0 | 100 | 26 | 68 |
|  | Hispanic/Latino | 2 | 98 | 18 | 80 |
|  | Native American | — | — | 7 | 93 |
| Party Affiliation | Democrat | 3 | 94 | 20 | 79 |
|  | Independent | <1 | 99 | 17 | 83 |
|  | Republican | 3 | 92 | 14 | 85 |
| Ideology | Liberal | — | — | 22 | 77 |
|  | Moderate | — | — | 18 | 81 |
|  | Conservative | — | — | 17 | 82 |

*Notes*: [a] American Farm Bureau Federation Survey, October 29–November 2, 2005, Zogby International. Question wording: "Do you strongly agree, somewhat agree, somewhat disagree, or strongly disagree with the recent Supreme Court ruling that allowed a city in Connecticut to take the private property of one citizen and give it to another citizen to use for private development?" The totals given here differ slightly from those published by Zogby because they correct a minor clerical error in Zogby's tabulation.
[b] The Saint Index Poll, October–November 2005, Center for Economic and Civic Opinion at University of Massachusetts/Lowell. Question wording: "The U.S. Supreme Court recently ruled that local governments can take homes, business and private property to make way for private economic development if officials believe it would benefit the public. How do you feel about this ruling?"
[c] The figures for Asians, Hispanics, and Native Americans may be unreliable because of small sample sizes.

**Table 7.2** State-by-State Public Opinion on *Kelo*

| State | % Agreeing with *Kelo* | % Disagreeing |
|---|---|---|
| Connecticut[a] | 8 | 88 |
| Florida[b] | 12 | 88 |
| Kansas[c] | 7 | 92 |
| New Hampshire[d] | 4 | 93 |
| Minnesota[e] | 5 | 91 |
| North Carolina[f] | 7 | 91 |
| Pennsylvania[g] | 9 | 90 |
| Tennessee[h] | 8 | 86 |

*Notes*: [a] Quinnipiac University Poll, July 19–25, 2005, Quinnipiac University Polling Institute, available at http://www.quinnipiac.edu/x11385.xml?ReleaseID=821. Question wording: "As you may know, the Court ruled that government can use eminent domain to buy a person's property and transfer it to private developers whose commercial projects could benefit the local economy. Do you agree or disagree with this ruling? Do you agree/disagree strongly or somewhat?"
[b] Coalition for Property Rights Survey, October 17–19, 2005, Mason Dixon Polling & Research Inc., available at http://www.rg4rb.org/surveyEmDom.html. Question wording: "In that Connecticut case, the U.S. Supreme Court ruled government can use the power of eminent domain to acquire a person's property and transfer it to private developers whose commercial projects could benefit the local economy. Do you agree or disagree with this ruling? (Is that strongly agree/disagree or somewhat agree/disagree?)"
[c] Americans for Prosperity Survey, January 2–5, 2006, Cole Hargrave Snodgrass and Associates, available at http://www.castlecoalition.org/pdf/polls/amcns-prosp-poll-KS.pdf. Question wording: "For years, governments have used the power of eminent domain to take control of private property and then using that property for schools, hospitals, roads, parks and other public services. Recently, the Kansas Supreme Court has expanded the government's ability to use eminent domain to include taking control of private property and transferring it not for public services, but to other private interests such as shopping centers or car lots. Do you favor or oppose the increased use of eminent domain to include taking private property and transferring ownership to other private interests? (After response, ask:) Would you say you strongly (favor/oppose) or only somewhat (favor/oppose)?"
[d] Granite State Poll, July 7–17, 2005, University of New Hampshire Survey Center, available at http://www.unh.edu/survey-center/sc072005.pdf#search=%22kelo%20poll%22. Question wording: "Recently, the Supreme Court ruled that towns and cities may take private land from people and make it available to businesses to develop under the principle of eminent domain. Some people favor this use of eminent domain because it allows for increased tax revenues from the new businesses and are an important part of economic redevelopment. Other people oppose this use of eminent domain because it reduces the value of private property and makes it easier for big businesses to take land. What about you? Do you think that towns and cities should be allowed to take private land from the owners and make it available to developers to develop or do you oppose this use of eminent domain?"
[e] Minnesota Auto Dealers Association Survey, February 9–17, 2006, Decision Resources Ltd., available at http://www.castlecoalition.org/pdf/polls/Survey-for-Strib.pdf. Question wording: "What is your opinion—do you support allowing local government to use eminent domain to take private property for another private development project? Do you feel strongly this way?"
[f] John William Pope Civitas Institute Survey, August 2005, Tel Opinion Research, available at http://www.jwpcivitasinstitute.org/keylinks/poll_august.html. Question wording: "The Supreme Court recently expanded the power of government to take private property for non-public use. Do you agree or disagree with this expansion of government's right to take private property?"
[g] Keystone Business Climate Survey, April 2–25, 2006, Lincoln Institute of Public Opinion Research, Inc., available at http://www.lincolninstitute.org/polls.php. Question wording: "A recent U.S. Supreme Court decision upheld the taking of private residential property by local municipalities to enable private developers to build higher tax-yielding structures on that land. Do you agree or disagree with this ruling?"
[h] Tennessee Poll, July 5–16, 2006, Social Science Research Institute at the University of Tennessee, Knoxville, available at http://web.utk.edu/~ssriweb/National_Issues.pdf. Question wording: "Sometimes the property taken through eminent domain is given to other private citizens for commercial development, rather than for public uses, such as road or schools. Would you say you favor or oppose this use of eminent domain?"

opposition to the decision cut across racial, ethnic, partisan, and gender lines. In the Saint Index survey, which has the better worded question of the two national polls,[21] *Kelo* was opposed by 77 percent of men, 84 percent of women, 82 percent of whites, 72 percent of African-Americans, and 80 percent of Hispanics (table 7.1). The decision was also opposed by 79 percent of Democrats, 85 percent of Republicans, and 83 percent of Independents. Moreover, public opposition to *Kelo* was deep as well as broad. In the Saint Index survey, 63 percent of respondents not only disagreed with the decision, but said they did so "strongly"[22] A later 2006 Saint Index survey found that 71 percent of respondents support reform laws intended to ban "the taking of private property for private development" projects, and 43 percent supported such laws "strongly" (See also Somin 2007a, Table 2).

Table 7.2 presents results for eight individual state surveys, all of which are similar to the national data, with opposition to *Kelo* ranging from 86 to 92 percent of respondents. The state surveys each use different question wording, and therefore are not completely comparable to the national surveys or to each other. Nevertheless, the national and state-by-state survey results collectively paint a picture of widespread and overwhelming opposition to *Kelo* and economic development takings.

The broad anti-*Kelo* consensus among political leaders, activists, and the general public leads one to expect that the ruling would be followed by the enactment of legislation abolishing or at least strictly limiting economic development takings. Yet, as we shall see in Part II, such a result has not occurred in most states.

## THE LEGISLATIVE RESPONSE

With some important exceptions, the legislative response to *Kelo* has fallen well short of expectations. At both the state and federal level, most of the newly enacted laws are likely to impose few if any meaningful restrictions on economic development takings.

### State Law

In analyzing the state law reforms enacted in the wake of *Kelo,* it is important to recognize that there is a significant difference in quality between laws enacted by referendum and those adopted by state legislatures. The former are generally much stronger than the latter. Therefore, I analyze the two categories separately. The overall results of the analysis are summarized in table 7.3. Table 7.4 describes the effectiveness and type of reform enacted in each state.

Table 7.5 shows that the enactment of effective post-*Kelo* reform seems unrelated to the degree to which the state in question engaged in private-to-private condemnation previously. Only seven of the twenty states with the greatest number of private-to-private takings in the five year period from 1998 to 2002 have enacted effective post-*Kelo* reforms. States in the top twenty that enacted effective reforms are identified in bold.

The data in table 7.5 is based on a study by the Institute for Justice, the libertarian public interest law firm that represented the property owners in *Kelo* (Berliner 2003).[23] The Institute for Justice figures are far from definitive. They likely

**Table 7.3** State Post-*Kelo* Reform Laws[a]

| | Type of Law | | Number of States |
|---|---|---|---|
| **Effective** | **Enacted by Legislature** | | 14 |
| | Enacted by Referendum | Citizen-initiated | 4 |
| | | Legislature-initiated | 2 or 3 |
| **Ineffective** | **Enacted by Legislature** | | 21 |
| | Enacted by Referendum | Citizen-initiated | 0 |
| | | Legislature-initiated | 3 or 4 |
| **No Post-*Kelo* Reforms Enacted** | | | 8[b] |

*Notes*: [a] The total number of states listed adds up to more than forty-two because a few states had effective legislative reforms followed by ineffective legislative referendum initiatives, and are thus counted in both of these categories. The state of Florida had legislative and referendum initiative reforms that were both effective and is also counted twice. Nevada had an effective referendum initiative followed by an ineffective legislative reform. [b] This figure does not include the state of Utah, which abolished both economic development and blight condemnations before Kelo. See note 42. I do include the state of Washington, despite the fact that it recently enacted a change in its eminent domain law unrelated to Kelo. See § II.A.1.b.vii.

underestimate the prevalence of condemnations for the benefit of private parties because they were compiled from news reports and court filings (Berliner 2003, 100). Many cases are unpublished, and many other condemnations go unreported in the press (Berliner 2003, 2). Many of the condemnations in the study involved the taking of multiple properties, sometimes hundreds at a time, while others only applied to a small amount of land. Finally, it is unfortunate that the figures do not separate out economic development takings from other private-to-private condemnations. Nonetheless, they do give a rough indication of which states engage in private-to-private condemnations more than others. And it is noteworthy that states with a relatively large number of private-to-private takings are not more likely to have enacted effective post-*Kelo* reforms than others.

A similar picture emerges if we compare states with large numbers of "threatened" private-to-private condemnations to those with few, or if we analyze the data with respect to the frequency of actual or threatened condemnations relative to the size of the state's population (appendix A). In each case, states with relatively large numbers of actual or threatened condemnations were not more likely to enact effective reforms than those with few or none. Only seven of the twenty states with the most "threatened" condemnations have enacted effective reforms. The same is true of just seven of the twenty states with the most private-to-private condemnations relative to population size (appendix A, tables 7A.1 and 7A.2).

To be sure, it is noteworthy that three of the four states with the largest number of takings–Pennsylvania, Kansas, and Michigan—have enacted effective reforms. However, the significance of this fact is diminished by the reality that Pennsylvania's reform law has a major loophole exempting those parts of the state where most condemnations occur.[24] Michigan's reform law, while quite strong,[25] came on the heels of a state supreme court decision that had already banned *Kelo*-style "economic development" takings.[26]

In addition, the Institute for Justice figures are only approximate and it is likely that they greatly underestimate the number of economic development condemnations in some states.[27] It is therefore difficult to know whether Pennsylvania, Kansas, and Michigan really were three of the top four states in this category.

**Table 7.4**  Effectiveness of Reform by State

| State | Effectiveness of Reform[a] |
| --- | --- |
| Alabama | Effective (L) |
| Alaska | Ineffective (L) |
| Arizona | Effective (CR) |
| Arkansas | No Reform |
| California | Ineffective (L) |
| Colorado | Ineffective (L) |
| Connecticut | Ineffective (L) |
| Delaware | Ineffective (L) |
| Florida | Effective (L & LR) |
| Georgia | Effective (L & LR) |
| Hawaii | No Reform |
| Idaho | Effective (L) |
| Illinois | Ineffective (L) |
| Indiana | Effective (L) |
| Iowa | Ineffective (L) |
| Kansas | Effective (L) |
| Kentucky | Ineffective (L) |
| Louisiana | Effective (LR) |
| Maine | Ineffective (L) |
| Maryland | Ineffective (L) |
| Massachusetts | No Reform |
| Michigan | Effective (L & LR) |
| Minnesota | Effective (L) |
| Mississippi | No Reform |
| Missouri | Ineffective (L) |
| Montana | Ineffective (L) |
| Nebraska | Ineffective (L) |
| Nevada | Effective (L & CR) |
| New Hampshire | Effective (L & LR) |
| New Jersey | No Reform |
| New Mexico | Effective (L) |
| New York | No Reform |
| North Carolina | Ineffective (L) |
| North Dakota | Effective (CR) |
| Ohio | Ineffective (L) |
| Oklahoma | No Reform |
| Oregon | Effective (CR) |
| Pennsylvania | Effective (L) |
| Rhode Island | No Reform |
| South Carolina | Ineffective (LR) |
| South Dakota | Effective (L) |
| Tennessee | Ineffective (L) |
| Texas | Ineffective (L) |
| Utah | Enacted Prior to Kelo |
| Vermont | Ineffective (L) |
| Virginia | Effective (L) |
| Washington | No Reform |
| West Virginia | Ineffective (L) |
| Wisconsin | Ineffective (L) |
| Wyoming | Effective (L) |

*Notes*: L = Reform enacted by state legislature; CR = Reform enacted by citizen-initiated referendum; LR = Reform enacted by legislature-initiated referendum.
[a] As of January 2008. "L" refers to legislation passed; "CR" refers to citizen initiated referenda passed; "LR" refers to legislative initiated referenda passed.

**Table 7.5** Post-*Kelo* Reforms in States Ranked by Number of Private-to-Private Condemnations, 1998–2002

| State | No. of Takings[a] | Effectiveness of Reform[b] |
|---|---|---|
| **Pennsylvania** | **2,517** | **Effective (L)** |
| California | 223 | Ineffective (L) |
| **Kansas** | **155** | **Effective (L)** |
| **Michigan** | **138** | **Effective (L & LR)** |
| Maryland | 127 | Ineffective (L) |
| Ohio | 90 | Ineffective (L) |
| **Florida** | **67** | **Effective (L & LR)** |
| **Virginia** | **58** | **Effective (L)** |
| New York | 57 | No Reform |
| New Jersey | 51 | No Reform |
| Connecticut | 31 | Ineffective (L) |
| Tennessee | 29 | Ineffective (L) |
| Colorado | 23 | Ineffective (L) |
| Oklahoma | 23 | No Reform |
| Missouri | 18 | Ineffective (L) |
| Rhode Island | 12 | No Reform |
| **Arizona** | **11** | **Effective (CR)** |
| Texas | 11 | Ineffective (L) |
| Washington | 11 | No Reform |
| **Minnesota** | **9** | **Effective (L)** |
| Alabama | 8 | Effective (L) |
| Illinois | 8 | Ineffective (L) |
| Kentucky | 7 | Ineffective (L) |
| Louisiana | 5 | Effective (LR) |
| Massachusetts | 5 | No Reform |
| Indiana | 4 | Effective (L) |
| Iowa | 4 | Ineffective (L) |
| Mississippi | 3 | No Reform |
| Nevada | 3 | Effective (L & CR) |
| Maine | 2 | Ineffective (L) |
| Arkansas | 1 | No Reform |
| Nebraska | 1 | Ineffective (L) |
| North Carolina | 1 | Ineffective (L) |
| North Dakota | 1 | Effective (CR) |
| Alaska | 0 | Ineffective (L) |
| Delaware | 0 | Ineffective (L) |
| Georgia | 0 | Effective (L & LR) |
| Idaho | 0 | Effective (L) |
| South Dakota | 0 | Effective (L) |
| Wyoming | 0 | Effective (L) |
| Hawaii | 0 | No Reform |
| Montana | 0 | Ineffective (L) |
| New Hampshire | 0 | Effective (L & LR) |
| New Mexico | 0 | Effective (L) |
| Oregon | 0 | Effective (CR) |
| South Carolina | 0 | Ineffective (LR) |
| Utah | 0 | Enacted Prior to *Kelo* |
| Vermont | 0 | Ineffective (L) |
| West Virginia | 0 | Ineffective (L) |
| Wisconsin | 0 | Ineffective (L) |

*Notes*: L = Reform enacted by state legislature; CR = Reform enacted by citizen-initiated referendum; LR = Reform enacted by legislature-initiated referendum.
[a] Some takings affected more than one property.
[b] As of January 2008.

Furthermore, it would be unwise to draw broad conclusions from just three cases, especially in light of the fact that nearly all the other states with large numbers of private-to-private takings in the Institute for Justice study either enacted ineffective reforms or none at all. For these reasons, the reforms in these states are not compelling evidence for the theory that the effectiveness of post-*Kelo* reform was driven by the extent to which the state in question made use of economic development condemnations prior to *Kelo*.

## REFORMS ENACTED BY STATE LEGISLATURES

As of January 2008, 35 state legislatures have enacted post-*Kelo* reforms. The state of Utah effectively banned economic development takings in a statute enacted several months before *Kelo* was decided by the Supreme Court.[28] However, 21 of the 35 new state laws provide little or no protection for property owners against economic development takings. Only 14 state legislatures have enacted laws that either ban economic development takings or significantly restrict them. The 21 ineffective state laws are of several types. By far the most common are laws that forbid takings for "economic development" but in fact allow them to continue under another name, such as "blight" or "community development" condemnations. Other post-*Kelo* reforms lack teeth because they either forbid only those takings that are for "private" development (thus permitting localities to condemn under the standard theory that any such takings are really intended to promote "public" benefit) or are purely symbolic in nature.

### a. Laws with Broad Exemptions for "Blight" Condemnations

Sixteen states have enacted post-*Kelo* reform laws whose effect is largely negated by exemptions for "blight" condemnations under definitions of "blight" that make it possible to include almost any property in that category. This is by far the most common factor undermining the potential effectiveness of post-*Kelo* reform laws.

Early blight cases in the 1940s and 1950s upheld condemnations in areas that closely fit the layperson's intuitive notion of "blight": dilapidated, dangerous, or disease-ridden neighborhoods. For example, in *Berman v. Parker,* the well-known 1954 case in which the Supreme Court upheld the constitutionality of blight condemnations under the Federal Public Use Clause, the condemned neighborhood was characterized by "[m]iserable and disreputable housing conditions" (348 U.S. 26, 32 [1954]). According to the Court, "64.3 percent of the dwellings [in the area] were beyond repair, 18.4 percent needed major repairs, only 17.3 percent were satisfactory; 57.8 percent of the dwellings had outside toilets, 60.3 percent had no baths, 29.3 percent lacked electricity, 82.2 percent had no wash basins or laundry tubs, [and] 83.8 percent lacked central heating" (qtd. at 32).

More recently, however, many states have expanded the concept of "blight" to encompass almost any area where economic development could potentially be increased. For example, recent state appellate court decisions have held that Times Square in New York City (*In re W. 41st St. Realty v. N.Y. State Urban Dev. Corp.,* 744 N.Y.S.2d 121 [N.Y. App. Div. 2002]), and downtown Las Vegas (*City of Las Vegas Downtown Redev. Agency v. Pappas,* 76 P.3d 1, 12–15 [Nev. 2003]) are "blighted," thereby justifying condemnations undertaken to acquire land for a new headquarters for the *New York Times* and parking lots for a consortium of local casinos respectively. All but three states permit condemnation for "blight" and most of these define the concept broadly.[29] For decades, courts have interpreted broad definitions of "blight" in ways that allow the condemnation of almost any property (Luce 2000; Gordon 2004). If virtually any property can be condemned as "blighted," a ban on "economic development" takings would be essentially irrelevant.

Sixteen post-*Kelo* reform laws continue this pattern, using definitions of "blight" that are either identical to those enshrined in preexisting law or very similar to them. These reform laws thereby undermine the effectiveness of their bans on private-to-private condemnations for "economic development." Ten of these followed a standard pattern of defining "blight" as any obstacle to "sound growth" or an "economic or social liability." Six have somewhat more idiosyncratic but comparably broad definitions of "blight."

### i. Defining "Blight" to Include Any Obstacle to "Sound Growth" or an "Economic or Social Liability"

Ten state post-*Kelo* laws leave in place definitions of "blight" that include any area where there are obstacles to "sound growth" or conditions that constitute an "economic or social liability." These include reform laws in Alaska,[30] Colorado,[31] Missouri,[32] Montana,[33] Nebraska,[34] North Carolina,[35] Ohio,[36] Texas,[37] Vermont,[38] and West Virginia.[39] Obviously, any obstacle to economic development can easily be defined as impairing "sound growth," making this definition of "blight" broad enough to justify virtually any condemnation under an economic development rationale. Similarly, an impediment to "economic development" can be considered an "economic or social liability." Several of the state laws listed above require that, in order to be blighted, an area that is an "economic or social liability" must also be "a menace to the public health, safety, morals, or welfare" (See statutes cited in notes 43–54). This additional condition is unlikely to be a significant constraint because almost any condition that impedes economic development could be considered a "menace" to public "welfare."

For example, under Florida's pre-reform blight statute which used this exact wording, the Florida Supreme Court found that even undeveloped land could be considered "blighted" because its current state impedes future development (*Panama City Beach Community Redev. Agency v. State,* 831 S0.2d 662, 688–69 [Fla. 2002]). The Supreme Court of Arizona has similarly described this language— which was present in Arizona's pre-*Kelo* blight statute, as an "extremely broad definition of … 'blighted area'" that gives condemning authorities "wide discretion in deciding what constitutes blight" (City of Phoenix v. Superior Ct., 671 P.2d 387 [Ariz. 1983] at 391, 393). Significantly, searches on Westlaw and Lexis do not reveal any published state court opinions that interpret this language as a meaningful constraint on the scope of blight condemnations. There are no published court decisions using it to strike down an attempted blight taking of any kind.[40]

### ii. Other Broad Blight Exemptions

Seven other states have similarly broad blight exemptions, albeit with different wording. Illinois' new law exempts blight condemnations from its ban on economic development takings and retains its preexisting definition of "blight," (Ill. S.B. 3086 [signed into law July 28, 2006]) which defines a blighted area as one where "industrial, commercial, and residential buildings or improvements are detrimental to the public safety, health, or welfare because of a combination of 5 or more of the following factors" (qtd. at 65 Ill. C. Stat. § 5/11–74.4–3). The list of factors include dilapidation; obsolescence; deterioration; below minimum code standards; illegal use of structures; excessive vacancies; lack of ventilation, light or sanitary facilities; inadequate utilities; excessive land coverage and overcrowding of structures and community facilities; deleterious land use or layout; environmental clean-up; lack of community planning; or an assessed value that has decline three of the last five years (§ 5/11–74.4–3). The concept of "detriment" to "public welfare" is extremely broad and surely includes detriment to local economic welfare and development. The list of factors, of which five must be present, includes numerous conditions, such as deterioration, "deleterious land use or layout," lack of community planning, a declining assessed value, "excessive" land coverage, and obsolescence that exist to some degree in most communities. Thus, Illinois' law would forbid few if any economic development takings.

The new Nevada statute bans all private-to-private condemnations,[41] but leaves open an exception for blight takings (§ 10). Current Nevada law defines "blight" very broadly, allowing an area to be declared blighted so long as it meets at least four of eleven factors (Nev. Rev. State § 279.388 [defining "blighted area"]. The possible factors included at least six that are extremely broad and could apply to almost any area: "economic dislocation, deterioration or disuse," "subdividing and sale of lots of irregular form and shape and inadequate size for proper usefulness and development," "[t]he laying out of lots in disregard of the contours and other physical characteristics of the ground," "[t]he existence of inadequate streets, open spaces and utilities," "[a] growing or total lack of proper utilization of some parts of the area, resulting in a stagnant and unproductive condition of land," and "[a] loss of population and a reduction of proper use of some parts of the area, result-ing in its further deterioration and added costs to the taxpayer" (Nev. Rev. State § 279.388). In 2003, the Nevada Supreme Court used this statute to declare down-town Las Vegas a blighted area, thereby justifying the condemnation of property for transfer to several casinos so that they could build new parking facilities for their customers (*City of Las Vegas Downtown Redev. Agency v. Pappas*, 76 P.3d 1, 12–15 [Nev. 2003])[42] However, the Nevada statute was enacted in the aftermath of a referendum that approved. a state constitutional amendment that will eventually provide much stronger protection for property owners than permitted under the legislative statute.[43]

Kentucky's post-*Kelo* reform law likewise retains a very broad preexisting defi-nition of "blight" (Ky. H.B. 508). The law allowed condemnation of property for "urban renewal and community development" in "blighted" or "slum" areas (Kan. Rev. Stat. §§ 99.330–590, 99.370). An area can be considered "blighted" or a "slum" if there are flaws in the "size" or "usefulness" of property lots in the area, or if there are conditions "constitut[ing] a menace to the public health safety or welfare" (Kan. Rev. Stat. § 99.340).

Maine's reform statute also incorporates a broad definition of "blight" from prior legislation.[44] Prior Maine law defines "blight" as including areas in which properties suffer from "[d]ilapidation, deterioration, age or obsolescence" (30 Me. Stat. Ann. §§ 203, 205). For condemnations that further "urban renewal" projects, detriment to "public health, safety, morals or welfare" may lead to a blight designa-tion (30 Me. Stat. Ann. § 203); condemnation for "community development" can occur in areas that are considered "blighted" under the same definition, except that threats to "morals" are not included (30 Me. Stat. Ann. § 205).

The new Tennessee law attempts to tighten the definition of "blight," but ultimately leaves it very broad. Under the new statute:

> "Blighted areas" are areas (including slum areas) with buildings or improvements which, by reason of dilapidation, obsolescence, overcrowding, lack of ventilation, light and sanitary facilities, deleterious land use, or any combination of these or other factors, are detrimental to the safety, health, morals, or welfare of the community. "Welfare of the community" does not include solely a loss of property value to surrounding properties nor does it include the need for increased tax revenues (Tenn. S.B. 3296, § 14[a] [signed into law June 6, 2006]).

The inclusion of the term "welfare of the community" seems to leave the door open to most economic development takings; after all, economic development is generally considered a component of community "welfare." This conclusion is not much affected by the stipulation that "'welfare'…does not include solely a loss of property value to surrounding properties nor does it include the need for increased tax revenues" (qtd. in § 14[a]). Condemnations that promote "development" by increasing property values are still permitted so long as there is some other claim of even a small economic benefit, such as an increase in employment, savings, or investment. Indeed, the provision of jobs and attraction of outside investors is a standard rationale for economic development condemnations.[45]

Finally, Iowa's and Wisconsin's post-*Kelo* laws are somewhat ambiguous cases, though tending toward a broad definition of "blight." The Iowa statute includes a less broad blight exemption but one that might still be extensive enough to allow a wide range of economic development takings. The Iowa statute permits condemnation of blighted areas, and defines "blight" as:

> [T]he presence of a substantial number of slum or deteriorated structures; insanitary or unsafe conditions; excessive and uncorrected deterioration of site or other improvements; tax or special assessment delinquency exceeding the fair value of the land; defective or unusual conditions of title; or the existence of conditions which endanger life or property by fire and other causes; or the existence of conditions which retard the provision of housing accommodations for low or moderate income families, or is a menace to the public health and safety in its present condition and use (Iowa H.F. 2351 [enacted into law July 14, 2006]).

Whether or not this is a broad definition of "blight" depends on the definition of such terms as "deteriorated structures" and "excessive and uncorrected deterioration of site." If the concept of "deterioration" is defined broadly, then virtually any area could be considered blighted because all structures gradually deteriorate over time. Since one of the conditions justifying a blight designation is "the presence of a substantial number of slum *or* deteriorated structures," (Iowa H.F. 2351, emphasis added) we might presume that the term "deteriorated" can be applied to structures that are not dilapidated enough to be considered "slum[s]." Otherwise, the inclusion of the term "deteriorated" would be superfluous. Thus, it is possible that courts will interpret the Iowa statute to permit a very broad definition of "blight" by virtue of the use of the term "deteriorated."

In addition, it is possible that a wide range of areas could be considered "blighted" by applying the statute's provision that an area is "blighted" if there are "conditions which retard the provision of housing accommodations for low or moderate income families" (Iowa H.F. 2351) Since the law does not state that the "retardation" must be of significant magnitude, it is possible that the existence of conditions that impair the provision of low and moderate income housing even slightly might be enough to justify a blight designation.

The Wisconsin statute is more restrictive than Iowa's. It too exempts blight condemnations from its ban on economic development takings and defines "blight" broadly. The definition includes:

> [A]ny property that, by reason of abandonment, dilapidation, deterioration, age or obsolescence, inadequate provisions for ventilation, light, air, or sanitation, high density of population and overcrowding, faulty lot layout in relation to size, adequacy, accessibility, or usefulness, unsanitary or unsafe conditions, deterioration of site or other improvements, or the existence of conditions that endanger life or property by fire or other causes, or any combination of such factors, is detrimental to the public health, safety, or welfare (Wisc. A.B. 657, § 1 [signed into law Mar. 31, 2006]).[46]

However, the statute also exempts residential property from condemnation for blight alleviation unless it has: 1) "been abandoned" or 2) has been "converted from a single dwelling unit to multiple dwelling units" and "the crime rate in [or near] the property is higher than in the remainder of the municipality" (qtd. in § 1). Thus, the Wisconsin law provides considerable protection for single family homes, but allows nonresidential properties and many multi-family homes to be condemned under a broad definition of "blight."

### b. State Laws that Are Ineffective for Other Reasons[47]

While broad blight exemptions are by far the most common type of loophole in post-*Kelo* laws, several post-*Kelo* statutes are ineffective for other reasons. The most notable of these are those of California, Connecticut, Maryland, and Delaware. The Texas and Ohio laws, already briefly discussed above, also have major loopholes besides those created by their blight exemptions. Each of these cases is analyzed below. I also briefly consider Washington's new eminent domain law, even though the latter is not truly a response to *Kelo*.

#### i. California

In September 2006, the California state legislature enacted a package of five post-*Kelo* eminent domain reform bills (Ca. S.B. 53, 1206, 1210, 1650, 1809 [signed into law Sept. 29, 2006]). None of the five even comes close to forbidding condemnations for economic development.

Four of the five new statutes create minor new procedural hurdles for local governments seeking to condemn property (Ca. S.B. 53, 1210, 1650, 1809 2006). As eminent domain scholar and litigator Timothy Sandefur has shown in a detailed analysis, none of the four impose restrictions that will significantly impede the exercise of eminent domain in California).[48]

Senate Bill 1206 attempts to narrow the definition of "blight," but still leaves a definition broad enough to permit the condemnation of almost any property that local governments might want for economic development purposes. The bill requires that a blighted area have both at least one "physical condition" that causes "blight" and one "economic" condition. Both the list of qualifying physical conditions and the list of qualifying economic ones includes vague criteria that apply to almost any neighborhood. The list of "physical conditions" includes "conditions that prevent or substantially hinder the viable use or capacity of buildings or lots," and "[a]djacent or nearby incompatible land uses that prevent the development of those parcels or other portions of the project area" (qtd. in Ca. S.B. 1206, § 3). Since "viable use" and "development" are left undefined, local officials will have broad discretion to designate areas as they see fit. The list of "economic conditions" is similar. Among other things, it includes "[d]epreciated or stagnant property values," abnormally high business vacancies," and "abnormally low lease rates" (qtd. in § 3) Since almost any area occasionally experiences stagnation or decline in property values and a declining business climate, this list too puts no meaningful restrictions on blight designations. Moreover, it is important to remember that a blight condemnation requires just one "condition" from each list, further increasing official discretion.

### ii. Connecticut

The new Connecticut law merely forbids the condemnation of property "for the primary purpose of increasing local tax revenue" (Conn. S.B. 167, § 1[b][1] [enacted June 25, 2007]). This restriction does not prevent condemnations for either economic development or blight purposes. Connecticut law allows local governments to condemn property for both economic development purposes and to alleviate blight-like conditions.[49] Even the goal of increasing tax revenue can still be pursued so long as it is part of a more general plan for local "redevelopment."[50] In practice, it is likely to be impossible to prove that a given property is being condemned primarily for the purpose of "increasing local tax revenue" as distinct from the goal of promoting economic development more generally. It is ironic that the state in which the *Kelo* case occurred has enacted one of the nation's weakest post-*Kelo* reform laws, one that would not have prevented the condemnations challenged by Susette *Kelo* and her fellow New London property owners.

### iii. Delaware

The Delaware bill is arguably the least effective of all the post-*Kelo* laws enacted so far. It does not restrict condemnations for economic development at all. The statute requires merely that the power of eminent domain only be exercised for "the purposes of a recognized public use as described at least six months in advance of the institution of condemnation proceedings: (i) in a certified planning document, (ii) at a public hearing held specifically to address the acquisition, or (iii) in a published report of the acquiring agency" (Del. Sen. Bill 217, § 1 [codified at 29 Del. Code § 9505(14)]. This bill does little more than restate current constitutional law, which already requires that condemnation be for a "recognized public use." Indeed, the *Kelo* majority notes that "'purely private taking[s]'" are constitutionally forbidden (*Kelo,* 545 U.S. 469, 477 [2005] [quoting *Midkiff,* 467 U.S. 229, 241, 245 [1984]). The real question, however, is what counts as a "recognized public use," and this issue is in no way addressed by the new Delaware law.

The requirement that the purpose of the condemnation be announced six months in advance provides a minor procedural protection for property owners, but one that can easily be circumvented simply by tucking away the required announcement in a "published report of the acquiring agency" (29 Del. Code § 9505 [14]).

### iv. Maryland

Maryland's new law does not forbid condemnations for either economic development or blight. Instead, it merely requires a condemnation to occur within four years of its authorization (Md. S.B. 3, §12–105.1 [signed into law May 8, 2007]). This restriction is unlikely to impede economic development takings. Not only is the four year period quite long, but reauthorization is likely to be easily obtained under the state's extremely broad definition of "blighted" and "slum" areas, both of which are eligible for condemnation under Maryland law.[51]

### v. Ohio

The main shortcoming of the Ohio law is its temporary nature. The new law mandated that "until December 31, 2006, no public body shall use eminent domain to take...private property that is not within a blighted area, as determined by the public body, when the primary purpose for the taking is economic development that will ultimately result in ownership of that property being vested in another private person" (qtd. in Oh. Gen. Assembly, Sen. Bill 167, § 2).

Even within the short period of its effect, the law probably only had a very limited impact. While it forbade condemnations where "economic development" is the "primary purpose," nothing prevented such takings if the community could cite some other objective to which the development objective is an adjunct or complement (§ 2). Creative local governments could easily come up with such proposals. Furthermore, the Ohio law explicitly exempted "blighted" areas from its scope; the definition of "blight" under Ohio law is broad enough to cover almost any area.[52] Finally, given the temporary nature of the legislation, a local government could get around it simply by postponing a given condemnation project for a few months.

The Ohio legislation also established a "Legislative Task Force to Study Eminent Domain and its Use and Application in the State" (Oh. Gen. Assembly, Sen. Bill 167, § 3). However, the twenty-five member commission was largely dominated by pro-eminent domain interests. Fourteen of the twenty-five members were required to be representatives of groups that tend to be supportive of broad eminent domain power. Only four were required to be members of groups likely to support strict limits on condemnation authority, and seven represented groups with mixed incentives.[53]

As was perhaps to be expected, the Commission's Final Report recommended only minor reforms in state law. For example, it recommended "tightening" the state's broad definition of "blight," but its proposed new definition is almost as broad as the old one.[54] In July 2007, the Ohio state legislature enacted a new reform law that adopted the definition of "blight" recommended by the Commission (Oh. Amended S.B. 7 [signed into law July 10, 2007]). That definition, however, provides little if any more protection for property owners than the old one.

### vi. Texas

Texas' post-*Kelo* legislation is likely to be almost completely ineffectual because of its major loopholes. It forbids condemnations if the taking:

(1) confers a private benefit on a particular private party through the use of the property; (2) is for a public use that is merely a pretext to confer a private benefit

on a particular private party; or (3) is for economic development purposes, unless the economic development is a secondary purpose resulting from municipal community development or municipal urban renewal activities to eliminate an existing affirmative harm on society from slum or blighted areas (Tex. Sen. Bill No. 7 2005 [codified at 10 Tex. Gov. Code §2206.001(b)]).

Taken literally, the first criterion in the act might be used to forbid almost all condemnations, since even traditional public uses often "confer a private benefit on a particular private party through the use of the property." Presumably, however, this prohibition is intended merely to forbid condemnations that create such a private benefit without also serving a public use. Otherwise, the state legislature would not be able to protect "community development" and "urban renewal" takings, which surely confer "private benefits" for "particular" persons (at §2206.001[b]).

The legislation's ban on pretextual takings merely reiterates current law. *Kelo* itself states that government is "no[t]...allowed to take property under the mere pretext of a public purpose, when [the] actual purpose was to bestow a private benefit" (*Kelo*, 545 U.S. 469, 478 [2005]).

The ban on takings for "economic development" purposes is largely vitiated by exemption for condemnations where "economic development is a secondary purpose resulting from municipal community development" (qtd. in 10 Tex. Gov. Code § 2206.001[b][3]). Virtually any "economic development" can be plausibly characterized as also advancing "community development." It is difficult to see how the two concepts can be meaningfully distinguished in real world situations. Indeed, Texas law defines "community development" to permit condemnation of any property that is "inappropriately developed from the standpoint of sound community development and growth" (qtd. in Tex. Local Gov. Code §373.005[b][1][A]). It is surely reasonable to suppose that "sound community development and growth" includes economic "development and growth."

The Texas legislation does contain two potentially effective elements. First, it eliminates judicial deference to governmental determinations that a challenged condemnation is for a legitimate public use (Tex. Local Gov. Code § 2206.001[e]). This shifts the burden of proof in public use cases to the condemning authority. Second, it seems to forbid private-to-private condemnations under statutes other than those allowing the use of eminent domain for blight alleviation and "community development."[55] However, as noted above, Texas' definition of "community development" is so broad that it can be used to justify almost any condemnation even under a nondeferential approach to judicial review. Judges are unlikely to find that very many takings run afoul of the community development statute's authorization of condemnation of property that is "inappropriately developed from the standpoint of sound community development and growth" (qtd. in Tex. Local Gov. Code §373.005[b][1][A]). This broad standard can also be used to defend a wide range of condemnations for various private development projects even without specific legislative authorization other than the community development law itself. Ultimately, the potentially effective new rules in the Texas law are swallowed up by the "community development" exception.[56]

### vii. Washington

The state of Washington's recent eminent domain law is not a true response to *Kelo* (See Wash. S.H.B. 1458 [signed into law April 4, 2007]). It does not even pretend to restrict economic development takings or cut back on the definition of "public use" in any other way. Instead, the new statute seems to be a response to a 2006 Washington Supreme Court decision which held that property owners are not entitled to personal notice of public meetings called to consider the necessity of initiating eminent domain proceedings against them.[57] Because the new law was neither a response to *Kelo* nor an attempt to narrow the definition of public use, I do not classify it as a post-*Kelo* reform. Changing this classification would not alter the quantitative data discussed in Part III,[58] nor would it alter the overall conclusions of this article. If the law were to be viewed as a post-*Kelo* reform, it would be classified as adding little or nothing to the protections Washington property owners already enjoyed before *Kelo*. The state supreme court banned economic development takings in 1959,[59] and Washington already had a narrow definition of "blight."[60]

## LEGISLATIVELY ENACTED LAWS THAT PROVIDE SUBSTANTIALLY INCREASED PROTECTION FOR PROPERTY OWNERS

Fourteen state legislatures have enacted laws that either abolish or significantly constrain economic development takings. The most sweeping of these laws are Florida's and New Mexico's, which not only abolished condemnations for economic development, but also banned all blight condemnations, even those that occur in areas that would meet a strict definition of the term (Fla. H.B. 1567 [signed into law May 11, 2006]; N.M. H.B. 393 [signed into law Apr. 3, 2007]).[61] Florida and New Mexico therefore became the second and third states to abolish blight condemnations, following in the footsteps of Utah, which did so prior to *Kelo*.[62] Unlike Utah and New Mexico, which made little use of economic development and blight takings even before the enactment of its new law,[63] Florida has an extensive record of dubious economic development and blight condemnations (Berliner 2003, 52–58). Due to its broad scope and location in a large state that previously made extensive use of private-to-private takings, the new Florida law is probably the most important post-*Kelo* legislative victory for property rights activists.

South Dakota's new law is only slightly less sweeping than Florida's. It continues to permit blight condemnations, but does not allow *any* takings—including those in blighted areas—that "transfer property to any private person, nongovernmental entity, or other public-private business entity" (2006 S.D. H.B. 1080 [signed into law Feb. 27, 2006]). This forbids economic development takings, and also greatly reduces the political incentive to engage in blight condemnations, since local governments can no longer use them to transfer property to politically influential interests.[64] Kansas' new law is similar to South Dakota's in so far as it bans nearly all private-to-private condemnations. It forbids condemnations "for the purpose of selling, leasing or otherwise transferring such property to any private entity" except in cases where needed for public utilities or where there is defective title (Kan. S.B. 323, §§1–2. [signed into law May 18, 2006]). Blight condemnations are limited to cases where the property in question is "unsafe for occupation by humans under the building codes"(§ 2[a]).

Eight state reform laws couple a ban on economic development condemnations with restrictions on the definition of "blight" that, roughly speaking, restrict blight condemnations to areas that fit the intuitive layperson's definition of the term. This formula was successfully used in the Alabama,[65] Georgia,[66] Idaho,[67] Indiana,[68]

Michigan,[69] New Hampshire,[70] Virginia,[71] and Wyoming statutes.[72] In the case of Nevada, the new legislation was enacted only in the aftermath of a referendum initiative that would ban both economic development and blight condemnations entirely.

Two state laws—Pennsylvania and Minnesota—forbid economic development takings and restrict the definition of "blight," but significantly undermine their effectiveness by exempting large parts of the state from the law's coverage. The Pennsylvania law forbids "the exercise by any condemnor of the power of eminent domain to take private property in order to use it for private commercial enterprise" (qtd. in Penn. House Bill No. 2054, ch. 2, § 204[a] [enacted May 4, 2006]), and imposes a restrictive definition of "blight" (at § 205). However, the scope of this provision is undermined by the effective exclusion of Philadelphia and Pittsburgh, as well as some other areas, from its coverage.[73] These two cities, by far the state's largest urban areas, are also the sites of many of the state's most extensive private-to-private takings.[74] Although the provision exempting the two cities is set to expire on December 31, 2012, (H.B. No. 2054, ch. 2, § 203[4]) by that time it is possible that legislators will be able to extend the deadline, once the public furor over *Kelo* has subsided.

Minnesota's law is similar. It too bans economic development takings and restricts the definition of "blight,"[75] while creating some major geographic exemptions. In this case, the exemptions include land located in some 2000 Tax Increment Financing Districts, including much of the territory of the Twin Cities of Minneapolis and St. Paul, where a high proportion of the state's condemnations take place (Minn. S.F. 2750, § 22). A recent survey by the pro-*Kelo* League of Minnesota Cities found that 27 of the 34 Minnesota cities that had used private-to-private takings for economic development purposes between 1999 and 2005 are located in the Twin Cities area, which is exempt from the new post-*Kelo* reform law.[76] Thus, the new law will impact only a small fraction of those cities that actually engage in the practices it seeks to curb. Like the Pennsylvania exemptions, the Minnesota ones are time-limited, scheduled to expire in five years (§ 22). But they too could be extended if the public furor over *Kelo* subsides over time.

Even many of the 14 state laws that do succeed in abolishing or curbing economic development takings have serious limitations. As already noted, the Minnesota and Pennsylvania laws are seriously weakened by geographic exemptions that exclude most of their largest urban areas. The laws enacted by Alabama, Georgia, and South Dakota were adopted by states that had little or no recent history of resorting to private-to-private condemnations;[77] thus, they forbid practices that local governments rarely engaged in. Overall, only seven states that had previously engaged in significant amounts of economic development and blight condemnations adopted legislative post-*Kelo* reform measures with any real teeth.

## REFORMS ENACTED BY POPULAR REFERENDUM

In sharp contrast to legislatively enacted post-*Kelo* reforms, those adopted by popular referendum are, on average, much stronger. In 2006, ten states adopted post-*Kelo* reforms by popular referendum.[78] All 10 passed by large margins ranging from 55 percent to 86 percent of the vote.[79] Of these, at least six and possibly seven provided significantly stronger protection for property owners than was available under existing law. Two other states—Georgia and New Hampshire—passed initiatives that added little or nothing to post-*Kelo* reforms already enacted by the state legislature. Finally, South Carolina voters adopted a largely ineffective reform law. It is crucial to recognize that referenda initiated by citizen groups were far more likely to lead to effective laws than those enacted by state legislatures. Indeed, only one state—Louisiana—passed a legislature-initiated referendum that provided significantly greater protection for property owners than that available under pre-existing statutory law enacted through the ordinary legislative process.

Three states—Arizona,[80] Louisiana,[81] and Oregon[82]—enacted referendum initiatives that essentially followed the standard formula of combining a ban on economic development takings with a restrictive definition of "blight." Nevada and North Dakota's initiatives went one step beyond this and would amend their state constitutions to ban virtually all condemnations that transfer property to a private owner; the Nevada law will not take effect until ratified by the voters a second time in 2008.[83]

Florida's referendum initiative could not add much in the way of substantive protections to the state's legislatively enacted post-*Kelo* law, already the strongest in the country (See II.A.1.). However, Constitutional Amendment 8 did alter the state constitution to provide an important procedural protection: no new law allowing "the transfer of private property taken by eminent domain to a natural person or private entity" can be passed without a three-fifths supermajority in the state legislature (Fla. Const. Amend. VIII [enacted November 7, 2006]). This could be an important safeguard for property owners against the erosion of public use protections by future state legislatures, after public attention has shifted away from eminent domain issues.

Georgia's new law adds little to that state's strong legislatively enacted post-*Kelo* statute, requiring only that any new private-to-private takings be approved by local elected officials (Ga. Amendment 1 [enacted November 7, 2006]). New Hampshire's referendum initiative also comes in the wake of a strong legislative proposal and adds nothing to it. Indeed, absent the earlier legislation, it would provide no real protection at all, since it only forbids condemnations "for the purpose of private development or other private use of the property" (qtd. in N.H. Question 1 [enacted November 7, 2006]). This wording is largely useless because it does not foreclose the argument that the transfer of property to a private party will promote "public development" that benefits the community as a whole, not just "private" individuals.[84]

South Carolina's referendum seems to forbid takings for economic development. However, the wording may actually permit such takings, since it states that "[p]rivate property shall not be condemned by eminent domain for any purpose or benefit, including, but not limited to, the purpose or benefit of economic development, unless the condemnation is for public use" (qtd. in S.C. Const. Amend. 5, § 13[2] [enacted November 7, 2006]). This, however, leaves open the question of whether "economic development" is in fact a "public use"—the very issue addressed by *Kelo* with respect to the federal Constitution. Current South Carolina case law already holds that economic development is not a public use under the state constitution.[85] However, the new constitutional amendment adds nothing to the case law and leaves open the possibility that future court decisions will be able to reverse it in the absence of a clear textual statement in the state constitution to the contrary. The South Carolina amendment also narrows the definition of "blight" to "property that constitutes a danger to the safety and health of the community by reason of lack of ventilation, light, and sanitary facilities, dilapidation, deleterious land use, or any combination of these factors" (qtd. in S.C. Amend. 5, § 13[B]). However, this provision also has a potential loophole, since "deleterious land use" and "health of the community" could both be interpreted broadly to include the community's "economic health" and "deleterious" land uses that undermine it. At best, the amendment modestly increases the protection provided by current law.

Finally, the new Michigan amendment is an ambiguous case. The amendment forbids condemnation of property "for transfer to a private entity for the purpose of economic development or enhancement of tax revenues" (Mich. Proposal 06–04, § Art. X, § 2). However, it did not change the state's previously broad definition of "blight." At this time, it is not clear whether or not the landmark 2004 state supreme court decision in *County of Wayne v. Hathcock* is interpreted to constrain condemnation of property under very broad blight designations (*County of Wayne v. Hathcock*, 684 N.W.2d 765, 779–86 [Mich. 2004]).[86] If *Hathcock* is held to limit broad blight designations, then the new constitutional amendment would have the modest but real advantage of providing explicit textual foundations for *Hathcock's* holding and reducing the chance of its reversal or erosion by future courts. If, on the other hand, *Hathcock* is interpreted to permit even very broad definitions of "blight," then the Michigan referendum initiative will be largely ineffective in its own right. At this point, however, the status of the Michigan referendum initiative is largely moot because Michigan's legislative reform had already narrowed the definition of "blight."[87] Thus, the Michigan constitutional amendment enacted by referendum reinforces the accomplishments of the previous statutory reform; but it might not have been effective as a stand-alone law.

In analyzing the ten post-*Kelo* referendum initiatives, it is important to note that four of the six clearly effective laws were enacted by means of initiative processes that allow activists to place a measure on the ballot without prior approval by the state legislature.[88] One of the other two (Florida) was sent to the voters by a legislature that had already enacted the nation's strongest post-*Kelo* reform law; only the Louisiana state legislature forwarded to the voters a referendum initiative without first enacting a strong legislative reform of its own. By contrast, all three largely ineffective initiatives required preapproval by state legislatures,[89] and the same was true of the ambiguous Michigan case.[90] Thus, the true contrast is not so much that between legislative reform and referendum initiatives, but that between referenda enacted without the need for approval by the state legislature and every other type of reform that does involve state legislators.

## FEDERAL LAW

### The Private Property Rights Protection Act

On November 3, 2005, the U.S. House of Representatives passed the Private Property Rights Protection Act of 2005 ("PRPA") by an overwhelming 376–38 margin (U.S. House of Representatives, 109 H.R. 4128 [enacted November 3, 2005]). Since early 2006,[91] the PRPA was bottled up in the Senate and the 109th Congress ended without its being enacted into law. As of this writing, it is not yet clear whether the PRPA will be enacted in the new Democratic Congress. In May 2007, it passed the Agriculture Committee of the House of Representatives; however, it has not yet been voted on by the full House as of January 2008.[92] Despite its failure to achieve passage so far, I consider it here because it is arguably the most important federal effort to provide increased protection for property owners in the aftermath of *Kelo*.

The Act would block state and local governments from "exercis[ing] [their] power of eminent domain or allow[ing] the exercise of such power by any person or entity to which such power has been delegated, over property to be used for economic development or over property that is subsequently used for economic development, if that State or political subdivision receives Federal economic development funds during any fiscal year in which it does so" (qtd. in § 2[a]). Violators are punished by the loss of all "Federal economic development funds for a period of 2 fiscal years" (qtd. in § 2[b]). Condemnation for "economic development" is broadly defined to include any taking that transfers property "from one private person or entity to another private person or entity for commercial enterprise carried on for profit, or to increase tax revenue, tax base, employment, or general economic health" (qtd. in § 8[1]).[93]

If adopted relatively intact by the Senate, the House bill might appear to create significant incentives to deter state and local governments from pursuing economic development takings. But any such appearance is deceptive because of the small amount of federal funds that offending state and local governments stand to lose.

States and localities that run afoul of the PRPA risk losing only "federal economic development funds," (109 H.R. 4218 § 2[b]) defined as "any Federal funds distributed to or through States or political subdivisions of States under Federal laws designed to improve or increase the size of economies of States or political subdivisions of States." The precise definition of "economic development funds" remains unclear, as it is difficult to tell precisely which federal programs are "designed to improve or increase the size of economies of States or political subdivisions of States" (at § 8[2]). A recent Congressional Research Service analysis concludes that the PRPA ultimately would delegate the task of identifying the relevant programs to the Attorney General (Meltz 2005).[94] It is hard to say whether the Bush administration or its successors would be willing to antagonize state and local governments by defining "economic development funds" broadly.

For present purposes, I count any grants to state and local governments that are designated as "development" programs in federal budget. The fiscal year 2005 federal budget defines only about 13.9 billion dollars of the annual total of the estimated 416.5 billion dollars in federal grants to states as designated for purposes of "community and regional development" (United States Government Budget Fiscal Year 2005, 123–30, Table 8–4).[95] This amount includes 3.5 billion dollars in "homeland security" grants and over 3 billion dollars in "emergency preparedness and response," (at 125, Table 8–4) funds that are unlikely to be categorized as "economic development" grants. Thus, it would seem that PRPA applies to at most just 7.4 billion dollars in federal grants to state and local governments, a mere 1.8 percent of all federal grants to states and localities.[96]

In some areas, of course, economic development grants might constitute an atypically large share of the local budget. So there are likely to be some parts of the country where PRPA has real bite. However, this effect is likely to be diminished by the ease with which offending localities can escape the sanction of loss of funding.

State or local authorities that run afoul of PRPA can avoid *all* loss of federal funds so long as they "return...all property the taking of which was found by a court of competent jurisdiction to have constituted a violation of the act" and replace or repair property damaged or destroyed "as a result of such violation" (109 H.R. 4128, § 2[c]). Thus, condemning authorities have an incentive to roll the dice on economic development takings projects in the hope that defendants will not contest the condemnation or will fail to raise the PRPA as a defense.[97] At worst, the offending government can simply give up the project, leaving itself and whatever private interests it sought to benefit not much worse off than they were to begin with. So long as it returns the condemned property, any such government stands to lose only the time and effort expended in litigation and the funds necessary to repair or pay for any property that has been damaged or destroyed.

While the PRPA may have some beneficial effects in deterring economic development condemnations in communities with an unusually high level of dependence on federal economic development funds, its impact if enacted is likely to be quite limited.

## The Bond Amendment

The Bond Amendment was enacted into law on November 30, 2005, as an amendment to the Transportation, Housing and Urban Development, District of Columbia, and Independent Agencies Appropriations Act. It forbids the use of funds allocated in the Act to "support" the use of eminent domain for "economic development that primarily benefits private entities" (P.L. 109–115, § 726 [enacted into law November 30, 2005]).[98]

For three interrelated reasons, the Bond Amendment is likely to have very little impact on the use of eminent domain by state and local governments. First, the Amendment forbids only those economic development takings that "primarily benefit...private entities" (qtd. in § 726). This restriction makes it possible for the condemning jurisdiction to argue that the primary benefit of the development will go to the public. Under *Kelo's* extremely lenient standards for evaluating government claims that takings create public benefits,[99] it is unlikely that such an argument will often fail in federal court.

Second, the Bond Amendment completely exempts condemnations for:

> mass transit, railroad, airport, seaport, or highway projects, as well as utility projects which benefit or serve the general public...other structures designated for use by the general public or which have other common-carrier or public-utility functions that serve the general public and are subject to regulation and oversight by the government, and projects for the removal of blight...or brownfields (qtd. in § 726).

While many of these exceptions are unproblematic because they fall within the traditional public use categories of facilities owned by the government or available for use by the general public as a matter of legal right, the listing of "utility projects which benefit...the general public" (qtd. in § 726) might open up the door to at least some private economic development projects.

Finally, an additional reason why the Bond Amendment's impact is likely to be small is that very few projects that do not fall within one of the Amendment's many exceptions are likely to be funded by federal transportation and housing grants in any event. The law completely excludes from coverage "mass transit" and "highway projects" and also excludes "the removal of blight" (which would presumably allow the use of eminent domain to build new housing in poor neighborhoods). There are few if any eminent domain projects previously funded by federal transportation or housing grants that the bill would actually forbid.

## President Bush's June 23, 2006 Executive Order

On June 23, 2006, the one year anniversary of the *Kelo* decision, President George W. Bush issued an executive order that purported to bar federal involvement in *Kelo*-style takings. On the surface, the order seems to forbid federal agencies from undertaking economic development condemnations. But its wording undercuts this goal. The key part of the order reads:

It is the policy of the United States to protect the rights of Americans to their private property, including by limiting the taking of private property by the Federal Government to situations in which the taking is for public use, with just compensation, and for the purpose of benefiting the general public and not merely for the purpose of advancing the economic interest of private parties to be given ownership or use of the property taken (Bush, Executive Order 13406).

Read carefully, the order does not in fact bar condemnations that transfer property to other private parties for economic development. Instead, it permits them to continue so long as they are "for the purpose of benefiting the general public and not merely for the purpose of advancing the economic interest of private parties to be given ownership or use of the property taken" (Bush, Executive Order 13406, Section 1).

Unfortunately, this language validates virtually any economic development condemnation that the feds might want to pursue. Officials can (and do) always claim that the goal of a taking is to benefit "the general public" and not "merely" the new owners. This is not a new pattern, but one that bedeviled takings litigation long before *Kelo*. Indeed, the New London authorities made such claims in *Kelo* itself and they were accepted by all nine Supreme Court justices, including the four dissenters, as well as by the Connecticut Supreme Court (including *its* three dissenters). The justices reached this conclusion despite considerable evidence that the takings were instigated by the Pfizer Corporation, which at the time hoped to benefit from them. Nonetheless, the courts accepted New London's claims that its officials acted in good faith, since they could have been intending to benefit the public as well as Pfizer.[100]

Even had President Bush's order been better worded, its impact would have been limited. The vast majority of economic development condemnations are undertaken by state and local governments, not by federal agencies. Nonetheless, it is noteworthy that the Bush Administration apparently chose to issue an executive order that is almost certain to have no effect even in the rare instances where the federal government does involve itself in *Kelo*-like takings.

## EXPLAINING THE PATTERN

Why, in the face of the massive public backlash against *Kelo*, has there been so much ineffective legislation? At this early date, it is difficult to provide a definitive answer. However, I would tentatively suggest that the weaknesses of much post-*Kelo* legislation are in large part due to widespread public ignorance. Survey data developed for this article show that the overwhelming majority of citizens know little or nothing about post-*Kelo* reform laws in their states. This widespread ignorance may well account for the ineffectiveness of many of the new laws. It also helps account for several other aspects of the *Kelo* backlash, including its timing and the relatively greater effectiveness of laws enacted by referenda relative to those adopted through the legislative process.

## PUBLIC IGNORANCE AND POST-*KELO* REFORM LAWS

### The Saint Index Survey Data

As noted earlier,[101] the majority of voters are "rationally ignorant" about most aspects of public policy because there is so little chance that an increase in any one voter's knowledge would have a significant impact on policy outcomes. No matter how knowledgeable a voter becomes, the chance that his or her better-informed vote will actually swing an electoral outcome is infinitesimally small. There is, therefore, very little incentive for most citizens to acquire information about politics and public policy, at least so long as their only reason to do so is to become better-informed voters.[102]

Recent survey data compiled at my request by the Saint Consulting Group, a firm that sponsors surveys on land use policy, confirm the hypothesis that most Americans have little or no knowledge of post-*Kelo* reform. The data compiled in table 7.6 are based on an August 2007 Saint Index national survey. They show that political ignorance about post-*Kelo* reform is widespread. Only 13 percent of respondents could both correctly answer whether or not their states had enacted eminent domain reform laws since 2005, and correctly answer a follow-up question about whether or not those laws were likely to be effective in preventing condemnations for economic development.[103] Only 21 percent could even correctly answer the first question in the sequence: whether or not their state had enacted eminent domain reform since *Kelo* was decided in 2005.[104]

It is also important to recognize that 6 percent of respondents believed that their states had enacted post-*Kelo* reforms that were likely to be "effective" in reducing economic development takings even though the state in fact had not. This is not a large number in absolute terms, but it still represents more than one-third of the 17 percent of respondents who expressed any opinion at all about the effectiveness of their state's reforms.[105] An additional 2 percent wrongly believed that their states' reform laws were ineffective even though the opposite was in fact true. Even among the small minority of Americans who paid close enough attention to post-*Kelo* reform legislation to have an opinion about its effectiveness, there was a high degree of ignorance.[106]

Table 7.6 indicates that ignorance about state post-*Kelo* reform cut across gender, racial, and political lines. Some 85 percent of men and 90 percent of women are ignorant about the condition of post-*Kelo* reform, as were 82 percent of African-Americans, 89 percent of whites, and similar overwhelming majorities of liberals and conservatives, Democrats and Republicans, and other groups. It is difficult to avoid the conclusion that most Americans were ignorant about the mere existence or lack thereof of post-*Kelo* reform in their states, and even fewer could tell whether the reform was effective or not.

The Saint Index data may even understate the amount of ignorance about post-*Kelo* reform. Some respondents may have gotten the right answers by guessing. In order to get a correct answer, respondents living in the eight states that have not passed any post-*Kelo* reform needed only to get one binary question and had a 50 percent chance of getting the right answer through random guessing; those living in the

Table 7.6　Public Knowledge of State Post-*Kelo* Reform

|  | Group | % Unaware of the Condition of Post-Kelo Reform in Their State[a] |
|---|---|---|
|  | Total | 87 |
| Gender | Male | 85 |
|  | Female | 90 |
| Racial/ Ethnic[b] Group | White | 89 |
|  | African American | 82 |
|  | Asian | 75 |
|  | Hispanic/Latino | 100 |
|  | Native American | 75 |
| Party Affiliation | Democrat | 89 |
|  | Independent | 83 |
|  | Republican | 89 |
| Ideology | Liberal | 88 |
|  | Moderate | 90 |
|  | Conservative | 87 |

*Notes*: [a] Calculated from answers to Saint Index August 2007 survey, questions 9 and 10. For question wording, see appendix B. I counted as "correct" those respondents who both (1) knew whether or not their states had passed post-*Kelo* eminent domain reform laws and (2) correctly answered the question about whether or not those laws were effective. Respondents from the eight states that had not enacted any post-*Kelo* laws at all were counted as giving correct answers to both questions if they correctly answered the first question by stating that their states had not adopted any reforms. Totals have been rounded off to the nearest whole number. The State of Utah presented a difficult methodological dilemma because it had banned economic development takings prior to *Kelo*. In the results in table 7.5, it is coded as having "effective" reforms and respondents who gave that answer were credited with a "correct" response. Coding the Utah results the other way does not significantly alter the overall results because of the extremely low number of Utah respondents in the sample.
[b] The results for Hispanics, Asians, and Native Americans may be unreliable because based on very small sample sizes of 24, 12, and 12 respondents respectively.

42 states that have passed reform laws needed to get two such questions correct, and thus had a 25 percent chance of doing so through random guessing.[107] Past research shows that many survey respondents will guess in order to avoid admitting ignorance about the subject matter of a poll question, and that may have happened in this case as well.[108] An additional factor biasing the knowledge levels found in the Saint Index survey upward is the fact that the pollsters only surveyed Americans over the age of 21. Political knowledge is generally correlated with age (Delli Carpini, and Keeter, 1996, 70; Somin 2004a), and young adults (people aged 18–29) have the highest incidence of ignorance of any age group.[109] The exclusion of 18–20 year olds from the sample reduces the representation of this group in the aggregate data.

The fact that most citizens are ignorant about post-*Kelo* reform is not surprising to researchers. Large majorities know little or nothing about far more important policies. For example, polls conducted around the time of the 2004 election showed that 70 percent of Americans did not know that Congress had recently enacted a massive prescription drug bill, and 58 percent admitted that they knew little or nothing about the controversial USA Patriot Act (Somin 2004c, Table 1). What may be somewhat surprising—especially to nonexpert observers—is that ignorance is so widespread despite the immense public outcry that the issue has generated.

## POSSIBLE ALTERNATIVE EXPLANATIONS OF THE DATA CONSISTENT WITH THE CLAIM THAT VOTERS WERE ADEQUATELY INFORMED

There are several possible objections to my theory that the Saint Index data prove the existence of widespread ignorance about post-*Kelo* reform that undermine the ability of voters to force through the sorts of policies favored by overwhelming majorities. I consider four such potential objections here and tentatively conclude that none of them withstand close scrutiny.

### a. The Possibility of Respondent Forgetting

Because post-*Kelo* reforms were enacted over a two-year period between the time *Kelo* was decided in June 2005 and the time the Saint Index data was collected in August 2007, it is conceivable that voters were well informed of the contents of their state's legislation at the time but later forgot that knowledge. To test that hypothesis, I checked to see whether respondents from Connecticut, Maryland, Montana, Nevada, New Mexico, Ohio, Virginia, and Wyoming, the eight states whose post-*Kelo* laws were enacted in 2007 had greater knowledge than those in states where reform legislation passed in 2005 and 2006. Two of these states, Nevada and Ohio passed their second post-*Kelo* reform laws during this time period. The eight states in question all enacted eminent domain reform laws between February 28 and July 10, 2007, just a few months or weeks before the Saint Index survey was conducted from August 1 to August 10, 2007.[110] The data show that the 122 respondents from those eight states had almost exactly the same knowledge levels as those in the rest of the country. Twenty-six percent of respondents in the eight 2007 states knew whether or not their states had passed post-*Kelo* reform laws, a figure only slightly higher than the 20 percent rate compiled by respondents from the other 44 states.[111] Similarly, 12 percent of respondents in these eight states could correctly answer both the question about the existence of reform laws and that about their effectiveness; the figure for the other 44 states was 13 percent.[112] While some forgetting could have taken place even in the few weeks between the passage of the 2007 laws and the time of the Saint Index survey, one would still expect that respondents in the eight states would be less likely to forget than those in states that had enacted their reforms earlier. The lack of any statistical differences between the two sets of respondents suggests that forgetting is not a major factor in accounting for the widespread ignorance revealed in the 2007 Saint Index data. Other data also show that those voters who do acquire political knowledge tend to retain it for many years.[113]

### b. The "Issue Public" Hypothesis

Public ignorance about post-*Kelo* reform might also be less bleak than I suggest if those who cared about the issue strongly were mostly well informed about it. This scenario would be consistent with the "issue public" hypothesis advanced by political scientists, which holds that citizens are likely to be well informed about a small number of issues that they care about intensely even if they remain ignorant about most others.[114] However, survey data show that the percentage of the public who care intensely about eminent domain reform is much greater than the mere 13 percent who know enough about it to be able to determine whether their states have passed effective post-*Kelo* laws or not. As discussed in Part I, 63 percent of respondents in a 2005 Saint Index survey said that they "strongly" opposed the *Kelo* decision. A 2006 Saint Index poll question showed that 43 percent "strongly" support reforms intended to ban economic development takings (Somin 2007b, 1940, Table 2). Even the smaller of these two figures is still almost four times greater than the percentage of respondents who knew whether or not their states had passed effective reforms as of the time of the August 2007 Saint Index survey.

Political ignorance greatly reduces the number of voters who could potentially use the level of post-*Kelo* reform in their state as a basis for electoral decisions. In other words, it greatly diminishes the size of the potential "issue public." Even if the 13 percent who gave accurate answers on the survey all feel strongly about the issue and make effective use of that knowledge in deciding which candidates to support in state and local elections, that still leaves several times that number of citizens who also feel strongly about banning economic development takings but lack the necessary knowledge to reward political leaders who support effective reform and punish those who oppose it.

## c. The "Miracle of Aggregation"

A third potentially benign interpretation of widespread ignorance of post-*Kelo* reform is the "miracle of aggregation."[115] Even if many or most voters are ignorant about a particular issue, that may be irrelevant to political outcomes if their errors are randomly distributed. In that situation, ignorance-driven votes for Candidate or policy A would be offset by a similar number of "mistaken" votes for alternative B, and electoral outcomes would be determined by the (potentially very small) minority of well-informed citizens.

With respect to post-*Kelo* reform, there are two serious problems with this scenario. First, even random error is likely to have an important impact on policy. Second, the errors are not in fact randomly distributed, but are skewed toward overestimation of the effectiveness of post-*Kelo* reform laws.

Even if errors really are randomly distributed, the existence of widespread ignorance still greatly diminishes the number of voters who can take account of post-*Kelo* reform in choosing candidates. It likely eliminates at least 70 percent of those voters who "strongly" support a ban on economic development takings.[116] This greatly reduces the potential pressure on officeholders to comply with overwhelming popular sentiment. If, for example, 10 percent of the 43 percent of Americans who say they strongly support effective post-*Kelo* reform would be willing to vote on the issue if they were informed about it, ignorance will have reduced the number willing to change their vote based on the issue from 4.3 percent of the adult population to a maximum of 1.3 percent.[117] And even that figure unrealistically assumes that the 13 percent with accurate knowledge of post-*Kelo* reform in their states were all drawn from among the 43 percent who care "strongly" about banning economic development takings.

It is also important to recognize that respondent mistakes about post-*Kelo* reform are not randomly distributed. It is far more common for voters to believe that their state has passed effective reform even if it has not than for them to believe that it has not done so in cases where it actually has. As discussed above,[118] some 6 percent of the 2007 Saint Index survey respondents wrongly believe that their state passed effective reform, whereas only 2 percent mistakenly believe that their state has failed to enact effective reform, even though it has. The 6 percent figure may not seem high in and of itself. But it constitutes more than one third of all those respondents (17 percent) who had any opinion on the effectiveness of post-*Kelo* reform in their states at all. Unfortunately, it is impossible to use the 2007 Saint Index data to determine whether these 17 percent were disproportionately drawn from the subset of respondents most interested in post-*Kelo* reform issues. However, it is plausible that they were. If so, it is possible that the 6 percent of respondents who mistakenly believe that their state has passed effective post-*Kelo* reform constitute a substantial percentage of those who would otherwise use the issue as a criterion for voting. Their ignorance deprived them of the opportunity to use their votes to reward politicians who support effective reform and punish those who oppose it.

### d. Opinion Leaders as Sources of Information

Finally, it is possible that voters could learn about the effectiveness or lack thereof of post-*Kelo* laws by relying on the statements of interest groups and other "opinion leaders" who have incentives to be better informed than ordinary citizens.[119] However, as I have argued at greater length elsewhere, (e.g. Somin 1999) reliance on opinion leaders itself requires considerable knowledge, including the knowledge needed to select opinion leaders to follow who are both knowledgeable and reliable. Moreover, the ways in which the *Kelo* issue cuts across traditional party and ideological lines makes it more difficult for voters to identify opinion leaders to follow based on traditional political cues, such as partisan or ideological affiliation.[120] In addition, the failure of the opinion leader "information shortcut" to alleviate ignorance on less complex and more important issues[121] than post-*Kelo* reform suggests that it will be of only limited utility in this case. Most important of all, the widespread ignorance revealed in the Saint Index survey shows that most citizens either did not acquire relevant information from opinion leaders or obtained information that turned out to be misleading about the true effectiveness of reform laws in their states.

## POLITICAL IGNORANCE AS AN EXPLANATION FOR THE ANOMALIES OF THE BACKLASH

The political ignorance hypothesis gains traction from the fact that it can account for three otherwise anomalous aspects of the *Kelo* controversy: the massive backlash against a decision that largely reaffirmed existing case law that had previously excited little public controversy; the paucity of effective reform measures despite widespread public opposition to economic development takings; and the striking divergence between citizen-initiated referendum initiatives and all other types of post-*Kelo* reform measures.

### Explaining the Timing of the *Kelo* Backlash

Some *Kelo* defenders complain that the backlash to the decision was grossly excessive in light of the fact that the case made little change in existing law.[122] After all, eminent domain was not a prominent national issue before *Kelo*, even though existing constitutional doctrine permitted economic development takings under the federal Constitution. A spokesman for the California Redevelopment Association lamented that *Kelo* had led to "a hue and cry about how bad things are in California, yet *Kelo* changed nothing."[123] But the reaction is understandable once we recognize that— for most of the public—*Kelo* was probably the first inkling they ever had that private property could be condemned merely to promote "economic development" by other private parties. This sudden realization led to outrage and a desire for change. Public ignorance helps explain why economic development takings could become so common despite the fact that the vast majority of citizens oppose condemnation of private property for such purposes (§ I.B.). It is likely that, prior to *Kelo,* most of the public did not even realize that economic development condemnations exist. The public ignorance hypothesis is the only explanation I know of for the suddenness of the *Kelo* backlash. It also helps explain why there was relatively little public pressure to reform eminent domain law before *Kelo.*

## Explaining the Paucity of Effective Reform Laws

Public ignorance is also the best available explanation for the seeming scarcity of effective post-*Kelo* reform laws. The highly publicized Supreme Court decision apparently increased awareness of the problem of eminent domain abuse, perhaps as a result of extensive press coverage. But while the publicity surrounding *Kelo* made much of the public at least somewhat aware of the issue of economic development takings, it probably did not lead voters to closely scrutinize the details of proposed reform legislation. The Saint Index survey showed that almost 80 percent of Americans do not even know whether their state has passed a reform law at all.

Few citizens have the time or inclination to delve into such matters and many are often ignorant of the very existence of even the most important legislative items.[124] Thus, it would not be difficult for state legislators to seek to satisfy voter demands by supporting "position-taking" legislation that purported to curb eminent domain,[125] while in reality having little effect. In this way, they can simultaneously cater to public outrage over *Kelo* and mollify developers and other interest groups that benefit from economic development condemnations.

This strategy seems to have been at the root of the failure of post-*Kelo* reform efforts in California. In that state, legislative reform efforts were initially sidetracked by the introduction of weak proposals that gave legislators "a chance . . . to side with anti-eminent domain sentiment without doing any real damage to redevelopment agencies."[126] At a later stage in the political battle, the Democratic majority in the state legislature tabled even these modest reforms by claiming that they were being blocked by the Republican minority, despite the fact that "the stalled bills required only simple majority votes and thus needed no Republicans to go along." As one Sacramento political reporter puts it, the entire process may have been "just a feint to pretend to do something about eminent domain without actually doing anything to upset the apple cart."[127] Eventually, California did enact some reforms, but only ones that are almost completely ineffective (See § II.A.1.b.i).[128] A leading advocate for eminent domain reform in Nevada also believes that, in his state as well, legislators sought to "look good while not upsetting anyone" (Interview with Steven Miller, Nevada Policy Research Institute, Mar. 14, 2007).[129]

As of the time of this writing the California League of Cities, an organization composed of local governments with an interest in preserving their eminent domain authority, has also sought to exploit political ignorance about post-*Kelo* reform. The CLC has succeeded in placing an essentially meaningless eminent domain "reform" referendum initiative on the state's 2008 ballot as a way of pre-empting a potential stronger referendum initiative sponsored by property rights advocates. The CLC initiative cleverly includes a provision stating that it would supersede any other eminent domain referendum enacted on the same day, so long as the latter gets fewer votes than the CLC proposal.[130]

Such maneuvers would be difficult to bring off if the public paid close attention to pending legislation. But they can be quite effective in the presence of widespread political ignorance. Unfortunately, public ignorance of the details of eminent domain policy is unlikely to be easily remedied.

A possible alternative explanation for the scarcity of effective reform laws is the political power of developers and other organized interest groups that benefit from the transfer of property condemned as a result of economic development and blight condemnations.[131] There is little question that this factor does play a role. Developers, local government planning officials, and other interest groups have indeed spearheaded opposition to post-*Kelo* reform (Sandefur 2006, 769–72). In Texas, for example, advocates of strong eminent domain reform concluded that lobbying by developers and local governments played a key role in ensuring that that state passed an essentially toothless reform law (Interview with Brooke Rollins, Texas Public Policy Foundation, March 17, 2007).

However, the mere existence of interest group opposition does not explain why state legislators would choose to satisfy a few small interest groups while going against the preferences of the vast majority of the electorate (See survey data cited in §I.B). It is possible that the pro-condemnation interest groups simply have more intense preferences about the issue than most of the opponents in the general public, and are therefore more likely to cast their votes based on politicians' stances on the issue. However, 63 percent of the respondents in the 2005 Saint Index survey said that they not only opposed *Kelo,* but felt "strongly" about it; more recent survey data shows that 43 percent of Americans "strongly" support reform legislation banning economic development takings (Somin 2007b, 1940, Table 2). If even a fraction of that 63 percent were willing to let post-*Kelo* reform influence their voting decisions, they would probably constitute a much larger voting bloc than all the pro-*Kelo* developers and government officials put together.

For this reason, it is likely that, to the extent that interest group opposition was able to stymie effective post-*Kelo* reform and force the passage of merely cosmetic legislation, this result occurred only because most ordinary voters are unaware of what is happening. Political ignorance is the handmaiden of interest group power in the political process. Absent widespread ignorance, interest groups at odds with the majority of the general public would find it more difficult to block eminent domain reform.

## EXPLAINING THE RELATIVE SUCCESS OF CITIZEN-INITIATED REFERENDUM INITIATIVES

As we have already seen, there is a great difference between the effectiveness of citizen-initiated referendum initiatives, and all other types of post-*Kelo* reforms. All four of the latter provide significant protection for property owners against economic development takings. By contrast, only 14 of 34 state legislative initiatives are comparably effective, and only two of six legislature-initiated referenda (Data compiled from table 7.3.) Reforms initiated by Congress and the President at the federal level are also largely cosmetic in nature (See § I.B).

The likely explanation for this striking pattern is consistent with the political ignorance hypothesis. Citizen-initiated referendum proposals are usually drafted by activists rather than by elected officials and their staffs. This was the case with all four of the post-*Kelo* citizen-initiated referenda enacted in 2006.[132] Unlike state legislators, the property rights activists who wrote the citizen-initiated anti-*Kelo* ballot initiatives have no need to appease powerful pro-condemnation interest groups in order to improve reelection chances. And they usually have little reason to promote reforms that fail to produce real changes in policy. Unlike ordinary citizens, committed activists in a position to draft referendum proposals and get them on the ballot have strong incentives to acquire detailed information about eminent domain law, since they have a real chance of influencing policy outcomes through their actions.

Obviously, property rights activists can and do attempt to influence legislatively enacted reforms as well. However, in this scenario, anything they propose is likely to be filtered through the legislative process, where organized interest groups will inevitably get a strong say.

The political ignorance hypothesis does not completely explain the pattern we have observed. For example, it does not account for the fact that a few state legislatures, notably Florida, enacted strong reforms. However, it is more consistent with the available evidence than any alternative theory proposed so far. Certainly, it is better supported than either the argument that interest groups have successfully stymied reform or the theory that elected officials will have little choice but to yield to the broad consensus of public opinion. Further research will be necessary to fully test the political ignorance hypothesis and compare it to rival theories.

## CONCLUSION

So far, the *Kelo* backlash has yielded far less effective reform than many expected. This result is striking in light of the overwhelming public opposition to the decision. Critics of *Kelo* will lament the result, while defenders may be heartened by it. Both can agree that the anti-*Kelo* backlash has not turned out to be a complete substitute for strong judicial enforcement of public use limits on eminent domain.

The evidence also supports the tentative conclusion that the relative paucity of effective reforms is in large part a result of widespread political ignorance. This hypothesis is the only one proposed so far that can account for the conjunction of three anomalies: the sudden and massive public outrage against *Kelo*, despite the fact that the decision made few changes in existing law; the scarcity of effective reforms, despite deep and broad public opposition to economic development takings; and the striking divergence between citizen-initiated referenda and all post-*Kelo* laws enacted by other means. It is also supported by recent Saint Index survey data documenting widespread public ignorance of post-*Kelo* reform.

There is also much room for future research. For example, scholars should make a systematic effort to explain why a few state legislatures, notably Florida, enacted very strong post-*Kelo* reforms. The political response to *Kelo* is a striking example of public backlash against an unpopular judicial decision. It also shows that backlash politics has its limits.

# APPENDIX A
## ADDITIONAL TABLES

**Table 7A.1**  Post-*Kelo* Reform in States Ranked by Number of "Threatened" Private-to-Private Condemnations

| State | Number of Threatened Takings[a] | Effectiveness of Reform[b] |
|---|---|---|
| **Florida** | **2,055** | **Effective (L & LR)** |
| Maryland | 1,110 | Ineffective (L) |
| California | 635 | Ineffective (L) |
| New Jersey | 589 | No Reform |
| Missouri | 437 | Ineffective (L) |
| Ohio | 331 | Ineffective (L) |
| **Michigan** | **173** | **Effective (L & LR)** |
| Utah | 167 | Enacted Prior to *Kelo* |
| Kentucky | 161 | Ineffective (L) |
| Texas | 118 | Ineffective (L) |
| Colorado | 114 | Ineffective (L) |
| **Pennsylvania** | **108** | **Effective (L)** |
| New York | 89 | No Reform |
| **Minnesota** | **83** | **Effective (L)** |
| Rhode Island | 65 | No Reform |
| Connecticut | 61 | Ineffective (L) |
| **Indiana** | **51** | **Effective (L)** |
| Arkansas | 40 | No Reform |
| Tennessee | 37 | Ineffective (L) |
| **Virginia** | **27** | **Effective (L)** |
| **Nevada** | **15** | **Effective (L & CR)** |
| Vermont | 15 | Ineffective (L) |
| West Virginia | 12 | Ineffective (L) |
| Nebraska | 11 | Ineffective (L) |
| Arizona | 10 | Effective (CR) |
| Illinois | 9 | Ineffective (L) |
| Kansas | 7 | Effective (L) |
| South Carolina | 7 | Ineffective (LR) |
| Hawaii | 5 | No Reform |
| Massachusetts | 4 | No Reform |
| Oregon | 2 | Effective (CR) |
| Delaware | 0 | Ineffective (L) |
| Georgia | 0 | Effective (L & LR) |
| Idaho | 0 | Effective (L) |
| South Dakota | 0 | Effective (L) |
| Wyoming | 0 | Effective (L) |
| Alabama | 0 | Effective (L) |
| Alaska | 0 | Ineffective (L) |
| Iowa | 0 | Ineffective (L) |
| Louisiana | 0 | Effective (LR) |
| Maine | 0 | Ineffective (L) |
| Mississippi | 0 | No Reform |
| Montana | 0 | Ineffective (L) |
| New Hampshire | 0 | Effective (L & LR) |
| New Mexico | 0 | Effective (L) |
| North Carolina | 0 | Ineffective (L) |

Continued

**Table 7A.1**  Continued

| State | Number of Threatened Takings[a] | Effectiveness of Reform[b] |
|---|---|---|
| North Dakota | 0 | Effective (CR) |
| Oklahoma | 0 | No Reform |
| Washington | 0 | No Reform |
| Wisconsin | 0 | Ineffective (L) |

*Notes*: L = Reform enacted by state legislature; CR = Reform enacted by citizen-initiated referendum; LR=Reform enacted by legislature-initiated referendum.

[a] The data on known eminent domain condemnations by state between from 1998–2002 is derived from Dana Berliner's study, *Public Power, Private Gain: A Five Year, State-by-State Report Examining the Abuse of Eminent Domain*, 196 (2003), *available at http://www.castlecoalition.org/publications/report/index. html* (last visited January 18, 2007).

[b] As of January 2008.

**Table 7A.2**  Post-*Kelo* Reform in States Ranked by Number of Private-to-Private Condemnations per 1 Million People

| State | Population[a] | Takings/1M People[b] | Effectiveness of Reform[c] |
|---|---|---|---|
| **Pennsylvania** | **12,429,616** | **202.5** | **Effective (L)** |
| **Kansas** | **2,744,687** | **56.5** | **Effective (L)** |
| Maryland | 5,600,388 | 22.7 | Ineffective (L) |
| **Michigan** | **10,120,860** | **13.6** | **Effective (L & LR)** |
| Rhode Island | 1,076,189 | 11.2 | No Reform |
| Connecticut | 3,510,297 | 8.8 | Ineffective (L) |
| Ohio | 11,464,042 | 7.9 | Ineffective (L) |
| **Virginia** | **7,567,465** | **7.7** | **Effective (L)** |
| Oklahoma | 3,547,884 | 6.5 | No Reform |
| California | 36,132,147 | 6.2 | Ineffective (L) |
| New Jersey | 8,717,925 | 5.9 | No Reform |
| Tennessee | 5,962,959 | 4.9 | Ineffective (L) |
| Colorado | 4,665,177 | 4.9 | Ineffective (L) |
| **Florida** | **17,789,864** | **3.8** | **Effective (L & LR)** |
| Missouri | 5,800,310 | 3.1 | Ineffective (L) |
| New York | 19,254,630 | 3 | No Reform |
| Arizona | 5,939,292 | 1.9 | Effective (CR) |
| **Minnesota** | **5,132,799** | **1.8** | **Effective (L)** |
| **Alabama** | **4,557,808** | **1.8** | **Effective (L)** |
| Washington | 6,287,759 | 1.7 | No Reform |
| Kentucky | 4,173,405 | 1.7 | Ineffective (L) |
| North Dakota | 636,677 | 1.6 | Effective (CR) |
| Maine | 1,321,505 | 1.5 | Ineffective (L) |
| Iowa | 2,966,334 | 1.3 | Ineffective (L) |
| Nevada | 2,414,807 | 1.2 | Effective (L & CR) |
| Louisiana | 4,523,628 | 1.1 | Effective (LR) |
| Mississippi | 2,921,088 | 1 | No Reform |
| Massachusetts | 6,398,743 | 0.8 | No Reform |
| Illinois | 12,763,371 | 0.6 | Ineffective (L) |
| Indiana | 6,271,973 | 0.6 | Effective (L) |
| Nebraska | 1,758,787 | 0.6 | Ineffective (L) |
| Texas | 22,859,968 | 0.5 | Ineffective (L) |

Continued

**Table 7A.2**  Continued

| State | Population[a] | Takings/1M People[b] | Effectiveness of Reform[c] |
|---|---|---|---|
| Arkansas | 2,779,154 | 0.4 | No Reform |
| North Carolina | 8,683,242 | 0.1 | Ineffective (L) |
| Alaska | 663,661 | 0 | Ineffective (L) |
| Delaware | 843,524 | 0 | Ineffective (L) |
| Georgia | 9,072,576 | 0 | Effective (L & LR) |
| Idaho | 1,429,096 | 0 | Effective (L) |
| South Dakota | 775,933 | 0 | Effective (L) |
| Wyoming | 509,294 | 0 | Effective (L) |
| Hawaii | 1,275,194 | 0 | No Reform |
| Montana | 935,670 | 0 | Ineffective (L) |
| New Hampshire | 1,309,940 | 0 | Effective (L & LR) |
| New Mexico | 1,928,384 | 0 | Effective (L) |
| Oregon | 3,641,056 | 0 | Effective (CR) |
| South Carolina | 4,255,083 | 0 | Ineffective (LR) |
| Utah | 2,469,585 | 0 | Enacted Prior to *Kelo* |
| Vermont | 623,050 | 0 | Ineffective (L) |
| West Virginia | 1,816,856 | 0 | Ineffective (L) |
| Wisconsin | 5,536,201 | 0 | Ineffective (L) |

*Notes*: L = Reform enacted by state legislature; CR = Reform enacted by citizen-initiated referendum; LR = Reform enacted by legislature-initiated referendum.

[a] *See U.S. Census Bureau: State and County Quick Facts.* Data derived from Population Estimates for 2005, available at http://www.census.gov/ (last visited January 18, 2007).

[b] Some takings affected more than one property.

[c] As of January 2008.

**Table 7A.3**  Post-*Kelo* Reform in States Ranked by Number of Threatened Private-to-Private Condemnations per 1 Million People

| State | Population[a] | Threatened Takings/ 1M People[b] | Effectiveness of Reform[c] |
|---|---|---|---|
| Maryland | 5,600,388 | 198.2 | Ineffective (L) |
| **Florida** | **17,789,864** | **115.5** | **Effective (L & LR)** |
| Missouri | 5,800,310 | 75.3 | Ineffective (L) |
| Utah | 2,469,585 | 67.6 | Enacted Prior to Kelo |
| New Jersey | 8,717,925 | 67.6 | No Reform |
| Rhode Island | 1,076,189 | 60.4 | No Reform |
| Kentucky | 4,173,405 | 38.6 | Ineffective (L) |
| Ohio | 11,464,042 | 28.9 | Ineffective (L) |
| Colorado | 4,665,177 | 24.4 | Ineffective (L) |
| Vermont | 623,050 | 24.1 | Ineffective (L) |
| California | 36,132,147 | 17.6 | Ineffective (L) |
| Connecticut | 3,510,297 | 17.4 | Ineffective (L) |
| **Michigan** | **10,120,860** | **17.1** | **Effective (L & LR)** |
| **Minnesota** | **5,132,799** | **16.2** | **Effective (L)** |
| Arkansas | 2,779,154 | 14.4 | No Reform |
| **Pennsylvania** | **12,429,616** | **8.7** | **Effective (L)** |
| **Indiana** | **6,271,973** | **8.1** | **Effective (L)** |
| West Virginia | 1,816,856 | 6.6 | Ineffective (L) |

Continued

**Table 7A.3**  Continued

| State | Population[a] | Threatened Takings/ 1M People[b] | Effectiveness of Reform[c] |
|---|---|---|---|
| Nebraska | 1,758,787 | 6.3 | Ineffective (L) |
| **Nevada** | **2,414,807** | **6.2** | **Effective (L & CR)** |
| Tennessee | 5,962,959 | 6.2 | Ineffective (L) |
| Texas | 22,859,968 | 5.2 | Ineffective (L) |
| New York | 19,254,630 | 4.6 | No Reform |
| Hawaii | 1,275,194 | 3.9 | No Reform |
| Virginia | 7,567,465 | 3.6 | Effective (L) |
| Kansas | 2,744,687 | 2.6 | Effective (L) |
| Arizona | 5,939,292 | 1.7 | Effective (CR) |
| South Carolina | 4,255,083 | 1.6 | Ineffective (LR) |
| Illinois | 12,763,371 | 0.7 | Ineffective (L) |
| Massachusetts | 6,398,743 | 0.6 | No Reform |
| Oregon | 3,641,056 | 0.5 | Effective (CR) |
| Delaware | 843,524 | 0.0 | Ineffective (L) |
| Georgia | 9,072,576 | 0.0 | Effective (L & LR) |
| Idaho | 1,429,096 | 0.0 | Effective (L) |
| South Dakota | 775,933 | 0.0 | Effective (L) |
| Wyoming | 509,294 | 0.0 | Effective (L) |
| Alabama | 4,557,808 | — | Effective (L) |
| Alaska | 663,661 | — | Ineffective (L) |
| Iowa | 2,966,334 | — | Ineffective (L) |
| Louisiana | 4,523,628 | — | Effective (LR) |
| Maine | 1,321,505 | — | Ineffective (L) |
| Mississippi | 2,921,088 | — | No Reform |
| Montana | 935,670 | — | Ineffective (L) |
| New Hampshire | 1,309,940 | — | Effective (L & LR) |
| New Mexico | 1,928,384 | — | Effective (L) |
| North Carolina | 8,683,242 | — | Ineffective (L) |
| North Dakota | 636,677 | — | Effective (CR) |
| Oklahoma | 3,547,884 | — | No Reform |
| Washington | 6,287,759 | — | No Reform |
| **Wisconsin** | **5,536,201** | **—** | **Ineffective (L)** |

*Notes*:  L = Reform enacted by state legislature; CR = Reform enacted by citizen-initiated referendum; LR = Reform enacted by legislature-initiated referendum.
[a] *See U.S. Census Bureau: State and County Quick Facts.* Data derived from Population Estimates for 2005, *available at* http://www.census.gov/ (last visited January 18, 2007).
[b] Some takings affected more than one property.
[c] As of January 2008.

# Appendix B
## 2007 Saint Index Survey Questions on Post-Kelo Reform

### Question 9

In 2005, the U.S. Supreme Court ruled that the government could take private property by eminent domain to give it to another private owner to promote economic development. Since that ruling, some states have passed new laws that restrict the government's power to take private property. Do you happen to know if your state is one of those that have passed such a law?

A. Yes, my state has enacted at least one such law
B. No, it has not enacted any laws like that
C. Don't know

## Question 10 (Asked Only of Those Who Chose Answer A on Question 9)

Do you think that the new laws in your state will be effective in preventing the condemnation of private property for economic development?
A. Very effective
B. Somewhat effective
C. Mostly ineffective
D. Completely ineffective
E. Don't know

*Note*: For purposes of table 7.6, I counted the first two answers as "effective" and the second two as "ineffective," and marked "don't know" as automatically mistaken. Respondents in states that had passed ineffective reforms were given credit for "correct" answers if they picked either C or D. Those in states with effective laws similarly counted as "correct" if they chose either A or B.

## NOTES

For helpful suggestions and comments, I would like to thank Bruce L. Benson, Dana Berliner, Steve Eagle, Jim Ely, Richard Epstein, Bruce Kobayashi, Andrew Koppelman, Janice Nadler, Paul Cargiuolo, Timothy Sandefur, and participants in the Northwestern University Law School Constitutional Law Colloqium, the George Mason University School of Law Levy Seminar, and the Florida State University conference on takings. Baran Alpturk, Susan Courtwright Rodriguez, Kari DiPalma, and Anthony Messuri provided valuable research assistance. Susan Courtwright Rodriguez deserves additional credit for helping to put together several of the tables in the Article. I would like also to thank the Saint Consulting Group for allowing me to use the data from their 2005 and 2006 Saint Index surveys, and particularly for permitting me to insert two questions about post-*Kelo* reform into their August 2007 survey.

1. For the most complete and up to date listing of state post-*Kelo* legislative initiatives see *Castle Coalition Enacted Legislation Since Kelo*. Retrieved February 3, 2008, from *http://www. castlecoalition.org/legislation/passed/index.html*. Other parts of the Web site also discuss proposed and enacted federal legislation.
2. The closest competitor is *Furman v. Georgia,* 408 U.S. 238 (1972), which struck down all then-existing state death penalty laws. In response, some 35 states and the federal government had enacted new death penalty statutes intended to conform to Furman's requirements between 1972 and 1976. See *Gregg v. Georgia,* 428 U.S. 153, 179–80 & n. 23 (1976) (noting that "at least 35 states" and the federal government had enacted new death penalty statutes in response to Furman, and listing the state laws in question).
3. See Posner 2005 (claiming that "the strong adverse public and legislative reactions to the *Kelo* decision" is a justification of the decision). At his confirmation hearing before the Senate, then-Judge John Roberts commented that the legislative reaction to *Kelo* shows that "this body [Congress] and legislative bodies in the states are protectors of the people's rights as well" and "can protect them in situations where the court has determined, as it did 5–4 in *Kelo,* that they are not going to draw that line." *The Washington Post, "Transcript: Day Three of the Roberts Confirmation Hearings,"* September 14, 2005.
4. See Sandefur 2006 for the most complete earlier analysis. Sandefur's article is an excellent contribution to the literature, but was written too soon to take account of the ten referendum initiatives enacted in 2006, as well as several legislative reforms enacted after the summer of

2006. I also provide a very different explanation of the pattern of effective and ineffective reforms than Sandefur does, as well as providing extensive public opinion data. A forthcoming article by Janice Nadler, Shari Diamond and Matthew Patton analyzes public opinion on *Kelo*, but does not examine the legislation passed as a result, and does not explain the three anomalies discussed in Part III of this paper. See Nadler, et al. forthcoming 2007. See also Campbell, et. al. 2007.

5. Because of submission deadlines and subsequent publication schedules, I was unable to include legislation enacted after January 2008 in this paper. I have considered several post-Kelo reform laws enacted since then in Somin 2009.

6. See Somin 2007a, where I address these issues at length.

7. Nader has been a longstanding critic of economic development takings. See, e.g., Nader and Hirsch 2004 (arguing that they should be banned in most cases). For his statement denouncing *Kelo*, see Nader 2005 (claiming that "the U.S. Supreme Court's decision in *Kelo v City of New London* mocks common sense, tarnishes constitutional law and is an affront to fundamental fairness.").

8. For Limbaugh's denunciation of *Kelo*, see Limbaugh 2005 (claiming that because of *Kelo*, "Government can kick the little guy out of his and her homes and sell those home to a big developer who's going to pay a higher tax base to the government. Well, that's not what the takings clause was about. It's not what it is about. It's just been bastardized, and it gets bastardized because you have justices on the court who will sit there and impose their personal policy preferences rather than try to get the original intent of the Constitution.").

9. See e.g., Erickson, et. al. 1993 (arguing that state public policy closely follows majority public opinion).

10. This figure does not include the state of Utah, which enacted effective eminent domain reform prior to *Kelo*.

11. See Somin 2004a (summarizing evidence of extensive voter ignorance); and Somin 1998.

12. For a more detailed discussion, see Somin 1998.

13. See the Saint Index Poll, August 2007, Center for Economic and Civic Opinion at University of Massachusetts/Lowell. The survey included 1000 respondents in a nationwide random sample.

14. For a more detailed discussion of *Kelo's* holding, from which this brief summary is drawn, see Somin 2007a.

15. See also Karlin 2005 (describing massive anti-*Kelo* backlash).

16. See, e.g., Limbaugh 2005 and note 7. The New London property owners were represented by the Institute for Justice, a prominent libertarian public interest law firm.

17. See Eric Kriss,"More Seek Curbs on Eminent Domain." *Syracuse Post-Standard*, July 31, 2005 (noting Clinton's opposition to the ruling).

18. See KSL TV [Salt Lake City]. *Howard Dean Comes to Utah to Discuss Politics*, July 16, 2005. Retrieved on December 5, 2006, from http://tv.ksl.com/index.php?nid=39&sid=219221 (quoting Dean as denouncing "a Republican appointed Supreme Court that decided they can take your house and put a Sheraton hotel in there").

19. See Charles Hurt, "Congress Assails Domain Ruling," *The Washington Times,* July 1, 2005 (quoting Waters denouncing *Kelo* as "the most un-American thing that can be done").

20. See references to table 7.1. The differences between the two surveys are likely due to a difference in question wording.

21. The Zogby survey question asked respondents whether they supported "the recent Supreme Court ruling that allowed a city in Connecticut to take the private property of one citizen and give it to another citizen to use for *private development?*" American Farm Bureau Federation Survey, October 29- November 2, 2005, Zogby International (emphasis added). This wording ignores the fact that the legal rationale for *Kelo* is that the takings are intended to promote "public" development. By contrast, the Saint Index survey asked respondents whether they agreed with the Court's decision "that local governments can take homes, business and private property to make way for private economic development if officials believe it *would benefit the public*." The Saint Index Poll 2005, Center for Economic and Civic Opinion at University of Massachusetts/Lowell (emphasis added).

22. See The Saint Index Poll 2005, Center for Economic and Civic Opinion at University of Massachusetts/Lowell and note 35.
23. Berliner was one of the two IJ lawyers who represented Susette Kelo and the other New London property owners.
24. See discussion of the Pennsylvania law in § II.A.2.
25. See discussion of the Michigan law in § II.A.2 and note 84.
26. See *County of Wayne v. Hathcock,* 684 N.W.2d 765 (Mich. 2004). For an analysis of *Hathcock,* see Somin 2004b. The new Michigan law does, however, go beyond *Hathcock* in limiting blight condemnations that might not have been prevented by the court decision. For analysis of the ambiguity of *Hathcock* on this score, see Somin 2004b, 1033–39.
27. See, for example, the discussion of the underestimation of the number of takings in Minnesota in § II.A.2.
28. See Utah Code § 17B-202–4 (amended March 21, 2005 by Utah Sen. Bill 184) (outlining powers of redevelopment agencies and omitting the power to use eminent domain for blight alleviation or development); See also Henry Lamb, "Utah Bans Eminent Domain Use by Redevelopment Agencies," *Environmental News,* June 1, 2005, available at http://www.heartland.org/article.cfm?artID=17162 (visited December 12, 2005) (describing the politics behind the Utah law). In March 2007, Utah partially rescinded its ban on blight condemnations. See Utah H.B. 365 (signed into law March 21, 2007) (permitting blight condemnations if approved by a supermajority of property owners in the affected area).
29. See generally Luce 2000 (describing definitions of blight used in various states). This article is slightly out of date because it does not account for the abolition of blight condemnations by Florida, New Mexico, and Utah, as well as the tightening of the definition of blight by other states in the aftermath of *Kelo.* See discussion of the relevant laws in this Article. See also Gordon 2004 (describing very broad use of blight designations to facilitate condemnation).
30. See Alaska H.B. 318 (Signed into law July 5, 2006) (exempting preexisting public uses declared in state law from a ban on economic development takings); Alaska Stat. § 18.55.950 (stating that "'blighted area' means an area, other than a slum area, that by reason of the predominance of defective or inadequate street layout, faulty lot layout in relation to size, adequacy, accessibility, or usefulness, unsanitary or unsafe conditions, deterioration of site or improvements, tax or special assessment delinquency exceeding the fair value of the land, improper subdivision or obsolete platting, or the existence of conditions that endanger life or property by fire and other causes, or any combination of these factors, substantially impairs or arrests the sound growth of the municipality, retards the provision of housing accommodations, or constitutes an economic or social liability and is a menace to the public health, safety, morals, or welfare in its condition and use.").
31. See Colorado H.B. 1411 (enacted into law June 6, 2006) (allowing condemnation for "eradication of blight"); Colo. Stat. § 31–25–103(2) (defining "blight" to include any condition that "substantially impairs or arrests the sound growth of the municipality, retards the provision of housing accommodations, or constitutes an economic or social liability, and is a menace to the public health, safety, morals, or welfare").
32. See Mo. S.B. 1944, § 523.271.2 (signed into law July 13, 2006) (exempting blight condemnations from ban on "economic development" takings); Mo. Stat. § 100.310(2) (defining "blight" as "an area which, by reason of the predominance of defective or inadequate street layout, insanitary or unsafe conditions, deterioration of site improvements, improper subdivision or obsolete platting, or the existence of conditions which endanger life or property by fire and other causes, or any combination of such factors, retards the provision of housing accommodations or constitutes an economic A recent Missouri Supreme Court decision has construed § 353.020 as requiring separate proof of "social liability" that goes beyond merely showing the existence of an "economic liability," in the sense of an obstacle to future growth and reduction of tax revenue. See *Centene Plaza Redev. Corp. v. Mint Properties,* 225 S.W. 3d 431 (Mo. 2007). The decision notes, however, that proof of the existence of "social liability" might be demonstrated by providing evidence "concerning the public health, safety, and welfare," which in this case was totally absent in the record (at 433–35). In any event, Missouri local governments also have the power to condemn property based on the definition of blight

in another statute that defines the concept as requiring proof of the existence of either an "economic" or a "social liability." See Mo. Stat. § 100.310(2) (defining "blight" as "an area which, by reason of the predominance of defective or inadequate street layout, insanitary or unsafe conditions, deterioration of site improvements, improper subdivision or obsolete platting, or the existence of conditions which endanger life or property by fire and other causes, or any combination of such factors, retards the provision of housing accommodations or constitutes an economic or social liability or a menace to the public health, safety, morals, or welfare in its present condition and use"); See *State ex rel. Atkinson v. Planned Indus. Expansion Authority of St. Louis*, 517 S.W.2d 36, 41 (Mo. 1975) (noting that industrial development projects undertaken in accordance with this section include the power to acquire property through the use of "eminent domain").

33. See Mont. S.B. 41, §§7–15–4206(2), 7–15–4206(2)(a) (signed into law May 8, 2007) (defining "blighted area" as "an area that is conducive to ill health, transmission of disease, infant mortality, juvenile delinquency, and crime; that substantially impairs or arrests the sound growth of the city or its environs; that retards the provision of housing accommodations; or that constitutes an economic or social liability or is detrimental or constitutes a menace to the public health, safety, welfare, and morals in its present condition and use by reason of "the substantial physical dilapidation; deterioration; age obsolescence, or defective construction, material, and arrangement of buildings or improvements, whether residential or nonresidential."); Mont. S.B. 363 (enacted into law May 16, 2007) (banning economic development condemnations, but retaining most of the broad definition of blight outlined in S.B. 41, § 7–15–4206(2)(a)).

34. See Neb. L.B. 924 (enacted into law April 13, 2006) (exempting "blight" condemnations from ban on economic development takings); Neb. Stat. § 18–2103 (defining blight as any area in a condition that "substantially impairs or arrests the sound growth of the community, retards the provision of housing accommodations, or constitutes an economic or social liability" and has "deteriorating" structures).

35. See N.C. H.B. 1965, § 2.1 (signed into law August 10, 2006) (exempting blight condemnations from restrictions on economic development takings and stating that "'Blighted area' shall mean an area in which there is a predominance of buildings or improvements (or which is predominantly residential in character), and which, by reason of dilapidation, deterioration, age or obsolescence, inadequate provision for ventilation, light, air, sanitation, or open spaces, high density of population and overcrowding, unsanitary or unsafe conditions, or the existence of conditions which endanger life or property by fire and other causes, or any combination of such factors, substantially impairs the sound growth of the community, is conducive to ill health, transmission of disease, infant mortality, juvenile delinquency and crime, and is detrimental to the public health, safety, morals or welfare.").

36. See 2005 Ohio S.B. 167 § 1(exempting "blight" condemnations from temporary moratorium on economic development takings); Oh. Rev. Code § 303.26(E) (defining blight to include ""deterioration" of structures or where the site "substantially impairs or arrests the sound growth of a county, retards the provision of housing accommodations, or constitutes an economic or social liability and is a menace to the public health, safety, morals, or welfare"). This language is retained in Ohio's more recent 2007 reform law. See 2007 Ohio Amended S.B. 7 (enacted into law July 10, 2007), § 1(A) (repeating this language). The new bill also requires that a "blighted parcel" meet at least two of 17 different conditions. Id., §1(B). However, these include such vague and general criteria as "deterioration," "age and obsolescence," "faulty lot layout," being "located in an area of defective or inadequate street layout," and "overcrowding of buildings." Virtually any area is likely to meet two or more of these criteria.

37. See Tex. S.B. 7B (enacted into law September 1, 2005) (exempting "blight" condemnations from ban on economic development takings); Tex. Local Gov. Code § 374 (defining a blighted area as one that "because of deteriorating buildings, structures, or other improvements; defective or inadequate streets, street layout, or accessibility; unsanitary conditions; or other hazardous conditions, adversely affects the public health, safety, morals, or welfare . . . or results in an economic or social liability to the municipality").

38. See 2006 Vt. S.B. 246 (exempting blight condemnations from ban on economic development takings, and defining blight to include any planning or layout condition that "substantially impairs or arrests the sound growth of a municipality, retards the provision of housing accommodations or constitutes an economic or social liability and is a menace to the public health, safety, morals, or welfare").

39. See 2006 W.V. H.B. 4048 (enacted into law April 2006) (exempting blight condemnation from ban and defining blight to include "an area that, for any number of factors such as deterioration or inadequate street layout, "substantially impairs or arrests the sound growth of a municipality, retards the provision of housing accommodations or constitutes an economic or social liability and is a menace to the public health, safety, morals, or welfare").

40. As far as I am aware, there are also no unpublished decisions with such a holding.

41. See Nev. Assembly Bill 102 (signed into law May 23, 2007) (forbidding private-to-private condemnations, but with exception for blight.)

42. However, it should be noted that the 2003 version of §279.388 required the presence of only one of the eleven factors to allow an area to be declared "blighted."

43. See discussion of Nevada's referendum initiative in § II.A.3.

44. See 2005 Maine H.B. 1310 (signed into law April 13, 2006) (exempting blight condemnations from ban on economic development condemnations).

45. The best-known such case is that of *Poletown Neighborhood Council v. City of Detroit*, 304 N.W.2d 455 (Mich. 1981), *overruled County of Wayne v. Hathcock*, 684 N.W.2d 765 (Mich. 2004), where some 4000 where uprooted in order to provide a site for a new General Motors factory in Detroit that was expected to create 6000 new jobs. For discussion, see Somin 2004b.

46. Wisc. A.B. 657, § 1 (signed into law March 31, 2006).

47. The analysis of the Delaware, Ohio, and Texas laws is in large part derived from Somin 2007a, 245–52.

48. See Parts 1, 3, 4, and 5 of Timothy Sandefur, *Gov. Schwarzenegger Signs Mealy-Mouthed Property Rights Protection,* Pacific Legal Foundation on Eminent Domain, available at http://eminentdomain.typepad.com/my_weblog/2006/09/gov_schwarzeneg.html (visited January 2, 2006).

49. See generally Conn. Gen. Stat. § 8–125(2) (allowing use of eminent domain within "redevelopment areas" that can be declared in any "area within the state that is deteriorated, deteriorating, substandard or detrimental to the safety, health, morals or welfare of the community"). The concept of "deteriorating" area is defined extremely broadly. See also § 8–125(7) (providing list of numerous conditions only one of which has to be met for an area to qualify as "deteriorating"; even this list is not exhaustive, since the statute says that possible conditions qualifying an area as "deteriorating" are "not limited" to those enumerated). See also, *Kelo,* at 475 (noting that Connecticut law permitted condemnation of the New London properties despite the fact that they were not "blighted" and were only sought for purposes of promoting economic growth in the area.

50. See Conn. Gen. Stat. §§ 8–125–33 (outlining procedures for condemning property in "redevelopment areas").

51. See Md. Const., Art. III, § 61 (allowing use of eminent domain in "slum or blighted areas" and defining these terms as follows: "The term 'slum area' shall mean any area where dwellings predominate which, by reason of depreciation, overcrowding, faulty arrangement or design, lack of ventilation, light or sanitary facilities, or any combination of these factors, are detrimental to the public safety, health or morals. The term 'blighted area' shall mean an area in which a majority of buildings have declined in productivity by reason of obsolescence, depreciation or other causes to an extent they no longer justify fundamental repairs and adequate maintenance").

52. See Oh. Rev. Code § 303.26(E) (defining blight to include "deterioration" of structures or where the site "substantially impairs or arrests the sound growth of a county, retards the provision of housing accommodations, or constitutes an economic or social liability and is a menace to the public health, safety, morals, or welfare").

53. For a detailed analysis of the commission's Composition, see Somin 2007a, 249.

54. See Final Report of the Task Force to Study Eminent Domain Aug. 1, 2006, 12 (on file with the author). The new definition of blight advocated by the Commission would allow the

designation of an area as "blighted" so long as it was characterized by any two of seventeen different conditions (Attachment 2). Many of these are vaguely defined and could apply to almost any property. For example, one of the seventeen conditions is "faulty lot layout in relation to size, adequacy accessibility, or usefulness." Others include "excessive dwelling unit density" (without defining what counts as "excessive"), and "age and obsolescence" (also undefined). Like the old definition, the new one would still permit virtually any property to be designated as "blighted." For the old definition, see note 67.

55. These latter two statutes are listed as the only broad exceptions to the bill's ban on takings "for economic development purposes." 10 Tex. Gov. Code §2206.001(b).

56. Sandefur (2006) is more optimistic about these two provisions, calling them "significant improvements." See also note 4. Sandefur does not, however, consider the possibility that they can be circumvented by means of the "community development" exception.

57. See *Central Puget Sound Regional Trans. Auth. v. Miller*, 128 P. 3d 588 (Wash. 2006). This decision was cited as the reason for the passage of the new Washington law by the state's Senate Committee on the Judiciary. See Senate Bill Report, S.H.B. 1458, Mar. 21, 2007, available at http://www.leg.wa.gov/pub/billinfo/2007–08/Pdf/Bill%20Reports/Senate/1458-S.SBR. pdf (visited January 28, 2008).

58. If I classified Washington State as having passed either an effective or ineffective reform law, that would not alter the political ignorance findings discussed in Part III because there are too few Washington respondents in the sample to make a statistically significant difference.

59. See *Hogue v. Port of Seattle*, 341 P.2d 171, 187 (Wash. 1959) (denying condemnation of residential property so that agency could "devote it to what it considers a higher and better economic use").

60. See Rev. Code of Wash. § 35.80A.010 (defining blight narrowly for purposes of condemnation).

61. The New Mexico bill does still permit the condemnation of property that is characterized by "obsolete or impractical planning and platting" and "(a) was platted prior to 1971; (b) has remained vacant and unimproved; and (c) threatens the health, safety and welfare of persons or property due to erosion, flooding and inadequate drainage." N.M. H.B.393, § 3–18–10(B)(3).

62. See § II.A.1, and note 43. However, Utah partially rescinded its ban on blight condemnations in a more recent bill. See Utah H.B. 365 (signed into law March 21, 2007) (permitting blight condemnations if approved by a supermajority of property owners in the affected area).

63. A report prepared Institute for Justice, the libertarian public interest law firm that represented the property owners in *Kelo*, does not list a single private-to-private condemnation in Utah during the entire five-year period from 1998 to 2002. See Berliner 2003. The IJ Report concluded (two years before the enactment of the 2005 reform law) that "Utah has done fairly well in avoiding the use of eminent domain for private parties" (at 196). New Mexico did not have any private-to-private condemnations during the 1998–2002 period (at 143).

64. For arguments that this is a major problem with economic development and blight condemnations, see Somin 2007a, 190–205, 264–271.

65. See Alabama H.B. 654 (signed into law April 25, 2006) (limiting definition of blight to a relatively narrow range of situations, such as property that is "unfit for human habitation," poses a public health risk, or has major tax delinquencies); See also Ala. Code § 11–47–170(b) (forbidding condemnations that "transfer" nonblighted property to private parties).

66. See Geo. H.B. 1313 (signed into law April 4, 2006) (forbidding economic development takings, and defining blight to include primarily risks to health, the environment, and safety, while excluding "esthetic" considerations).

67. See Id. H.B. 555 (signed into law March 21, 2006) (forbidding condemnations "For the purpose of promoting or effectuating economic development" and for the acquisition of non-blighted property, and defining blight as a condition that poses physical risks to the occupants of a building, spreads disease or crime, or poses "an actual threat of harm" to public safety, health, morals, or welfare). The burden of proof for showing that blight exists is imposed on the government. Nonetheless, there is some room for potential slippage in the Idaho law because of the possibility that property could be condemned merely for posing an "actual

threat of harm" to public "morals" or "welfare," concepts that could be defined broadly enough to include most economic development takings.

68. See Ind. H.B. 1010 (signed into law March 24, 2006) (forbidding most private to private condemnations and defining blight as an area that "constitutes a public nuisance," is unfit for habitation, does not meet the building code, is a fire hazard, or "otherwise dangerous").

69. See Mich. H.B. 5060, § 3 (signed into law September 20, 2006) (banning condemnations for "general economic development" and limiting definition of "blight" to property that is a "public nuisance," an "attractive nuisance," poses a threat to public safety, such as a fire hazard, or is abandoned. The law does have a potential loophole in so far as it permits the condemnation of property as "blighted" if "it is not maintained in accordance with applicable local housing or property maintenance codes or ordinances" (at § 3[8][a][vii]). This could allow local governments to manipulate the content of local property codes in such a way as to make it impossible for all or most property owners to fully comply, thus potentially opening the door to sweeping condemnation authority for economic development purposes. My tentative judgment is that this loophole is not broad enough to completely negate the impact of the new statute.

70. N.H. S.B. 287, §205–3-b (signed into law June 23, 2006) (defining public use as "exclusively" limited to government ownership, public utilities and common carriers, and blight-like condemnations needed to "remove structures beyond repair, public nuisances, structures unfit for human habitation or use, and abandoned property when such structures or property constitute a menace to health and safety").

71. See Va. H.B. 2954, § 1–237.1(A) (signed into law April 4, 2007) (permitting condemnation of private property only if "(i) the property is taken for the possession, ownership, occupation, and enjoyment of property by the public or a public corporation; (ii) the property is taken for construction, maintenance, or operation of public facilities by public corporations or by private entities provided that there is a written agreement with a public corporation providing for use of the facility by the public; (iii) the property is taken for the creation or functioning of any public service corporation, public service company, or railroad; (iv) the property is taken for the provision of any authorized utility service by a government utility corporation; (v) the property is taken for the elimination of blight provided that the property itself is a blighted property; or (vi) the property taken is in a redevelopment or conservation area and is abandoned or the acquisition is needed to clear title where one of the owners agrees to such acquisition or the acquisition is by agreement of all the owners"). The new law also narrows the definition of "blight" to include only "property that endangers the public health or safety in its condition at the time of the filing of the petition for condemnation and is (i) a public nuisance or (ii) an individual commercial, industrial, or residential structure or improvement that is beyond repair or unfit for human occupancy or use." (at § § 1–237.1[B]).

72. Wyo. House Bill No. 124, § 1–26–801(c) (signed into law February 28, 2007) (requiring that "[a]s used in and for purposes of this section only, 'public purpose' means the possession, occupation and enjoyment of the land by a public entity. 'Public purpose' shall not include the taking of private property by a public entity for the purpose of transferring the property to another private individual or private entity except in the case of condemnation for the purpose of protecting the public health and safety"). Technically, this law seems to forbid blight condemnations. However, the provision permitting condemnations for the purpose protecting "public health and safety" is functionally equivalent to allowing condemnation under an extremely narrow definition of blight.

73. See § 203(4-) (excluding areas designated as blighted within "a city of the First or Second Class," which under Pennsylvania law turn out to be Pittsburgh and Philadelphia).

74. See Berliner 2003, 173, 179–81 (describing major condemnation projects in the two cities).

75. See Minn. S.F. 2750 (signed into law May 19, 2006) (defining "public use" to mean exclusively direct public use or mitigation of blight or a public nuisance and *not* "the public benefits of economic development" and defining a "blighted area" as an urban area where more than half of the buildings are "structurally substandard" in the sense of having two or more building code violations).

76. League of Minnesota Cities, *Research on Cities' Use of Eminent Domain*, available at http://www.lmnc.org/pdfs/EminentDomain/ResearchOnEminentDomain.pdf (visited

January 25, 2007). The LMC study claims that these cities use eminent domain only rarely and judiciously. However, it also notes that the 34 cities engaged in an average of 12 economic development takings per year, many of them involving "multiple parcels" of land. This yields a total of over 400 economic development takings per year in the state of Minnesota, a fairly large number for a state with a population of only 5.1 million. See table 7.A3. If each of these takings impacted about twelve people (a conservative estimate in view of the fact that many involved multiple parcels), then about 5000 Minnesotans lose property to economic development takings per year, for a total of 35,000 during the seven year period studied by the LMC. Between 1999 and 2005, economic development takings, some 0.7 percent of the Minnesota population may have lost property or been displaced by economic development condemnations.

77. See Berliner 2003, 10–11 (noting that Alabama "has mostly refrained from abusing the power of eminent domain in recent years" and had only one documented private-to-private condemnation in 2002); (at 59) (noting that Georgia is "one of a handful of states with no reported instances" of such condemnations during the same period); (at 189) (same as to South Dakota).

78. For a complete list and other details, see National Council of State Legislatures, *Property Rights Issues on the 2006 Ballot*, November 12, 2006, available at http://www.ncsl.org/statevote/prop_rights_06.htm (visited November 20, 2006).

79. Only two post-*Kelo* ballot initiatives were defeated—one in Idaho and one in California. Id. Both lost primarily because they were tied to controversial measures limiting "regulatory takings." See, e.g., Sandefur 2007 (attributing the defeat of California's Proposition 90 primarily to the shortcomings of the regulatory takings element of the proposal and strategic errors of its supporters). No stand-alone post-*Kelo* public use referendum initiative was defeated anywhere in the country.

80. See Ariz. Proposition 207 (enacted November 7, 2006) (forbidding condemnations for "economic development" and limiting blight-like condemnations to cases where there is "a direct threat to the public health or safety caused by the current condition of the property.").

81. See La. Const. Amend. 5 (enacted September 30, 2006) (forbidding condemnations for "economic development" and tax revenue purposes; and confining blight condemnations to cases where there is a threat to public health or safety).

82. See Ore. Measure 39 (enacted November 7, 2006) (forbidding most private-to-private condemnations and limiting blight-like condemnations to cases where they are needed to eliminate dangers to public health or safety).

83. See Nev. Ballot Question 2 (enacted November 7, 2006) (forbidding the "direct or indirect transfer of any interest in property taken in an eminent domain proceeding from one private party to another private party"); N.D. Measure 2 (enacted November 7, 2006) (mandating that "public use or a public purpose does not include public benefits of economic development, including an increase in tax base, tax revenues, employment, or general economic health. Private property shall not be taken for the use of, or ownership by, any private individual or entity, unless that property is necessary for conducting a common carrier or utility business.").

84. See the discussion of a similar problem in President Bush's executive order on takings in § II.B.3.

85. See *Karesh v. City of Charleston*, 247 S.E.2d 342, 345 (S.C. 1978) (striking down taking justified only by economic development).

86. The status of blight condemnations in under *Hathcock* is analyzed in Somin 2004a.

87. See note 84.

88. The four are Arizona, Nevada, North Dakota and Oregon. See note 93 on the National Council of State Legislatures, *Property Rights Issues on the 2006 Ballot*.

89. The three were Georgia, New Hampshire, and South Carolina. See note 93 on the National Council of State Legislatures, *Property Rights Issues on the 2006 Ballot*.

90. See note 93 on the National Council of State Legislatures, *Property Rights Issues on the 2006 Ballot*.

91. See Bullock 2006 (explaining how the PRPA was held up by Senator Arlen Specter, then Chairman of the Senate Judiciary Committee).

92. The PRPA has been renamed s as the "Strengthening the Ownership of Private Property Act of 2007." Text available at http://thomas.loc.gov/home/gpoxmlc110/h926_ih.xml (visited January 11, 2008). On June 5, 2007, it was referred to the House Subcommittee on Healthy Families and Communities. No further action has been taken as of this writing. See http://thomas.loc.gov/cgi-bin/bdquery/z?d110:HR00926:@@@L&summ2=m& (visited January 12, 2008).

93. The Act goes on to establish several exemptions, but these are relatively narrow. See also § 8(1)(A-G) (exempting condemnations that transfer property to public ownership and several other traditional public uses).

94. The report bases this conclusion on Section 5(a)(2) of the PRPA, which requires the Attorney General to compile a list of economic development grants, but does not explicitly state that the list should be used as a guide for determining which funds to cut off in the event of PRPA violations (Meltz 2005, 4 & n.7). Section 11 of the Act does require that Act "be construed in favor of a broad protection of private property rights." 109 H.R. 4128, § 11. However, it is unclear whether this requirement will bind the Attorney General in his determination of the range of programs covered by the Act's funding cutoff.

95. I have used the estimated figures for the 2005 fiscal year.

96. The figure is arrived at by dividing 7.4 billion by 416.5 billion.

97. This may not be an unlikely occurrence, given that many property owners targeted for condemnation are likely to be poor and legally unsophisticated.

98. The full text of the Amendment is reprinted in Meltz 2005, 12.

99. See *Kelo*, 545 U.S. 469, 488 (2005) (holding that courts should not "second-guess [a] City's considered judgments about the efficacy of its development plan").

100. For a detailed discussion of these aspects of *Kelo*, see Somin 2007a, 235–40.

101. See the discussion of this point in the Introduction.

102. For a more detailed discussion of the theory of rational ignorance, see Somin 2006 and Somin 2004a.

103. For the exact wording of the two questions involved, see appendix B.

104. Data calculated from Saint Index 2007, Question 9. See appendix B for question wording.

105. Data calculated Saint Index 2007, Question 10. See appendix B for question wording.

106. Only 17 percent of respondents expressed any opinion at all about the effectiveness of post-*Kelo* reform in their states. Data calculated from Saint Index 2007.

107. Question 10 on the Saint Index Survey 2007 has four possible answers in addition to "don't know." However, as described in appendix B, in each case I coded two different answers as "correct" for purposes of table 7.6. Respondents living in states that had passed effective laws could get a "correct" answer by choosing either A or B, while those in states with ineffective reforms could pick either C or D.

108. For the classic survey result showing that many respondents will express opinions even about completely fictitious legislation invented by researchers rather than admit ignorance, see Stanley Payne's (1951) famous finding that 70 percent of respondents expressed opinions regarding the nonexistent "Metallic Metals Act."

109. See Wattenberg 2007, 79–90 (summarizing evidence indicating that the young have the lowest levels of political information of any age group).

110. See dates for the enactment of the six states' laws in Part II.

111. Data calculated from Saint Index 2007, Question 9. Standard tests showed that the difference between the 26 percent and 20 percent figures is not statistically significant; the relevant data is available from the author.

112. Data calculated from Saint Index 2007, Questions 9 and 10.

113. See Somin 2003, 639–40 (discussing relevant evidence on retention of political knowledge); Jennings 1996, 243–45 (same).

114. For discussion and criticism of this theory, see Somin 1998, 427–29. For a recent defense of the theory, see Hutchings, 2003.

115. For defenses of this theory, see e.g., Wittman 1995; John Ferejohn and James Kuklinski 1990.

116. See notes 37–39 and accompanying text.

117. For the 4.3 percent figure, see the data cited in § I.B and Somin 2007b, 1940. The 1.3 percent figure is calculated by taking 10 percent of the 13 percent who could correctly identify the state of post-*Kelo* reform in their state.
118. See nn. 120–21 and accompanying text.
119. For the argument that reliance on opinion leaders can alleviate the problem of political ignorance, see, e.g. Lupia and McCubbins 1998.
120. See Lupia and McCubbins 1998 (arguing that voters often choose opinion leaders based on ideological affinity).
121. For a more detailed discussion, see Somin 1998, 424–27.
122. See, e.g., Heller and Hills 2005, 1 (complaining that the reaction to *Kelo* was excessive in light of the fact that it merely reaffirmed existing law and told state legislatures "that they may do what they see fit"); See also § I.A (explaining how *Kelo* made little change in existing doctrine).
123. Quoted in Michael Gardner, "Lawmakers Rethink Land-Seizure Laws: High Court Ruling Leads to Groundswell in State, Proposed Moratorium," *San Diego Union-Tribune*, August 17, 2005, at A1.
124. See, e.g., Somin 2004a, Table 1 (providing data that the majority of citizens are unaware of the very existence of several of the most important pieces of legislation adopted by Congress in recent years).
125. For the concept of position-taking legislation, see Mayhew 1974.
126. Quoted at Dan Walters, "Eminent Domain Bills Are Stalled—Except One for Casino Tribe," *Sacramento Bee*, September 16, 2005, at A3.
127. Ibid.
128. Ibid.
129 Nevada eventually passed effective eminent domain reform by referendum. See discussion of the Nevada law in § II.A.3.
130. For the text of the CLC initiative, see http://ag.ca.gov/cms_pdfs/initiatives/2007–05–14_07–0018_Initiative.pdf (visited January 15, 2007). The provision negating other eminent domain reform laws passed the same is Section 9. For discussion of the reasons why the CLC initiative would not actually provide any meaningful protection for property owners, see Ilya Somin, *The California League of Cities' Deceptive Eminent Domain "Reform" Referendum Initiative,* Volokh Conspiracy, April 1, 2007, available at http://volokh.com/posts/1175462916.shtml (visited January 17, 2008).
131. See, e.g., Sandefur 2006, 769–72 (arguing that interest group opposition accounts for the failures of the *Kelo* backlash).
132. The Arizona initiative was undertaken by an activist group known as the Arizona Homeowners' Protection Effort. See Arizona Secretary of State, *Proposition 207,* available at http://www.azsos.gov/election/2006/Info/PubPamphlet/english/Prop207.htm (visited January 30, 2007); The Nevada law was put on the ballot by the People's Initiative to Stop the Taking of our Land ("PISTOL"), headed by former state judge Don Chairez, a longtime property rights advocate. See PISTOL, *Property Bill of Rights,* available at http://www.propertybillofrights.com/your_rights.html (visited January 30, 2007). In North Dakota, the ballot initiative was drawn up by a group known as Citizens to Restrict Eminent Domain) ("C-RED"). See C-RED Web site, available at http://c-red.org/ (visited January 30, 2007). In Oregon, the post-*Kelo* initiative was filed by the Oregonians in Action Political Action Committee. See Measure Argument for State Voters' Pamphlet for Measure 39 (on file with the author). Oregonians in Action is a property rights activist group. See Oregonians in Action Web site, available at http://www.oia.org/ (visited January 30, 2007).

## R<small>EFERENCES</small>

Berliner, Dana. 2003. *Public Power, Private Gain: A Fiver Year, State-By-State Report Examining the Abuse of Eminent Domain.* Retrieved on February 13, 2007, from http://www.castlecoalition.org/publications/report/index.html.
Bullock, Scott. The Specter of Condemnation. *The Wall Street Journal,* June 24, 2006.

Campbell, Noel D., R. Todd Jewell, and Edward J. López. 2007. Pass a Law, Any Law, Fast! The States' (Somewhat) Symbolic Response to the *Kelo* Backlash. Retrieved January 12, 2008, from http://papers.ssrn.com/s013/papers.cfm?abstract_id=1022385.

Delli Carpini, Michael X. and Scott Keeter. 1996. *What Americans Know about Politics and Why It Matters*. New Haven: Yale University Press.

Erickson, Robert S., Gerald C. Wright, and John P. McIver. 1993. *Statehouse Democracy: Public Opinion and Policy in the American States*. New York: Cambridge University Press.

Ferejohn, John A. and James Kuklinski. 1990. *Information and Democratic Processes*. Urbana: University of Illinois Press.

Gordon, Colin. 2004. Blighting the Way: Urban Renewal, Economic Development, and the Elusive Definition of Blight. *Fordham Urban Law Journal*. 31: 305–337.

Heller, Michael A. and Roderick M. Hills, Jr. 2005. *LADs and the Art of Land Assembly* (unpublished paper on file with author).

Hutchings, Vincent L. 2003. *Public Opinion and Democratic Accountability: How Citizens Learn About Politics*. Princeton: Princeton University Press.

Jennings, M. Kent. 1996. Political Knowledge over Time and across Generations, *Public Opinion Quarterly* 60: 228–252.

Karlin, Adam. Property Seizure Backlash. *The Christian Science Monitor* July 6, 2005.

Limbaugh, Rush. 2005. Liberals Like Stephen Breyer Have Bastardized the Constitution. Retrieved February 3, 2008, from http://www.freerepublic.com/focus/f-news/1501453/posts.

Luce, Hudson Hayes. 2000. The Meaning of Blight: A Survey of Statutory and Case Law. *Real Property, Probate & Trust Journal* 35: 389–478.

Lupia, Arthur and Mathew D. McCubbins. 1998. *The Democratic Dilemma: Can Citizens Learn What They Need To Know?* New York: Cambridge University Press.

Mayhew, David R. 1974. *Congress: The Electoral Connection*. New Haven: Yale University Press.

Meltz, Robert. 2005. Condemnation of Private Property for Economic Development: Legal Comments on the House-Passed Bill (H.R. 4128) and Bond Amendment. *Congressional Research Service*. Retrieved on February 3, 2008, from http://www.opencrs.com/document/RL33208.

Nader, Ralph. 2005. Statement on *Kelo*. Retrieved February 3, 2008, from http://ml.greens.org/pipermail/ctgp-news/2005-June/000507.html.

Nader, Ralph and Alan Hirsch. 2004. Making Eminent Domain Humane. *Villanova Law Review* 49: 207–231.

Nadler, Janice, Shari Diamond, and Matthew Patton. 2008. Government Takings of Private Property: *Kelo* and the Perfect Storm. In *Public Opinion and Constitutional Controversy*, edited by Nathaniel Persily, Jack Citrin, and Patrick Egan. New York: Oxford University Press, 287–310.

Payne, Stanley LeBaron. 1951. *The Art of Asking Questions*. Princeton: Princeton University Press.

Posner, Richard A. 2005. Foreword: A Political Court. *Harvard Law Review* 119: 31–102.

Sandefur, Timothy. 2006. The Backlash So Far: Will Citizens Get Meaningful Eminent Domain Reform. *Michigan State Law Review:* 709–777.

———. 2007. The California Crackup. *Liberty* 21 (2): Retrieved on February 4, 2007, from http://libertyunbound.com/archive/2007_02/sandefur-california.html.

Somin, Ilya. 1998. Voter Ignorance and the Democratic Idea. *Critical Review* 12: 413–438.

———. 1999. Resolving the Democratic Dilemma? *Yale Journal on Regulation* 16: 401–414.

———. 2003. Voter Knowledge and Constitutional Change: Assessing the New Deal Experience. *William and Mary Law Review*. 45: 595–637.

———. 2004a. Political Ignorance and the Countermajoritarian Difficulty: A New Perspective on the Central Obsession of Constitutional Theory. *Iowa Law Review* 89: 1287–1371.

———. 2004b. Overcoming *Poletown: County of Wayne v. Hathcock*, Economic Development Takings, and the Future of Public Use. *Michigan State Law Review* 1005–1039.

———. 2004c. *Political Ignorance Is No Bliss*. Washington, DC: Cato Institute Policy Analysis No. 525.

———. 2007a. Controlling the Grasping Hand: Economic Development Takings after *Kelo*. *Supreme Court Economic Review* 15: 183–271.

Somin, Ilya. 2007b. Is Post-*Kelo* Eminent Domain Reform Bad for the Poor? *Northwestern University Law Review* 101: 1931–1943.

————.2009. The Limits of Backlash: Assessing the Political Response to *Kelo*. *Minnesota Law Review* 93: 2100–2178.

U.S. Government Budget Fiscal Year 2005. *Analytical Perspectives*. Washington, DC: U.S. Government Printing Office.

Wattenberg, Martin P. 2007. *Is Voting for Young People?* New York: Pearson/Longman.

Wittman, Donald A. 1995. *The Myth of Democratic Failure: Why Political Institutions are Efficient.* Chicago: University of Chicago Press.

# 8

# EMINENT DOMAIN FOR PRIVATE USE

## IS IT JUSTIFIED BY MARKET FAILURE OR AN EXAMPLE OF GOVERNMENT FAILURE?

*Bruce L. Benson and Matthew Brown*

## INTRODUCTION

The alleged market-failure "justification" for using eminent domain to obtain property for a private development is that compulsory transfers are necessary in order to overcome holdout problems. After all, this argument continues, only the state has such power, so the private sector would be unable to supply the efficient amount of land-extensive developments. This market-failure justification is examined from two different perspectives in order to demonstrate that it is not efficacious. Section 2 provides a direct examination of the alleged holdout problem to demonstrate that, while government entities may face significant holdouts, the magnitude of any market failure that might actually exist with a private development is much less significant than this argument assumes. Section 3 follows with an examination of the actual historical evolution of eminent domain powers and its accompanying requirement for compensation to illustrate that the actual development reflects repeated efforts to constrain government rather than to solve market failures. Section 4 explains that, as with earlier efforts to constrain government, the United States' constitutional requirements of public use and just compensation have gradually broken down. As a consequence, eminent domain powers actually result in substantial government failure. Therefore, even if there is a potential market-failure, the high likelihood of government failure undermines the claim that eminent domain is an appropriate solution to the market failure. The concluding comments in Section 5 point out, however, that eminent domain is only one type of government takings. Takings also occur through the regulatory process (police powers), for instance. Thus, potential limitations on eminent domain should be considered in the broader context of government failure and takings. If local governments' abilities to transfer wealth through eminent domain condemnation with compensation are limited, it could lead to a substitution of uncompensated takings.

## The Alleged Market Failure Justification for Eminent Domain: Holdouts[1]

Suppose one person, individual A, wants to obtain possession of a tract of land that is currently legally controlled by another person, individual B, perhaps to combine with other parcels currently owned by still other people. There are two ways for A to obtain the property. One is through bargaining in an effort to achieve a mutually advantageous exchange. The other is through coercion if the person desiring the land has the power to force a transfer or the ability to call on someone (e.g., a government official) who has. Suppose that A values the land at $X and B values it at $Y, X > Y. A and B are therefore likely to find mutually advantageous terms to make the exchange, i.e., A will pay price $P to B where X > P > Y. In general, successful voluntary exchange is likely to be Pareto efficient,[2] but such exchange is not costless. If transactions costs prevent some valuable exchanges from occurring, then in theory, a substitute for bargaining, such as regulation or compulsory sale, may increase social welfare.[3] The primary source of transactions costs that allegedly justify eminent domain powers is the so-called holdout problem (Posner 1977, 40–41; Fischel 1995, 68; Miceli and Segerson 2000, 330). This problem is explained quite succinctly by Posner (1977, 40–41):

> An economic reason for eminent domain, although one applicable to its use by railroads and other right-of-way companies rather than by government, is that it is necessary to prevent monopoly. Once the railroad or pipeline has begun to build its line, the cost of abandoning it for an alternative route becomes very high. Knowing this, people owning land in the path of the advancing line will be tempted to hold out for a very high price—a price in excess of the actual opportunity cost of the land. The high cost of acquiring land will, by increasing the costs of right-of-way companies, induce them to raise the prices of their services; the higher prices will induce some consumers to shift to substitute services; the companies will therefore have a smaller output; and a result the companies will need, and will purchase, less land than they would have purchased at prices equal to (or slightly above) the opportunity costs of the land. Furthermore, higher land prices will give the companies an incentive to substitute other inputs for some of the land that they would ordinarily purchase. As a result of these factors land that would have been more valuable to the right-of-way company than to its present owners remain in its existing, less valuable uses, and this is inefficient.

Indeed, a holdout problem presumably could be so severe that it prevents the transfers of any property. This may be particularly likely when a buyer is trying to purchase several contiguous pieces of land in order to create a private (or public) development. If a large number of landowners know about the intended purchase ahead of time, they will all want to be the last individual to sell in order to be in a monopoly position and extract the highest possible price. Such strategic behavior on the part of sellers would result in expected transactions costs for the buyer being so high that she gives up the effort and the potentially welfare enhancing development is never undertaken. Thus, Fischel (1995, 68) suggests that "Preventing time-consuming strategic bargaining is an important justification for eminent domain."

Holdout incentives for sellers actually may be weaker than they are often assumed to be, however, particularly if an individual sells only part of his land for the development. After all, the increase in the rental value of his remaining land due to proximity and access to the development easily can be substantially more than the price of the land that is sold for the development. Thus, there clearly are strong incentives for many landowners to sell part of their land, offsetting the incentives to hold out [e.g., see Engel, Fischer, and Galetovic (2002)].

Further note that Posner's description of the holdout problem explicitly assumes that there is only one combination of property that can be used for the project and that the project is begun before all of the land for the project is purchased. These two assumptions lead to the potential for a single seller to act like a monopolist because the buyer has no substitute to consider. If this is not the case then, once again, holdouts may not be a serious concern, as Posner (1977, 43) observes. In this regard, for instance, Miceli and Segerson (2000, 330) note that the land could, in theory, be acquired prior to construction. They recognize that when projects are publicly funded plans are not likely to be kept secret until after the land is obtained because of the need to appropriate the funds. There often are many other requirements associated with government projects, such as mandated public hearings, environmental review, and so on, that preclude secrecy (and, we might add, the prevalence of corruption as public officials sell information to speculators). On the other hand, Miceli and Segerson (2000, 330) also note that private developers who want to assemble large tracts of land generally do not have the power of eminent domain (except through manipulation of the political process), perhaps because it is "easier for them to acquire the property while disguising their ultimate intent, for example, through the use of 'dummy' buyers."

Private buyers of multiple parcels can also make their deals much more quickly than public buyers. They do not have to get budgets approved by legislatures, deal with time-delaying statutory procedures, or operate under rules that limit the amount that they can pay on each piece of land (e.g., rules that constrain bureaucrats to paying assessed values, for instance). Therefore, the likelihood that a private firm's plans are discovered is much lower than the similar plans by a government agency. Not surprisingly, private developers frequently consolidate large parcels of land without being held up (Starkie 1990).

A private buyer's secret efforts to obtain multiple parcels of land may be discovered, of course,[4] and if this happens, holdout incentives can arise. Can such transactions costs be avoided? Landsburg (1993, 29) provides an interesting solution to what might appear initially to be an intractable problem analogous to the holdout problem by citing a situation from Joseph Conrad's novel, *Typhoon*. A number of sailors stored their gold coins in personal boxes in the ship's safe, but a severe storm caused the boxes to break open and all of the coins were mixed together. Everyone knew how many coins he had placed in the safe but no one knew how many others had placed there. Therefore, everyone's incentives were to claim that they had more coins in the safe than they actually had and the problem for the captain was to determine how to divide the coins to give each sailor his actual savings. Landsburg's (1993, 29) proposed solution: "Have each sailor write down the number of coins he is entitled to. Collect the papers and distribute the coins. [But] Announce in advance that if the numbers on the papers don't add up to the correct total, you will throw all of the coins overboard." This clearly reduces, and perhaps eliminates the incentives to holdout for more coins than had actually been contributed.

A similar strategy might be used by the private buyer of a number of contiguous parcels of land, even if it is known that a development of some sort is going to be constructed. Suppose, for example, that the developer chooses more than one potential site for development. She then informs the land owners within the two or more sites that she would like to purchase specified parcels from each of them, and that each should submit the price at which they are willing to sell (alternatively she might make initial bids that can be accepted, but indicate that each seller has an opportunity to make one take-it-or-leave-it counter offer). In addition, potential sellers are informed that the buyer will only purchase the parcel that has the lowest total cost associated with it (a maximum might also be specified, and/or information provided about the total acreage required at each site). The precise nature of the strategy may be quite different than this, but the fact is that pipeline builders, for instance, "routinely consider alternative routes, negotiate with different groups of owners, and settle with the first group that comes up with an acceptable arrangement. Where buyers compete with competing groups of sellers, there is extra pressure on the sellers to agree to reasonable deals" (Roth 1996, 199). When a private buyer structures the bargain appropriately (e.g., by secretly buying land or by simultaneously considering alternative sites and buying the parcels only after every seller has agreed and before the project starts, by choosing sites where landowners only give up part of their land so they can collect rents on the rest, etc.),[5] holdouts are not likely to prevent acquisition.

Fischel (1995, 70), in criticizing arguments against the use of eminent domain, notes that the literature has not indicated how the holdout problem is to be dealt with, and suggests that the theoretical progress made regarding methods to induce people to reveal their preferences involve complicated voting rules. These arguments either presume that the purchase is being made by the government or that private entities face the same holdout problems that government does. However, if private developers do not have the option of asking government to consolidate land for them, the incentives to find solutions to potential holdout problems would be very strong, and methods for doing so might be forthcoming quite quickly. For instance, several large firms (e.g., Sears, Walmart, Kmart, Ford Motor Company) use combinatorial auctions to select transportation carriers in order to construct routes that avoid empty back hauls and other unnecessary costs.[6] The fact is that actual market participants have discovered many ways to induce people to reveal their relative preferences in situations similar to those that would characterize purchases of contiguous parcels of land from multiple owners by private firms. This really is the relevant issue, even if theorists do not fully understand how these processes work, or might work if local governments' eminent domain powers were not available for private developers with political influence.[7] Indeed, the growing literature on combinatorial auctions is developing as theorists are attempting to understand the actual processes that are already being implemented. Of course, incentives to develop methods to avoid holdout problems are diminished when developers know that they can call upon local governments to use eminent domain powers to condemn the desired property and transfer it to the private developer. Thus, as long as this option remains open, holdout problems are likely to appear to be more severe than they actually would be in the absence of the eminent domain option. In other words, while Posner (1977, 41) explicitly recognizes that the economic justification for eminent domain based on the holdout problem actually is "applicable" to private purchasers of multiple contiguous properties "rather than the government," private sector purchasers are actually much more likely than government to be able to avoid the problem.

The final point to note in this context is that the holdout justification for eminent domain powers does not actually explain why government has those powers. That is, the holdout justification is an ex post rationalization of the existing government power, not an ex ante explanation for why the power exists. If it is assumed that government is simply a benevolent mechanism for solving market failure problems, then it follows that there must be some market failure reason for an existing government power. If, on the other hand, it is assumed that those with power are likely to use that power in pursuit of their own preferred objectives, then the possibility of other explanations for eminent domain powers should be considered. In order to "test" these alternative theories of government, let us consider the historical evolution of eminent domain powers.

## The Evolution of Eminent Domain: Market Failure or an Effort to Limit Government Failure[8]

The roots of the law of eminent domain trace to England (Stoebuck 1977, 7–9), as much of American property law does (Eagle 2002). Indeed, eminent domain clearly reflects the feudal underpinnings of English property law (Paul 1988, 8–9). Early Norman Kings retained absolute authority over the allocation of land: landholders controlled land only as long as they performed their required duties and paid their required fees. This tenurial system, whereby a landholder simply held the land of those higher in the feudal pyramid, was designed for military and political purposes. Land-use decisions were clearly not central to the process, but the implication was that landholders were "stewards" for feudal lords and kings, rather than being free to determine how land should be used or disposed of. Landholders wanted more secure property rights, of course, and some felt that they were powerful enough to obtain them. Increasingly tenants were regarded as having ownership rights rather than simply possessionary rights, and they expected to hold the land as long as they fulfilled their various feudal obligations. The effort to establish such rights is one reason for the long series of Baronial revolts to limit royal power. The most famous of these revolts occurred in 1215, when powerful barons renounced their homage to John; as a result, on June 19 *Magna Carta* was issued with both John and the barons swearing to abide by its provisions. The struggle for power between Kings and the barons (as well as the church, and other groups that became influential, such as the growing merchant class) continued for centuries, however, with some Kings ignoring *Magna Carta* and others forced to recognize it. Gradually the Kings' powers were reduced and feudal relationships were broken down. In the process, a right to compensation was extracted from the Crown in the event that property was condemned (seized).

The practices of condemnation and compensation were transplanted from England into the American colonies. Condemnation was regularly used to obtain highway right-of-ways (compensation was not always paid,, as in at least some colonies no payments were made if the land was unimproved, partly due to the fact that such land was abundant so property owners could easily obtain replacements at very low costs), for example. Many of the roads of the period were privately financed, built, and maintained, however, often by charging tolls (Gunderson 1989; Klein 1990). Nonetheless, government condemnation was used at times to obtain rights-of-way (Paul 1988, 73). Land was condemned for other private purposes too, such as the drainage of lowlands and the erection of private mills run by water power that required dams and flooding of land up river from a mill. As Paul (1988, 73) suggests, "The various mill acts enacted by the New England and several southern colonies are interesting because they afford an early example of the delegation of sovereign "taking" authority to private businesses."

The power of government to take property was clearly well established by the American Revolution, a remnant of sovereign powers established under feudalism in England. It was also customary for the government to pay compensation, however, a result of the long struggle to limit the power of the King in England, so such payments were clearly expected. The culmination of that struggle in North America was the revolution and the establishment of a new set of governments (13 states under the *Articles of Confederation*, and then the stronger federal government under the U.S. Constitution). Yet, just as parliament retained the power to take property when they wrestled control of the government of England away from the kings, the new governments in North America did not explicitly give up that power either. Note, however, that the United States Constitution does not explicitly grant condemnation powers to the federal government. Today it is generally assumed that this power is implied by such clauses as 7 and 17 of Article 1, Section 8, and especially, by the taking clause of the Fifth Amendment. In fact, however, the clauses in Article 1 appear to limit federal takings by requiring the "Consent of the Legislature of the State." In this context, one of the arguments against including the Bill of Rights raised by Alexander Hamilton (1788 [1961], 513) was that "it would contain various exceptions to power which are not granted." The takings clause of the Fifth Amendment may well fit this concern given the limits on federal takings implied by Article 1.

Some of the founding fathers actually argued for an explicit recognition of private property rights that could not be taken by the government. For instance, Thomas Jefferson contended that all remnants of feudalism in regard to property should be eliminated. He vigorously pushed for allodial ownership wherein land owners would hold absolute dominion over their property. In other words, he contended that land holders should not be treated as stewards, with property ultimately controlled by the prerogative of the state (Paul 1988, 9). He felt that if the state was considered to be the ultimate owner of land, freedom could not be secure, as the state would be in a position to reduce men to poverty or even serfdom. Others obviously had a different view, of course. One reason may well have been that the former colonies had been actively confiscating property to benefit powerful business interests, and their leaders did not want to repudiate their actions. Similarly, the property of loyalists had been seized during the Revolution, debts owed to British subjects by the tobacco producing states were cancelled, and a number of other takings had been made (Paul 1988, 74), so if the new governments did not have similar powers, claims by former owners might have had legal standing.

## GOVERNMENT FAILURE THROUGH EMINENT DOMAIN POWERS[9]

In light of the preceding discussion, recall individual A introduced earlier who valued a parcel of land at $X. In the earlier hypothetical, A obtained control of the land through voluntary bargaining, and paid $P where $X > P > Y$, but this is not his only choice. Assume that by spending $T, a small fraction of $X (e.g., on a lobbyist, a bribe, or some other method of influencing the city council), he is quite sure that he can get local government officials to decide that the business he is going to establish on the land is in the "public interest" because it will generate employment in the community and increase the tax base (see the discussion of the actual purposes of eminent domain condemnations below where it becomes clear that this could be an adequate justification for such political action). He negotiates with the local officials who decide to condemn the land and sell it to him for \$Z where $T+Z<P$—i.e., below market value, because they are convinced (or claim to be convinced) that the project will benefit the community. The city's land appraiser determines that the "fair compensation" for the parcel is \$W and this is paid to B (note that the assessor cannot determine B's actual subjective value; furthermore, as explained below, there is an under-valuation bias in such assessment processes in that it is likely that $W<Y$) which is paid to B. The land, in this case, is still transferred to a higher valued use, but the transfer is not Pareto optimal. Even if B is fully compensated (an unlikely outcome), taxpayers who pay any difference between the compensation payment and the sales price ($W<Z$ is clearly possible, and probably likely, as explained below), are worse off. A is clearly much better off, of course. Indeed, he could fully compensate B and the taxpayers for their losses if he wanted to (his decision to choose condemnation rather than bargaining suggests that he is not willing to, however). Thus, the "net" gain in social welfare is as large as it was under voluntary exchange but the gain is now distributed so unequally that the "transaction" makes some people worse off. In this light, note that some economists suggest that the Pareto criterion is too constraining in the public policy arena and that an alternative, called Kaldor-Hicks efficiency (a transfer is said to be efficient if the gainers gain enough to compensate the losers, even if no compensation is paid), is preferable. Recognize, however, that if full compensation is not required when a "Kaldor-Hicks efficient" transfer is made through the government, then the incentives for the buyer to bargain in the first place are weakened, as a subsidized political transfer is a more attractive option. Why bargain and pay for a property that can be obtained without full payment through the use of political influence (unless the political influence is more expensive than the property would be)? Furthermore, and importantly, under voluntary exchange both parties are likely to be made better off by the exchange, but there is no guarantee that land under compulsory purchase is actually moved to its highest valued use. The example just given would work just as well if B valued the land at $Y>X$, in which case any forced transfer would fail even the Kaldor-Hicks test and lower net welfare.

Can inefficient transfers be avoided by constraining the use of compulsory purchase powers to a limited set of circumstances? Suppose such purchases can only be made if the benefits to the "public" are clearly very large, for instance and where sufficient compensation is paid to avoid making the individual worse off when her property is condemned (i.e., meeting the Pareto criterion). The U.S. Constitutions' Fifth Amendment states, for instance, "nor shall private property be taken for *public use*, without *just compensation*" (emphasis added). Thus, it appears that the framers wanted government's takings powers to be constrained to "public use" purposes (presumably, uses with substantial benefits for many members of the public at large, as opposed to narrowly focused private uses, perhaps with some public purpose such as higher tax revenues as a secondary goal), and they expected such takings to involve "just compensation." Let us consider the effectiveness of these constraints on transfer activity. First, consider the way that "public use" has been interpreted by U.S. courts to see if it might prevent compulsory purchase for purposes that produce relatively small concentrated benefits, and after that, the "justness" of compensation will be examined.

## The Deterioration of the "Public Use" Constraint; Or Why *Kelo* Was Not a Surprise[10]

James Madison, who wrote the Fifth Amendment, and those who supported him, clearly hoped to restrict the takings behavior that had been going on in the colonies under British rule. Therefore, along with *just* compensation, the amendment explicitly requires that takings be for "public use" rather than public purpose, interest, benefit, or some other term. "Public use" was recognized at the time as a narrower and more objective requirement that such alternative terms might imply (Jones 2000, 290). Indeed, this wording was, at the time, conceived of as a strong constraint, since the Framers did not recognize a non-public authority in government; "an express prohibition on 'private' taking would [therefore] have been superfluous" (Jones 2000, 289, note 23).

Before 1875 all eminent domain condemnations in the United States were performed by state or local governments, and therefore, most early litigation over the constitutional limits implied by "public use" in the United States took place in state courts.[11] Evidence from this litigation illustrates that even though state constitutions had takings clauses similar to the U.S. Constitution's Fifth Amendment, there were two interpretations of public use across the states. The narrow interpretation required that the project for which the condemned property was used had to be open to the public (Jones 2000, 293) while the broader interpretation "equated *public use* with more nebulous terms such as *public advantage, public purpose, public benefit,* or *public welfare*" (Paul 1988, 93). States adopting this broader interpretation allowed transfers of condemned land to private commercial activities under the assumption that "the public" benefited from economic development (Jones 2000, 292). Thus, many states used eminent domain powers to transfer property from one private entity to another for a variety of private purposes. In other states, however, public use was interpreted by courts to mean "use by the public" (Paul 1988, 93). State treatment of the concept of public use still varies, both across states and within states over time,[12] although for the most part, state court treatment of public use has closely mirrored federal court views (Kulick 2000, 654).[13] The focus here will be on the effectiveness of the Federal Constitution as a constraint on eminent domain practices, however.

When the United States Supreme Court began considering eminent domain issues, it adopted the narrow view of public use (Jones 2000, 292). In *Kohl v. United States* (91 U.S. 367 (1875)), for instance, the Court explicitly stated that this power could be used by "a sovereign to take private property for its own public use, and not for those of another" (at 373–374). Furthermore, in *Missouri Pacific Railway Co. v Nebraska* (164 U.S. 403 (1896)), ruling on a condemnation of railroad property by the state of Nebraska in order to transfer it to a private grain elevator, the court concluded that the taking was an unconstitutional violation of the Due Process Clause of the Fourteenth Amendment, as well as being "in essence and effect, a taking of private property [for a] private use."[14] Two decades later, however, the court reversed itself. The opinion in *Mount Vernon-Woodberry Cotton Duck C. v Alabama Interstate Power Co.* (240 U.S. 30 (1916)) explained

that the Court would exercise great deference when reviewing a state court's findings regarding public use, and in *Old Dominion Land Co. v. United States* (269 U.S.
55 (1929)) the court began to suggest that it would exercise similar deference with
regard to legislative decisions about public use. Indeed, a relatively broad definition was explicitly adopted in *Rindge C. v. Los Angeles County* (262 U.S. 700, 707
(1923)): "It is not essential that the entire community, nor even any considerable
portion, should directly enjoy or participate in any improvement in order to constitute a public use."

*United States ex. re. TVA v. Welch* (327 U.S. 546 (1946)) came close to with-
drawing the federal court from even considering the question of public use when
Justice Black wrote "We think it is the function of Congress to decide what type
of taking is for a public use and that the agency authorized to do the taking may
do so to the full extent of its statutory authority" (at 551–552). Whatever limitation might have remained was severely undermined by Justice Douglas's decision in
*Berman v. Parker* (348 U.S. 26 (1954)). The case involved a District of Columbia
condemnation of land in areas of the city that were apparently dominated by slums,
with the land subsequently transferred to private developers. The petitioner was
the executor of the estate of the deceased owner of a department store in one of
the areas, and among other things, he objected to the fact that the seized property
could be transferred to another private party who would then redevelop it and sell
it for private gain. Douglas wrote, "The concept of the public welfare is broad and
inclusive..... It is within the power of the legislature to determine that the community should be beautiful as well as healthy, spacious as well as clean, well balanced as
well as carefully patrolled....there is nothing in the Fifth Amendment that stands
in the way" (at 33). Paul (1988, 94) describes the implications of *Berman v. Parker*
as follows:

> In a decision remarkable for its confusion of the central issues, Douglas and his col-
> leagues concluded that the appellants' "innocuous and unoffending" property could
> be taken for the larger "public purpose" of remediating urban blight....traditionally
> the limitation on the exercise of the police power, the power of the states to regulate
> property, has been something called the "public purpose." This broad phase allows
> quite a wide range of state regulatory behavior...so long as they serve some loosely
> defined notion of the public purpose....What Douglas accomplished by his confusion
> of the more permissive criterion of the police power's public purpose with eminent
> domain in *Berman v. Parker* was the application of the more permissive criterion of
> the police power's public purpose to eminent domain. Public use as a constraint on
> governmental seizures suffered a crippling blow as the result of Douglas's confusion.
>
> ....If the legislature is "well nigh" the final arbiter of "public needs," then what is the
> purpose of the Bill of Rights or the Constitution? The Court apparently lost sight of
> the purposes behind the Fifth Amendment's property clauses: to limit congressional
> seizures of property; to place conditions on those seizures that are necessary for a
> "public use," and to protect individual property rights.

Similarly, Epstein (1985, 161) suggests that the public use constraint was given
"a mortal blow in *Berman v. Parker* when [the Court] noted that 'the concept of
the public welfare is broad and inclusive' enough to allow the use of the eminent
domain power to achieve any end otherwise within the authority of Congress."
The decision essentially implies that whatever the legislature says is a public purpose
(which now is the meaning of public use) is a public purpose and this "opened a

Pandora's Box of state interference with individual property rights" (Jones 2000, 294). If this decision did not completely eliminate the public use constraint, then subsequent decisions have.

Jones (2000, 296–297) notes that "In *Hawaii Housing Authority v. Midkiff,* the United States Supreme Court dealt the public use requirement a final mortal wound." Hawaii passed a Land Reform Act which transferred property from private-land owners to the lessees of that land. While the Ninth Circuit Court of Appeals [*Hawaii Housing Authority v. Midkiff* (702 F.2d. at 798)] declared the Act to be "a naked attempt on the part of the state to take land from A and give it to B solely for B's private use and benefit," the Supreme Court declared the Act to be Constitutional [*Hawaii Housing Authority v. Midkiff* (476 U.S. 229 (1984))]. The Court ruled, once again, that if a legislature has determined that an eminent domain taking involves "a conceivable public purpose" then the public use requirement has been met. As Kulick (2000, 653) explains, "a legislature, under the Supreme Court's guidance from *Midkiff,* can legitimately effectuate public-private takings by merely making some legislative pronouncement that the taking will serve some public purpose or goal."[15] Clearly, this ruling "effectively [rendered that [the public use] requirement nugatory" (Eagle 1005, 164).

This non-constraint was reaffirmed in the 2005 U.S. Supreme Court case, *Kelo et al. v. City of New London,* 545 U.S. 469 (2005). This case involves the New London Development Corporation, a public corporation created in the City of New London, Connecticut, condemnation of privately owned real property in order to lease it to Pfizer Corporation for economic redevelopment. In a ruling consistent with *Berman v. Parker* (1954), the majority held that a more broadly defined "public purpose," such as proposed economic development, was consistent with the takings clause. This decision is not surprising, given past rulings, although two dissenting opinions contended, in different ways, that the decision was contrary to earlier precedents.[16]

The changes in the constitutional public-use constraint has been criticized from a number of perspectives [efficiency, liberty, equity—e.g., Epstein (1985, 2001); Paul (1988); Jones (2000); Kulick (2000)].[17] The focus here is on economic efficiency, however. One efficiency implication is that the lack of a public use constraint increases the chance that the benefits of an involuntary transfer will be less than the losses, implying inefficiency even with the weak Kaldor-Hicks standard, and clearly from a Pareto perspective, particularly if the individuals who lose their property are under compensated.

## THE SYSTEMATIC UNDER-VALUATION BIAS FOR EMINENT DOMAIN CONDEMNATIONS

The Fifth Amendment to the U.S. Constitution requires "just" compensation for takings by the federal government. The federal courts actually did not constrain state or local compensation awards in eminent domain situations at all, however, until the Fourteenth Amendment and its due process clause, applicable to the States, was adopted. Prior to that, the Supreme court ruled that the Fifth Amendment's taking clause only applied to the federal government [*Baron v. Baltimore* 7 Pet. 243, 247 (U.S. 1833)].[18] The Fourteenth Amendment states: "nor shall any state deprive any person of life, liberty, or property without due process of law; nor deny any person within its jurisdiction the equal protection of the law," however, and this suggests that at least some subsequent legislative actions and bureaucratic applications may not meet constitutional standards. Therefore, in *Chicago Burlington and Quincy Railroad Company v. Chicago* (166 U. S. 226 (1897)) the Supreme Court considered a claim that payment of a just compensation for a takings was an essential ownership right, implying that any takings without such compensation was a violation of due process. The fact that the Supreme Court decided to consider this issue could have been important since it implied that state court decisions regarding compensation in eminent domain takings could be appealed to the federal level on due process grounds, suggesting a potential constraint on compensation assessments. However, the potential constraint did not materialize. The court ruled that it was improper for it to review state court rulings on matters of fact (under the Seventh Amendment), and that the Illinois court's conclusion that no significant property had been taken was an issue of fact, not law. The City of Chicago had opened a public street on the railroad's land and compensated it with a payment of one dollar. The contention was that no significant property had been taken because the land's railroad purposes were not impaired (ignoring the fact that the railroad erected a gateway to make the street crossing safe—the court ruled that "Such expenses must be regarded as incidental to the exercise of the police powers of the state").

The Supreme Court has considered federal, state and local eminent domain compensation cases since *Chicago Burlington and Quincy Railroad Company v. Chicago* in 1897. First recognize that the concept of significant property (i.e., what really constitutes a takings) and just compensation are intertwined. Compensation could be generous, for instance, but if the view of what constitutes a significant property taking is extremely narrow so most government actions that affect property uses and values are not considered to be a takings worthy of compensation (e.g., as in *Chicago Burlington and Quincy Railroad Company v. Chicago;* the courts phrase this as a two-part inquiry: does the plaintiff possess a property interest, and if so, was it taken). In this regard, the U.S. Supreme Court's view of property appears to have broadened since 1897. Indeed, the Court has been quite explicit in some instances, stating for example, that the meaning of property is not interpreted in the "vulgar and untechnical sense of the physical thing with respect to which citizens exercise rights recognized by law...[Property refers to] the group of rights inhering in the citizen's relation to the physical thing...The constitutional provision is addressed to every sort of interest the citizen may possess" (*United States v. General Motors* 323 U.S. 373, 377–78 (1945)).[19]

In *Olson v. United States* (292 U.S. 246 (1934)), the Court explained that compensation should put an owner "in as good a position pecuniarily as if his property had not been taken. He must be made whole but is not entitled to more. It is the property and not the cost of it that is safeguarded by the state and federal constitutions." Epstein (1985, 182) notes that this is an appropriate standard from an economic perspective, as the Pareto criterion is met. If compensation really comes close to making the loser whole, however, then one must wonder why so many people who have property taken continue to protest and even sue? One obvious conclusion is that the compensation is actually less than what a willing seller would accept, as Epstein (1985) observes, because in reality courts do not follow this standard.[20] Indeed, they have chosen to ignore subjective value in most cases. This stems from *Monongahela Navigation Co. v. Untied State* (148 U.S. 312 (1893), at 325–326) wherein the Supreme Court recognized that one of the important reasons for awarding "just compensation" is that "it prevents the public from loading upon one individual more than his just share of the burdens of government, and says that when he surrenders to the public something more and different from that which is exacted from other members of the public, a full and just equivalent shall be returned to him." Yet, the Court went on to hedge this statement by stressing that "this just compensation, it will be noticed, is for the property, and not the owner" (Ibid., 326). This qualification has been interpreted to mean that the compensation is for the property taken, and not for losses to the owner that are a consequence of that taking (Epstein 2001, 12). In other words, any losses that are collateral to or a result of the taking of property are borne by the landowner.

While the *Monongahela* standard might still imply that the person whose property is taken is entitled to be compensated for losses in subjective value, subsequent interpretation has denied such an interpretation. For instance, in *United States v. 564.54 Acres of Land* (442 U.S. 506, 511 (1979)) the Court stated that "the owner is entitled to receive 'what a willing buyer would pay in cash to a willing seller' at the time of the taking."[21] However, as Epstein (2001, 12–13) explains,

> There is a good reason why 'for sale' signs do not sprout from every front lawn in the Untied States. In a well-ordered society most individuals are content with their personal living or business situation. They do not put their property up for sale because they do not think that there is any other person out there who is likely to value it for a sum greater than they do. In the normal case, use value is greater than exchange value. So the property is kept off the market. The use of the market value standard therefore results in a situation in which the party who owns the property, even if he shares in the social gain generated by the project, is still left worse off than his peers. He is forced to sacrifice the subjective values associated with his property, values which almost by definition he could not recreate through his next best use for the funds received.

After all, an owner purchases property because she values it at more than the purchase price and/or holds onto the property because she places more valuable on it than the market price she could get for it. Thus, even an accurate assessment of market value "does not leave the owner indifferent between sale and condemnation" (Epstein 1985, 183). Indeed, the court has explicitly recognized that compensations are lower than the level that would actually restore the landowner. In *Kimball Laundry v. United States* (338 U.S. 1 (1949)) Justice Frankfurter noted that "the value of property springs from subjective needs and attitudes; its value to the owner may therefore differ widely from its value to the taker.... In view, however, of the liability of all property to condemnation for the common good, loss to the owner if nontransferable values deriving form his unique need for property or idiosyncratic attachment to it, like loss due to an exercise of the police power, is properly treated as part of the burden of common citizenship." Thus, for instance, the laundry owner in *Kimball* could not recover for the dissipation of the "good will" that he had built up at his location because it was not transferred to the State (it was simply destroyed). More recently, Judge Richard Posner, in *Coniston Corp. v. Village of Hoffman Estates,* 844 F.2d 461, 464 (7th Cir. 1988) explained:

> Compensation in the constitutional sense is therefore not full compensation, for market value is not the value that every owner of property attaches to his property but merely the value that the marginal owner attaches to his property. Many owners are "intramarginal," meaning that because of relocation costs, sentimental attachments,

or the special suitability of the property for their particular (perhaps idiosyncratic) needs, they value their property at more than its market value (i.e., it is not "for sale"). Such owners are hurt when the government takes their property and gives them just its market value in return. The taking in effect confiscates the additional (call it "personal") value that they obtain from the property, but this limited confiscation is permitted provided the taking is for a public use.

Clearly, "The disregard for non-market values...creates a systematic downward bias in the priced paid in eminent domain proceedings" (Posner 1977, 43). Beyond that, the Supreme Court has frequently stated that the fair-market-value standard is not "absolute."[22] In fact, a number of doctrines have been developed by the courts that allow compensation substantially below market value, and even lower than the owner actually paid for the property, thereby guaranteeing that compensation must be below the value that the owner places on the condemned property [e.g., *United State v Commodities Trading Corp.* 339 U.S. 121 (1950), and *United States v. Fuller* 409 U.S. 488 (1973)]. As a result, "the fact is that 'just' compensation hardly ever is 'full' compensation. The landowner almost invariably loses more than the government takes" (Eagle 2005, 189).

The under-compensation bias creates significant incentives for under-valuation by condemning agencies, and this is a common practice (Starkman 2001). In fact, "initial compensation offers by the government often pale in comparison to the market value of the land" (Kulick 2000, 665, note 159) and compared to the value that the victim might ultimately receive through litigation. Consider Vera Coking's situation, for instance. She had lived in her ocean-front home in Atlantic City for almost four decades when, in May of 1996, she received notice that her property had been condemned by the Casino Redevelopment Authority. She had 90 days to move so her land could be used by the Trump Plaza Hotel and Casino to build a parking area and put in a lawn. The "fair market value" of her home was appraised to be $251,250. However, she had actually turned down a $1,000,000 offer by another casino operator in 1983, suggesting that the actual market value was much higher than the assessed value, but still lower than Coking's personal subjective evaluation. This appraisal was quite consistent with other condemnation assessments done in the same community, however. For instance, a pawn shop that had recently been purchased by the owners for $500,000 (an obvious indicator of actual market value) was assessed at $174,000, and a neighboring restaurant was assessed at $700,000, a value that would not even cover the legal fees and start up costs for the restaurant owners to relocate. Of course, the victims of an under-compensated takings can sue in an effort to overturn the condemnation or increase the compensation (and the victims of the Atlantic City condemnations just mentioned have done so), but this is clearly a costly and time consuming process, with considerable risks involved. A land owner who sues for just compensation is likely to have to pay his lawyer around 30 to 40 percent of the award, so the actual gain from litigating may be very small.

The power of eminent domain combined with an under-compensation bias and the high cost of litigation gives substantial bargaining power to government entities. Not surprisingly, "institutionally, government behavior will take advantage of the background legal rules. The eminent domain power thus allows the state to push hard so that the landowner will take a price which is...lower than he would have taken in any voluntary exchange" (Epstein 2001, 7). Indeed, as a result of this bargaining power, "government officials are becoming increasingly brazen in invoking eminent domain" to transfer land to private for-profit organizations (NCPA 2002, 1), in part because "many owners cave in to the pressure and settle" (Berliner 2002, 1). The fact is that the prospect (and expected costs) of fighting a threatened eminent domain condemnation through the courts in an effort to get more money than was offered by a government official can be sufficiently frightening for many individuals to induce people to accept substantially lower prices than they would otherwise be willing to take. Thus, there is an under-evaluation bias even for so-called voluntary sales of property to the government, at least for individuals who do not have sufficient political influence to counter such a bargaining power advantage. Note that even if a holdout problem arises in the absence of eminent domain powers, because sellers have "excessive" bargaining power, the ability for buyers to use eminent domain provides excessive bargaining power to these buyers, creating the opposite and potentially equally inefficient result. Under the Kaldor-Hicks criteria, holdouts may mean that some potentially desirable property transfers may never occur through bargaining, but eminent domain powers mean that some undesirable property transfers may occur through bargaining in the shadow of eminent domain, as well as through actual takings.

## INEFFICIENT TRANSFERS THROUGH EMINENT DOMAIN

As the public use constraint on eminent domain powers has been undermined, it has become easier for government to use this power to transfer land to other private entities, thus encouraging the use of the process by those with political power to gain transfers for substantially less than they would have to pay through a voluntary purchase. This political transfer seeking activity, often called "rent seeking" (Kulick 2000, 673–675),[23] can involve government condemnation of property for subsidized transfer to other private entities, after all. In one widely cited example (the condemnation that lead to the *Poletown* case in Michigan), the City of Detroit displaced 3,438 residents of Poletown so General Motors could have the land for a Cadillac assembly plant, paid the residents $62 million in compensation for their condemned homes, spent another $138 million in other costs including improvements to the land required by General Motors, and then resold the property to General Motors for $8 million. Or consider the more recent use of compulsory purchase to attract a Nissan plant to Mississippi (see *Percy Lee Bouldin and Minnie Pearl Bouldin et al. v. Mississippi Major Economic Impact Authority*, Case No. 2001-CA-01296 (Mississippi Supreme Court)), which included more than $300 million in subsidies and tax breaks along with condemnation of the property in question (*Wall Street Journal: WSJ.com—From the Archives,* January 4, 2002). This clearly creates excess demand for condemnations relative to what would be necessary with a strong public use constraint. Subsidies also give the private recipient of the transfer a competitive advantage over others who have not obtained similar subsidies, creating incentives for everyone who may want to obtain property for a new, expanded, or relocated business to look seriously at the political process to obtain the transfer rather than directly bargaining.

Subsidies are often explicit, as in the *Poletown* example, but even if the recipient of a condemned property repays the full amount that the government pays as compensation, there is an implicit subsidy if the victims of the condemnation (or condemnation threat) are not fully compensated for their losses, as suggested above. In this regard, what apparently is the only empirical study of the use of compulsory purchase found that low valued parcels (note that these are the parcels most likely to belong to individuals with little political influence, in part because litigation costs are likely to limit the chances that such owners will challenge the payment) systematically received less than estimated market prices through eminent domain in Chicago's urban renewal program (Munch 1976, 473).[24] Clearly, such transfers are not efficient in a Pareto sense, and there is no way of knowing whether they are efficient in a Kaldor-Hicks sense, as Epstein (2001, 6) notes: the under-compensation bias "has the unfortunate effect of inviting government initiatives that do not even meet the hypothetical compensation [Kaldor-Hicks] requirement." But inefficiencies from such transfers go well beyond those implied by under-compensation (Pareto inefficiency) or possible a net reduction in "social welfare" (Kaldor-Hicks inefficiency) arising from the specific transfers of resources through eminent domain. "The inequitable treatment, of course, leads to profound allocative distortions: the lower prices stipulated by government lead to an excessive level of takings, and thereby alters for the worse the balance between public and private control" (Epstein 2001, 15).

## GOVERNMENT FAILURE: THE COSTS OF INVOLUNTARY TRANSFERS

Political wealth transfers reduce wealth (i.e., are inefficient) for at least five reasons. First, involuntary transfers (e.g., through regulations under the police powers, through condemnation and reallocation of property as in *Poletown*) generally produce deadweight losses (e.g., a net reduction in wealth). For instance, when explicit subsidies such as those in Detroit (*Poletown*) or implicit subsidies due to under-valuation are implemented, they "encourage economic markets to operate in an economically inefficient state by lowering the cost for firms to purchase property for corporate activities" (Kulick 2000, 662). Standard neoclassical production theory suggests that a subsidy to a producer in obtaining a particular input (e.g., land) leads to inefficient over use of the subsidized input relative to other inputs (e.g., in the Mississippi-Nissan arrangement mentioned above, for instance, the Mississippi Supreme Court actually ruled *Percy Lee Bouldin and Minnie Pearl Bouldin et al. v. Mississippi Major Economic Impact Authority* that the state may have taken more land than it needed to in order to meet the alleged public use), and therefore, to inefficient input combinations. These inefficient methods of production mean that less is produced given the true opportunity cost of production than could be if the prices paid for resources reflected full opportunity costs—there is a "deadweight loss" to society because resources are allocated inefficiently.

Second, Tullock (1967) explains that the resources consumed in the process of seeking such transfers also have opportunity costs. He emphasizes the striking analogy between monopoly achieved through regulation, tariffs achieved through legislation, and theft. Thieves use resources, particularly their time, in order to steal, and potential victims employ resources (e.g., locks, alarms, private security, public police) in an effort to deter or prevent theft. Tullock then points out that precisely the same analysis applies to the political transfer process, or what has come to be known as "rent seeking" (Krueger 1974). Some individuals and groups expend resources (e.g., time to organize interest groups, lobbyists, investments in political campaigns to exchange support for those who have the discretionary power to create transfers) in an effort to gain wealth in the form of subsidies or artificial rents created by government actions (e.g., monopoly franchises, licenses, quotas, tariffs, subsidized purchase of property),[25] and others expend resources in an effort to defend against such transfers. These rent-avoidance costs, arising through investments in political information and influence by potential losers in the political transfer process, can be considered as a third source of costs arising in the involuntary transfer process. Because resources used in both rent seeking and rent avoidance have opportunity costs (they could be used to produce new wealth rather than to transfer existing wealth), they are "wasted" (Tullock 1967, Krueger 1974). Yet, individuals and groups have incentives to invest time and resources in an effort to gain wealth through the political process if the net gains are expected to be greater for them (but not for "society") than they can obtain through investments of the resources they control in actual wealth creation alternatives. Clearly, the use of condemnation powers to provide subsidized transfers of property from one private entity to another is part of this rent-seeking process.

Exit is another option for potential victims, perhaps by moving to an alternative political jurisdiction or by hiding economic activity and wealth (e.g., moving transactions underground into black markets). While immobile resources like land cannot be hidden in a gross sense, many attributes of land can be hidden (or destroyed) in order to make it less attractive for taking. Rapid development or exploitation of land might be attractive, for instance, if an under-compensated transfer (or regulatory taking) is anticipated, perhaps because such development at least raises the cost of pursuing the project through a takings. The rapid development also can eliminate alternative potentially more valuable future uses. Essentially, the incentives are to capture whatever benefits from the property can be extracted relatively quickly before the property it is taken away (or before police powers are exercised through zoning or some other regulatory process that attenuates use rights). Therefore, for instance, a landholder might develop (e.g., create a residential or commercial development) or exploit the property (e.g., plant crops that consume the soils nutrients, harvest its trees and/or minerals) much more quickly than she otherwise would, even though greater benefits potentially exist from later development or exploitation.

In order to reduce such "exit" actions and induce compliance with discriminatory transfer rules, other rules are likely to develop, and furthermore the rule makers will generally have to rely on courts and bureaucracies to implement and enforce the myriad of rules that are produced. Governments all over the United States are creating development authorities, zoning commissions, growth-management commissions, environmental authorities, and other agencies in order to implement controls on land use, for instance. Furthermore, lawyers representing land owners, developers, and government authorities are involved in millions of hours of negotiation and litigation, experts (e.g., assessors), land owners, and many other parties devote many more hours in control and compliance costs, and so on. These implementation, enforcement, and compliance costs are a fourth source of opportunity costs that accompany an involuntary wealth transfer process.[26]

The fifth source of costs may be the most significant. The takings power (including police powers and eminent domain) undermines the security of private property rights (Kulick 2000, 663), and importantly, insecure private property rights result in the same kinds of "tragedies" as those which arise in a common pool: rapid use (as suggested above) along with under maintenance of resources relative to the efficient level of conservation. The more frequent and arbitrary transfers are expected to be, the more significant these costs become. The trends in the use or threatened use of eminent domain discussed above suggest that this power is being used increasingly frequently and arbitrarily. Perhaps these actions may not have a tremendous impact on property rights security, at least by themselves, but when they are put into the context of overall trends in government takings (e.g., through regulatory actions under the police powers), it is clear that property rights to land in the United States are becoming less secure.[27]

Clearly, government taking powers have substantial costs. Indeed, as Epstein (2001, 18) concludes, "The consequences are quite sobering. Whatever the theoretical promise of taking property only with compensation, that gain has been nullified in large measure [if not entirely] by the troubling circumstances of its application." Therefore, any justification for such powers (e.g., the holdout problem that may prevent obtaining a beneficial transfer), that does not also recognize the potential government-failure consequences when such powers exist should be questioned.

## CONCLUSIONS

The rhetoric of market failure used to justify government takings assumes that the starting point in the analysis is private property rights, since this assumption underlies the models of perfect competition and general equilibrium against which market failures are compared. Then, given the potential for holdout problems that can prevent beneficial (efficient) transfers of property through voluntary agreements, it follows that private property rights should be modified to the degree that government can take property under certain limited circumstances. The limited circumstances specified by the constitution are that the property is for "public use" and "just compensation" is paid. As explained above, the strength of these limitations have been substantially undermined by the U.S. Supreme Court, but an entirely different point is also made above. The assumptions underlying the market failure rhetoric in support of eminent domain powers actually have the story about the evolution of eminent domain powers backward. The starting point was government ownership of property. Kings in England granted stewardship to individuals, but maintained the "right" (or more accurately, power) to take the property back. Gradually, over a long history of struggle to limit the power of government, property rights evolved in the direction of private property by placing various constraints on government. Government in England and then in the United States never fully relinquished its power to take property, but efforts continued to limit such power through revolts and efforts to constrain the feudal powers of the subsequent government through contracts (*Magna Carta*, The U.S. Constitution). The U.S. Constitution therefore included the Fifth Amendment's requirements of just compensation and public use, which have since been undermined to a substantial degree. It also successfully limited the federal government's power to condemn for almost a century while not constraining state governments. The federal government was not allowed to condemn property directly (it had to ask a state government to use its eminent domain powers) until *Kohl v United*

*States* (91 U.S. 367 (1875)). In *Kohl*, however, the court declared that the takings power is an attribute of sovereignty, and that (*Kohl,* 91 U.S. at 372) the federal government

> is as sovereign within its sphere as the States are within theirs. True, its sphere is limited. Certain subjects only are committed to it; but its power over those subjects is as full and complete as is the power of the States over the subjects to which their sovereignty extends. The power is not changed by its transfer to another holder.
>
> But, if the right of eminent domain exists in the Federal government, it is a right which may be exercised within the States, so far as is necessary to the enjoyment of the powers conferred upon it by the Constitution.

As Paul (1988, 73) explains "Justice Strong deduced a federal power to condemn in its own name both from the very nature of sovereignty and, more concretely, from the Fifth Amendment's taking clause...The latter inference was, undoubtedly, inventive. The requirement that the government must pay compensation when it takes was construed to imply a power to take in the first place. This clause, as virtually all commentators agree, is a restriction on government's powers, not a concession."

Whether the U.S. constitution constrains the federal government's takings powers or not is not directly relevant to the issue of takings for retransfer for development, of course, since these actions are virtually all undertaken by local governments pursuant to State law. It is relevant to the point that constitutional constraints on governments are not binding, however. As governments find ways around such constraints, or simply reinterpret them, property rights are increasingly threatened. The backlash against the *Kelo* decision that is playing out in state legislatures all over the country (López and Totah 2007; Somin, this volume) actually is another in a long chain of backlashes against the ever-present incentive that those in government have to expand the scope and strength of the claim that the state is the actual property owner and that the population simply serve as stewards for the state.

Criticism of uses of eminent domain powers is once again widespread and growing.[28] Much like the barons who demanded *Magna Carta,* the critics tend to demand reestablishment of constraints on the power of the state that have been eroding. The evidence and analysis presented above clearly support reestablishing the constitutional constraints. Indeed, they suggest that much stronger constraints on government takings are justified (perhaps to the degree that the sovereign authority that underlies eminent domain and police powers is not justifiable at all?). The government-failure perspective taken here also should suggest some caution in this regard, however.

The evolution of eminent domain powers and compensation requirements reflect an ongoing effort to constrain government powers to transfer wealth rather than to resolve market failure. Eminent domain is just one of many ways for government to take property and transfer rents, however, and it may be the most desirable method of transfer from an efficiency (and equity) perspective. After all, takings through eminent domain do require some compensation, even though it is likely to be inefficiently (and unfairly) low. Other methods of transferring property that are available to government do not even require compensation.

Regulatory takings involve similar government failure problems (Eagle 2005, 21–28; Benson 2002, 2004, 2005a) and do not require compensation. Thus, potential limitations on eminent domain should be considered in the broader context of takings. If local governments' abilities to transfer wealth through eminent domain condemnation with compensation are limited, it could lead to a substitution of uncompensated regulatory takings. Suppose a local government wants to encourage construction of a large power plant (or a low income housing development, manufacturing plant, retail store, etc.) in a particular area, for instance. It could encourage a private firm to build the plant (or developer to provide the desired housing, etc.) by using eminent domain to take the desired land, and transferring it to a private firm at a relatively low price. If the local government' use of eminent domain is effectively constrained by a true "public use" requirement that prevents a transfer to a private firm, however, it has alternatives. It could establish sufficiently strong regulatory requirements instead, which zone the land for industrial use, require lot size restrictions that dictate a plant of the size desired, and require sufficient regulatory approvals and oversight that would lead to the land being used as desired (or require any developer to provide a substantial number of low income housing units, etc.), without compensating for the reduced land value that results. Thus, for the public use constraint to prevent the transfer, it should be accompanied by restrictions on the use of police powers (e.g., a requirement of compensation for regulatory takings).

# NOTES

This paper was written for the Critical Issues Symposium on "Takings: The Uses and Abuses of Eminent Domain and Land Use Regulation" sponsored by The DeVoe Moore Center, College of Social Sciences and The Program in Law, Economics and Business, College of Law, Florida State University held at The Florida State University College of Law, Tallahassee, Florida, April 20–21, 2007. We wish to thank all of the symposium participants for their comments and suggestions, and particularly Steve Eagle, who served as discussant for the paper and also provided detailed and thoughtful written comments. In addition, we want to thank Alex Tabarrok for his helpful suggestions in his capacity of Research Director for the Independent Institute, and Laura Schonmuller, who provided research assistance. Nothing in this paper should be construed to represent the views of the Charles G. Koch Charitable Foundation.

1. This section draws from and expands on Benson (2005b, 2006).
2. A fundamental fact is that *voluntary* exchange takes place only when *both parties expect to be better off* as a consequence. And of course, if those expectations are met, the *voluntary exchange increases "wealth"* (subjective well-being) in what economists refer to as a *Pareto efficient* way. Use of Pareto efficiency as a criterion indicates that an action is desirable if it makes someone better off without making anyone else worse off. Naturally, fraud can lead to non-Pareto improving exchanges, so trust or recourse (e.g., to a legal system) may be required to alleviate this problem when there are significant asymmetries in information (Benson 2001). Pareto inefficiency may also arise in voluntary exchange if significant externalities arise through the exchange.
3. See discussion of the Kaldor-Hicks welfare concept below.
4. One reason for this could be that government approval of the development is required. Changes in zoning classification may be needed, for instance.
5. In a given project, private developers may also acquire options to purchase on speculation—something that public officials generally cannot do.
6. See De Vries and Vohra (2001) for a review of combinatorial auctions.
7. Tabarrok (1998, 345) offers a theoretical mechanism for a private profit-seeking entrepreneur to provide a public good using a "modified form of an assurance contract, called a dominant assurance contract," for instance, and similar contracts could be used to purchase multiple contiguous parcels of land.

8. For more details on the evolution of the roots of eminent domain, see Benson (2008), from which this section draws.

9. This section draws from and expands on material in Benson (2005b. 2006).

10. This subsection draws heavily from Paul (1988), Jones (2000) and Kulick (2000). For similar analysis and conclusions regarding the public-use issue and police powers, see Epstein (1985, 161–181) and Eagle (2005, 153–188).

11. See the discussion relating to *Kohl v United States* (91 U.S. 367 (1875)) in the concluding section of this paper for an indication of why this was the practice even for properties to be used for federal purposes.

12. See *Poletown Neighborhood Council v. City of Detroit* (304 N.W. 2d 455 (1981)), for instance and compare it with *County of Wayne v. Hathcock* (684 N.W. 2d 765 (Mich. 2004)).

13. *County of Wayne v. Hathcock* (2004) is one example of recent state court departures from this pattern. Also see, for example, *99 Cents Only Stores v. Lancaster Redevelopment Agency*, 237 F. Supp. 2d 1123 (C.D. Cal. 2001). Indeed, while the focus below is primarily on federal court decisions, it must be noted that most of the takings for private developments are done under state law. Furthermore, state treatment of the public use concept clearly varies considerably, both across states and within states over time (see Eagle 2005, 175–187). Therefore, in one sense, this discussion is illustrative of changes in constitutional constraints rather than a direct discussion of all constraints relevant to the use of eminent domain for private development. Over the last 130 years, however, many states' courts have made similar changes in the interpretation of public use to those that have occurred in federal courts.

14. Such rulings were consistent with earlier Supreme Court views of Constitutional constraints. For instance, in *Calder v. Bull* (3 U.S. 386, 388 (1798)) the court stated that there "are acts which the Federal or State Legislature cannot do, without exceeding their authority. There are certain vital principles in our free Republican Governments, which will determine and overrule an apparent and flagrant abuse of legislative power...[For example, a] law that punishes a citizen for innocent action...a law that destroys, or impairs, the lawful private contracts of citizens,...*or a law that takes property from A and Gives it to B*: it is against all reason and justice, for people to entrust a Legislature with such powers" (emphasis added).

15. Since *Midkiff* the Supreme Court has reconfirmed the same public use standard (or perhaps non-standard would be more appropriate). See *National R. .R. Passenger Corp. v. Boston & Maine Corp.* 503 U.S. 407, 422 (1992).

16. Justice O'Connor's decent contended that a narrower interpretation of public use was appropriate, along the lines taken by the Michigan Court in its 2004 *Hathcock* decision. Justice Thomas was more direct in that he essentially contended that *Kelo* was simply one in a series of rulings which are misguided, as they ignore the original meaning of the public use concept.

17. This conclusion is far from universally accepted of course. For instance, Fischel (1995, 74) contends that the broad interpretation of public use is desirable, in part because he sees two other constraints on the use of compulsory purchase. One is that the transactions costs of using it are high, so the "budget-preserving instincts of government agencies may usually be depended upon to limit eminent domain," and the other is that the use of compulsory purchase to transfer property for private uses "are also limited by popular revulsion at the government's action." The Constitution is supposed to protect people even when there is not a "popular revulsion" however (i.e., even when the majority supports some action that harms a minority) so it is presumably suppose to be a stronger constraint than popular beliefs. Moreover, the budget preserving tendency are not a relevant constraint when powerful political interests are seeking benefits through the political process, particularly if the "fair compensation" constraint is also relatively weak (in addition, revenues matter, for instance, where a condemnation of one business to help another is motivated, at least in part, by fear of losing sales tax revenues). Finally, some bureaucracies have found ways to actually enhance their budgets through compulsory purchase. When the Southwestern Illinois Development Authority seized property to transfer it to Gateway International Raceway, for instance, Gateway used the Development Authority's standard "application form" for seeking a condemnation for "private use" and paid the $2,500 application fee. The authority also charged a percentage commission for the land: $56,500, a sum greater than the Authority's appropriated budget (officials from the Authority also got free tickets to Gateway events) (Berliner 2002, 3).

18. The only other eminent domain case to reach the Supreme Court during the first several decades of the country's existence was *West River Bridge v. Dix* (6 How. 507 (U.S. 1848)), but that case was based on Article 1, Section 10 of the Constitution where the states are barred from impairing the obligation of contracts. Vermont had granted an exclusive franchise to operate a bridge for 100 years. The private firm was clearly willing to operate the bridge, but the state decided to take it over anyway. West River Bridge sued, contending that the franchise charter was a contract, and while the Supreme Court agreed that the charter was a contract, it ruled that the state's breach of contract and seizure of the bridge did not violate Article I, Section 10. Instead, the court stated that the state's eminent domain powers were "paramount to all private rights vested under the government, and these last are by necessary implication, held in subordination to this power, and must yield in every instance to its proper exercise." In other words, contracts, including contracts entered into by a state legislature, can be taken through compulsory purchase, "a rather odd conclusion, one among many that served to eviscerate the contract clause, while strengthening the states' power to take all kinds of interests in property" (Paul 1988, 78).

19. *General Motors* has proven largely aspirational, although some relatively recent Supreme Court decisions appear to be broadening the concept of property rights takings that require at least some compensation (e.g., *Lucas v. South Carolina Coastal Council*). The overall trend in such requirements is far from clear, however, particularly given the decision in *Tahoe-Sierra Preservation Council v. Tahoe Regional Planning Agency* (2002). See Greenhouse (2002) for discussion. Also see Paul (1988, 82–91).

20. Another conclusion addressed above is that the incentives that motivate holdout also motivate political action and litigation, but the answer suggested here clearly is relevant in many cases. After all, "abuses in practice are legion" (Paul 1988, 81). Furthermore, many loses are still considered to be "incidental," as in *Chicago Burlington and Quincy Railroad Company v. Chicago*. For instance, in *United States v. General Motors* the court ruled that the loss of business goodwill or other injury to a business is not recoverable. Other losses that the court considers to be unrecoverable included future loss of profits and the expenses associated with removing fixtures or personal property from the condemned property (even though expenses for moving are supposedly recoverable). As Paul (1988, 165) explains, "the Court reasoning that such losses would be the same as might ensue upon the sale of property to a private buyer…because when business persons sell their buildings…they have presumably factored in these ancillary costs and found the deals satisfactory despite such costs. No such assumption, of course, can be made where the government forcibly takes property…over the owner's objection…and, indeed, the opposite assumption is far more likely." The Court actually recognized this, however, when it stated that "No doubt all those elements would be considered by an owner in determining whether, and at what price, to sell. No doubt, therefore, if the owner is to be made whole for the loss consequent of the sovereigns' seizure of his property, these elements should properly be considered. But the courts have generally held that they are not to be reckoned as part of the compensation for the fee taken by the government" (at 379). In other words, in the past such property takings have not been compensated for so compensation is not required. As a result, loses arising in many condemnations are considered to be incidental due to the interpretation of "property," and therefore, not warranting compensation.

21. The opinion quotes an earlier ruling, *United States v. Miller* (317 U.S. 369, 374 (1943)), which stated this market value rule.

22. There is another source of systematic under compensation as well: "the expense in finding, obtaining, and relocating to other premises" (Eagle 2005, 154). Some of these costs may be compensated under state or federal laws, under some circumstances, but many are not.

23. This rent-seeking process and its consequences are discussed in more detail below.

24. Individuals who have political connections are less likely to suffer such losses, however, or at least, less likely to suffer large losses. In the empirical study of eminent domain practices in Chicago's urban renewal program, high valued parcels (e.g., those owned by individuals who probably had political clout, in part at least, because of their financial capacity and incentives to challenge payments through litigation) were systematically paid more than estimated market prices (Munch 1976, 473). This problem of discriminatory pricing based on political

influence is inevitable given the flexibility of the assessment standards and the ease with which some (but not all) individuals and groups are able to influence political decisions.

25. Note that rents are not necessarily all captured by firms like General Motors. Many of the rents will be diverted to politicians who are in a position to create them, and to other parties such as labor unions (Benson 2002, 2005a).

26. Rules that facilitate voluntary production and exchange (e.g., private property rights, enforceable contracts) also require some enforcement costs, of course, but the level of these costs (e.g., litigation costs, assessment costs, policing costs that arise when individuals attempt to hide their wealth, etc.) increases dramatically when laws are also imposed in order to generate involuntary wealth transfers.

27. When property rights are relatively insecure, bargaining is also less likely (Coase 1960). When the insecurity arises because of government's power to take, however, there is an additional reason for expecting bargaining to decline. People who can effectively operate in the political arena essentially have potential claims on other people's property. Seeking control of the desired land through political channels is costly, of course, but if it is expected to be less costly than direct bargaining and voluntary exchange, incentives to seek involuntary transfers are strong. Thus, individuals who are active in and familiar with the political process are likely to choose that arena (i.e., the marginal cost of seeking condemnation is very low once someone has invested in building political connections and influence), while individuals who are not politically connected are relatively likely to choose direct bargaining. Furthermore, as the level of state transfer activity increases, more people will be forced to learn about the political process, so over time, political takings will tend to replace voluntary exchange. On the other hand, increasing the constraints on the state and reducing the ease of transfers would lead to the substitution of voluntary exchange for political actions. Indeed, the fact that eminent domain may appear to be necessary to obtain property rights under the existing property regime does not mean that it would be necessary with very secure allodial rights.

28. For instance, the Castle Coalition has been developed by the Institute for Justice as a nationwide network of property owners and community activists dedicated to the prevention of the use of eminent domain powers in the United States for transfers to private parties for private uses. See *www.castecoalition.org*. Note that this anti-eminent domain movement is just one of the "property rights" movements in the United States. See Eagle (2002), for instance.

# REFERENCES

Austin, Page. 2002. Cypress Invokes Eminent Domain to Seize Church Land. *Orange County Register.* OCRegister.com, May 29.

Barnes, David W. and Lynn A. Stout. 1992. *Cases and Materials on Law and Economics.* St. Paul, MN: West Publishing Company.

Benson, Bruce L. 1994. Are Public Goods Really Common Pools: Considerations of the Evolution of Policing and Highways in England. *Economic Inquiry* 32 (2): 249–271.

———. 1996. Uncertainty, the Race for Property Rights, and Rent Dissipation due to Judicial Changes in Product Liability Tort Law. *Cultural Dynamics* 8 (3): 333–351.

———. 2001. Knowledge, Trust, and Recourse: Imperfect Substitutes as Sources of Assurance in Emerging Economies. *Economic Affairs* 21 (1): 12–17.

———. 2002. Regulatory Disequilibrium and Inefficiency: The Case of Interstate Trucking. *Review of Austrian Economics* 15 (2–3): 229–255.

———. 2004. Opportunities Forgone: the Unmeasurable Costs of Regulation. *Journal of Private Enterprise* 19 (2): 1–25.

———. 2005a. Regulation, More Regulation, Partial Deregulation, and Reregulation: The Dynamics of a Rent-Seeking Society. *Advances in Austrian Economics* 8: 107–146.

———. 2005b. The Mythology of Holdout as Justification for Eminent Domain and Public Provision of Roads. *The Independent Review: A Journal of Political Economy* 10 (2): 165–194.

———. 2006. Do Holdout Problems Justify Compulsory Right-of-Way Purchase and Public Provision of Roads? In *Street Smart: Competition, Entrepreneurship and the Future of Roads,* Gabriel Roth, ed. New Brunswick, NJ: Transaction, 43–78.

———. 2008. The Evolution of Eminent Domain: Market Failure or an Effort to Limit Government Power and Government Failure. *The Independent Review: A Journal of Political Economy* 12 (3): 423–432.

Berliner, Dana. 2002. Government Theft: The Top 10 Abuses of Eminent Domain, 1998–2002. Report from the Castle Coalition: Citizens Fighting Eminent Domain Abuse (March), *www.CastleCoalition.org.*

Calabresi, Guido and A. Douglas Melamed. 1972. Property Rules, Liability Rules and Inalienability: One View of the Cathedral. *Harvard Law Review* 85: 1089–1128.

Coase, Ronald H. 1960. The Problem of Social Cost. *Journal of Law and Economics* 3: 1–44.

De Vries, S. and R.V. Vohra. 2001. Combination Auctions: A Survey. *Zentrum Mathematik Working Paper.* October.

Eagle, Steven J. 2002. The Development of Property Rights in America and the Property Rights Movement. *Georgetown Journal of Law and Public Policy* 1: 77–129.

———. 2006. *Regulatory Takings,* 3d ed. Newark, NJ: LexisNexis.

Engel, Eduardo, Ronald Fischer, and Alexander Galetovic. 2002. Highway Franchising and Real Estate Values. *NBER Working Paper No. 8803,* Cambridge, MA: National Bureau of Economic Research, February.

Epstein, Richard A. 1985. *Takings: Private Property and the Power of Eminent Domain.* Cambridge, MA: Harvard University Press.

———. 2001. In and Out of Public Solution: The Hidden Perils of Property Transfer. *John M. Olin Law & Economics Working Paper No. 129.* Chicago: Law School, University of Chicago.

Fischel, William A. 1995. *Regulatory Takings: Law, Economics, and Politics.* Cambridge, MA: Harvard University Press.

Gordon, H. Scott. 1954. The Economic Theory of a Common Property Resource: The Fishery. *Journal of Political Economy* 62: 124–142.

Greenhouse, Linda. 2002. Justice Weaken Movement Backing Property Rights. *New York Times,* (April 24). www.nytimes.com.

Gunderson, Gerald. 1989. Privatization and the 19th-Century Turnpike. *Cato Journal* 9: 191–200.

Hamilton, Alexander. 1788 [1961]. The Federalist No. 84. *The Fderalist Papers.* Ed. C. Rossiter. New York: Mentor.

Hardin, Garrett. 1968. The Tragedy of the Commons. *Science* 162: 1243–1248.

Johnson, Ronald N. and Gary D. Libecap. 1982. Contracting Problems and Regulation: The Case of the Fishery. *American Economic Review* 72: 1005–1022.

Jones, Stephen J. 2000. Trumping Eminent Domain Law: An Argument for Strict Scrutiny Analysis under the Public Use Requirement of the Fifth Amendment. *Syracuse Law Review* 50: 285–314.

Klein, Daniel. 1990. The Voluntary Provision of Public Goods? The Turnpike Companies of Early America. *Economic Inquiry* 28: 788–812.

Krier, James E. and Stewart J. Schwab. 1995. Property Rules and Liability Rules: The Cathedral in Another Light. *New York University Law Review* 70: 440–483.

Kraus, Michael I. 2000. Property Rules vs. Liability Rules. In the *Encyclopedia of Law and Economics,* Vol. 3, edited by B. Bouckaert and G. De Geest. Chelthenham, UK: Edward Elgar, 782–794.

Krueger, Anne O. 1974. The Political Economy of a Rent-Seeking Society. *American Economic Review* 64: 291–303.

Kulick, Peter J. 2000. Rolling the Dice: Determining Public Use in Order to Effectuate a "Public-Private Taking"—a Proposal to Redefine "Public Use." *Law Review of Michigan State University—Detroit College of Law* 3: 639–691.

Landsburg, Steven E. 1993. *The Armchair Economist: Economics & Everyday Life.* New York: Free Press.

Laster, Richard E. 1970. Criminal Restitution: A Survey of Its Past History and an Analysis of Its Present Usefulness. *University of Richmond Law Review* (Fall): 71–80.

Levi, Margaret. 1988. *Of Rule and Revenue.* Berkeley: University of California Press.

Libecap, Gary D. 1984. The Political Allocation of Mineral Rights: a Reevaluation of Teapot Dome. *Journal of Economic History* 44: 381–391.

López, Edward J. and Sasha M. Totah. 2007. Kelo and Its Discontents: The Worst (or Best) Thing to Happen to Property Rights. *The Independent Review: A Journal of Political Economy* 11 (3): 397–416.

Lyon, Bryce. 1980. *A Constitutional and Legal History of Medieval England*, 2nd ed. New York: W.W. Norton.

Mansnerus, Laura. 2001. Refusing to Let Go, Property Owners Test Eminent Domain's Limits. *New York Times:* July 25.

Miceli, Thomas J. and Kathleen Segerson. 2000. In the *Encyclopedia of Law and Economics,* Vol. 3., edited by B. Bouckaert and G. De Geest. Chelthenham, UK: Edward Elgar, 328–357.

Munch, Patricia. 1976. An Economic Analysis of Eminent Domain. *Journal of Political Economy* 84: 473–497.

NCPA (National Center for Policy Analysis). 2002. State and Local Issues: Eminent Domain Used for Economic Development. *National Center for Policy Analysis: Idea House* (March 5): www.ncpa.org/pd/state/pd12298b.html

Paul, Ellen F. 1988. *Property Rights and Eminent Domain.* New Brunswick, NJ: Transactions Books.

Pollock, Frederick and Frederick William Maitland. 1959. *The History of English Law.* Washington, DC: Lawyers' Literary Club.

Polinsky, A. Mitchell. 1980. Resolving Nuisance Disputes: The Simple Economics of Injunctive and Damage Remedies. *Stanford Law Review.* 32: 1075–1112.

Roth, Gabriel. 1996. *Roads in a Market Economy.* Aldershot, UK: Avebury Technical.

Starkie, David N. M. 1990. The Private Financing of Road Infrastructure. *Transportation and Society Discussion Paper No. 11.* Oxford University.

Starkman, Dean. 2001. In the Clash of Eminent Domain and Private Property, Courts are Sending Cities a Message: Enough. *The Wall Street Journal: WSJ.com—From the Archives* (July 23).

———. 2002. Most Important Case in Years to Curb Local Government Use of Eminent Domain Powers. *Wall Street Journal: WSJ.com-Law* (April 5).

Stephen, James F. 1883. *A History of the Criminal Law of England.* New York: Burt Franklin.

Stoebuck, William B. 1977. *Nontrespassory Takings in Eminent Domain.* Charlottesville, VA.: Michie Company.

Tabarrok, Alexander. 1998. The Private Provision of Public Goods via Dominant Assurance Contracts. *Public Choice* 96: 345–362.

Tullock, Gordon. 1967. The Welfare Costs of Tariffs, Monopolies and Theft. *Western Economic Journal* 5: 224–232.

# 9

# LAND GRAB

## TAKINGS, THE MARKET PROCESS, AND REGIME UNCERTAINTY

*Peter J. Boettke, Christopher J. Coyne, and Peter T. Leeson*

### INTRODUCTION

Eminent domain is the power of the state to confiscate private property for its own use without the owner's consent. The takings clause of the Fifth Amendment grants the U.S. federal government the authority to use eminent domain provided the taking is for "public use" and the property's owner is "justly compensated."[1] The Fourteenth Amendment extends right to state and local governments.

The logic behind granting government the power of eminent domain is that it will occasionally need large tracts of land for public projects such as highways, schools, parks, hospitals, etc. The main problem is that acquiring adjacent pieces of property may result in a holdout problem whereby a project is delayed by a small number of owners who refuse to sell their property to the government. Granting government the right to confiscate the property of holdouts is meant to overcome this problem.[2]

The associated conditions of "public use" and "just compensation" aim to prevent political abuse by placing constraints on the government's power of eminent domain. For instance, the condition that the confiscated property must be for public use is meant to limit government's ability to interfere with the private market and the valuations of private individuals. Stated differently, the public use requirement is intended to prevent the state from using its coercive power to bypass the market and transfer property from one private owner to another. Likewise, the condition of just compensation, which requires government to pay the market rate for confiscated property, aims to prevent government from arbitrarily taking private property to finance state operations. The logic here is that if the government is required to pay the market price for the confiscated property, there can be no profit from takings.

Of course the conditions of public use and just compensation are broad in nature and often pose significant difficulties in practice. For instance, what projects fall under the category of public use? Similarly, how is just compensation to be determined given that compensation from government will, almost inevitably, be different from how the owner values the property? Given the vagueness of these conditions, there is much room for interpretation by both governments and courts. Although the recent case of *Kelo v. City of New London*[3] has made the government's power of eminent domain front-page news, the interpretation of the conditions associated with government takings has a long and controversial history (see Paul 1985).

For example, in the case of *Berman v. Parker*[4] the United States Supreme Court upheld the rights of the District of Columbia to seize and demolish properties that were partially blighted in order to replace them with a privately owned department store. In doing so, the Court broadened the interpretation of public use to include redevelopment. In *Poletown Neighborhood Council v. City of Detroit*,[5] the Michigan Supreme Court upheld the right of the City of Detroit to use eminent domain to displace several thousand private residents for the construction of a General Motors factory. The justification was that the expected creation of jobs and associated economic benefit were for the public use. For decades, state Supreme Courts have referenced the *Poletown* decision (including the Connecticut Supreme Court in *Kelo*) in deciding similar cases.

The issues associated with government takings become even murkier when one includes cases of regulatory takings. Regulatory takings refer to situations where government regulations severely reduce the value of a property such that it effectively involves government takings. Examples of these types of indirect takings include zoning laws and land-use regulations. In a 1987 decision, the U.S. Supreme Court held that regulation is the equivalent of a government taking when regulation deprives the property owner of economically viable use of the property.[6] Given this, the central issue is determining when a regulation has sufficiently infringed upon property rights such that it amounts to takings by the government. Typically, in order to receive compensation, the owner must demonstrate he has been deprived all value of the property or that he was required to dedicate part of his property to government use without a justifiable reason. In reality, most government regulations may reduce the value of the property to its owners while not fully reducing the value to zero. In these cases, the owner bears the cost of the regulations.

In this paper, we examine a subsidiary cost of government takings. Specifically, we focus on the impact of government takings on entrepreneurship and the market process. Takings redirect the market process along a new path, generating costs that are often overlooked. These costs manifest themselves in forgone entrepreneurial opportunities as well as the emergence of undesirable consequences.[7] We use the term government takings in the broadest sense to include both direct (i.e., eminent domain) and indirect (i.e., regulatory takings) takings.

The starting point of our analysis is the basic premise that institutional context and the resulting "rules of the game" matter for economic, political, and social outcomes. All interactions presuppose some rules of the game and players must know what the rules are and agree to them for the game to function properly. When rules become unclear, unstable, or are altogether absent, the game tends to break down resulting in dysfunction or chaos. To provide an example of this latter point consider that a central issue facing countries transitioning from centrally planned economies to market-based systems was the absence of clear and accepted rules for the new game that was being adopted (see Boettke 1993). The absence of clear rules not only slowed the transition, but in many cases also led to corruption, inflation, and black market activity.

Property rights are a critical aspect of the broader rules of the game.[8] By deciding what belongs to whom under which circumstance, property rights provide individuals with dependable information and incentives. Well-defined and stable property rights encourage the effective use of existing scarce resources and also provide an incentive to innovate by discovering new resources, introducing new cost-cutting technologies, and developing human capital. It is in this context that we analyze the impact of government takings.

We focus on the role of property rights as a central part of the market process. Government takings change the rules of the game and hence the opportunities and incentives that entrepreneurs face. Moreover, the use of government takings introduces regime uncertainty whereby the predictability of the rules of the game is weakened. In many cases the unintended subsidiary costs of takings cannot be captured in standard cost-benefit analysis because they consist of entrepreneurial opportunities and activities that are never realized due to changes in the rules of the game.

In order to pursue this analysis we proceed as follows. In the next section we discuss the market process and the adverse impact that intervention and regulation in general has on this process. We pay particular attention to the institutional context within which entrepreneurs act and discuss how changes in the rules of the game change the relative payoff to certain types of behaviors. We then extend this logic and focus specifically on the impact of takings on the rules of the game and the market process. We conclude by considering the implications of the analysis.

## THE MARKET PROCESS AND THE PERILS OF INTERVENTION

### The Market Process

The market is best viewed as a dynamic process driven by entrepreneurs seeking pure profit (see Kirzner 1973, 1979a). Given that interventions, such as takings, distort the nature of the market process, it makes sense to briefly review the key aspects of the process view of the market. This will provide a context to better understand some of the significant, but often unrealized, subsidiary costs of government takings.

The existence of competition, defined as the freedom of entry and exit, is the essence of the dynamic market process. This freedom serves to continually pressure market participants to reallocate resources in pursuit of perceived profit opportunities. Those that perceive potential profit opportunities must be free to enter the market to pursue them and those that do enter the market but fail to successfully exploit perceived opportunities must be free to exit.

The central participant in the market process is the entrepreneur (Kirzner 1973). Acting on perceived profit opportunities, entrepreneurs serve the dual role of pushing the economy toward the production possibility frontier and shifting the frontier outward (an increase in real output due to an increase in real productivity). For the entrepreneur, yesterday's inefficiencies are today's profit opportunities and, in exploiting those opportunities, entrepreneurs serve as the catalyst of economic change. In an institutional context characterized by well-defined property rights and minimal to no government regulation, entrepreneurship will be *productive* in continually reallocating resources to their most highly valued use known to the entrepreneur at the moment of action. Moreover, productive entrepreneurial actions create new opportunities to produce more goods and services by introducing new or cost-cutting production techniques and technologies.

Every economic action has an element of entrepreneurship to it. Economic decision-makers do not simply react to given data and allocate their scarce means to realize given ends. The entrepreneurial element in human action entails the discovery of new data and information, discovering anew not only the appropriate means, but also the ends that are to be pursued. As such, entrepreneurs are the central mechanism through which market inefficiencies are corrected. Of course, market inefficiencies are never completely eradicated; but entrepreneurs are the most effective means for correcting existing errors (see Leeson, Coyne, and Boettke 2006).

Entrepreneurs lack perfect information and face constant uncertainty. As such, the market process view emphasizes "competition as a discovery procedure." As F.A. Hayek notes, competition is a "procedure for discovering facts which, if the procedure did not exist, would remain unknown or at least would not be used" (2002, 9). The competitive market process described above affords market participants the opportunity to act on existing knowledge and information and also the ability to generate previously unknown knowledge and information.[9] Much of this knowledge is context specific or knowledge of time and place that cannot possibly be known by those other than the actor (Hayek 1945). In other words, the market process allows participants the opportunity to utilize existing knowledge and information while engaging in the ongoing process of discovering new knowledge and information and opportunities for profit.

Yet another critical realization is that the market process takes place within an institutional context. Institutions can be understood as the formal and informal rules governing human behavior and their enforcement. This enforcement can occur through the internalization of certain norms of behavior, the social pressure exerted on the individual by the group, or the power of third party enforcers who can utilize force on violators of the rules. Institutions can be traditional values or codified laws. However, as binding constraints on human action, they govern human affairs for good or bad, and as they change, so will the course of economic and social development.

Both formal and informal institutional regimes provide the rules of the game that create incentives for market participants. A regime of stable and predictable property rights is critical for creating an environment where market participants can continually reallocate resources to pursue new profit opportunities. For instance, it is the lure of profit which provides an incentive for entrepreneurs to enter the market to pursue a perceived opportunity. In order for this incentive to persist, entrepreneurs must be confident that their property and any profits generated from their actions will be secure.

In addition to providing incentives, a stable and predictable regime of property rights also serves the central role in communicating information to all market participants. Ludwig von Mises (1920) emphasized that private property in the means of production were necessary for the emergence of prices.[10] These prices reflect relative scarcities, which are the very result of entrepreneurial activity. As such, the existing prices at any point in time reflect the entrepreneurial discoveries that have been made until that point. At the same time, existing prices reflect entrepreneurial errors and the potential for profit opportunities. It is the existence of the opportunity for profit that drives entrepreneurial activity and hence the market process. As the market process unfolds and entrepreneurs make adjustments to the allocation of resources, prices will adjust accordingly to reflect those changes.

## The Perils of Government Intervention

Government interventions are implemented to influence the outcome of the market process. For instance, price controls seek to influence the nature of the prices that the market process would generate absent that intervention. Similarly, zoning laws, which are regulations that restrict the uses of land and buildings, are meant to constrain the outcomes generated in real estate markets. The key point for our purposes is that interventions change the institutional context and hence the rules of the game. These interventions distort the market process relative to what would have unfolded if those regulations had not been implemented. As Israel Kirzner indicates, "government controls constrain and constrict; they rearrange and repattern the structure of incentives; they redistribute incomes and wealth and sharply modify both the process of production and composition of consumption" (1979b, 134–135).

Although interventions change the nature of the market process, they do not eradicate that process or associated profit opportunities. Instead, in altering the rules of the game, interventions and regulations alter the opportunities and incentives that entrepreneurs face. Entrepreneurs responding to the new incentives created by intervention shift their activities to take advantage of the new profit opportunities. While the exact nature and magnitude of the distortions caused by interventions will vary from case to case, there are some general insights that we can postulate regarding government intervention in the market process. Kirzner (1979b, 136–145) considers four distinct ways in which government intervention and regulation adversely impacts the market process. We consider each category in turn.

First, the use of government interventions to correct market outcomes assumes that the manipulated process will be superior to the unregulated future outcome of the market process. This, however, neglects the fact that market process is just that, a process. Future states of the world (i.e., market outcomes) are unknown, which is why the market process is inherently one of continuous discovery, as discussed earlier. Government interventions assume that a desired or perhaps even a superior, yet unknown, outcome cannot be expected to emerge as the market process continually unfolds.

In discussing this category of government intervention, Kirzner (1979b, 137–138) highlights two central misunderstandings. First, the call for government intervention overlooks the fact that it may very well be the case that that entrepreneurs have discovered everything that is currently efficient to discover at a specific point in time. In this case, what appear to be inefficiencies to those outside the market process are really not inefficiencies given the context-specific knowledge possessed by market participants. The second key misunderstanding is that without government interventions the market process will fail to correct existing inefficiencies in the future. This misunderstanding fundamentally fails to appreciate the nature of the market process. As we discussed above, the very existence of inefficiencies is what provides the incentive for future entrepreneurial action.

Kirzner's second category of government intervention in the market process deals with the fundamental knowledge problem faced by regulators. Specifically, any government intervention intended to generate a desired outcome assumes a level of knowledge on the part of government officials that they cannot possibly possess. Even if regulators have the best of intentions, how will they know the specifics of how to bring about the desired outcome? Whether it is price controls, mandated standards, redistribution, or urban development and planning, regulators cannot possibly know the "right" or "correct" levels of intervention required to generate the desired allocation of resources. Further, outside the feedback loop of profit and loss, regulators will be unable to judge if earlier decisions were correct or not. In the absence of profit and loss, there is no way for regulators to discover inefficiencies and determine if their actions generated corrections or subsequent errors in the market process.[11] As such, one should expect inefficiencies to emerge and persist when government intervenes in the market because "nothing within the regulatory process seems able to simulate even remotely well the discovery process that is so integral to the unregulated market" (Kirzner 1979b, 141).

The third impact of government regulation is that it stifles the process of discovery. As Kirzner notes, "the most serious effect of government regulation on the market discovery process well might be the likelihood that regulation, in a variety of ways, may discourage, hamper, and even completely stifle the discovery process of the unregulated market" (Kirzner 1979b, 141). The exact nature and magnitude of the stifling of the market process will depend on the specific type of intervention. For instance, some regulations may raise the cost of engaging in certain activities while others may actually restrict competition and freedom of entry and exit.

It is important to note the impact of interventions and regulations on *yet undiscovered* opportunities. Government regulation not only hampers the market for existing goods and services; it also hampers the very process by which previously nonexistent goods and services are discovered. Regulations tend to distort or constrain profit opportunities for productive activities that provide the incentive for the discovery of entirely new opportunities for profit from such activities. This negative consequence of government regulation is often neglected because it is unobservable by its very nature. For instance, one can observe the shortages or surpluses associated with price controls, but one cannot similarly observe an opportunity for discovery that would have taken place absent government intervention but which goes unrealized because of intervention. Precisely because they cannot be observed or quantified, the subsidiary costs of intervention in terms of foregone entrepreneurial opportunities that are never realized due to the intervention are rarely considered or even recognized.

Yet another way that intervention may stifle the entrepreneurial discovery process is by introducing uncertainty into the rules of the game. For example, government interventions in the present period may create uncertainty regarding the likelihood and magnitude of future government interventions. In his analysis of why the Great Depression lasted as long as it did, Robert Higgs (1997) introduced the notion of "regime uncertainty." Higgs argues that the length of the Great Depression was due to a slow recovery in private investment which "...reflected a pervasive uncertainty among investors about the security of their property rights in their capital and its prospective returns" (1997, 563).

Similar reasoning can be extended to government interventions in general, including takings. Interventions create uncertainty in the institutional regime in which entrepreneurs must act. As a result, the incentives for entrepreneurs to pursue perceived profit opportunities are weakened. The full effects of this regime uncertainty cannot be known since opportunities that would have existed absent that uncertainty will no longer be exploited. In the case of takings, the perceived uncertainty by the American public is evident from their response to the *Kelo* decision. In many states this backlash has produced laws placing restrictions on government takings (see López and Totah 2007 and Somin, this volume).[12]

The fourth and final impact of government intervention in the market process is that "whether intended by regulatory authorities or not and whether suspected by them or not, the imposition of regulatory restraints and requirements tends to create entirely new, and not necessarily desirable opportunities for entrepreneurial discovery" (Kirzner 1979b, 144). Government interventions alter the pattern of profit opportunities and the full effects of this alteration cannot possibly be known in advance by those designing and implementing the intervention. Productive entrepreneurial activities either push the economy toward the production possibility frontier or shift the frontier outward. As discussed, one adverse effect of intervention is that it stifles some of these productive activities. However, another unintended consequence of intervention is that it may create undesirable profit opportunities. Interventions, in altering the pattern of profit opportunities, tend not just to stifle productive activities but also to create opportunities for *unproductive* activities.

In contrast to productive activities, unproductive activities include crime, rent-seeking, and the destruction of existing resources among other socially destructive activities (Baumol 1990, Boettke and Coyne 2003, Coyne and Leeson 2004). In the case of unproductive entrepreneurship it is possible that profits are being earned, but by activities that do not shift the production possibility frontier outward. As an example, consider resources dedicated to rent-seeking. Rent-seeking occurs when actors seek to extract uncompensated value from others by manipulating the economic and political environment. While rent-seeking activities often lead to increased profit for the entrepreneur undertaking the activity, they result in inefficiencies for society as a whole.

Given this understanding of the perils of government intervention, we next turn to a consideration of takings. We argue that government intervention through the use of takings suffers from the problems discussed by Kirzner and is therefore more costly than most people think. Some specific examples will illuminate these claims.

## The Perils of Government Takings

William Minnich and his nephew, Bill Minnich, are the owners of Minic Custom Woodwork, a small family business over 75 years old. In 1981 they bought a run-down building in East Harlem to relocate their business. In addition to buying the building, the Minnichs also invested more than $250,000 in renovating and updating the building. All was going well with the business until William Minnich read in the *New York Times* that the Empire State Development Corporation (ESDC)—a public authority of the State of New York that finances and operates state projects—planned to redevelop the East Harlem area. Upon closer inspection of the map associated with this project, Minnich realized that the area for redevelopment included his building. The government planned to use eminent domain to seize the property and sell it to the Blumenfeld Development Corporation to build a Home Depot, Costco, and other retail stores. The justification was that the transfer of property would be a net benefit to the community in terms of jobs and tax revenue (Berliner 2003, 145–146; Carney 2006, 91–96).

Much of the maneuvering between the ESDC and the Blumenfeld Development Corporation was done behind closed doors, leaving the Minnichs in a position where they could not defend their property until it was too late. This lack of transparency became clear when the New York Supreme Court dismissed the Minnichs' lawsuit to prevent the project because they had missed the 30-day period to appeal based on a previous notice of "determination and findings," which authorized the confiscation of their property at some future time. The problem, William Minnich claimed, was that he never knew the project had been officially approved and therefore was unaware that the 30-day period had actually begun. A federal court confirmed this decision and after exhausting all efforts at appeals, the Minnichs were forced to sell their building (Berliner 2003, 145–146; Carney 2006, 91–96).

The Minnichs' story illuminates the perils of intervention discussed earlier and can be generalized to understand the adverse impacts of government takings. Takings are fundamentally an exercise in central planning in which government officials intervene to change the outcome of the natural market process. As the Minnich case indicates, the condition of "public use" has been broadly interpreted to include economic benefits (i.e., job creation, tax revenue, etc.) to the community. As discussed in the Introduction, this interpretation has historical precedent in *Berman v. Parker* (1954), *Poletown Neighborhood Council v. City of Detroit* (1981), and more recently in *Kelo v. City of New London* (2005). These economic benefits are typically calculated by carrying out an "impact analysis" that considers the associated costs and benefits of an intervention. Such an analysis attempts to place a monetary value on all of the costs of confiscating property and compares it to the expected benefits of redevelopment. However, this approach poses several key problems.

In assigning monetary values to expected costs and benefits, those carrying out the study must consider situations that have not even occurred yet. In producing these calculations, assumptions about the future must be made regarding profitability, associated tax revenue, and job creation. Typically, assumptions are also made about the "multiplier effect" of each dollar spent on the redeveloped property. Recall that Israel Kirzner noted that interventions of all types assume that government planners have superior information as compared to market participants and that interventions will produce superior outcomes compared to the unregulated market process. It is far from clear that either of these assumptions is accurate in the case of takings. Further, because the use of takings does not entail a penalty on private developers for failing to deliver on the estimated benefits, there is an incentive to overstate the estimates to support the case for takings.

As an example to illustrate some of these points, consider a study published by the Cato Institute regarding the economic benefits of bringing a Major League Baseball team to Washington, DC (Coates and Humphreys 2004). A key aspect of the negotiations between the city and baseball team was the promise of a new stadium using direct takings to acquire the land if necessary.[13] Regarding the impact studies conducted in these types of situations, the authors of the Cato report note that "The results of those studies invariably reflect the desires of the people who commission them, and advocates of stadiums and franchises typically produce impact studies that find large economic benefits from building a stadium or enticing a team to relocate to the city" (2004, 3). In an analysis of 37 cities with sports teams over a 35-year period, the authors of the report found no positive effect on overall growth rates of real per capita income and a statistically significant, negative impact on the level of real per capita income (2004, 5). The authors attribute these findings to the tax breaks that these sports teams often receive to entice them to locate to a certain city in the first place. Also, influencing this outcome is the presence of a substitution effect whereby spending on the sports team increases but spending in other areas in the community simultaneously declines.

For our purposes the important point of this study is that it is a mistake to assume that government officials, and developers attempting to convince government to utilize takings, have information superior to market participants. Similarly, it is a mistake to assume that the outcome from intervention will be superior to the outcome produced absent that intervention. As the aforementioned report indicates, there is some evidence to suggest that many cities have taken land to give to sports franchises expecting economic growth only to have a negative or no effect. Moreover, since governments act outside the market context of profit and loss, there is no means of correcting these errors where they do occur.

In general, the use of takings distorts the structure of production that arises naturally from the market process. As Murray Rothbard notes, when government uses eminent domain "the result is an overextension of resources (a malinvestment) in the privileged firm or industry and an underinvestment in other firms and industries" (1977, 77). Rothbard's point is that government takings shifts the relative payoffs associated with various entrepreneurial opportunities. The taking of property by government raises the cost of investing in certain types of business ventures and lowers the cost of investing in others. The structure of production that arises on the unhampered market is a function of consumer preferences and prices. Government intervention distorts this process by creating incentives to divert resources into other firms and industries that may not represent consumer preferences. Further, because the structure of production is an emergent process, these distortions to the structure of production, or the associated costs, are not readily evident to the outside observer because they represent forgone opportunities that never actually took place.

In changing the rules of the game, government intervention through takings also generates an unintended consequence in the form of uncertainty in formal and informal institutional regimes. This has adverse effects the magnitude of which, similar to the impact on the structure of production, cannot be measured or even realized by government bureaucrats. For instance, in those areas where it is relatively easy for government to use takings, it provides a disincentive to purchase land or make improvements to existing land. Sandy Ikeda (2004) has analyzed how government interventions not only distort the price system itself but also erode the norms and trust levels that facilitate interpersonal interaction through the price system. Focusing his analysis on interventions in the form of "urban renewal," Ikeda emphasizes that such interventions "can threaten the stability of local communities because of the drastic changes it brings to an area in a time period too short for the informal networks to form that are needed for healthy economic development" (2004, 258). Similar logic can be extended to intervention in the form of takings, which can destroy existing social networks and norms and introduce uncertainty into informal institutional regimes. As Jane Jacobs notes, takings for economic development destroy "thousands upon thousands of small businesses....whole communities are torn apart and sown to the winds, with a reaping of cynicism, resentment and despair that must be seen to be believed" (1961, 5).

To the extent that regime uncertainty exists, it lowers the payoff to productive entrepreneurial activities (Benson 2004). As such, productive activities that would have existed and been exploited absent the possibility of intervention no longer take place. For example, in the case of environmental regulations, uncompensated regulatory takings tend to increase uncertainty while discouraging private, voluntary conservation, and encourage the destruction of certain environmental resources. Further, the absence of compensation lowers the cost associated with government use of environmental regulations (see the chapter in this volume by Jonathan Adler).

It is well known that secure property rights are a critical ingredient for economic development. This is evident from both empirical studies (Acemoglu and Johnson 2005; Acemoglu, Johnson. and Robinson 2001, 2002; Hoskins and Eiras 2002; Rodrik, Subramanian, and Trebbi 2004) and fieldwork in underdeveloped countries. For instance, in his study of Peru, Hernando de Soto (1989) noted how the regime uncertainty created in the form of poorly defined and enforced property rights, corruption, and burdensome regulations, drove a majority of productive activities underground. The fundamental problem for poor countries, de Soto concludes, is transforming "dead capital" into "live capital" (2000). This process can only take place through the recognition and enforcement of stable and predictable property rights.

Of course, the United States does not suffer from the extent of regime uncertainty present in Peru and other underdeveloped countries. Nonetheless, the existence of takings in the United States is a less extreme variant of the more extreme land-use policies that exist in many third world countries where governments expropriate property as they see fit. One can see the connection between the instability created by the land and property rights policies in these third world countries and confiscatory policies, such as government takings in the United States. While the uncertainty created by takings in the United States is not as great as the uncertainty in those countries where property rights are almost nonexistent, it still exists and any movement in the direction of weakening the strength and predictability of property rights serves to increase regime uncertainty on the margin.

Between 1998 and 2002, The Institute for Justice documented over 10,000 cases nationwide of the threatened or actual use of eminent domain for private development (Berliner 2003). Perhaps a bigger issue than the large number of cases identified is that each of these cases is different in its specific characteristics. This makes it for difficult for entrepreneurs to determine any kind of general and predictable characteristics of when property will be taken for public use. There are cases of larger development corporations and "big box" retailers using eminent domain to seize land; but there are also many cases of smaller businesses using political means to avoid private markets and secure property through eminent domain (see, for instance, Staley 2003; Staley and Blair 2005). The general vagueness of when and how takings laws are applied contributes further to the distortion of the market process as well as regime uncertainty at all levels.

In his analysis of land use regulation, Bruce L. Benson suggests that "land use regulations are the result of public sector responses to demands of politically powerful special interest groups, rather than attempts to correct for market failures" (1981, 435). Benson's main point is that government interventions regarding land use regulations should not be assumed to be benevolent in nature but rather must be viewed as the outcome of the political decision-making process. This process is largely influenced by special interest groups, which attempt to manipulate political outcomes in their favor. Similarly, Jane Jacobs (1961, 270–290, 311–314) argues that the use of eminent domain for the economic development and urban renewal often serves private interests at the expense of the communities it is intended to help. Donald Kochan contends that the "public use doctrine is no longer an impediment to interest-group capture of the condemnation power in order to acquire private land by employing the power of the state to that end..." (1998, 51). The result, according to Kochan, is that legislatures can sell their power of takings to special interest groups because of the low probability that the judiciary will overturn it on the grounds that it violates public use.

In general, when the rules of the game allow for the use of the political decision-making process to secure transfers of private property, the payoff associated with unproductive activities such as rent-seeking increases. Recall that in his analysis of government intervention in the market process, Kirzner noted that government intervention not only stifles existing entrepreneurial opportunities but also creates new and often undesirable opportunities as well. This is indeed the case with government takings.

In order to provide a concrete example of the dynamics of the political decision-making process as they relate to government takings, return to the example of New York, where the Minnich case took place. Recall that the Empire State Development Corporation (ESDC) used the state's power of eminent domain to take the Minnichs' property to transfer it to the Blumenfeld Development Corporation under the guise of "economic redevelopment." However, a closer look at the ESDC and Blumenfeld indicates that there were close political connections that most likely played some role in the takings.

A 1996 report issued by the office of Democratic State Senator Franz Leichter indicated that "Since Pataki took office, more than 25 firms that made campaign contributions to Pataki, U.S. senator Al D'Amato and other State Republican political committee members have received grants and loans from the Empire State Development Corporation" (quoted in Carney 2006, 97). Indeed, since 1989, Blumenfeld had made political contributions to New York Mayor Ed Koch, Charles Schumer, Rudy Giuliani, and Al D'Amato, among many others (Carney 2006, 98). The resources that Blumenfeld invested in developing relationships with the political leaders of New York seem to have paid off. In addition to obtaining the land in East Harlem via direct takings, he also received subsidies for the redevelopment project itself in the form of tax-breaks and low-interest loans from the state.

The fact that the use of takings is heavily influenced by the political decision-making process further contributes to the perils of government interventions of this form. Decisions in the public realm are not guided by market prices and profit and loss but by political pressures. Further, when takings become a tool of first resort for private parties to acquire private property, they create new opportunities for profit through political means. As such, resources are reallocated to influencing the outcome of political decisions.

## CONCLUSION

F. A. Hayek emphasized that the main issue facing social scientists was "how the spontaneous interaction of a number of people, each possessing only bits of knowledge, brings about a state of affairs in which prices correspond to costs, etc. and

which could be brought about by deliberate direction only by somebody who possessed the combined knowledge of all those individuals" (1937, 50–51). Precisely
because individuals face incomplete and dispersed knowledge, Hayek argued for
general rules that would create an environment where individuals could discover
and act on new experiences. Hayek went on to argue that in order for this learning
process to take place, institutions and rules must be predictable so that people can
foresee the consequences of their actions and engage in interactions and transactions with confidence (1960, 148–161). Unpredictable and unstable rules create
regime uncertainty, preventing this learning process from taking place. Takings are
an example of a government power that has such an effect.

We have explored the dynamics of the market process and how the use of
government takings can distort that process and generate unintended subsidiary
costs. The use of takings to correct market outcomes assumes that the outcome
generated by the intervention will be superior to the market outcome. However,
because government actors suffer from a fundamental knowledge problem regarding future entrepreneurial opportunities and the true costs and benefits of the
redistribution, there is no reason to assume this will be the case. When one also
considers that the use of takings is heavily influenced by the political-decision
making process, we have good reason to assume that the outcome may very well
be worse than that which would be generated absent the intervention. The costs
of government takings identified in our analysis are excluded from standard cost-
benefit impact analysis because they represent forgone opportunities that were
never actually realized. Further, the unintended consequences of regime uncertainty will be neglected in these studies because such costs cannot be captured
using conventional means.

Whether the debate is focused on if the government should have the power of
takings, or on the scope of the state's existing power, the issues addressed in our
analysis must be realized and taken into consideration. To date, these issues have
received little to no attention. It is our hope that this paper is a first step in correcting this state of affairs.

## NOTES

The authors thank participants in the "Takings: The Uses and Abuses of Eminent Domain and
Land Use Regulations" symposium for useful comments and suggestions. We are especially
grateful to Bruce L. Benson and Edward Stringham for their detailed comments and suggestions.

1. For almost a century, the U.S. Constitution was actually interpreted to prevent federal government use of eminent domain, while not constraining state governments. The federal government was not allowed to condemn property directly (it had to ask a state government to use its
   eminent domain powers) until *Kohl v United States* (91 U.S. 367 (1875)). In *Kohl*, however,
   the court concluded that the Fifth Amendment implies that federal takings are constitutional.
   See Benson and Brown (this volume).
2. For a critique of the "holdout problem," see Benson (2005) and Benson and Brown (this
   volume).
3. 125 S. Ct. 2655 (2005).
4. 348 U.S. 26 (1954).
5. 410 Mich. 616 (1981).
6. *First Lutheran Church v. Los Angeles County,* 482 U.S. 304 (1987). The courts recognition that
   a statue or ordinance may impose restrictions on the use of property that are so burdensome
   that they amount to takings by the government can be traced back to *Pennsylvania Coal Co.
   v. Mahon,* 260 U.S. 393 (1922) (see Fischel 1998).

7. Benson (2004) considers the costs of forgone opportunities associated with government regulation in general.
8. We fully recognize that rules facilitating social and economic interactions are beneficial only up to a point. Too few rules will lead to chaos and dysfunction, but too many rules can be stifling. For instance, Michael Heller (1998) has identified the "tragedy of the anticommons," whereby individuals collectively waste a resource by underutilizing it because too many individuals have the right of exclusion. Heller and Eisenberg (1998) apply this logic to biomedical research and conclude that competition over patent rights may prevent beneficial products from reaching market. While fully recognizing that rules have diminishing returns, it is not our purpose here to determine the "optimal" level of rules and property rights. Instead, our focus is on exploring the costs of eminent domain and regulatory takings on the entrepreneurial process.
9. On the important distinction between knowledge and information, see Boettke (2002).
10. For an overview of the socialist calculation debate and the parallels with the issue of government intervention, see Kirzner (1979b, 121–129).
11. This is a fundamentally different point than the "dynamics of intervention" criticism of government intervention which holds that one intervention will lead to a series of subsequent interventions (see Mises 1929, Ikeda 1997, and Benson (conclusion, this volume). While this criticism is relevant, our point here is one regarding fundamental discovery. Regulators have no means of discovering the means of correcting inefficiencies in the market process.
12. For a similar response from the American public regarding the uncertainty created by regulatory takings in the 1990s, see Boudreaux, Lipford and Yandle (1995).
13. In fact it was ultimately necessary for the city of Washington, DC, to employ eminent domain to secure the property for the new stadium (see Lemke 2005).

## REFERENCES

Acemoglu, Daron and Simon Johnson. 2005. Unbundling Institutions. *Journal of Political Economy* 113: 949–995.

Acemoglu, Daron, Simon Johnson, and James Robinson. 2001. The Colonial Origins of Comparative Development: An Empirical Investigation. *The American Economics Review* 91 (5): 1369–1401.

———. 2002. Reversal of Fortunes: Geography and Institutions in the Making of the Modern World Income. *Quarterly Journal of Economics* 117 (4): 1231–1294.

Baumol, William J. 1990. Productive, Unproductive and Destructive. *Journal of Political Economy* 98 (5): 893–921.

Boettke, Peter J. 1993. *Why Perestroika Failed: The Politics and Economics of Socialist Transformation*. New York: Routledge.

———. 2002. Information and Knowledge: Austrian Economics in Search of its Uniqueness. *The Review of Austrian Economics* 15 (4): 263–274.

Boettke, Peter J. and Christopher J. Coyne. 2003. Entrepreneurship and Development: Cause or Consequence? *Advances in Austrian Economics* 6: 67–88.

Benson, Bruce L. 1981. Land Use Regulation: A Supply and Demand Analysis of Changing Property Rights. *Journal of Libertarian Studies* 5 (4): 435–451.

———. 2004. Opportunities Forgone: The Unmeasurable Costs of Regulation. *The Journal of Private Enterprise* 19 (2): 1–25.

———. 2005. The Mythology of Holdout as a Justification for Eminent Domain and Public Provision of Roads. *The Independent Review* 10 (2): 165–194.

Berliner, Dana. 2003. *Public Power, Private Gain*. Arlington, VA: Institute for Justice.

Boudreaux, Donald J., Jody Lipford, and Bruce Yandle. 1995. Regulatory Takings and Constitutional Repair: The 1990s' Property-Rights Rebellion. *Constitutional Political Economy* 6 (2): 171–190.

Carney, Timothy P. 2006. *The Big Ripoff*. New Jersey: John Wiley & Sons.

Coates, Dennis and Brad R. Humphreys. 2004. Caught Stealing: Debunking the Economic Case for D.C. Baseball. Cato Institute Briefing Paper No. 89.

Coyne, Christopher J. and Peter T. Leeson. 2004. The Plight of Underdeveloped Countries. *Cato Journal* 24 (3): 235–249.

De Soto, Hernando. 1989. *The Other Path*. New York: Basic Books.
———. 2000. *The Mystery of Capital*. New York: Basic Books.
Fischel, William A. 1998. *Regulatory Takings: Law, Economics and Politics*. Cambridge, MA: Harvard University Press.
Hayek, Friedrich A. 1937. Economics and Knowledge. *Economica* 4: 33–54.
———. 1945. The Use of Knowledge in Society. *American Economic Review*, 35 (4): 519–530.
———. [1960] (1978). *The Constitution of Liberty*. Chicago: University of Chicago Press.
———. 2002. Competition as a Discovery Procedure. *Quarterly Journal of Austrian Economics* 5 (3): 9–23.
Heller, Michael. 1998. The Tragedy of the Anticommons: Property in transition from Marx to Markets. *Harvard Law Review* 111 (3): 621–688.
Heller, Michael A. and Rebecca Eisenberg. 1998. Can Patents Deter Innovation? The Anticommons in Biomedical Research. *Science* 280 (5364): 698–701.
Higgs, Robert. 1997. Regime Uncertainty: Why the Great Depression Lasted So Long and Why Prosperity Resumed After the War. *The Independent Review* 1 (4): 561–590.
Hoskins, Lee and Ana I. Eiras. 2002. Property Rights: The Key to Economic Growth. In *2002 Index of Economic Freedom*. Washington, DC: Heritage Foundation, 37–48.
Ikeda, Sanford. 1997. *Dynamics of the Mixed Economy: Toward a Theory of Interventionism*. New York: Routledge.
———. 2004. Urban Interventionism and Local Knowledge. *The Review of Austrian Economics* 17 (2/3): 247–264.
Jacobs, Jane. 1961. *The Death and Life of Great American Cities*. New York: Random House.
Kirzner, Israel M. 1973. *Competition and Entrepreneurship*. Chicago: University of Chicago Press.
———. 1979a. *Perception, Opportunity, and Profit*. Chicago: University of Chicago Press.
———. 1979b [1985]. The Perils of Regulation: A Market-Process Approach. In, *Discovery and the Capitalist Process,* pp. 119–149. Chicago: Chicago University Press.
Kochan, Donald J. 1998. Public Use and the Independent Judiciary: Condemnation in an Interest Group Perspective. *Texas Review of Law & Politics* 3 (1): 49–116.
Leeson, Peter T., Christopher J. Coyne, and Peter J. Boettke. 2006. Does the Market Self Correct? Asymmetrical Adjustment and the Structure of Economic Error. *Review of Political Economy* 18 (1): 79–90.
Lemke, Tim. 2005. Landowners must yield to ballpark. *The Washington Times,* October 6.
López, Edward J. and Sasha M. Totah. 2007. *Kelo* and Its Discontents: The Worst (or Best?) Thing to Happen to Property Rights. *The Independent Review* 11 (3): 397–416.
Mises, Ludwig von. [1920] (1935) Economic Calulation in the Socialist Commonwealth. In *Collectivist Economic Planning,* edited by F.A. Hayek. London: George Routledge & Sons, 87–130.
———. [1929] (1977) A Critique of Interventionism: Inquiries into Economic Policy and the *Economic Ideology of the Present,* translated by Hans F. Sennholz. New York: Arlington House.
Paul, Ellen Frankel. 1985. Public Use: A Vanishing Limitation on Government Takings. *Cato Journal* 4 (3): 835–851.
Rodrik, Dani, Arvind Subramanian, and Francesco Trebbi. 2004. Institutions Rule: The Primacy of Institutions over Geography and Integration in Economic Development. *Journal of Economic Growth* 9 (2): 131–165.
Rothbard, Murray N. 1977. *Power & Market: Government and the Economy*. Kansas City: Sheed Andrews and McMeel.
Staley, Samuel R. 2003. Wrecking Property Rights: How cities use Eminent Domain to seize property for private developers. *Reason* (February): 33–38.
———. 2004. Urban Planning, Smart Growth, and Economic Calculation: An Austrian Critique and Extension. *The Review of Austrian Economics* 17 (2/3): 265–284.
Staley, Samuel R. and John P. Blair. 2005. *Eminent Domain, Private Property, and Redevelopment: An Economic Development Analysis*. Reason Foundation, Policy Study 331.

# 10

# The Adverse Environmental Consequences of Uncompensated Land-Use Controls

## Jonathan H. Adler

Private land is indispensable to environmental conservation. Over three-fourths of those species currently listed as threatened or endangered under the Endangered Species Act rely upon private land for some or all of their habitat (USGAO 1994). Most wetlands are in private hands as well (Kusler 1992, 29). In addition, a disproportionate amount of many important ecological services are provided by private lands (Thompson 2002, 249). Without conservation on private lands, meaningful ecological conservation cannot be achieved.

Recognizing private land's importance for the achievement of environmental goals, federal, state, and local governments impose extensive regulations on private land use. Such regulations typically restrict or prohibit the modification of ecologically valuable lands without government permission. The impact on property values can be significant, but landowners are rarely compensated for the costs of such rules. So long as a given regulation, by itself, does not cause a "total wipeout," government agencies rarely need to compensate landowners when preventing them from making productive use of their land.

Though well intentioned, environmental land-use controls do not always advance environmental values. Economic theory predicts and empirical research demonstrates that failing to compensate private landowners for the costs of environmental regulations discourages voluntary conservation efforts and can encourage the destruction of environmental resources. Uncompensated environmental land-use controls cause many landowners to view environmental protection as a burdensome or hostile enterprise. At the same time, failing to require compensation means that land-use regulation is "underpriced" as compared to other environmental protection measures for which government agencies must pay. This results in the "overconsumption" of land-use regulations relative to other environmental protection measures and less efficient environmental policies. Taken together, these effects suggest that *uncompensated* regulatory takings are themselves a threat to greater environmental protection.

## Perverse Incentives for Landowners

Environmental regulations that impose limits on a private landowner's ability to use land due to the environmental value of that land, discourage the production

and maintenance of ecological amenities on private land. In the traditional eminent domain context, where governments seize property so as to devote it to some
public use deemed more valuable for the community, it is possible that compensation may create a "moral hazard" for landowners (Fischel 1995). A property owner
who knows he will be compensated for any eventual taking of his land may discount the risk of an eventual taking, and therefore will be more likely to invest in
improvements to their land that could be taken for public use (Blume, Rubenfeld,
and Shapiro 1984). This causes landowners to over-invest in improvements to their
land. The threat of over-investment in development from the moral hazard created
by a compensation rule appears to be small in comparison to the inefficiencies and
costs of under-compensation, however (Fischel 2003).

The moral hazard problem that may exist in other contexts is absent where land-
use regulations seek to preserve land in an undeveloped condition. In the conservation context, it is the threat of an uncompensated taking, not the potential for
compensation, that will induce landowners to over-invest in development of their
lands (Innes 2000). This is because it is the undeveloped nature of the land—and
its value as wetlands, species habitat, or something else—that prompts the government regulation in the first place. The negative effect of uncompensated land-use
regulations on environmental conservation is best observed in the context of species
conservation. Under the Endangered Species Act (ESA), landowners are prohibited
from modifying or destroying habitat on their own land without a federal permit.
This has had significant effects on landowner willingness to provide habitat for
endangered species. As Brown and Shogren (1998, 7) explain "[s]ince owning land
which is hospitable to endangered species can dramatically circumscribe any development plans for that land, owners have an incentive to destroy the habitat before
listing occurs, sometimes known as the 'shoot, shove, and shut-up' strategy." This
is because the imposition of uncompensated restrictions on productive land use can
have a significant negative effect on land values (Miceli and Segerson 1995).

Unlike in the standard eminent domain context, where environmental preservation is at issue, "investors have available to them an alternative to reducing their
level of investment in response to the risk of future natural preservation regulation:
they can accelerate their investments and, in essence, beat the regulatory clock"
(Dana 1995, 681). Once a wetland is filled or species habitat is cleared, the land will
not be regulated for its ecological value (Turnbull 2005, 369). The surest way for
a landowner to avoid regulation under the ESA is to ensure that her land does not
constitute suitable habitat for a listed endangered species. Under current law, it is
perfectly legal for a landowner to take preventative action to make conservation of
her land less desirable. The landowner who defers the decision to develop is "opening himself to the risk that the development prohibition will be imposed at some
point in the future before the land is developed" (Turnbull 2005, 369).

The value of compensation is that it reduces the incentives to alter development
decisions so as to reduce the risk of being regulated. If a landowner knew he would
be compensated were his right to develop his land in the future effectively taken by
the government, he would feel less pressure to develop his land today. Innes (1997,
406) argues that "it is not compensation per se that is necessary for the achievement
of efficient development incentives but rather the 'equal treatment' of developed
and undeveloped property owners." In the environmental conservation context,
however, there is no "equal treatment." Land use regulations are invariably focused

on undeveloped, as opposed to developed, parcels, resulting in inefficient levels of development.

The economic effects of uncompensated land-use regulation are not confined to those land parcels that are actually regulated. The prospect of additional regulation on other lands has economic effects as well. "The *threat* of regulation, whether or not the taking actually occurs, introduces uncertainty into property rights, and as a consequence, alters investment incentives...even when not imposed, the threat of regulation itself alters private property rights by restricting landowners' perceived options" (Turnbull 2005, 367). Although development permits are potentially available, landowners and investors cannot know beforehand whether their permit applications will be granted. Indeed, there is little assurance that they will even receive a formal approval or rejection within a definite time period. This creates substantial uncertainty for landowners and investors.

Not only is preemptive habitat destruction economically inefficient and socially wasteful, but it can be environmentally devastating as well. Such "efforts inherently threaten the continued existence of the very species that the ESA is designed to protect" (Thompson 1997, 351). Habitat conservation under the ESA is the most obvious example of this phenomenon, but the same principles should apply in other conservation contexts. Writing in *Conservation Biology,* a group of wildlife biologists observed that "the regulatory approach to conserving endangered species and diminishing habitats has created anti-conservation sentiment among many private landowners who view endangered species as economic liabilities." (Main, Roka, and Noss 1999, 1263) As they explain:

> Landowners fear a decline in the value of their properties because the ESA restricts future land-use options where threatened or endangered species are found but makes no provisions for compensation. Consequently, endangered species are perceived by many landowners as a financial liability, resulting in anticonservation incentives because maintaining high-quality habitats that harbor or attract endangered species would represent a gamble against loss of future opportunities (Main, Roka, and Noss 1999, 1265).

The problem is not simply that some landowners have the incentive to engage in "scorched earth" practices to prevent their land from becoming inhabited by endangered species, there is also a greater reluctance to manage land to enhance or restore habitat. This is a problem because, "in numerous cases, the absence of harmful behavior may not be enough" to conserve and recover endangered species (Langpap and Wu 2004, 436). As the Fish and Wildlife Service (FWS) has acknowledged, the costs imposed by habitat modification restrictions "actually generate disincentives for private landowner support for threatened species conservation."[1] As a consequence of these negative incentives there is less and lower-quality available habitat for endangered species.

Anecdotal accounts of private landowners induced to take "anti-environmental" action in response to environmental land-use regulations are legion.

- In California's Central Valley, farmers plow fallow fields to destroy potential habitat and prevent the growth of vegetation that could attract endangered species (Warren 1997). In Kern County, California, landowners regularly disced their lands to prevent the regrowth of species habitat. As one landowner explained, "Because of the Endangered Species Act we disc everything all the time. We are afraid of an endangered species moving in. It [discing] costs $25 per acre. It's not cheap. But the risk of not doing it is too great" (Parrish 1995).

- In the Pacific Northwest, the FWS found that land-use restrictions imposed to protect the northern spotted owl scared private landowners enough that they "accelerated harvest rotations in an effort to avoid the regrowth of habitat that is usable by owls."[2] In some logging communities, the recommended response to a spotted owl siting is to "shoot, shovel, and shut up."

- In Texas Hill Country, landowners razed hundreds of acres of juniper tree stands after the golden-cheeked warbler was listed as an endangered species to prevent their occupation (Wright 1992; Delong 1997, 103).

- In Boiling Springs Lakes, North Carolina, landowners began clearing timber from their property while the FWS drew up maps of red-cockaded woodpecker nests. Once these maps were issued, landowners feared, more land would be placed off limits to logging or development (Rawlins 2006). In just eight months, the city issued 368 logging permits, even though few landowners sought building permits. In an ironic twist, the primary reason the small town was so attractive to red-cockaded woodpeckers in the first place was because tree notches left from local turpentine production made the pines better potential nesting sites (NY Times, 2006).

- When the Fish and Wildlife Service proposed listing the San Diego Mesa Mint as endangered, land containing the plant was bulldozed before the listing could take effect[3] (Mann and Plummer 1995a, Mann and Plummer 1995b).

Some environmental activist groups have sought to discount or deny anecdotal accounts of the ESA's perverse incentives and their implications for successful species conservation. John Echeverria (2005, 22), for example, argues the "perverse environmental costs of the regulatory approach are probably overstated." A lawyer with the National Wildlife Federation even maintained that the ESA "has never prevented property owners from developing their land" (Kostyack 1994).

As anecdotal evidence of the ESA's anti-environmental incentives mounted, however, and species dependent on private land failed to improve, some environmental leaders took notice. Among them was wildlife law expert Michael Bean of Environmental Defense. In a 1994 speech to FWS personnel, Bean (1994) acknowledged:

> increasing evidence that at least some private landowners are actively managing their land so as to avoid potential endangered species problems. The problems they're trying to avoid are the problems stemming from the Act's prohibition against people taking endangered species by adverse modification of habitat. And they're trying to avoid those problems by avoiding having endangered species on their property.

As Bean recounted, the incentives of the ESA created a race to clear potential habitat before the FWS would impose additional requirements.

Bean observed that landowners could take a number of different steps to avoid "endangered species problems," including "deliberately harvesting their trees before they reach sufficient age to attract woodpeckers," even if this meant harvesting timber "before they reach the optimum age from an economic point of view." Moreover, "simply by refraining from understory management," or replanting alternate tree species, landowners could further make their lands less attractive to red cockaded woodpeckers (Bean 1994). While Bean characterized these effects as "surprising" in a subsequent article (Bean 1998), in 1994 he characterized landowner responses as "fairly rational decisions motivated by a desire to avoid potentially significant economic constraints," and "nothing more than a predictable response to the familiar perverse incentives that sometimes accompany regulatory programs" (Bean 1994).

## EMPIRICAL EVIDENCE OF ANTI-ENVIRONMENTAL EFFECTS

For the purposes of environmental conservation, the important question is whether the negative effects of environmental land-use controls are isolated or more widespread. In 1993, Dr. Larry McKinney (1993, 74), Director of Resource Protection for the Texas Parks and Wildlife Department stated his belief that "more habitat for the black-capped vireo, and especially the golden-cheeked warbler, has been lost in those areas of Texas since the listing of these birds than would have been lost without the ESA at all." Yet he also acknowledged that he lacked the empirical evidence to substantiate his belief. In the past several years, however, researchers have undertaken more systematic analyses of the incentives created by uncompensated land-use controls.

The first study providing solid empirical evidence of the negative environmental effects of uncompensated land-use regulations was an examination of how private timber owners respond to the presence of endangered red-cockaded woodpeckers (RCWs) in North Carolina. Lueck and Michael (2003) examined the rate of preemptive habitat destruction by owners of private timberland at risk of federal regulation. Their findings confirmed that the ESA creates negative incentives for private landowners, and that these incentives have a significant effect on habitat for the red-cockaded woodpecker, a species dependent upon private timberland in the southeastern United States.

Lueck and Michael (2003, 31) reported that "increases in the probability of ESA land-use restrictions, as measured by a landowner's proximity to existing RCW colonies, increase the probability of forest harvest and decrease the age at which timber is harvested." Providing habitat for a single red-cockaded woodpecker colony can cost up to $200,000 in foregone timber harvests. To avoid this cost, those landowners at greatest risk of ESA-imposed restrictions were most likely to prematurely harvest their forestlands and to reduce the length of their timber harvesting rotations. The ultimate consequences were potentially significant as RCWs rely upon older trees for nesting cavities. When timber rotations are shortened, this deprives RCWs of potential habitat, as trees are not allowed to age enough to provide suitable habitat. Lueck and Michael estimate that several thousand acres of woodpecker habitat is lost in this way, enough to provide habitat for between 25 and 76 red-cockaded woodpecker colonies in the state of North Carolina alone. Given that the ESA only provided protection for 84 woodpecker colonies on private land at the time of the Lueck and Michael study, their findings are quite significant.

A second study on red-cockaded woodpecker habitat reinforced the Lueck and Michael findings. Zhang (2004, 151) found that "regulatory uncertainty and lack of positive economic incentives alter landowner timber harvesting behavior and hinder endangered species conservation on private lands." Absent the regulatory uncertainty created by the ESA, "landowners choose among harvesting methods to maximize stumpage revenue...subject to constraints such as forest stand characteristics..., aesthetics, management objective, and tax liability" (Zhang 2004, 155). The threat of regulatory prohibitions on timber activity, however, alters the landowners' calculation. Zhang (2004, 160) found that "a landowner is 25 percent more likely to cut forests when he or she knows or perceives that a RCW cluster is within a mile of the land than otherwise." The threat of ESA regulation also increased the likelihood that a landowner would engage in clear-cutting when harvesting the timber, as opposed to a selective harvesting technique that may have less severe ecological impacts. Thus, Zhang (2004, 162) concluded, "at least for the RCW, the ESA has a strong negative effect on habitat," and this effect appears to be "substantial."

The Zhang study, like the Lueck and Michael study, confirms the anecdotal observations about the effect of uncompensated environmental land-use restrictions.

> Despite the use of different data, the basic conclusions reached in these two studies are similar: the ESA regulations actually lead landowners [to] cut their timber sooner, to the detriment of the RCW, than they otherwise would do. As a consequence, RCW habitats have been reduced on private lands because of the ESA. In this case the ESA imposes costs but does not generate conservation benefits (Zhang 2004, 162).

These findings are further supported by data showing that the rate and magnitude of reforestation investment is reduced by the risk of environmental land-use regulation, and that government incentive programs may alleviate the magnitude of these negative incentives (Zhang and Flick 2001, 454).

A study of landowner responses to the listing of the endangered Preble's Meadow jumping mouse in *Conservation Biology* provides still more empirical evidence that the ESA discourages private landowner cooperation with federal conservation efforts. Brook, Zinto, and De Young (2003) conducted a survey of private owners of Preble's Meadow jumping mouse habitat, finding that a significant number of landowners took actions to make their lands less hospitable to the mouse when it was listed as an endangered species. While some landowners sought to improve the quality of the habitat on their land, the data suggested that "the efforts of landowners who acted to help the Preble's were cancelled by those who sought to harm it" (Brook, Zinto, and De Young 2003, 1643). This led Brook, Zinto, and De Young (2003, 1644) to conclude that "[t]he current regulatory approach to the conservation of rare species is insufficient to protect the Preble's mouse," and that "as more landowners become aware that their land contains Preble's habitat, it is likely that the impact on the species may be negative."

Brook, Zinto and De Young (2003) further illustrates that the imposition of land-use regulations can have a negative environmental effect. Those landowners who undertook conservation activities did so in response to the species' listing. Given their support for environmental stewardship, these landowners responded positively to the information that their land was important to an endangered species. Unless one believes that there is widespread visceral hostility to endangered species, as such, those who took negative actions almost certainly did so due to the threat of regulation, and its economic consequences, and not because the species was endangered. Thus, it is the imposition of uncompensated regulatory controls on private land-use that encourages landowners to take actions adverse to the survival of endangered species such as the Preble's Meadow jumping mouse.

A fourth recent study of uncompensated ESA regulation sought to measure "the extent to which landowners act to preempt regulation during the urban growth process" by accelerating the rate at which land is developed (List, Margolis, and Osgood 2006, 1–2). This study focused on landowner responses to the threat of regulation of habitat for the Cactus Ferruginous pygmy owl near Tucson, Arizona. List, Margolis, and Osgood (2006) found that land designated as critical owl habitat was, on average, developed one year earlier than equivalent parcels that were not designated as habitat. When the pygmy owl was listed, and proposed critical habitat was published, months before regulatory responses were imposed, "allowing landowners ample time to respond" (List, Margolis, and Osgood 2006, 16). These findings are reinforced by additional data showing that the value of undeveloped land designated as critical habitat fell relative to other lands in the study area.

One potential criticism of the List, Margolis, and Osgood analysis is that it overstates the importance of critical habitat designations. Unpermitted land modifications that could alter or destroy habitat are prohibited under Section 9 whether or not a given parcel is identified as "critical habitat." Habitat designations nonetheless provide information about the likelihood of a given land parcel's being regulated. As such, when proposed a critical habitat designation is published, it could induce landowners to take preemptive action, as their study found.

While List, Margolis, and Osgood (2006) focused on the timing of development, it should be noted that government actions that encourage more rapid development can be expected to result in more development. For ecological purposes, the decision to develop land is largely irreversible. At the same time, land that is not developed today can still be conserved or protected before it is developed tomorrow. Thus preventing—or, at least, avoiding creating incentives for—premature development is important to the ultimate goal of ecological conservation.

Most of the available evidence on the perverse incentives created by uncompensated land-use restrictions focuses on the ESA. This does not mean that other environmental regulations that limit or prohibit the development or productive use of ecologically valuable lands do not induce the same sorts of effects. For example, in 1999, when North Carolina regulators proposed more stringent wetland drainage regulations, the rate of wetland drainage and development on private land increased dramatically, as landowners sought to act before the new rules came into effect (Lueck and Michael 2003, 51). In other cases, landowners have sought to develop wetlands on private land before they are discovered by federal regulators.[4]

Such anecdotal accounts notwithstanding, it is possible that wetlands conservation measures under section 404 may not produce the same level of preemptive destruction. It is quite likely, however, that section 404 can discourage the voluntary creation and restoration of wetlands on private land in a similar fashion. Federal wetland regulations apply equally to human-created as naturally formed wetlands, and private landowners have faced criminal prosecution for altering artificially created wetlands without federal permits. As a consequence, there is no reason why federal wetland regulations would not discourage wetland creation and restoration on private land in much the same fashion as the ESA discourages habitat creation and maintenance on such lands.

## Compromising Scientific Research

The perverse, anti-environmental incentives of uncompensated environmental land-use regulation are not limited to the provision and maintenance of habitat. The threat of land-use regulation also discourages private landowners from cooperating with scientific research on their land, further compromising conservation efforts. As Polasky and Doremus (1998, 41) observe, "[t]he current ESA...gives landowners little incentive to cooperate with information collection activity. Under these conditions, both information collection and species conservation on private lands are likely to occur at less than optimal levels."

Despite the importance of private land for species preservation, most research on endangered species occurs on government land (Hilty and Merenlender 2003, 133). Private landowners may be reluctant to allow wildlife biologists and other researchers onto their land, fearing the discovery of endangered or threatened species populations will result in the imposition of land-use controls. "Under current conservation rules, information is a prerequisite to regulation. Therefore, as a result, property owners and regulators have sharply divergent views of the desirability of increased information about species status and distribution" (Polasky and Doremus 1998, 23). Regulators want greater information about the status and location of endangered species and their habitat, whereas property owners fear the disclosure of such information could lead to costly regulation.

The lack of more complete data on endangered species and their habitat complicates species conservation efforts. In some cases, "a private landowner might be the only individual who knows a listed species is on his or her land" (Shogren, Smith, and Tschirhart 2005, 217). This information asymmetry makes enforcement of the ESA's habitat modification prohibition particularly difficult. There is little question that some species populations and ecological resources are neglected because they reside on private lands, and private landowners are reluctant to cooperate with conservation officials due to the fear of environmental regulation. Indeed, the more important a given parcel of private land is to species conservation efforts, the more important is accurate information about the ecological condition of the land—and the greater potential negative consequences of uncompensated land-use controls.

Brook et al. (2003) provide empirical evidence that these incentives are significant. Specifically, it found that more landowners would refuse to give biologists permission to conduct research on their land to assess mouse populations, out of fear that land-use restrictions would follow the discovery of a mouse on their land, than would allow such research. "Many landowners appeared to defend themselves against having their land-management options restricted by refusing to allow surveys for the Preble's" (Brook, et al. 2003, 1644).

The incentives against habitat conservation created by federal land-use regulation interact with the incentives against allowing scientific research on private land. Regulatory uncertainty can discourage private landowners from participating in conservation banking and other efforts to facilitate private land conservation. Specifically, landowners "fear that investigating opportunities will reveal previously unrecognized endangered species and, in the event that a bank is not established, result in increased enforcement of the ESA" (Fox and Nino-Murcia 2005, 1006).

## From Conscription to Enlistment

If endangered species habitat is not preserved on private land, many endangered species will not survive. "Habitat destruction and degradation are by far the leading threats to biodiversity, contributing to the endangerment of at least eighty-eight percent of the plants and animals on the endangered species list" (Wilcove 1998, 277–278). Yet the ESA and other regulatory measures have not been particularly effective at preserving habitat on private land (Main et al. 1999, 1263). One reason for this is that "the consistent exclusion of economic behavior in the calculus of endangered species protection has led to ineffective and, in some instances, counterproductive conservation policy" (Shogren et al, 1999, 1258). Even strong advocates of regulatory measures to protect endangered species habitat acknowledge that "[n]o one...suggests that the federal ESA is realizing Congressional intent or that it has been implemented rationally or responsibly" (Dwyer, Murphy, and Erhlich 1995, 736).

Providing compensation to landowners who are denied the productive use of their land by habitat-conservation regulations would go a long way toward reducing the resentment and hostility many landowners feel toward endangered species. As Thompson (1997, 351–352) summarizes: "A system of complete compensation would reduce both political and economic investment by landowners. Property owners would have little incentive to oppose the ESA, prematurely develop their property, or otherwise destroy habitat." Compensation at fair-market value will not always fully compensate landowners as such compensation will often fail to compensate landowners for the subjective value they place on the land. Nor will such compensation reflect the land's nonmarket value as species habitat. Nonetheless, compensation would make an important contribution to species conservation efforts.

If those who value the preservation of species habitat are required to pay for its protection—either through government compensation or voluntary private transactions—the incentive to destroy habitat, hide information about species populations, and oppose science-based listing decisions largely disappears. Moreover, the prospect of economic gain from the cost-effective provision of species habitat will direct private energies in more positive directions. Much as IP Timberlands learned to manage their lands so as to maximize recreation revenue on timberlands during decades-long timber rotations, habitat owners will learn to appreciate the economic—and perhaps even the ecological—value of their lands (Anderson and Leal 2001, 4–8). One does not need to share the ecological values held by many Americans to recognize the potential to gain through meeting the demands such values create. Some landowners undertake conservation efforts not because ecological conservation is an important value to them, but because it is an important value to others.

Compensation can also help transform the relationship between the government and private landowners so as to encourage greater trust and openness in environmental policy. Many landowners are very willing to cooperate with conservation goals, so long as they are not forced to bear the lion's share of the cost. Landowners are often willing to learn about, and even enhance, the ecological value of their land. Again, however, this must be something for which they will not be punished economically. Providing compensation reduces the threat posed by scientific information about the location and status of endangered species. Compensation can help encourage landowners to act as if motivated by a conservation ethic in part because it treats them as respected conservationists, as opposed to the government's uncompensated conscripts. Indeed, the threat of uncompensated regulatory takings under existing environmental regulations increases the potential costs of inducing greater voluntary conservation on such lands (Zhang 2004, 151, n.1).

## PERVERSE INCENTIVES FOR GOVERNMENT AGENCIES

The anti-environmental consequences of uncompensated environmental land-use regulations are not limited to the effects of such measures on private landowners. The lack of a compensation requirement also creates incentives for government agencies to adopt suboptimal conservation strategies and creates political distortions that further frustrate the achievement of environmental goals.

Regulators and government bureaucrats are as much economic actors as anyone else, in that they respond to changes in economic incentives on the margin. Changes in economic incentives can influence the behavior of government agencies (Anderson 1982). The reactions of government agencies to changes in incentives may be more complicated to model and predict than those of private firms, but this does not mean the effects of such incentives can be ignored. Legal changes that alter the incentives faced by agency personnel will alter the agency's behavior.

When government agencies impose conservation restrictions on private land without paying compensation, they create an incentive for private landowners not to maintain ecological amenities on their land. At the same time, when government agencies are not required to pay for the costs of such regulatory controls, they may suffer from "fiscal illusion" and over-rely upon such measures as compared with potentially available alternatives. Because agencies are not required to pay for the costs of their regulatory restrictions, such measures are underpriced relative to available alternatives. The resulting perversities are two-fold. The federal government simultaneously "seizes more property rights than it needs to protect a given habitat" while providing "too little habitat protection over all, as the government avoids the political costs of the ESA by dragging its feet on actions such as listing species" (Morriss and Stroup 2000, 789).

Environmental land-use regulations often enable the government to obtain the benefits of land acquisition without bearing the full cost of such actions. Therefore, the government acts under the "illusion" that land-use controls are less costly than they actually are.[5] When a government agency seeks to advance conservation values by purchasing lands, acquiring non-possessory property interests, or providing technical assistance or monetary incentives, it must pay for such measures. When the same agency seeks to advance conservation by imposing regulatory limits on private land use, however, no payment is required. The economic costs of such regulations borne by the landowners are "off-budget expenditures" (Thompson 2002, 288). As a consequence, there is little assurance that the government "will truly value the resources it takes from the private sector," (Fischel 1995, 144) particularly as compared to those resources that are accounted for within agency budgets. The failure to account for private costs is not simply a "mistake" by the government. Indeed, it may be a deliberate consequence of majoritarian decision-making, as political majorities (or influential interest groups) impose the costs of their preference for land conservation on a minority of landowners.

Where expenditures are on budget, funds must be appropriated by Congress and, insofar as legislatively authorized, agencies must allocate funds to competing agency priorities and programs. The adoption of land-use controls, such as are authorized under section 9 of the ESA or section 404 of the Clean Water Act (CWA), does not impose additional costs on agencies.[6] As a result, agencies are likely to "over-invest" in such measures, as compared to potential alternative measures. As viewed from the agency perspective, "land is 'free,'" but alternatives are not. Much as conscription resulted in the military's over-reliance on labor as a factor input, a no-compensation rule encourages the government to over-use land as an input into environmental conservation. This is not meant to diminish the importance of land in environmental conservation, but only to note that it can be overused like any factor input.

Fiscal illusion is a problem insofar as it prevents government agencies from considering the trade-offs inherent in environmental policy. As Professors Morriss and Stroup (2000, 788–789) observe:

> Unlike private land managers, government biologists face no opportunity costs for their decisions to place restrictions on the use of private land.... Because they are not required to compensate a private landowner for reducing the value of the landowner's property, they need not consider the value of the alternative uses of the land. Indeed, the [Endangered Species] Act forbids such considerations.

Environmentalist organizations and citizen groups are likely to suffer from fiscal illusion as well. Such groups often sue federal agencies to force greater regulation of private land. Such suits can trigger regulatory action and limits on private land use, but this does not come at the expense of other conservation measures. Just as regulators can be expected to over-use land-use regulation as compared to other conservation measures, environmentalist groups can be expected to seek the imposition of such measures more than would be optimal both because they do not bear the opportunity costs to conservation of such action, and because the existing regulatory structure does not provide public interest organizations with equivalent means of triggering alternative conservation measures. Even an organization that seeks to ensure the optimal use of agency resources can suffer from fiscal illusion because of the "off-budget" nature of land-use regulations.

The by-now familiar case of *Lucas v. South Carolina Coastal Council*[7] is a good example of how regulatory agencies can suffer from "fiscal illusion." The *Lucas* story illustrates that when agencies do not bear the costs of their regulatory measures, they have a more difficult time identifying whether a given land-use control is actually worthwhile. After David Lucas purchased two beachfront lots on the South Carolina Coast, the state legislature adopted a new Beachfront Management Act and created a coastal regulatory agency, the South Carolina Coastal Council. Although there were homes on either side of each of his lots, the council denied Lucas permission to make similar use of his land, claiming the addition of two homes along the coast would threaten significant public harm (Rinehart and Pompe 1995; Been 2004).

Lucas' challenge to the council's regulatory restrictions as uncompensated takings of his land was ultimately successful. The U.S. Supreme Court held that unless the development restrictions could be justified as inhering in the title to the land itself, the prohibition amounted to a taking under the Fifth Amendment. In such cases, the court observed, there is a particular risk that government-imposed land-use controls are, in actuality, efforts to produce public benefits at private expense. As Justice Scalia noted in his opinion for the Court in *Lucas,*

> regulations that leave the owner of land without economically beneficial or productive options for its use—typically, as here, by requiring land to be left substantially in

its natural state—carry within them a heightened risk that private property is being pressed into some form of public service under the guise of mitigating serious public harm.[8]

After additional legal skirmishing over damages, the South Carolina Coastal Council agreed to purchase the lots for $1.5 million (Rinehart and Pompe 1995, 82). Yet now that the South Carolina Coastal Council was required to pay for the land upon which it sought to prohibit development, it determined that prohibition was not so important after all, promptly selling the property to developers. Large houses were subsequently built on each lot, amidst the row of houses that already occupied the beachfront block.

As the owner of the lots, the state would now bear the costs of its decisions as to how the land would be used. The Council was no longer operating under the "illusion" that its actions were cost-free, and its behavior changed accordingly. As one state official explained, "We felt that we had an obligation to offer the property to the public and get the highest price" (Rinehart and Pompe 1995, 82). The resources necessary to prevent development of two beachfront lots on an already developed beachfront could better serve the Council's conservation mission if devoted to some other purpose. Even those who defended the council's regulations acknowledged that this decision "opens the state to charges of hypocrisy when it is willing to have an economic burden fall on an individual but not when the funds have to come out of an agency's budget" (Lehrman 1993).

Some critics of the "fiscal illusion" argument suggest that "the common view of takings payments as an instrument to deter excessive regulation depends upon important implicit and, upon examination, implausible assumptions regarding the incentives regulators face" (Brennan and Boyd 2005, 200). Specifically, "regulators are not independent principals; they make policy decisions at the behest of environmentalists and property owners affected by such decisions" (Brennan and Boyd 2005, 190). Others claim that "[t]he notion that governments must be forced to pay compensation to ensure that they enact only efficient regulation implicitly assumes that government actors are the equivalent of rational profit-maximizing firms" (Been and Beauvais 2003, 92).

Such critiques of "fiscal illusion" adopt the wrong standard of measure. The relevant policy question in the real world is not whether a given policy reform will result in *the* paradigmatic efficient outcome. Such outcomes only exist in theoretical models. Rather, the question is whether, given realistic assumptions, a specific reform will move policy in a preferable direction on the margin. The suggestion here is that requiring compensation to be paid by the agency responsible for the land-use restriction will improve the agency decision-making process on the margin, generating a more desirable policy outcome.

Professor Farber suggests that "if we adopt a public interest theory of government, internalizing a cost makes no difference," because public spirited policymakers would "take into account all the costs and benefits" of government action irrespective of whether those costs are borne by the government" (Farber 1992, 288). Yet this is only the case if one assumes away many of the problems that even the most public-spirited government will face in policy development and implementation. Among the most serious of these difficulties is the information problem. Government agencies face tremendous difficulty in accumulating and processing all of the information relevant to centralized policy decisions (Hayek 1945).

The problem of "fiscal illusion" is not dependent on the assumption that "the regulator is nonbenevolent" (Polasky and Doremus 1998, 42). Rather, it is dependent only upon the assumption that even the best intentioned of regulators have limited capacities and will, on the margin, be influenced by changes in the costs and benefits of given actions. This proposition should be indisputable. When one recognizes that even well-intentioned and proficient regulators will suffer from information problems and other government failures, the likelihood of some amount of "fiscal illusion" increases greatly. Indeed, insofar as some costs of government action are off-budget, this increases the information problem for agencies.

To calculate the costs and benefits of a given government project, the government decision-maker needs access to information about the preferences and circumstances of all those who are gong to be affected by the decision. In practice, no government agency has access to such information, nor could it (Hayek 1945). A compensation mechanism can lessen this problem at the margin insofar as the potential for compensation facilitates the generation of prices that are an important and effective means of transmitting dispersed information about costs and benefits in the marketplace. Requiring compensation does not completely cure the information problem, to be sure, but it does reduce it at the margin. Further, Tollison (1992, 139) observes,

> The market for alternative uses of land is highly efficient....A compensation policy basically insures that land prices will not be distorted by government projects and that government will face relevant market prices for its land acquisitions. Thus, compensation allows private markets in land to work efficiently, conveying the correct information about opportunity cost to investors and so forth. A no-compensation policy would lower the price of land throughout the economy and inject uncertainty into the process of investing in real property.

Critics of "fiscal illusion" further argue that the theory is dependent upon the government treating "a requirement to pay compensation as a cost to itself rather than to the taxpayers who support it. In practice, of course, the costs of compensation are borne by tax-payers, not the regulators who actually make decisions" (Brennan and Boyd 2006, 190–191). Taxpayers, the argument continues, may not be particularly responsive to the marginal increase or reallocation of government spending caused by a compensation requirement. "Taxpayers are an extremely large, diffuse group. History provides little reason to think they will be a powerful political force in resisting small increases in government spending" (Farber 1992, 293). The money required to compensate landowners for the consequences of environmental land-use regulation is easily lost in the federal budget, such that no taxpayer will feel the consequence.

The discipline imposed on regulatory agencies derives less from the political opposition of taxpayers, however, than from the agencies own desire to command resources to achieve its goals. Regulatory agencies have set budgets. As a result, they *will* feel the consequences of a compensation requirement if it places a constraint on agency activities. Insofar as a compensation requirement forces an agency to consider trade-offs in resource allocation that it did not have to consider in the past, it can be expected to weigh the opportunity costs of different conservation strategies. It can also facilitate greater oversight of agency behavior, as placing the costs of regulatory controls "on budget" makes it easier to evaluate how an agency is expending its resources.

While the empirical evidence of "fiscal illusion" is not as robust as that demonstrating the perverse incentives created by uncompensated takings under Section 9 of the ESA, observed agency behavior seems to support the claim. There is no statutory requirement that the FWS provide compensation, nor have landowners brought successful challenges to land-use restrictions under section 9 of the ESA in federal court.[9] Moreover, there are various procedural obstacles to bringing successful takings challenges under the ESA, including the FWS' reluctance to issue a final determination on whether a proposed use of land will violate the ESA (Thompson 1997, 325–326).

A review of "Takings Implication Assessments" conducted by the FWS "suggests that the FWS does not believe current takings law significantly constrains their actions under the ESA" (Thompson 1997, 336). It also appears that private landowners are aware of the long odds against a successful takings claim under the ESA. Worse, the government has no incentive—if even the ability—to make trade-offs when implementing current policy. Under the ESA, "there is no explicit recognition of relative costs and benefits. . . . A species with high economic costs of recovery and possibly low economic benefits has the same standing as a species with palpably large economic benefits and small costs" (Brown and Shogren 1998, 6). Similarly, if the FWS declines to regulate one area, this does not release resources that can be devoted to a more pressing conservation priority.

Despite the ample evidence that land-use restrictions may do more harm than good—evidence of which federal agencies are explicitly aware—the FWS and other agencies continue to impose such restrictions at the expense of other measures. For instance, "[b]efore the decision in *Sweet Home,* the government over a 25-year period spent $253,900,000 to purchase about 360,000 acres of land for critical habitat. Yet a single designation for the coastal California gnat-catcher brought 3.8 million acres of coastal scrub habitat beneath the jurisdiction of the FWS" (Epstein 1997, 25). At present, there is no incentive to consider the alternative ways of allocating agency resources to maximize attainment the agency's overall conservation objectives because some inputs are underpriced, and the existing statutory structure does not provide for such flexibility. Requiring compensation and enabling agencies to consider alternatives to land-use controls could improve upon this situation.

## MONEY FOR SOMETHING

It is not entirely true that "the incentive effects of compensation are *only* desirable . . . to the extent that inefficient projects are deterred" (Farber 1992, 129). This is an unduly narrow view of how a compensation requirement can change the way in which government agencies operate. A compensation requirement can encourage government agencies to consider most cost-effective means of implementing specific projects, help overcome the information problems faced by centralized government agencies, and improve transparency and accountability. In this way, compensation may not *reduce* the amount of conservation activity as much as it could lead to more optimal conservation measures.

The positive effect of a compensation requirement on the incentives faced by government agencies may be less obvious, but it is no less important than those for private landowners. Requiring compensation transforms private land from an off-budget acquisition to a conservation policy input that must be paid for like any other. As Fischel and Shapiro (1988, 269) explain, requiring compensation "serves the dual purpose of offering a substantial amount of protection to private entitlements, while disciplining the power of the state, which would otherwise over-expand unless made to pay for the resources that it consumes." If agencies have sufficient latitude to act upon the incentives this change creates—an assumption that does not always hold—they can consider the trade-offs inherent in developing conservation policy, and allocate scarce government resources so as to achieve the maximum return. Contrary to the claim of some compensation opponents, the result is less likely to be a lessening of environmental conservation than a greater consideration of the relative cost-effectiveness of various strategies leading to more optimal conservation policies. Once a federal agency is forced to face its true budget constraint, it is more likely to optimize its function by devoting its resources to their best uses.

There are always trade-offs when government agencies devote greater resources to one matter over another. For example, the traditional emphasis on enforcement at the U.S. Environmental Protection Agency came at the expense of scientific and technical research, policy development, and other agency priorities (Landy, Roberts, and Thomas 1994, 36). Just as the aim of pollution control can sometimes be advanced by substituting compliance assurance and technical assistance for greater enforcement efforts, shifting resources from land-use control to other policy initiatives could yield greater environmental returns. One of the problems of current conservation policy is that agencies act as if such trade-offs do not exist because they do not bear the full costs of certain policy measures. While this facilitates greater land-use control, it is not always to the benefit of environmental conservation reducing land-use regulations need not reduce environmental conservation.

A compensation rule "gives the government a choice. It can continue the regulation if it values it above the market price." (Fischel 2003, 364). If not, it may devote the relevant resources to some other goal. If agencies are allowed some discretion in the selection of means to achieve statutory goals, a compensation rule also places land-use control on the same plane as other conservation tools, so that the costs and benefits of each may be evaluated, and the agency may adopt the most cost-effective combination of measures.

Federal officials argue that proposals to fund payment out of individual agency budgets are "clearly intended to punish a federal agency for any action that would inconvenience any property owner to the slightest degree" (Tiefer 1996, 511). Yet the aim is not to "punish" federal officials so much as to discipline them, and force them to recognize trade-offs and the social costs of their decisions. In testimony before the U.S. House of Representatives, then-FWS Director Jamie Rappaport-Clark reported that, "taxpayer money spent on compensation for legally required agency actions is money not spent on protection and recovering the species needing the protections of the ESA" (Morriss and Stroup 2000, 788). This is precisely the point. Forcing agency expenditures to be on-budget forces agencies to report on the true costs of their regulatory actions and to acknowledge the trade-offs their policy decisions impose.

Opponents of takings compensation fear that a compensation requirement would produce the de facto repeal of existing environmental laws. They warn that "judicial decisions that find permit denials constitute takings may alter agency behavior. . . . As large takings judgments mount, agencies will become reluctant to engage in strict enforcement of laws and regulations designed to protect wetlands" (Gardner 1996, 543). Such requirements "provide a powerful incentive for agencies to grant permits that will harm the health, safety and property of neighbors" rather than risk a negative court judgment (Sugameli 1997, 80; Gardner 1996, 547).

Where the imposition of land-use controls is economically efficient, compensation is not an obstacle to sound policy, as the "losing" landowners can be compensated out of the surplus (Fischel 2003, 352–53). There is also reason to believe that agencies could revise easement acquisition and voluntary conservation programs so as to both increase landowner participation rates as well as to lower compensation payments. In the species conservation context, there are many different mechanisms that can be used to encourage or ensure conservation on private land, short of outright acquisition. The cost of a conservation easement can be as little as 30 percent of the cost of acquiring a fee simple interest in land (Shaffer, et al. 2002). Some studies indicate that voluntary conservation agreements can achieve many of the results of more permanent measures at a fraction of the cost (Main, Roka, and Noss 1999, 1270).

The potential to substitute government land-use control with more effective conservation strategies can readily be seen in the context of wetlands regulation. Land acquisition or retirement programs are not always the best value. In some cases, "the adoption of conservation practices on working land" will be more cost-effective, even if the overall conservation benefits seem smaller (Feng, et al. 2004, 601). The costs imposed by the section 404 permitting scheme are far greater than the costs of various wetland conservation and restoration efforts engaged in by both government and private actors. There also is little evidence that wetland regulators account for the ecological functions provided by given wetlands when making permitting decisions (Sunding and Silberman 2002, 86; Mortimer 1998).

As recent analyses demonstrate, "[f]ederal regulation of wetlands can be enormously expensive when considered in terms of total economic impacts per acre of wetlands conserved" (Sunding 2003, 31). In some instances, the total economic losses imposed by federal wetland regulation can reach $1 million per acre of wetlands conserved. Yet this is only part of the picture. "Traditional measures of the cost of regulation, namely out-of-pocket cost of obtaining a permit and performing mitigation," dramatically understate the total economic costs of wetland regulations (Sunding 2003, 32). Insofar as the nation has approached, or even achieved, the stated goal of "no net loss" of wetlands, it does not appear to be the result of increased regulatory stringency (Sunding and Silberman 2002, 84).

Non-regulatory wetland conservation programs look like a bargain when compared to available regulatory alternatives. Wetland conservation through the purchase of easements or other partial interests in land is significantly less expensive than the total costs of conserving wetlands through Section 404, and the "restoration of wetlands is usually much less expensive than conservation" (Sunding and Silberman 2002, 84). U.S. Department of Agriculture programs that restore and conserve wetlands by obtaining partial interest in land cost an average of $1,300 per acre (Sunding 2003, 34). The Wetland Reserve Program is even more cost-effective, restoring wetlands at approximately $600 per acre (Sunding 2003, 34). The North American Waterfowl Management Plan has conserved or restored an estimated three million acres of waterfowl habitat at a cost of approximately $230 per acre (Turner and Rylander 1998, 124). Partners for Wildlife has likewise funded the restoration of over 300,000 acres of wetland habitat and 350 miles of riparian habitat at a cost as low as $100 or less (Turner and Rylander 1998, 126). Compared to existing regulatory programs, these approaches seem quite cost-effective—and are far less controversial. Privately funded conservation efforts, dollar-for-dollar, appear to be even more cost-effective. This should not be surprising. "The Corps is not forced to pay attention to factor prices. Private groups have better incentives to target the land with the highest level of environmental amenities per dollar spent" (Sunding 2003, 35).

There is reason to believe that there is an equivalent range in the cost-effectiveness of various species conservation measures. Land parcels, and their ecological functions, vary greatly from place to place. Not every acre of habitat for a given species will provide the same level of ecosystem services, and therefore not every acre should be valued the same. Faced with budget constraints, agencies will have a greater incentive to consider which acres are most important to conserve, and can increase the conservation returns of their investment. Shogren et al. (1999, 1259) report "[b]y taking into account that land values vary across the United States instead of treating land as homogenous, the costs of protecting half the species on the list can be cut by two-thirds."

The existence of compensation and the consideration of non-regulatory conservation efforts may also lower the costs of such efforts insofar as they facilitate voluntary landowner cooperation. "By lowering or removing property owner opposition, increased compensation might well free Congress and the FWS to pursue greater habitat regulation." At some level, the precise response of individual agencies is difficult to predict. However, "[w]hat one can conclude, with a reasonable degree of confidence, is that broader compensation would lead to a more efficient balance among the resources devoted to species protection and recovery" (Thompson 1997, 366).

Requiring compensation, by itself, is not sufficient to encourage more efficient regulatory action if the agency itself is not liable for compensation. As Been and Beauvais (2003, 92) note, "[b]ecause politicians and bureaucrats do not maximize profits, having to expend funds to cover a compensation award will not necessarily have any effect on their decision, unless those expenditures make it harder for the decisionmaker to achieve whatever it is trying to maximize." This means agencies must themselves bear the costs of their decisions. Without question, "the charging of agency appropriations for such claims radically alters the politics of controlling agency operations." Under such an approach, "adjudication of private claims also affects the amount of funds left over for other objects of funding" (Tiefer 1996, 516).

At present, the federal government pays court-awarded takings compensation claims out of the federal "judgment fund," rather than out of specific agency appropriations or land-acquisition funds. Thus it is a fair criticism that "the cost-internalization argument . . . is undermined by the fact that regulatory agencies often do not directly bear the costs of takings judgments" (Tiefer 1996, 516). Compensation is mandatory, but it does not affect agency operations; "Congress allows agencies to execute their legal responsibilities without operational instability or insecurity." The current system "completely insulates agencies from the fiscal impact of constitutional takings suits" (Tiefer 1996, 512). It further enables agencies to implement their environmental programs without any meaningful conservation of costs imposed on landowners or the cost-effectiveness of alternative conservation strategies.

If conservation agencies are required to pay compensation, and face a meaningful budget constraint, they will seek lower-cost means of achieving their conservation objectives. At the same time, private landowners will have greater incentives to find ways of providing conservation benefits at a cost government can afford (Stroup 1997, 55). As in private markets, there are potential economic rewards for environmental entrepreneurs who uncover means of providing better services at a lower cost. This encourages an organic market-driven discovery process that leads to greater innovation and cost-effective means of achieving societal goals.

Critics of a compensation requirement are correct that a regulator "may pay little attention to a compensation award unless having to pay compensation to property owners makes it harder for the decision-maker to achieve whatever he or she is trying to maximize" (Been 2004, 248). This is precisely why allowing mandated compensation to be paid from a separate account, such as the federal judgment fund, is insufficient. It also points to the need for a compensation requirement to be paired with programmatic reforms that ensure conservation agencies have the freedom and discretion to make policy trade-offs and substitute other conservation measures for compensated land-use controls. If compensation is required *and* if agencies are in position to evaluate alternatives to regulation, there is the potential for improved priority-setting and greater adoption of more optimal conservation strategies.

## INCREASING TRANSPARENCY AND IMPROVING ACCOUNTABILITY

Compensation paid directly from the relevant agency's budget would have several likely effects. First, it would reduce political opposition to government actions to achieve conservation goals, such as the listing of endangered species or the adoption of more expansive definitions of wetlands and valuable ecosystems. Second, and perhaps more important, it would encourage a greater consideration of trade-offs and cost-effectiveness in agency decision-making. Further, a compensation requirement can increase transparency in agency decision-making and improve public accountability.

Insofar as the costs of regulation are brought to bear in the policy-making process, it is only indirectly. Those burdened by such regulations may seek to intervene politically to alter agency priorities. But this does not further the goal of efficient resource allocation nor does it support "open consideration of costs and benefits." "Where the government directly finances the cost of conservation, it will generally engage in a reasoned, albeit political, balancing of the costs and benefits of various levels of conservation." Whatever the imperfections or pathologies of the existing appropriations process, it at least frames resource allocations as involving questions of trade-offs. Funds devoted to program A are not available for program B, and vice-versa. This furthers transparency and accountability in government decision-making. In contrast "regulatory programs generally eschew full consideration of costs, and thus the costs of regulatory programs are addressed in political skirmishes that occur behind closed doors rather than in an open, rational fashion" (Thompson 2002, 289–390). Further, requiring compensation can also affect interest-group behavior and discipline the government tendency to prefer some constituencies over others.

As Wilson (1989, 155) observed, it is often difficult to measure the effectiveness of government action. "Suppose a police officer walking a beat makes no arrest. That can mean either that no crime occurred or that the officer could solve none of the dozens of crimes that did in fact occur." The actual environmental performance of various conservation programs should not be measured by the number of enforcement actions, or even the amount of regulatory activity. What actually matters are the results on the ground: Are species being conserved? Are ecological resources protected? And so on. To the extent that agency policies are off-budget, it is more difficult to evaluate the effectiveness and efficiency of their various programs and weigh potential alternatives.

It is well understood that "bureaucrats also tend to favor programs with visible benefits and invisible costs" (Copeland 1990, 17–18). As Wilson (1989, 161) notes, "[t]here is a kind of Gresham's Law at work in many government bureaus: Work that produces measurable outcomes tends to drive out work that produces unmeasurable outcomes." This problem is magnified when landowners are not compensated for their land, and agencies can treat private land as a free, off-budget factor input. "The just compensation requirement forces the government and the public to make explicit trade-offs between different goods, in order to determine their value to the polity at large" (Epstein 1997, 37). With land conservation on-budget alongside other conservation tools, it would be easier for the public—and their political agents—to determine whether conservation agencies are acting in an effective and responsive manner.

## CONCLUSION

Most environmental regulation proceeds from the assumption that government action is a necessary and appropriate response to the negative environmental consequences of private activities. If private economic activities create harmful effects on other persons and their properties, the reasoning goes, then government regulation is necessary to limit such harms. In economic terms, government action is necessary to control or "internalize" the externalities associated with private land use. In the language of the common law, the government should prohibit those activities that constitute a trespass or nuisance to private or public rights.

In the pollution context, this conventional reasoning is straightforward. Since the earliest days of the common law, it has been understood that one's right to use one's own land only extends so far as one is not infringing upon a neighbor's equivalent right. In the resource conservation context, this approach is more far-reaching. In modern environmental law, government regulation is expected to control private land uses that do not impose harms on neighboring properties. Rather, these activities undermine the provision of public goods—such as species habitat or ecosystem services—or transgress commonly held environmental preferences. The result is far more extensive regulation of private land use than traditional rationales for government intervention would have contemplated.

An additional, unstated, premise of much contemporary environmental regulation is that government intervention is an effective means of addressing environmental concerns. Upon identifying an externality or alleged "market failure," policymakers routinely jump to the conclusion that government regulation or some other intervention is warranted, without first considering whether such action will be effective or represent an improvement over the *status quo ante*. As a consequence, much environmental regulation has been adopted with insufficient attention to its consequences and potential alternatives.

This paper has sought to demonstrate that there are serious negative environmental consequences to certain land-conservation measures, particularly those that regulate private land use in an effort to ensure the adequate provision of species habitat and other ecological goods. The costly nature of contemporary land-use controls, such as those imposed under Section 9 of the ESA, combined with the lack of compensation for those landowners who find their property rights effectively redefined by government edict, has made these measures particularly ineffective at achieving their stated environmental goals. In the context of habitat conservation under the ESA, economic theory and increasing empirical evidence suggest that, at least in the context of private land, land-use regulations are doing more harm than good.

Providing compensation for private landowners whose rights to make productive use of their land are restrained by non-nuisance-related environmental land-use controls has several potential environmental benefits. First, providing compensation could significantly reduce the perverse incentives landowners have to destroy habitat, refrain from habitat creation, and refuse to cooperate with scientific research about the condition of imperiled species. Second, a compensation requirement can facilitate greater consideration of which environmental conservation measures will be most cost effective. If agencies are forced to pay for the acquisition or extinguishment of traditional land use rights, the costs of these actions may be compared with available alternatives, ranging from the voluntary acquisition of easements to conservation incentives to the direct subsidization of conservation and ecological restoration activities. This has the potential to improve internal agency decision-making, enhance agency accountability, and facilitate greater public participation in relevant environmental policy decisions. More broadly, a legal regime that provides greater protection for property rights provides a stronger institutional framework for the pursuit of environmental and other social goals.

Compensation for regulatory takings is hardly a panacea to the ails of environmental protection. Many environmental programs are failing, either because they have become outdated or because they were never particularly effective. Solving today's environmental challenges requires a willingness to reconsider the presumptions and prejudices that have guided environmental policy to date. In this regard, it is time for environmental policy leaders to reconsider their opposition to compensating landowners for regulatory takings in environmental law. Such a policy is anything but "anti-environmental." Indeed, for some resources and imperiled species, it may be the most pro-environmental option on the table.

## NOTES

Portions of this chapter are adapted from Jonathan H. Adler, 2006, "Money or Nothing: The Adverse Environmental Consequences of Uncompensated Land-Use Controls," *Boston College Law Review* 49 (2): 301–366.

1. *See* Endangered and Threatened Wildlife and Plants; Proposed Rule Exempting Certain Small Landowners and Low-Impact Activities from Endangered species Act Requirements for Threatened Species, 60 Fed. Reg. 37,420 (1995).
2. 60 *Federal Register* 9507–8 (February 17, 1995). See also Bean (1998, 10706 n45).
3. The irony in this case is that the presence of endangered plants does not trigger the same level of regulation as does the presence of endangered animal species.
4. John Rapanos, for example, sought to destroy federally regulated wetlands without the knowledge of federal regulators. See *Rapanos v. United States*, 126 S.Ct. 2208, 2238–39 (2006).

5. William Fischel (1995, 206) defines "fiscal illusion" as "the systematic underestimating of costs by government decision makers when full compensation does not have to be paid" See also Blume and Rubinfeld (1984).
6. Certainly the adoption or enforcement of regulatory measures entails *some* costs, in terms of personnel time and other agency resources. Such costs are involved in *any* agency action. The point here is that the agency is not bearing the economic cost of the policy measure itself, only the costs of implementing or adopting *any* policy measure.
7. 505 U.S. 1003 (1992).
8. *Lucas,* 505 U.S. at 1018.
9. The only successful takings claims have involved ESA restrictions on water rights. In some cases, however, the federal government has settled cases in which property owners appeared to have potentially meritorious takings claims. See, e.g., 61 Fed. Reg. 36390 (July 10, 1996); 62 Fed. Reg. 54122 (October 17, 1997) (granting an incidental take permit to Ben Cone).

# REFERENCES

Anderson, Terry L. 1982. The New Resource Economics: Old Ideas and New Applications. *American Journal of Agricultural Economics* 64: 928–934.

Anderson, Terry L. and Donald R. Leal. 2001. *Free Market Environmentalism.* New York: Palgrave Macmillan.

Bean, Michael J. 1994. Ecosystem Approaches to Fish and Wildlife Conservation: "Rediscovering the Land Ethic." *U.S. Fish and Wildlife Service Office of Training and Education Seminar Series,* November 3.

———. 1998. The Endangered Species Act and Private Land: Four Lessons Learned From the Past Quarter Century. *The Environmental Law Reporter* 28 (12): 10701–10710.

Been Vicki. 2004. Lucas v. The Green Machine: Using the Takings Clause to Promote More Efficient Regulation? In *Property Stories,* edited by G. Korngold and A.P. Morriss. New York: Foundation Press, 221–258.

Been Vicki and Joel C. Beauvais. 2003. The Global Fifth Amendment? NAFTA's Investment Protections and the Misguided Quest for an International "Regulatory Takings" Doctrine. *New York Law Review* 78: 30–143.

Blume, Lawrence E. and Daniel L. Rubenfeld. 1984. Compensation for Takings: An Economic Analysis. *California Law Review* 72: 569–624.

Blume, Lawrence E., Daniel L. Rubenfeld, and Perry Shapiro. 1984. Taking of Land: When Should Compensation Be Paid? *Quarterly Journal of Economics* 99 (1): 71–92.

Brennan, Timothy J. and James Boyd. 2006. Political Economy and the Efficiency of Compensation for Takings. *Contemporary Economic Policy* 24 (1): 188–202.

Brook, Amara, Michaela Zint, and Raymond De Young. 2003. Landowners' Responses to an Endangered Species Act Listing and Implications for Encouraging Conservation. *Conservation Biology* 17 (6): 1638–1649.

Brown, Gardner M., Jr. and Jason F. Shogren. 1998. Economics of the Endangered Species Act. *Journal of Economic Perspectives* 12 (3): 3–20.

Copeland, Michael. 1990. The New Resource Economics. In *The Yellowstone Primer,* edited by J.A. Baden and Donald Leal. San Francisco, CA: Pacific Research Institute for Public Policy, 13–23.

Dana, David A. 1995. Natural Preservation and the Race to Develop. *University of Pennsylvania Law Review* 143: 655–708.

De Long, James V. 1997. *Property Matters.* New York: Free Press.

Dwyer, Lynn E., Dennis D. Murphy, and Paul R. Ehrlich. 1995. Property Rights Case Law and the Challenges to the Endangered Species Act. *Conservation Biology* 9 (4): 725–741.

Echeverria, John D. 2005. Regulating Versus Paying Landowners to Protect the Environment. *Journal of Land, Resources, and Environmental Law* 26: 1–46.

Epstein, Richard A. 1997. Babbitt v. Sweet Home Chapters of Oregon: The Law and Economics of Habitat Preservation. *Supreme Court Economic Review* 5: 1–57.

Farber, Daniel A. 1992a. Economic Analysis and Just Compensation. *International Review of Law and Economics* 12 (2): 125–138.

———— 1992b. Public Choice and Just Compensation. *Constitutional Commentary* 9: 279–308.

Feng, Hongli, Lyubov Kurkalova, Catherine L. Kling, and Philip W. Gassman. 2004. Environmental Conservation in Agriculture: Land Retirement versus Changing Practices on Working Land. *Journal of Environmental Economics and Management* 52: 600–614.

Fischel, William A. 1995. *Regulatory Takings: Law, Economics, and Politics.* Cambridge, MA: Harvard University Press.

————. 2003. Public Goods and Property Rights: Of Coase, Tiebout, and Just Compensation. In *Property Rights: Cooperation, Conflict & Law,* edited by T.L. Anderson and F.S. McChesney. Princeton: Princeton University Press, 343–364.

Fischel, William A. and Perry Shapiro. 1988. Takings, Insurance, and Michelman: Comments on Economic Interpretations of "Just Compensation" Law. *The Journal of Legal Studies* 17: 269–293.

Fox, Jessica and Anamaria Nino-Murcia. 2005. Status of Species Conservation Banking in the United States. *Conservation Biology* 19 (4): 996–1007.

Gardner, Royal C. 1996. Banking on Entrepreneurs: Wetlands, Mitigation Banking, and Takings. *Iowa Law Review* 81: 527–587.

Hayek, Friedrich A. 1945. The Use of Knowledge in Society. *American Economic Review* 35 (4): 519–530.

Hilty, Jodi and Adina M. Merenlender. 2003. Studying Biodiversity on Private Lands. *Conservation Biology* 17 (1): 132–137.

Innes, Robert. 1997. Takings, Compensation, and Equal Treatment for Owners of Developed and Undeveloped Property. *Journal of Law and Economics* 40 (2): 403–432.

————. 2000. Economics of Takings and Compensation When Land and Its Public Use Value Are in Private Hands. *Land Economics* 76 (2): 195–212.

Innes, Robert, Stephen Polasky, and John Tschirhart. 1998. Takings, Compensation, and Endangered Species Protection on Private Lands. *Journal of Economic Perspectives* 12 (3): 35–52.

Kostyack, John. 1994. If Ecosystem Is Harmed, We're All Endangered. *Wall Street Journal.* May 12.

Kusler, John. 1992. Wetland Delineation: An Issue of Science or Politics? *Environment* 32 (2): 7–11, 29–37.

Landy, Marc. K., Marc J. Roberts, and Stephen R. Thomas. 1994. *The Environmental Protection Agency: Asking the Wrong Questions From Nixon to Clinton.* New York: Oxford University Press.

Langpap, Christian. 2004. Conservation Incentive Programs for Endangered Species: An Analysis of Landowner Participation. *Land Economics* 80 (3): 375–388.

Langpap, Christian and Junjie Wu. 2004. Voluntary Conservation of Endangered Species: When Does No Regulatory Assurance Mean No Conservation? *Journal of Environmental Economics and Management* 47 (3): 435–457.

Lehrman, H. Jane. 1993. Case Closed: Settlement Ends Property Rights Lawsuit. *Chicago Tribune,* July 25, sec. 3G.

List, John A., Michael Margolis, and Daniel E. Osgood. 2006. Is the Endangered Species Act Endangering Species? *NBER* Working Paper No. 12777, from http://www.nber.org/papers/w12777.

Lueck, Daniel, and Jeffrey A. Michael. 2003. Preemptive Habitat Destruction under the Endangered Species Act. *Journal of Law and Economics* 46 (1): 27–60.

Main, Martin B., Fritz M. Roka, and Reed F. Noss. 1999. Evaluating Costs of Conservation. *Conservation Biology* 13 (6): 1262–1272.

Mann, Charles C. and Mark L. Plummer. 1995. Is the Endangered Species Act in Danger? *Science* 267 (5202): 1256–58.

————. 1995. *Noah's Choice: The Future of Endangered Species.* New York: Knopf.

McKinney, Larry. 1993. Reauthorizing the Endangered Species Act—Incentives for Rural Landowners. In *Building Incentives Into the Endangered Species Act,* pp. 71–78. Washington, DC: Defenders of Wildlife.

Metrick, Andrew and Martin L. Weitzman. 1996. Patterns of Behavior in Endangered Species Preservation. *Land Economics* 71 (1): 1–16.

Miceli, Thomas J. and Kathleen Segerson. 1995. Government Regulation and Compensation for Takings: Implications for Agriculture. *American Journal of Agricultural Economics* 77 (5): 1177–83.

Morriss, Andrew P. and Richard L. Stroup. 2000. Quartering Species: The "Living Constitution," the Third Amendment, and the Endangered Species Act. *Environmental Law* 30 (4): 769–809.

Mortimer, Michael J. 1998. Irregular Regulation Under Section 404 of the Clean Water Act: Is the Congress or the Army Corp of Engineers to Blame? *Journal of Environmental Law and Litigation* 13: 445–74.

Niskanen, William. 2004. *Policy Analysis and Public Choice: Selected Papers by William A. Niskanen*. North Hampton, MA: Edward Elgar.

Olson, Todd G. 1996. Biodiversity and Private Property: Conflict or Opportunity? In *Biodiversity and the Law*, edited by W.J. Snape, III. Washington, DC: Island Press, 67–92.

Parrish, David. 1995. Environmental Dilemma. *Los Angeles Daily News*, March 19: 10.

Parkhurst, Gregory M. and Jason F. Shogren. 2005. An Economic Review of Incentive Mechanisms to Protect Species on Private Lands. In *Species at Risk: Using Economic Incentives to Shelter Endangered Species on Private Lands*, edited by J. F. Shogren. Austin: University of Texas Press, 67–92.

Polasky, Stephen and Holly Doremus. 1998. When the Truth Hurts: Endangered Species Policy on Private Land with Imperfect Information. *Journal of Environmental Economics and Management* 35 (1): 22–47.

Rare Woodpecker Sends a Town Running for Its Chainsaws. 2006. *New York Times* September 26.

Rawlins, Wade. 2006. Woodpecker Mapping Gets Chainsaw Buzzing. *News & Observer* August 7.

Rinehart, James R. and Jeffrey J. Pompe. 1995. The Lucas Case and the Conflict over Property Rights. In *Land Rights*, edited by B. Yandle. Lanham, MD: Rowman & Littlefield, 67–102.

Shaffer, Mark L., J. Michael Scott, and Frank Casey. 2002. Noah's Options: Initial Cost Estimates of a National System of Habitat Conservation Areas in the United States. *Bioscience* 52 (5): 439–443.

Shogren, Jason F. 2005. Introduction. In *Species at Risk: Using Economic Incentives to Shelter Endangered Species on Private Lands*, edited by J. F. Shogren. Austin: University of Texas Press, 3–22.

Shogren, Jason F., Rodney B.W. Smith, and John Tschirhart. 2005. The Role of Private Information in Designing Conservation Incentives for Property Owners. In *Species at Risk: Using Economic Incentives to Shelter Endangered Species on Private Lands*, edited by J. F. Shogren. Austin: University of Texas Press, 217–234.

Shogren, Jason F., John Tschirhart, Terry Anderson, Amy Whritenour Ando, Terry Anderson, Steven R. Beissinger, David Brookshire et al. 1999. Why Economics Matters for Endangered Species Protection. *Conservation Biology* 13 (6): 1257–1261.

Sugameli, Glenn P. 1997. Takings Bills Threaten Private Property, People and the Environment. *Fordham Environmental Law Journal* 8: 521–587.

Sunding, David. An Opening for Meaningful Reform? *Regulation Magazine* 26 (2) (summer 2003): 30–35.

Sunding, David and David Zilberman. 2002. The Economics of Environmental Regulation by Licensing: An Assessment of Recent Changes to the Wetland Permitting Process. *Natural Resources Journal* 42: 59–89.

Thompson, Barton H., Jr. 1997. The Endangered Species Act: A Case Study in Takings and Incentives. *Stanford Law Review* 49: 305–78.

———. 2001. Protecting Biodiversity on Private Lands. *Idaho Law Review* 38: 355–84.

———. 2002. Conservation Options: Toward a Greater Private Role. *Virginia Environmental Law Journal* 21: 245–315.

Tiefer, Charles. 1996. Controlling Federal Agencies by Claims on Their Appropriations? The Takings Bill and the Power of the Purse. *Yale Journal on Regulations* 13: 501–534.

Tollison, Robert D. 1992. A Comment on Economic Analysis and Just Compensation. *International Review of Law and Economics* 12 (2): 139–140.

Turnbull, Geoffrey K. 2005. The Investment Incentive Effects of Land Use Regulations. *Journal of Real Estate Finance and Economics* 31 (4): 357–395.

Turner, John F. and Jason C. Rylander. 1998. The Private Lands Challenge: Integrating Biodiversity Conservation and Private Property. In *Private Property and the Endangered Species Act: Saving Habitats, Protecting Homes,* edited by J.F. Shogren. Austin: University of Texas Press, 92–137.

U.S. General Accounting Office (USGAO). 1994. *Endangered Species Act: Information on Species Protection on Nonfederal Lands.* Washington, DC: U.S. General Accounting Office.

Warren, Jennifer. 1997. Revised Species Protection Law Eases Farmers' Anxiety. *Los Angeles Times,* October 11, sec. A1.

Wilcove, David S. 1998. The Promise and the Disappointment of the Endangered Species Act. *New York University Environmental Law Journal* 6: 275–78.

Wilson, James Q. 1989. *Bureaucracy: What Government Agencies Do and Why They Do It.* New York: Basic Books.

Wright, David. 1992. Death to Tweety. *New Republic,* July 6: 9–10.

Zhang, Daowei. 2004. Endangered Species and Timber Harvesting: The Case of Red-Cockaded Woodpeckers. *Economic Inquiry* 42 (1): 150–165.

Zhang, Daowei and Warren A. Flick. 2001. Sticks, Carrots, and Reforestation Investment. *Land Economics* 77 (3): 443–456.

# 11

# MARKETS VERSUS TAKINGS AND REGULATION

## DECIDING THE FUTURE OF THE PAST

*Matthew Brown and Richard L. Stroup*

## INTRODUCTION

On February 18, 1999, the Miami-Dade County Commission voted 10–1 to seize land surrounding the Miami Circle by eminent domain. Like many archaeological finds, the Miami Circle is unremarkable to the casual observer. A ring of 24 carved basins speckled by 200 smaller "postholes" of no obvious pattern, the 38-foot wide circle cuts into the limestone bedrock of Brickell Point, where the Miami River pours into Biscayne Bay. According to archaeologist John Ricisak, the site was the foundation for a temple or hut constructed by the Tequesta Indians, a tribe devastated by the wars and disease of European explorers. When developer Michael Baumann bought the 2.2 acres for $8 million, the site was home to a 1950s-era apartment complex.

Commercial development can unearth and sometimes destroy remnants of the past. The same wealth that drives development, however, also increases demand for preservation; as incomes rise, demand for archaeological finds, a luxury and positional good, increases (Kaiser 1990, 209–210; Nye 2002). The competing interests of development and preservation can be reconciled by voluntary exchange in the market or by government intervention in the form of takings and regulation. This paper examines the unintended consequences of takings and regulation on archaeological preservation. By making archaeological finds a costly liability, as opposed to a valued resource, takings, and regulation motivates landowners to destroy artifacts while perversely increasing demand and rewards for looted artifacts. Takings and regulation also generates uncertainty, making development less attractive and thereby chilling economic growth.

Archaeology, however, does not have to conflict with the interest of property owners who seek the highest value of their property. This article recommends market reforms that would grant property owners clear and transferable property rights to archaeological finds and allow the free import, export, and sale of legally owned artifacts. The opportunity to profit from artifact sales would encourage public participation and appreciation of archaeology while also motivating landowners to cooperate with archeologists to explore, research, and protect promising sites from looters. In a free market, archaeology would reap a financial boon and more artifacts in greater diversity would be preserved. Unlike archaeology today, landowners, developers, collectors, and archaeologists would seldom be in acrimonious conflict and often engaged in mutually beneficial cooperation.

## HISTORY OF ARCHAEOLOGY AND ITS RELATIONSHIP TO ECONOMIC GROWTH

Change is often viewed as a defining characteristic of modern society. Until the eighteenth century, many gauged the time by the sun, organized their lives by the seasons, and lived by the accumulated wisdom of their ancestors. The average life span was about thirty (Stille 2002, pp. xvi-xvii). As agricultural economies shifted to industrialism, the "past" emerged as a distinct cultural phenomenon, and "change" became synonymous with "progress." With a zeal akin to the Renaissance's revival of classical antiquity, explorers, governments, and armies (most famously Napoleon's expedition to Egypt in 1798) collected artifacts of past cultures to symbolize "progress" (Brown 2004, 439).

By the mid-to-late nineteenth century, the wealth of the Victorian era fueled private and public efforts to unearth cultural sites and artifacts. Financed by personal wealth, German banker Heinrich Schliemann set out on a quest with the *Iliad* in hand to unearth the fabled Troy in Turkey. In the 1840s, the French and the British, under Paul Emile Botta and Austen Henry Layard, competed for the "largest number of works of art with the least possible outlay of time and money" from Mesopotamian ruins (Bahn and Renfrew 1997, 27–30). As a symbol of progress, artifacts from the past also legitimated the present and reinforced national identity. In 1858, Ann Pamela Cunningham organized the Mount Vernon Ladies Association to purchase Mount Vernon, the first private preservation initiative in the United States.[1]

At the turn of the century, skepticism about change and anxiety about the loss of tradition eroded the optimism of the Victorian era. On the one hand, economic growth funded preservation efforts and technological advancement brought previously unimagined tools for the study of the past. Development unearthed historic and pre-historic sites. But construction occasionally destroyed historic sites. Railway construction between Lahore and Multan unearthed kiln-fired bricks from the ancient cities of Harappa and Mohenjo-daro, but British officials took consideration of the bricks' ancient origin after laying them as foundation across swampy patches of track.

The same wealth that allowed consumers of the past to demand more preservation also increased demand for looted artifacts. In the United States, an explosion of interest in Native Americans in the late nineteenth century was followed by looting at archaeological sites, such as the cliff dwellings of Mesa Verde in Colorado. Looting is problematic because looters destroy seemingly less valuable artifacts, such as pottery shards, bones, pollen, and seed samples, in the rush to obtain the most financially attractive pieces. The remaining artifacts are less valuable to archeologists; only when discovered within proper context can archaeological artifacts yield the most information about the past.

The double-edged relationship between economic growth and preservation continues to exist today largely because the places where people live and work now are, in many cases, the same places people have occupied for thousands of years. Construction in cities with long histories—London, Rome, or Istanbul—often unearth archaeological artifacts ranging from cemeteries to ancient buildings. In Japan, more than 6,200 sites were destroyed or exposed to destruction by developers in 1980, (Bahn and Renfrew 1997, 525). The ancient Chinese capital of Xi'an, home of the terracotta soldiers, has also become a focal point for the conflict between development and preservation. The typical Chinese citizen is proud of the fabled army, but having known famine and hardship is also concerned about economic development and growth. In Xi'an and other parts of China, the government plans to demolish most historic courtyard houses to make way for high-rise apartment buildings, leaving a few old neighborhoods for tourists. According to one conservation student in Xi'an, "Xi'an is changing, but it needs to change more quickly" (Stille 2002, 49–58).

In the West, the modernist idea of perpetual change leading to progress competes with a post-modernist view that change is bad and preservation a higher good. Under a post-modernist lens, the past is a distinct reality endangered by "progress," rather than a prop to support progress. This reinterpretation of the past has not only fueled the debate on cultural artifacts, but also debates about environmental protection and the extinction of native languages. Artifacts as well as resources have become "endangered," prompting questions about who decides what merits protection (Brown 2004, 440–441).

## GOVERNMENTS AND THE WORLD ANTIQUITIES TRADE

By the twentieth century, the increased pace of looting led many countries to enact restrictions on the excavation and sale of artifacts. Laws generally criminalize the antiquities trade and occur in three varieties: export and import controls, laws vesting ownership of antiquities to the government, and private property regulation. It is worthwhile to examine the treatment of artifacts and cultural property around the world as international norms have increasingly influenced U.S. policy.

### Nationalized Artifacts

Many nations rich with archaeological resources have passed laws vesting ownership of cultural artifacts to the government. The laws vary in substance. Mexico and Egypt have vested all cultural property, whether discovered or not, to the State. Some countries, such as Italy, vest all antiquities discovered prior to a specified date. New Zealand vests for unauthorized export. England has a preemptive right of purchase (Pearlstein 2005). Nepal has banned archaeological excavations almost entirely. Because the local population buried their valuables over the centuries during repeated invasions, the Kathmandu Valley may be home to unimaginably rich treasures. The fear that such treasures will be looted and sold abroad led the government to conclude that they should not be discovered. "If we cannot provide such security, it might be a good idea not to encourage such excavation work: our treasures may be safest under 20 feet of earth," said the government's newspaper (Sason 1999).

Under the National Stolen Property Act (NSPA) (18 U.S.C. §§ 2314–2314 (1988 & Supp. II 1990).), states may seek restitution in U.S. courts for artifacts taken in violation of national vesting laws (*United States v. McClain*, 593 F.2d 658

(5th Cir. 1979).).[2] The first suit filed by a foreign government followed by restitution was *United States v. Hollinshead*, where the Ninth Circuit held the taking of a Maya stele was in violation of Guatemala's vesting law and constituted theft (*United States v. Hollinshead*, 495 F.2d 1154 (9th Cir. 1974).). Countries such as Turkey and Italy have since filed successful claims to ownership of antiquities, while other countries such as Lebanon and Peru have failed (Gerstenblith 2001, 217).

## Import and Export Controls

Although the World Trade Organization and European Union treaties prohibit export controls on "goods" (Merryman 2005, 281) many states have enacted export and import controls on cultural artifacts. Both the General Agreement on Tariffs and Trade and the Treaty of Rome admit exceptions for "the protection of national treasures of artistic, historic, or archaeological value," which has yet to be judicially interpreted (Merryman 2005, 281).[3] The North American Free Trade Agreement, following the GATT, also exempts "national treasures" from liberalization.

As of 2003, 102 governments have ratified the 1970 UNESCO Convention on the Means of Prohibiting and Preventing the Illicit Import, Export and Transfer of Ownership of Cultural Property. UNESCO 1970 calls upon "market" and "source"[4] states to respect export restrictions on cultural property. Cultural property is defined as "property which, on religious or secular grounds, is specifically designated by each State as being of importance for archaeology, prehistory, history, literature, art or science," which as John Merryman has observed translates into "anything that the authorities of a State so designate" (Convention 1970, Merryman I.J.C.P. 2005, 23).

While a few major source nations, such as the United Kingdom and Japan, apply export restrictions moderately to objects of particular importance to the nation's history and culture, the majority of source nations, particularly within the Mediterranean, apply export restrictions broadly and in wholesale. As a result, the "protection of cultural heritage" sought by the UNESCO 1970 has stymied the international circulation of cultural property, even for privately held works that bear little relation to the owner's culture.

Italy has denied their owners export permission for watercolors painted in Austria by Adolf Hitler and for Matisse and van Gogh paintings painted in France. The French have refused to permit their owners to export a collection of drawings by Italian masters, a Yuan-dynasty vase, and a painting of a Turkish scene by a Swiss artist (Merryman 2005, 275).

Since the ratification of UNESCO 1970, source nations have shifted focus to "repatriation," the return of cultural objects to alleged nations of origin. In the early nineties, Turkey successfully regained the Lydian Hoard, a famous cache of coins from the Metropolitan Museum of Art in New York (*Republic of Turkey v. Metropolitan Museum of Art*, 762 F.Supp 44 (S.D.N.Y. 1990).). Greece has less successfully attempted through diplomatic channels to obtain the Elgin Marbles from the British Museum in London. In 1806, Thomas Bruce, seventh Earl of Elgin, removed sections of the Parthenon frieze in Greece. The Greek government claims the Elgin Marbles represent an irreplaceable part of Greek culture and should be returned. Those who advocate keeping the Elgin Marbles in London point out the painstaking care and efforts of the British Museum, starkly evidenced by the deteriorated condition of the remaining frieze in Athens (Fitz Gibbon 2005).

The United States first began to regulate the importation of artifacts in the 1970s. In response to looting in Central America, the United States entered a treaty with Mexico, passed executive agreements with Peru, Ecuador and Guatemala, and passed the Pre-Columbian Art Act (1972), which requires certification of imported pre-Columbian artifacts from source countries verifying compliance with domestic law (Pearlstein 2005, 13). After more than ten years of lengthy debate, Congress passed the Convention on Cultural Property Implementation Act (1983) as a response to UNESCO 1970. The Act allows foreign nations to request import restrictions on categories of unprovenanced objects, but also preserves the United States' ability to limit those categories of restricted objects (Convention on Cul. 2000),[5] thereby limiting the scope of UNESCO 1970 and the "broadest declarations of ownership and historical or scientific value made by other nations."[6]

The relationship between the Implementation Act and the National Stolen Property Act, which allows for the extraterritorial enforcement of national patrimony laws, has yet to be resolved. In *United States v. Schultz,* the Court of Appeals acknowledged the "overlap" between the two Acts, but failed to resolve the tension (*United States v. Schultz,* 333 F.3d 393 (2d Cir. 2003).). According to William Pearlstein, *Schultz* "casts a cloud over title to every cultural object otherwise lawfully imported into the United States, including objects imported and subsequently exhibited in compliance with the Implementation Act" (Pearlstein 2005, 22).

## GOVERNMENT INTERVENTION IN ARCHAEOLOGY IN THE UNITED STATES

Like many nations, the United States vests ownership of artifacts on public lands to the government, but unlike many source nations, does not vest blanket ownership of artifacts discovered on private land. However, the use of eminent domain and growing "historic" and "archaeological"[7] regulation in recent decades has diminished property owners' control over the use, possession, and sale of sites and artifacts, often without compensation.

### Public Land

Spurred by looting at the Casa Grande ruins in Arizona (Phelan 1993, 63, 67), Theodore Roosevelt signed into law the Antiquities Act in 1906, which grants the President "the authority to designate historic landmarks and structures situated on federally controlled land" and provide criminal and civil penalties to deter artifact looting. Following suit, states have since vested ownership of archaeological objects on state land to state governments (Gerstenblith 2001, 232).

In 1935, the Historic Sites, Buildings, and Antiquities Act [HSA] codified the government's role in preservation by declaring it "national policy to preserve for public use historic sites, buildings, and objects of national significance for the inspiration and benefit of the people of the United States" (Historic Sites, Buildings, and Antiquities Act, 16 U.S.C. §§ 461–467 (1988 & Supp. I 1989).). Among other powers, the Act granted the Secretary the power to purchase property in the name of the United States. Fours years after its enactment, the Eighth Circuit ruled that, under the auspices of HSA, the federal government could acquire by eminent domain sites of national historic significance (*Barnidge v. United States*, 101 F.2d 295 (8th Cir. 1939).).

The next landmark preservation legislation occurred after World War II, when Congress passed the National Historic Preservation Act of 1966 (Historic Preservation Act of 1966, 16 U.S.C. §§ 470–470a-2 (1991).). The Act established a National Register of Historic Places, the Historic Preservation Fund, and the Advisory Council on Historic Preservation. Among other duties, the Council requires federal agencies to evaluate the impact of construction projects on historic sites.

Congress first folded historical concerns into environmental concerns in the National Environmental Policy Act of 1969 (National Environmental Policy Act of 1969, 42 U.S.C. §§ 4321–4370a (1988 & Supp. III 1991).). The Act requires federal agencies to consider environmental, cultural, and historical values when federally owned land is modified or federal funds are used on private land. The Historical and Archaeological Data Preservation Act of 1974 authorizes federal agencies to provide up to 1 percent of a federal projects cost to recover archaeological resources from a federal project.[8]

In recent decades, preservation legislation has centered on Native American artifacts and sites, ironically in response to Native American claims that historic and environmental laws have compromised the preservation of cultural practices (Phelan 1993, 8). In 1979, Congress passed the Archaeological Resources Protection Act, mandating stiff penalties for excavating Native American objects from Indian lands without consent from Indian tribes.[9] The Native American Graves Protection and Repatriation Act of 1990 [NAGPRA] requires federal agencies and museums to inventory and, upon request, return holdings of cultural items to Indian tribes and other Native American groups.[10] NAGPRA does not apply to artifacts discovered on private land or amassed in private collections before 1990. Despite its limited scope, NAGPRA has resulted in a number of controversies between archeologists and Native Americans, such as the controversy surrounding "Kennewick Man" where Indian groups attempted to block scientific research on a nine-thousand-year old skeleton discovered in Washington (Vincent 2005, 33–44).

## Private Property

### Eminent Domain

The Fifth Amendment to the Constitution provides that "private property [shall not] be taken for public use, without just compensation." (U.S. Const. amend. V.). The Fifth Amendment imposes two conditions on exercise of eminent domain: "the taking must be for a 'public use' and 'just compensation' must be paid to the owner" (*Brown v. Legal Found. of Wash.*, 538 U. S. 216, 231–232 (2003); *Kelo v. City of New London*, 545 U.S. 469 (2005).). The Supreme Court first considered whether historic preservation served a legitimate public use in *United States v. Gettysburg Electric Railway Co.* when Congress condemned private property to establish a national memorial at the Gettysburg battlefield. The Court upheld the condemnation, reasoning that "such a use seems necessarily not only a public use, but one so closely connected with the welfare of the republic itself as to be within the powers granted Congress by the Constitution for the purpose of protecting and preserving the whole country" (*United States v. Gettysburg E. R. Co.*, 160 U.S. 668, 682 (U.S. 1896).)[11] The scope of public use has only widened since *Gettysburg*.

At the close of the nineteenth century, the view that "public use" required "use by the public" gave way to the broader interpretation of "public use" as "public purpose," opening the door to a wider range of takings" (*Kelo*, 545 U.S. at 479–480.). In *Berman v. Parker*, the Court upheld the constitutionality of the District of Columbia Redevelopment Act of 1945, a plan to eliminate a blighted area of Washington, D.C., affirming that "if those who govern the District of Columbia decide the Nation's Capital should be beautiful as well as sanitary, there is nothing in the *Fifth Amendment* that stands in the way" (*Berman v. Parker*, 348 U.S. 26, 33 (1954).). The owner of a non-blighted department store had challenged the condemnation on the grounds that creating a "better balanced, more attractive community" was not a valid public use. *Berman* triggered the most active period in historic preservation. Local governments enacted preservation ordinances. By 1964, almost every state had enacted a preservation program (Fein 1985, 74).

Thirty years later, the Court reaffirmed *Berman*'s deferential approach to legislative judgments in *Hawaii Housing Authority v. Midkiff* when it upheld Hawaii's Land Reform Act of 1974, a statute intended to eliminate the "social and economic evils of land oligopoly" by redistribution. Echoing *Berman*, the Court reasoned that "judicial deference is required because, in our system of government, legislatures are better able to assess what public purposes should be advanced by an exercise of the taking power" (*Hawaii Housing Authority v. Midkiff*, 467 U.S. 229, 241 (1984).).

In the most recent takings decision, *Kelo v. New London*, the Court found no ground for exempting economic development as a valid public purpose. The decision validated the government's power to arbitrate between preservation *and* development goals with "broad latitude in determining what public needs justify the use of the takings power" (*Kelo*, 545 U.S. at 469). While the use of eminent domain has sometimes resulted in the preservation of historic properties, such as the Gettysburg battlefield, it has also resulted in razed historic properties for the sake of economic development.[12]

### Regulatory Takings and Penn Central

In the early twentieth century, the Supreme Court recognized that "while property may be regulated to a certain extent, if regulation goes too far it will be recognized as a taking" (*Penn Coal* 1922, 415). In *Penn Central Transportation Co. v. New York City*, the Court asked whether a historical preservation law could limit the use of private property so extensively as to constitute a taking (*Penn Central* 1978, 104). At the time, over 500 municipalities had historic preservation laws (*Penn Central* 1978, 108). In New York City, the Landmarks Preservation Commission had designated over 31 historic districts and 400 individual landmarks, the vast majority of which were privately owned, including the Grand Central Terminal (*Penn Central* 1978, at 2653). When the Commission rejected Penn Central Transportation Company's proposals to construct a skyscraper above the Terminal, concluding that "to balance a 55-story office tower above a flamboyant Beaux-Arts façade seems nothing more than an aesthetic joke ... reduc[ing] the Landmark itself to the status of a curiosity," Penn Central filed suit, claiming that the application of the Landmarks Preservation Law had taken their property without just compensation in violation of the Fifth and Fourteenth Amendments (*Penn Central* 1978, at 2656 and 119).

Before *Penn Central,* state courts generally decided when regulation went so far as to constitute a taking, engaging in "essentially *ad hoc,* factual inquiries" (*Lucas* 1992, 1015). The *Penn Central* Court attempted to take a step forward and identify a three-part criterion, requiring analysis of (1) the economic impact of the regulation on the claimant, (2) the extent to which the regulation interfered with distinct investment-backed expectations and (3) the character of the government action (*Penn Central* 1978, 124).

The Court's three factor balancing test, however, has done little to remedy the *ad hoc* approach, evidenced starkly by the Court's reasoning in *Penn Central.* Regarding economic impact, the Court arbitrarily concluded that Penn Central would not only continue to profit from the Terminal, but also obtain a "reasonable return." Regarding investment-backed expectations, the law did not interfere with Penn Central's "primary expectation" because present uses of the Terminal remained. Deprivation of air rights was not so bound up with the investment-backed expectations so as to constitute a taking, particularly since the Landmark Preservation Commission might have permitted another structure. In response to the appellants' challenge to the character of the government action, an argument for a "fair and equitable distribution of benefits and burdens," the Court responded that the "appellants" were not *solely* burdened or unbenefited; the New York City law applied to *all* the structures in the 31 historical districts and over 400 landmarks. Applying these factors, the Court held the prohibition to construct a skyscraper atop Grand Central Terminal to not constitute a taking (*Penn Central, 438 U.S.* at, 131–137).

Despite *Penn Central's ad hoc* criterion, it remains the "polestar" for partial takings analysis (*Palazzolo* 2001, 633; *Tahoe-Sierra Pres. Council v. Tahoe Reg'l Planning Agency, 535 U.S. at 336 (2002)*), which has reinforced the widespread view that regulatory takings is a confused field of law (Echeverria 2005, 171–172). According to Gideon Kanner, an appellate lawyer specializing in eminent domain and inverse condemnation, "under the *Penn Central* approach, lawyers are unable to ascertain which facts of the controversy will prove to be the operative, much less decisive, nor the prospective likelihood of litigational success or failure. They are thus handicapped when trying to advise clients, plan contemplated litigation, and marshal evidence likely to satisfy judges" (Kanner 2005, 679, 692). Individuals seeking compensation for partial takings resulting from archaeological and historical regulation of private property cannot hope to know the prospects of success under *Penn Central.*

### *Loretto, Lucas, and Lingle: Safeguards against Uncompensated Regulatory Takings?*

Since *Penn Central,* the Court has identified two categories of *per se* regulatory action as compensable under the Fifth Amendment irrespective of the public interest advanced by the regulation (*Lucas* 1992, 1015). Under *Loretto v. Teleprompter Manhattan CATV Corp.,* when the government requires an owner to suffer a permanent physical invasion of property—however minor—it must provide just compensation (*Loretto* 1982, 434–435). Under *Lucas v. S.C. Coastal Council* (1992), when regulation deprives *all* economically beneficial use of a property, just compensation is due unless the "background principles of nuisance and property law" independently restrict the owner's intended use (*Lucas* 1992, 1027).

*Lucas'* qualifications hedge the protection it affords to property owners seeking compensation for lost economic uses due to archaeological and historical regulation. To be consistent with *Andrus v. Allard*, (*Andrus v. Allard 444 U.S. 51* (1979)) the Court narrowed *Lucas'* holding to "land" and acknowledged that regulations could render "personal property," such as discovered historical artifacts, worthless without compensation (*Lucas* 1992, 1027). Rarely, however, does regulation deprive *all* economically viable uses of land, particularly when the "property interest" against which the loss of value is to be measured is unclear—100 percent of *what?* (Rose 1984, 566–569; see also Fee 1994 and Epstein 1987)

*Lucas'* requirement that the owner's intended use be consistent with "background principles of the State's law of property and nuisance" further diminishes the prospects for compensation. A regulation does not become a background principle by its mere enactment (*Palazzolo* 2001, 615), but it remains unclear when exactly a regulation does fall under the panoply "background principles." In *Hunziker v. Iowa*, Iowa's Supreme Court denied compensation to property owners that discovered a protected Indian burial mound after the property's purchase (*Hunziker* 1994). Under existing property law, the Court held that the "property owner's 'bundle of rights' never included the right to use the land in the way that the regulation forbids" (*Hunziker* 1994, 370). Roughly half of the states now control Native American burials located on private land. Some vest ownership in the state government while others recognize a right of restitution to lineal descendants or culturally affiliated tribes (Gerstenblith 2001). Some states have revived the public trust doctrine (Burling 2002)[13] and the law of custom[14] in an analysis of "background principles," further complicating the *Lucas* analysis.

In the most recent takings case, *Lingle v. Chevron,* the Court reaffirmed a fourth category of regulatory action as potentially compensable under the Takings Clause: "adjudicative land-use exactions," when the government conditions a development permit on the landowner dedicating an easement for public access through the property. For a land-use exaction to pass constitutional muster, the permit condition (i.e., easement) must, in accordance with *Nollan v. California Coastal Comm'n* (*Nollan v. California Coastal Comm'n 483 U.S. 825* (1987)) 1) substantially advance the *same* government interest that would justify a permit denial and, following *Dolan v. City of Tigard*, (*Dolan v. City of Tigard, 512 U.S. 374* (1994)) 2) be roughly proportional to the nature and extent of the proposed development's impact (*Lingle v. Chevron U.S.A. Inc, 544 U.S. 528* (2005)).

While *Nollan* and *Dolan* might thwart government extortion (Pollak 2006), it is unclear what protection the tests afford to property owners seeking compensation for a land-use exaction. *Nollan* requires an "essential nexus" between the permit condition and the government interest, but it does not limit the universe of legitimate government interests; in *Nollan*, "protecting the public's ability to see a beach" was a legitimate public purpose which would have warranted a permit condition of a public "viewing spot." Given the unpredictability of development outcomes and changing public preferences, the *Dolan* test, requiring "roughly proportional[ity]" between the public easement and proposed development's impact, seems a necessarily *ad hoc* determination. To the extent that *Dolan* offers a safeguard to exactions, it arguably applies only to cases of adjudicative land use exactions, as opposed to legislative determinations classifying areas of a city.

## CASE STUDY: THE MIAMI CIRCLE

In the early 1980s, Miami-Dade County and the City of Miami enacted historic preservation ordinances, making Miami one of the first local jurisdictions to regulate archaeological finds on private property.[15] Miami's code requires landowners to apply for a Certificate of Appropriateness before "construction, excavation, tree removal, or any other ground disturbing activity project" within archaeological zones, areas expected by the Historic and Environmental Preservation Board to "yield information on local history or prehistory based upon prehistoric or historic settlement patterns" (Miami Code Sec 23–2). On the basis of the landowner's or developer's application, the county archaeologist recommends archaeological work. If archeologists unearth artifacts during pre-construction excavations, the board may halt construction and require an archaeological survey assessing the site's significance and the proposed activity's impact at the applicant's expense. Alternatively, the board may issue the certificate with a delay that would allow archaeological work, or it may require the project to be redesigned (Miami Code Sec 23–5).

When pre-construction excavations unearthed the Miami Circle formation, the City halted Michael Baumann's development. Local government archaeologists concluded that the site was the foundation for a temple or hut constructed by the Tequesta Indians. As part of the Glades Culture, the Tequestas might have numbered as many as 10,000. According to archaeologist Jerald T. Milanich, the Glades Indians inhabited "a variety of wetlands: the Everglades, the large sawgrass marsh in Hen[d]ry, Palm Beach, Broward, Miami-Dade and Monroe counties." The last members of the culture are believed to have left the area when Spanish colonists abandoned the state to England in 1763. Yet, evidence of their inhabitance is scarce. According to Milanich, "only a small sample of sites remains. Even sites recorded in the 1950s have been lost to development" (Milanich 1998, 123).

As word spread that the Circle was probably of American Indian origin, saving it became a cause célèbre among environmental activists, school children, preservationists, and American Indians. Bobbie Billie, spiritual leader of Florida's Seminole Indians, declared the site sacred ground. Giving weight to Billie's statement, Archaeologist Carr later quoted to the *Miami Herald*, "It's some kind of sacred place" (Whoriskey February 14, 1999). City and county leadership had differing views. Mayor Carollo, anxious for the city government to receive the tax revenue from Baumann's project, led efforts to continue development. With neighbors like the Sheraton Biscayne Bay Hotel and the Dupont Plaza Hotel, estimates of the value of Baumann's twin tower apartment buildings ranged from $90 to $126 million. Miami-Dade County Mayor Alex Penelas, whose budget would receive less of the tax revenue from Brickell Pointe, advocated preservation.

While public attention surrounding the site's fate grew, the City granted Baumann the necessary permits to resume construction. Acknowledging widespread public desire to preserve the Circle, Miami Mayor Joe Carollo announced plans to move the Circle to another site, which would allow archaeologists to continue their research. Dissatisfied with the possibility that the Circle would be moved, however, attorneys for Dade Heritage Trust unsuccessfully filed for an injunction to prevent further construction. Despite their failure, Baumann agreed to delay work and allow archaeologists to remain for several more weeks (Chardy 1999).

On February 18, 1999, the Miami-Dade County Commission voted 10–1 in favor of using eminent domain to seize the land surrounding the Miami Circle. The county voted to pursue a "slow take," which would allow it to opt out of purchasing the site if the price determined by a jury trial was too high. Baumann's appraisers had estimated the value of the land to be as high as $42 million. County hopes for purchasing the site were given a boost when the state cabinet voted to make the Circle a priority for purchase under a state land acquisition program. Under the agreement, the cabinet would contribute funds for the purchase "at its appraised value or at 50 percent of the developer's selling price, whichever [was] cheaper" (Bridges 1999).

To avoid the costs and uncertainties of a jury trial, last-minute negotiations resulted in a $26.7 million dollar settlement. The state agreed to provide $15 million and the county the remainder. Originally, the county raised only $3 million, but a loan from the San Francisco-based Trust for Public Land organization provided the remaining funds. While the state and local governments were ready to pay millions of dollars for the land, the public seemed unwilling to put forth any substantial sum. Six months after the cause became widespread, the acquisition fund created to raise public money for the Circle's purchase had a balance of $4,012.12 (Whoriskey June 1999). County Commissioner Natacha Millan singled out Indian tribes for failing to raise funds. "Where are the people who say this is sacred?" Millan said. "It does not seem like any of these tribes or the nations have any problems with money" (Fienfrock 1999).

While state and local governments moved forward with pledges, questions about the authenticity of the site lingered. Florida Attorney General Bob Butterworth asked, "if this thing turns out to be a septic tank, we've just bought a $15 million septic tank, right?" (Bousquet 1999). Milanich, curator of archaeology at the Florida Museum of Natural History at the University of Florida in Gainesville, stated his intention in a leading archaeology magazine to "remain skeptical until sufficient evidence is collected to prove that the Miami Circle was built by Native Americans one or two thousand years ago and is not a 20th-century artifact." Only after the settlement between Baumann and the county did renewed research confirm the Circle's ancient origin (Milanich 1999).

Since the Circle's purchase in 1999, the State and Miami Dade County continue to debate its fate. Proposals range from building a small park at the site to digging up the stone formation and moving it to another site for display. Until an agreement is brokered, the Circle will remain buried beneath "a foot of sandbags, fills and tarps." In 2003, the County filled the Circle because sun, rain, and heat had damaged the limestone newly exposed after two millennia underground (Kleinberg 2006).

## UNINTENDED CONSEQUENCES OF REGULATION AND TAKINGS

Government intervention in the form of regulations and takings constrains the outcomes of the market process, but does not eradicate it (Boettke, Coyne, and Leeson, this volume). Intervention that forces archaeological preservation generates uncertainty in the market process and alters the incentives of market participants, whether they are archeologists, collectors, developers, or landowners. Individuals, however, continue to seek profit opportunities. Occasionally, these new opportunities are undesirable and lead to unintended outcomes counterproductive to archaeological preservation, such as fewer archaeological discoveries, destruction of artifacts, and looting.

## Uncertainty and the Chilling Effect on Economic Development and Archaeological Discovery

The use of eminent domain and regulation to force outcomes that would not otherwise be obtained by voluntary exchange generates uncertainty for landowners and developers. Without general characteristics and conditions for takings by eminent domain, individuals are not able to predict with certainty when property will be taken for economic development *or* historic preservation. "Big box" retailers, development corporations, and small businesses, for example, have all successfully used eminent domain to avoid voluntary exchange, evidenced by the over 10,000 cases of eminent domain abuse for private development documented by the Institute for Justice between 1998 and 2002 (Berliner 2003). Similarly, the prospect of a property falling under the purview of regulation generates uncertainty for landowners, who subsequently face lost economic uses and potentially decreased property values.

Economic research has confirmed that property rights are critical for long-term economic growth (Acemoglu and Johnson 2003; Acemoglu, Johnson, and Robinson 2000; Hoskins and Eiras 2002); "when investors believe their property rights are protected, the economy ends up richer" (Rodrik, Subramanian, and Trebbi 2002, 24). The uncertainty generated by takings and regulation, however, provides disincentives to purchase, improve, and develop property (Boettke, Coyne, and Leeson, this volume). Investment capital, unlike land, is mobile and can move to more profitable, less uncertain uses. When developers and landowners bear the risk from regulation and eminent domain proceedings, they look elsewhere to invest. Alternatively put, development in regulated areas must provide a return as high as other potential developments to attract investment. An attorney for Baumann's project implied a chilling effect on economic growth when he told the *Miami Herald* that potential developers would "be watching how this [the Miami Circle] is handled... it clearly gives a developer a pause" (Grow Downtown 1999). The chilling effect became apparent after construction of the nearby "One Miami Center" unearthed artifacts. Developers abandoned the $1 billion multi-use development across the river from the Circle and sold the site off in parcels (Kleinberg 2006).

While the full chilling effect on economic growth and development is difficult to measure because many of the foregone opportunities are not counterfactually observable, one can estimate foregone tax revenue from the cancellation of the Brickell Pointe development. According to estimates published in the *Miami Herald,* the project could have been worth approximately $90 million when completed. According to Baumann's attorneys, the value of the project was closer to $126 million, which would have generated tax revenues of about $1.1 million per year for the city, $647,000 for the Miami-Dade County government and more than $900,000 for the Miami-Dade County school district (Chardy and Finefrock 1999).

Chilled economic development impacts archaeology in two ways. Since artifacts are a luxury good—people tend to demand more as incomes rise—lost economic growth dampens demand for archaeology. By discouraging development of potentially archaeologically rich areas, takings and regulation also stymie archaeological discovery. According to Kate Fitz Gibbon, a specialist in Asian art and world heritage issues, "the majority of finds of antiquities are accidental or the result of infrastructure development and construction" (Fitz Gibbon 2005, 291) including the Rosetta

Stone.[16] While construction threatens archaeology by destroying potential sites, it simultaneously advances archaeology by uncovering sites that might otherwise remain unknown, like the Miami Circle. As archaeological regulation and potential takings makes Miami a more uncertain investment, however, developers will look for alternative sites less likely to contain artifacts, stymieing serendipitous discoveries.

## Supply Side Problems: Perverse Incentives to Hide or Destroy Artifacts

Forcing archaeological preservation by takings and regulation motivates undesirable and counterproductive behavior. Takings and regulation—whether it be use restrictions or requirements for salvage archaeology, inspections, and monitoring—results in greater uncertainty, higher development costs, and potentially decreased property values, all of which encourage landowners and developers to ensure that no artifacts are discovered. Many archaeologists fail to recognize this incentive problem. Some have encouraged it unwittingly and advocated treating cultural property like endangered species. According to one leading advocate of archaeological regulation:

> So-called cultural properties are like environmentally endangered species. First, they are non-renewable resources: once exhausted or destroyed, they cannot be replenished or replaced. Second, they are not anyone's property and no one can properly be said to own them. . . . Hence, no one has a claim to restitution or restriction based on an alleged right (for example, right of ownership) to them (Warren 1989, 19).

Research has documented the counterproductive effect of laws, such as the Endangered Species Act (ESA), designed to protect endangered species (Stroup 1995; Stroup 1997, 55–65; Lueck, Dean, and Michael 2003). When landowners are forced to pay the price of protection, either directly or in terms of lost uses and value of land, they are motivated to not become host to endangered species and engage in "preemptive habitat destruction." According to Michael Bean of the Environmental Defense Fund, who is often accredited for writing the Endangered Species Act, there is "increasing evidence that at least some private landowners are actively managing their land so as to avoid potential endangered species problems." People act not out of "malice toward the environment," but because of "fairly rational decisions, motivated by a desire to avoid potentially significant economic constraints." This behavior, according to Bean, is a "predictable response to the familiar perverse incentives that sometimes accompany regulatory programs, not just the endangered species program but others" (Stroup 1995).

As laws lean toward treating archaeological treasures like endangered species—penalizing the owners on whose land they appear—we should expect similar results. Without a financial interest in artifacts' preservation, we should expect landowners to actively avoid archaeological finds and invest little in security measures to ward off looters (Brown and Stroup 2001, 44–46). While any developer might cooperate with archaeologists when costs are low, a risk-averse developer has an incentive to prevent cooperation from causing unexpected delays, a cancellation of a project, or decreased revenues that accrue upon project completion. One professional archaeologist has confirmed this result, attesting that "some builders even offer me money not to find anything" (White cite in Stroup and Brown 1999).

The perverse incentives to destroy artifacts have surfaced ironically in historic revival efforts. Egypt's reconstruction of the ancient library of Alexandria, partially funded by the United Nations, has resulted in its partial destruction. To avoid costly delays, builders bulldozed during the middle of the night, presumably to prevent onlookers from observing the destruction of the library's foundation. According to Alexander Stille, "the revival of the library of Alexandria could be burying the ancient library once and for all" (Stille 2002, 268)

In the case of the Miami Circle, Baumann was initially cooperative with archaeologists, allowing them to continue research (albeit with restrictions) although a judge denied an attempt to halt Brickell Pointe's development; he "work[ed] side-by-side with Carr's crew, clearing out the post holes, helping to get the area prepped for mapping and photographs" (Ancrum 1999). However, the incentive to cooperate with archeologists quickly diminished. According to Baumann's attorney, "everyone talk[ed], but no one dip[ped] into their pocketbook, other than the developer" (Garcia-Toledo cited in Merzer, Martin and Alfonso Chardy 1999).

## GOVERNMENT FAILURE AND THE MISALLOCATION OF PUBLIC RESOURCES

From the perspective of public choice theory, there are strong reasons to doubt the political system's ability to effectively allocate resources for archaeology. Politicians are typically concerned with the impact of their decisions on election day and therefore "select policy with the idea that the customer, who is the voter, will reward the politician in the next election" (Tullock, Seldon, and Brady 2002, 8). Yet voters know very little about archaeology and the cultural values at stake or the relative value of other sites or other public services such as hospitals and schools. Worse, voters have little incentive to become informed on policy since their vote will have almost no impact. Voters' limited information contrasts with the much greater knowledge special interests have about specific policies. The asymmetrical information bias leads to the rise of special-interest groups and encourages politicians to pay heed to them (Tullock, Seldon, and Brady 2002, 9).

In the field of archaeology, the sensitive nature of ethnic or religious differences and the injustices of earlier generations further complicate voter preferences and political decision-making. As archeologists Renfrew and Bahn point out, "archaeology has become a focal point for complaints about the wrongdoing of the past" (Bahn and Renfrew 1997, 516). In testimony before the state cabinet during the Miami Circle debate, one American Indian declared that "if no one took on the responsibility to save this [Miami] Circle and the Circle was destroyed, it would be the same as a statement that we are destroying life here on earth with development." As a response, State Agricultural Commissioner Bob Crawford proclaimed, "I like Indians" (Brown and Stroup 2000, 16). Given the incentives politicians face to please or at least to not offend voters, cultural and scientific understanding played a secondary role to political calculations. Concerns over Miami Circle's authenticity, including the Florida Attorney General's comment that the Circle may be a $15 million dollar septic tank, did not stop the state or county governments from pledging millions of dollars for its purchase (Bousquet 1999).

Next, consider the incentives facing the Archaeological Conservancy[17] or a consortium of groups that seek to privately secure and investigate sites, perhaps later selling the artifacts after research and documentation. Private groups compete for resources from knowledgeable donors who know far more about the relevant tradeoffs than the average voter. They are therefore less likely to err as they are accountable to knowledgeable, even passionate, donors who sacrifice to finance the work. Organizations that have made sound decisions and few errors recruit alert donors from competing groups. As a result, successful organizations thrive while unsuccessful organizations generally lose funding.

Because the decision to preserve the Circle was made politically to meet short-term voter demands, rather than long-term preservation goals, resources were not effectively allocated. The opportunity cost to archaeological knowledge is significant. Spending $26 million on the Miami Circle has not secured the preservation of the Circle or future discoveries. Shortly after the Circle's purchase, archeologists unearthed a nearby ancient cemetery and another ancient circle of comparable size. Because the county government insisted on a $26.7 million dollar all-or-nothing taking to preserve the Miami Circle, as opposed to rescue archaeology, neither of the new sites will be excavated or saved from development. Meanwhile, eight years after the Circle's purchase in 1999, the State and Miami Dade County continue to debate its fate while it lies beneath "a foot of sandbags, fills and tarps." Even if an agreement is brokered, the Circle will remain under sandbags until the county acquires $2 million from the legislature to restore the crumbling seawall along the Miami River, a more pressing public demand (Kleinberg 2006). Scarce resources and competing public demands require trade-offs, even in a relatively wealthy place like Miami.

In many cases, the market process would better serve preservation interests by endowing artifacts with value when politicians see little or no value. Economic interests occasionally trump preservation interests in political calculations. As Mayor Carollo pointed out, "I have the responsibility to do what is right for past civilizations. But I have a greater responsibility to the present civilization" (Whoriskey February 16, 1999). Italy has licensed the destruction of its past by selling dispensations to real estate developers (Pearlstein 2005, 12). The Turkish government's construction of Birecek Dam flooded remnants of Zeugma, a two-thousand-year-old city holding one of the world's richest collections of Roman mosaics. The Three Gorges Dam in China submerged as many as thirteen hundred sites from the Paleolithic and Neolithic periods and the Ming and Qing dynasties (Emmerich 2005, 248–249). When the competing interests are military or ideological, the market may be the only protector of archaeological resources from deliberate acts of cultural annihilation. During Mao Zedong's Cultural Revolution, the "Red Guards" destroyed some 4,922 out of 6,843 officially designated sites of historic significance (Stille 2002, 44). Recent examples of cultural annihilation include the Khmer Rouge's looting of Angkor Wat and the Taliban's predicted destruction of the Bamiyan Buddhas and pre-Islamic art treasures in Afganistan's National Museum.[18] Rather than enlarging government powers for determining what merits preservation and what does not, preservationists ought to seek greater funding for private groups that have a stronger incentive to effectively allocate resources to meet preservation goals.

## PROTECTING THE PAST THROUGH MARKETS

Faced with challenges of funding, looting, and the threat of lost research opportunities due to economic development, many archaeologists believe that a free market for artifacts is the enemy of archaeology and advocate government intervention to eradicate the market process. Intervention, however, does not eradicate the process, but merely constrains the outcomes of the market process and perversely fuels a black market for looted, unprovenanced artifacts.

Because demand for historical artifacts will always stubbornly exist, when ethical archaeologists refuse to participate in markets, unethical archaeologists will. Greater controls and regulation might remove some buyers from the market, but they do not deter all. Supply continues, albeit at a decreased pace, and the price of looted artifacts rises, increasing the rewards for looters and thereby strengthening the economic incentives to loot (Bator 1981, 318–319; Brown and Stroup 2001, 45). If organized and better-financed attempts to suppress trade in controlled goods (e.g., arms, narcotics, alcohol) with strong demand have failed, bringing unintended consequences, unanticipated costs, and ever-receding goals, it is unlikely that the trade in antiquities will cease. As long as countries prosper, and demand for artifacts, which are luxury goods, grows, so will the black market (Merryman 1986, 848).

While governments alone can never fully stymie the flow of looted treasures into the black market, there is a class of individuals with a long history of protecting resources more effectively than the government: property owners. When individuals have a financial interest in a valued resource, they generally preserve and protect the resource. Assigning property rights to archaeological finds would make them a valued resource, as opposed to a costly liability. Contrary to popular opinion, a free market in artifacts could become the greatest booster and protector to archaeology.

## Using Market Incentives to Preserve Natural Resources

Using markets to preserve natural resources, including wildlife, is not new (Anderson and Leal 1991). Drawing upon the parallel between endangered species and historical artifacts, one can look to the CAMPFIRE program in Zimbabwe as a model of success. Under CAMPFIRE, local communities are allowed to profit from fee hunting and recreation programs that involve elephants and other wild animals. Prior to the program, villagers found it difficult to protect their crops, homes, and sometimes their lives. Wild elephants were dangerous competitors. Poaching was rampant, as villagers ignored and occasionally helped poachers. Under CAMPFIRE villagers receive an ownership stake in the elephants. The fees generated by hunting expeditions ($12,000 or more for a single elephant) are a financial boon to a village where the average income per family of eight is about $150 per year (Brown and Stroup 2000, 17).

The results have been dramatic. Despite hunting, from 1989 to 1995, elephant populations in Zimbabwe grew by 14 percent. In parts of Africa that relied upon traditional regulations, the herds decreased by 24 percent. The financial incentives to not allow over-hunting and poaching have ensured that adequate numbers of elephants exist for future hunts. Poaching has decreased and villagers have become the protectors of elephants. As the fruits of stewardship have increased for villagers, buyers from the general public have also benefited from paid for access to the elephants, photo opportunities, and hunting experiences. Today, there is a saying in Africa about wildlife: "If it pays, it stays" (Anderson and Grewell 2000).

The Zimbabwe experience is not an isolated instance. A report by the President's Council on Environmental Quality (CoEQ 1984, 362–429) and a book,

*Enviro-Capitalists: Doing Good While Doing Well* (Anderson and Leal 1997), cite numerous examples of private organizations, both nonprofit and profit-making, that protect the environment privately using the marketplace.

## Using Market Incentives for Archaeological Preservation

Just as the CAMPFIRE program in Zimbabwe has made wildlife a friend rather than enemy of local villagers, market reforms could make archaeological finds a benefit to landowners and developers rather than a burden. Making archaeological resources valuable to landowners requires 1) granting clear and transferable property rights to the artifacts found on their land and 2) allowing the free import, export, and sale of legally owned artifacts. The opportunity to profit from the sale of artifacts would motivate productive behavior that maximizes artifacts' value, such as exploration, research, careful storage, and security measures to ward off looters. As a result, a greater number of artifacts at diverse sites would be preserved.

### Archaeological Exploration

Ownership over archaeological finds and an opportunity to profit from its sale would motivate landowners to discover valuable artifacts and hire skilled archaeologists to explore promising sites, including sites slated for development. Archaeologists would be appreciated, not resented, as the discoverers and creators of value.[19] In some instances, we could expect contractual arrangements akin to contractual arrangements with petroleum exploration companies, specifying up-front payments, bonuses, and royalties. Such exploratory contracts would be a boon to archaeology, which lacks funding and has become more expensive as methods have advanced; new techniques such as infrared imagery, radio carbon dating, DNA analysis, and potassium-argon dating adds value to knowledge, but at a cost.

Skeptics might argue that the incentives for hiring archeologists to explore promising sites are weak given that many excavations would unearth few or no marketable artifacts, just as drilling operations sometimes fail to turn up marketable petroleum reserves. Even when no marketable petroleum is found, however, drilling produces valuable information about the local area. Similarly, even if no artifacts were discovered, archaeological exploration would yield information to archeologists seeking promising digs and developers seeking unique terrains.

The products of excavation need not be limited to artifacts. Just as cattle ranching produces multiple products, such as meat, hides, and cowboy tourist experiences, yielding multiple revenue streams, exploratory excavations could also be opportunities for tourism and fieldwork by university-affiliated archaeology students. Even if developers and collectors did not seize these alternative revenue opportunities, they would still reap rewards in publicity and prestige by exploratory, philanthropic excavations (Brown and Stroup 2001, 46).

### Gains in Archaeological Knowledge and Stewardship

Because undamaged, researched artifacts are worth more than damaged artifacts bereft of context, property owners, collectors and dealers would have a strong incentive to maximize the artifacts' value through careful excavation, storage, and research. The confidence that the artifact is authentic and not a fake, increases an artifact's value, which is why current antiquities dealers are quick to point that their artifacts have been properly researched.

As rewards (i.e., sale prices) for better preserved and researched artifacts increased in the marketplace, demand for archaeological science would also increase. Archaeologists with positive track records would reap greater funding for their successful discovery and research, while archeologists lacking successful track records would be motivated to improve their skills and knowledge. Competitive firms would have an incentive to develop low-cost technology that preserves and yields information about the artifacts. The opportunity to profit from the discovery of artifacts would encourage laypersons to acquire more archaeological knowledge and become collectors, thereby increasing public participation and knowledge of archaeology.

The price system generated by the voluntary exchange of artifacts would reflect agreement on historical significance and value; those artifacts valued the most would command higher prices. While the price of some rare and unique artifacts would increase over time, prices for the most plentiful would decline, even while certificates of legitimacy, explanations of context, and interpretations of historical significance increased the artifacts' value. To the extent that speculation affects prices, it might just as easily cause prices to fall as to rise. Reputation would also influence the price of an artifact. If marketed by a reputable firm affiliated with a museum, an artifact would be worth more to collectors. Much as the market for paintings of the masters or the market for antiques works today, museums or collectors would purchase those antiquities of highest value. It would be reasonable to assume that those prepared to pay the most would be the most likely to take the necessary precautions to protect their investment. Archaeological resources and cultural property, like other forms of property, are valuable to the extent that people care for them and, by extension, are willing to pay for them. In a free market for artifacts, consumers, as well as scholars and museums, would have a say on what is preserved.

### Greater Diversity in Archaeology

A market in properly researched artifacts would increase the diversity of artifacts that are preserved and studied. When preservation decisions are made in the political arena, by "majority rules," diverse views often are poorly represented. The debate over the fate of the Miami Circle, much like the debate about archaeological preservation in the rest of the world, has been characterized by charges of one culture dominating or destroying the history of others.

Markets, in contrast, by their voluntary nature cater to individual tastes and preferences. Unconstrained from purchasing and selling artifacts, demand for artifacts would increase in a free market, pulling more collectors, hobbyists, amateurs, professionals, and museums into the market. A wide variety of tastes and values would be reflected. While some collectors would only be interested in Egyptian artifacts, others would value Roman or Greek relics, and others would prefer artifacts of American Indian origin. Niche markets, which would never be supported by a majority-rule political calculus, would flourish.

If other nations liberalized artifacts trade, markets would protect diverse artifacts that might otherwise be destroyed in war. Cultural property that is currently locked in poor, corrupt states with inefficient law enforcement would be stored in wealthy, secure states. As Eric Posner laments, "if the contents of Baghdad Museum had been owned and held by museums in New York, Tokyo, London or Chicago, they would never have been stolen or destroyed during the second Gulf War" (Posner 2006, 15).

### Diminished Incentives to Loot

According to one estimate, the worldwide trade in illicit antiquities is valued between $2 billion and $6 billion a year, ranking third in size after drugs and arms among the world's black markets (Stille 2002, 77; Nafziger 1985, 835–852). Archaeologists employed by universities or governments who rely on public funding often are financially unable to keep up with the speed and resources of looters. Once significant artifacts have been discovered, Bahn explains, "the choice is simple: Either we excavate and protect it, or we abandon it to looting" (Bahn 1999). Yet, campaigns to put antiquities dealers out of business and to discourage private ownership by vilifying collectors have not had any significant effect on looting (Shanks 1999).

A free market for artifacts would deter looting in two ways. Currently, landowners must bear a cost to prevent looting and are therefore indifferent. With the opportunity to profit from the discovery and sale of archaeological resources, however, landowners would be more likely to invest in security measures and zealously protect valuable sites from looters. As collectors placed a higher premium on sellable, certified artifacts with an explanation of context, the reduced demand for looted artifacts and increased supply of legitimate artifacts would reduce the prices of looted artifacts. Looted artifacts would become less valuable, making plunder less rewarding.

In a free market, looters could be gainfully employed in productive archaeology under the supervision of an archeologist. Looting often provides a profitable escape from poverty or traditional methods of employment such as farming. According to Dr. David Matsuda's anthropological research amongst subsistence farmers in Central America, "in these outback areas with marginal land, no seed crops, and unstable weather patterns, the demand for artifacts found in unchartered archaeological ruins offer[s] a viable alternative to starvation." According to one subsistence digger, "these gifts from our ancestors mean seed corn, food, clothes, and security" (Matsuda 2005, 258 and 264). The cost to archaeology is that looters, fearing detection by police, rummage through sites at night, destroying much of a find's valuable contextual information. Working voluntarily under archaeologists' supervision, however, looters could be taught proper technique, extracting artifacts from the soil in daylight with more care and attention to context, while also increasing their standard of living (Shanks Looting 1999). Archeologists would benefit from employing looters by harnessing the often superior knowledge of local areas that looters possess, whether they be bone hunters of the American West, the *tamboroli* of Italy, or the *huecheros* of Central America.

## CHALLENGES

### Access to Artifacts?

As knowledge of the past and scientific tools improve, archaeologists sometimes revisit a trove of artifacts from a given site. If the artifacts were scattered between collectors, how would archeologists gain access? Under the current black market regime, owners of artifacts have little incentive to publicize their ownership. For artifacts purchased abroad, owners risk confiscation by source nations that claim all antiquities belong to the state. In the United States, regulation can becloud owner-ship rights over antiquities, making the fidelity to law uncertain and unrewarding[20] and motivating collectors, dealers and owners to sell the artifacts in a black market, "where the antiquity is handsomely paid for with no questions asked" and "conveniently disappears" (Bator 1981, 318).

A free market would be more transparent than the existing black market. When owners and traders are free to purchase and sell goods secured by property rights, they generally become more willing to publicize their identities and ownership to attract buyers. To reinforce the buyer's title and thereby maximize the artifact's value, owners would face an additional incentive to insure their assets against theft or destruction and participate in a voluntary registry of artifacts. Such a registry could also evolve from insurance practices requiring that the location of insured objects be recorded. Subsequent buyers' desire for clear and transferable title and insurability would encourage them to keep the registry current (Brown and Stroup 2001, 46). If the market for artifacts were relatively thick, we could also expect information markets regarding the whereabouts of artifacts to spring up to meet collector's demands.

Where museums and governments sell surplus artifacts that crowd warehouses,[21] artifact sales could stipulate temporary, non-destructive research return upon request (or repurchase if the research altered the artifact). Many collectors would prefer artifacts deemed unique and important enough to be subject to such a stipulation. A final alternative would be light regulation requiring that artifact sales be recorded.

## Under-provision of a Public Good?

Some argue that a free market for archaeology would result in the under-provision of a public good and advocate "public archaeology," the view that governments must provide money for archaeological excavation and preservation. As David Haddock argues, the remedy of government intervention does not logically or empirically follow.

Public goods are a subset of economic goods that are non-excludable and non-rivalrous; non-payers cannot be excluded from consuming the good and its benefit does not diminish with consumption. Archaeological resources provide two public goods: knowledge of the past and existence value, the benefit of simply knowing the resources exist. The use of archaeological knowledge does not diminish its utility to another, and an archeologist's joy in knowing archaeological resources are buried under Pompeii does not interfere with a collector's in New York. Advocates of "public archaeology" argue that because non-payers cannot be excluded from consuming public goods, beneficiaries will refuse to pay for it, private suppliers will not be able to make money and as a result, the public good's provision will not materialize or will be inadequate.

A public good, however, creates no policy issue if other people are satiated by the most avid demander's voluntary decisions or if transaction cost does not seriously burden negotiations between that person and the others whose interests are nearly as strong. Because a public good is not used up as an individual enjoys it, the appropriate amount cannot be determined from the population of users, particularly since many positive externalities are irrelevant (Haddock 2003). Instead, the provision depends on the relatively strong preferences of the most avid user(s) which, given enough variance among preferences, will sometimes consist of only one or a few people (Haddock 2003, 19). Thus, with private provision of archaeological resources and knowledge, most people may be beyond satiety even as they make no donation themselves and have purchased very little. Most can enjoy the preservation of enthusiasts, without the need to spend anything.

Skeptics might complain that private provision does not inevitably lead to an efficient level of every public good. While true, government provision is more likely to fall even shorter from the ideal due to high information costs and decision-making complicated by special interest groups who have a greater interest in personal than public benefits. Collecting information on changing subjective preferences is costly and any determination of provision is likely to change. Since one or a few strong demands determine the actual or ideal provision, Haddock argues that transaction costs for public goods, even if enjoyed by millions, are overestimated. "Private individuals often better resolve low transaction problems than any diligent, honest bureaucracy" (Haddock 2003, 10–11).

The privatization of religion during the disestablishment era in the early nineteenth century provides a historical illustration of how government provision, complicated by information costs and special interests, fell short of private provision. Like the argument for public archaeology, the argument for public churches was based on its positive externalities; "consuming religion not only benefited individuals but made them good neighbors and upstanding citizens as well. Good churches were supposed to raise property values and increase commerce by promoting honesty" (Olds 1994, 280). As one state after another cut off all tax dollars to the state's established religion, however, religion flourished. Demand for preachers, church memberships, and budgets rose rapidly. It did not wane, but waxed instead because only the faithful—doers and donors—had any influence in each church. Preachers performed for the faithful or lost membership or financial support. To this day, the United States has a far greater religious services sector than Europe and any other industrial democracy, most of which provide state support to their state religions (Olds 1994, 277).

## CONCLUSION

The discovery in 1998 of an ancient American Indian formation in downtown Miami sparked a debate about modern society's ability to preserve and appreciate past cultures while also moving forward with economic growth. The question of approach toward archaeological preservation is not limited to Florida. As economies grow around the world, construction will continue to unearth remnants of past cultures and civilizations.

When governments arbitrate between development and preservation interests through regulation and takings, however, both development into the future and preservation of the past are compromised. The problem is not simply the zero-sum nature of all-or-nothing intervention; when economic development is legislated, historic sites are destroyed and lost, and vice-versa. Takings for historic preservation *or* economic development, generate uncertainty, which chills economic development and, by extension, archaeological discoveries unearthed by construction. Regulations that limit landowners' rights over the transfer and possession of archaeological finds motivate artifact destruction, which inadvertently fuels a black market for looted artifacts and compounds the losses of archaeological knowledge. The opportunity costs are substantial. Mutually beneficial cooperation between landowners and archeologists to explore, research and preserve prospective sights are never realized and archaeology, as a discipline, remains under-funded. Intervention results in less future development, less preservation of the past, and more of the status quo. Government programs designed to stop the growth and change that threaten valuable remnants of the past are not the solution. Ironically, those societies most open to change, through the embrace of vibrant free markets, may be the most likely to succeed in providing the best future for the past.

## NOTES

The authors thank Matt Mitchell, Angela Redding, Mark Lavoie and seminar participants at Florida State University for helpful comments. Nothing in this paper should be construed to represent the views of the Charles G. Koch Charitable Foundation.

 1. For a history of collecting antiquities, see Mayo (2005, 133–142).
 2. Under the *McClain* cases, the knowing importation of cultural property subject a clear declaration of national ownership by a source nation constitutes grounds for criminal prosecution by the United States under the National Stolen Property Act. The Court articulated three restitution principles, known as the *McClain* doctrine: the ownership legislation must have provided adequate notice of its effect, the antiquities must have been proven to have been found within the modern territory of the nation which has declared ownership, and the act of conversion must have taken place after the effective date of the vesting legislation. *See also* (Bator 1981, 346–354).
 3. In *Commission v. Italy*, the European Court of Justice held that works of art are "goods" within the meaning of the Treaty of Rome and thus subject to the same trade liberalizing rules as other "goods." "National cultural treasures," however, has yet to be judicially interpreted.
 4. In "source" nations, the supply of desirable cultural artifacts exceeds the internal demand; examples include Mexico, Egypt, Greece, and India. In "market" nations, demand exceeds supply; examples include France, Japan, Switzerland, and the United States (Merryman 1986).
 5. The United States may impose import restrictions only on "significant" archaeological or "important" ethnological materials (Pearlstein 2005, 8).
 6. According to William Pearlstein, the Implementation Act was intended to facilitate international exchange; "the carrot of US import restrictions would be used as a stick to negotiate agreements for *partage*, museum loans, excavation permits for US archeologists, cooperation and exchange among curators and art historians, and even export permits for redundant, noncritical objects" (Pearlstein 2005, 8).
 7. Since both "historic" and "archaeological" regulation and takings seek to preserve the past, this article will treat both categories as functionally equivalent.
 8. Historical and Archaeological Data Preservation Act of 1974, 16 U.S.C. § 469c (2000); (Bahn and Renfrew 1997, 523).
 9. Archaeological Resources Protection Act of 1979, 16 U.S.C. §§ 470aa-470mm (1988).
10. Native American Graves Protection and Repatriation Act of 1990, 25 U.S.C. §§ 3001–3013 (1991).
11. Years later, in *Roe v. Kansas*, the Court relied on *Gettysburg* to reject an owner's challenge to the state's condemnation of an Indian Mission. The Court upheld the State's power "to condemn places of unusual historical interest for the use and benefit of the public" (Roe v. Kansas, 278 U.S. 191, 193 (U.S. 1929)).

12. *See* Tierney 2005, for a discussion of the destruction of Pittsburgh's historic Lower Hill District, famous for its jazz.

13. In *Marks v. Whitney*, the California Supreme Court interpreted the public trust doctrine to include the "preservation of those lands in their natural state, so that they may serve as eco-logical units for scientific study, as open space, and as environments which provide food and habitat for birds and marine life, and which favorably affect the scenery and climate of the area." (*Marks v. Whitney*, 491 P.2d 374, 380 (Cal. 1971)).

14. The law of custom, in a nutshell, "provides that if the public has always used property for a certain purpose, it may continue to do so," (Burling 2002, 514).

15. This section draws from (Brown and Stroup, 2000).

16. Although Napoleon took more than 60 scientists to explore Egypt, an army officer made the discovery during the construction of a fort ("Rock of Ages" 1999, 12).

17. The Archaeological Conservancy, founded 20 years ago, is the largest private archaeological con-servation group. Modeled after a successful environmental organization, The Nature Conservancy, the Conservancy's goal is to acquire by purchase or negotiation archaeological sites on private lands and convert them into archaeological preserves. In many cases, landowners are willing to donate historically significant land, though the organization also purchases land from willing sellers, with revenue generated from its 16,000 members and private foundations.

18. The museum's art director had warned UNESCO of the impending destruction, but UNESCO replied that it was against its policy to remove from any country art that might be described as part of that country's cultural heritage (Solomon 2005, 240).

19. While public interest in archaeology is at record levels, this interest is not without controversy; archaeologists are constantly forced to answer what Bahn called "the predictable claim that archaeologists are nothing more than grave robbers" (Bahn 1999).

20. In *Andrus v. Allard*, for example, the Court held a prohibition on the sale of artifacts com-posed of protected bird feathers to not effect a taking, even though the artifacts were lawfully acquired *before* the prohibition (*Andrus v. Allard*, 444 U.S. 51 (1979)).

21. Managing growing troves has become problematic. The Museum of London, for example, has only 10,000 items on display but more than a million are in storage, inaccessible to schol-ars. According to *The Daily Telegraph*, "England's archaeological archives are in crisis due to a lack of storage and display space." (Behan 1998). Over-retention of artifacts by governments limits scholarly research and public learning and can lead to "destructive retention" where countries do not catalogue, inventory, or properly preserve artifacts. Where security is half-hazard, over-retention can also lead to theft. (Merryman 1986, 846). According to Gordon Gaskill, "Italian archeologists laugh hollowly when newspapers report of the theft of some 'unique, priceless' Estrucan vase. They know, but the public does not, how many thousands of these 'unique, priceless' vases they already have in storage and quite literally don't know what to do with." (Gaskill 1969).

# REFERENCES

16 U.S.C. § 469c

18 U.S.C. §§ 2314–2315 (1988 & Supp. II 1990).

Acemoglu, Daron and Simon Johnson. 2003. Unbundling Institutions. *MIT Department of Economics Working Paper No. 03–29,* July 2003.

Acemoglu, Daron, Simon Johnson, and James A. Robinson. 2000. The Colonial Origins of Comparative Development: An Empirical Investigation. *The American Economic Review* 95 (3): 546–579.

Ancrum, Nancy. Miami Circle Mysteries Pose Dilemma for Developer, *Miami Herald,* 4 February 1999.

Anderson, Terry L. and Donald R. Leal. 1991. *Free Market Environmentalism.* San Francisco: Pacific Research Institute.

Anderson, Terry L. and J. Bishop Grewell. 2000. Property Rights Solutions for the Global Commons from the Bottom-up or the Top-down? *The Duke Environmental Law and Policy Forum,* Duke University, Durham, N.C. April 2000.

Anderson, Terry L. and Donald R. Leal. 1997. *Enviro-Capitalists: Doing Good While Doing Well.* Lanham, MD: Rowman & Littlefield.

*Andrus v. Allard*, 444 U.S. 51, 66–67 (1979).

Antiquities Act of 1906 (Antiquities Act 1988), 16 U.S.C. §§ 431–433mm (1988).

Archaeological Resources Protection Act of 1979 (Archaeological Act 1988), 16 U.S.C. §§ 470aa–470mm (1988).

Bahn, Paul G. 1999. Digging Up the Past—Without Recriminations. *Wall Street Journal*, September 7.

Bahn, Paul and Colin Renfrew. 1997. *Archaeology: Theories, Method and Practice*. London: Thames and Hudson Ltd.

*Barnidge v. United States*, 101 F.2d 295 (8th Cir. 1939).

Bator, Paul M. 1981. An Essay on the International Trade in Art. *Stanford Law Review* 34 (2): 275–384.

Behan, Rosemary. 1998. Ancient Artifacts Buried in Archives. *The Daily Telegraph*, 22 July 1998.

Berliner, Dana. 2003. *Public Power, Private Gain: A Five-Year, State-by-State Report Examining the Abuse of Eminent Domain*, Washington DC: Castle Coalition.

*Berman v. Parker*, 348 U.S. 26 (1954).

Bousquet, Steve. 1999. State's Cost Rise in Deal for Circle. *Miami Herald*, 29 September 1999.

Bridges, Tyler. 1999. Miami Circle Given Priority for State Purchase. *Miami Herald*, 26 May 1999.

*Brown v. Legal Foundation of Washington*, 538 U. S. 216 (2003).

Brown, Matthew and Richard L. Stroup. 2000. Deciding the Future of the Past: The Miami Circle and Archeological Preservation. Policy Report #26, July 2000, The James Madison Institute.

———. 2001. How to Reduce Archaeological Looting. *Archaeological Odyssey*, March/April 2001.

Brown, Matthew. 2004. Can the Past and the Future Coexist? *The Independent Review* 8 (3): 439.

Burling, James S. 2002. The Latest Take on Background Principles and the States' Law of Property after Lucas and Palazzolo. *University of Hawaii Law Review* 24 (508–510) p. 497.

Carnett, Carol L. 1995. A Survey of State Statutes Protecting Archeological Resources. *Preservation Law Reporter:* Special Report 3 Archeological Assistance Study.

Chardy, Alfonso and Don Finefrock. 1999. It's History vs. Taxes. *Miami Herald*, 5 February 1999.

Chardy, Alfonso. 1999. Penelas Suggests Buying Circle Site. *Miami Herald*, 6 February 1999.

*Commission of the European Communities v. The Italian Republic*. Court of Justice of the European Communities. Case 7–68. Judgment of December 10, 1968.

Convention on Cultural Property (Convention on Cul. 2000), 19 U.S.C. §§ 2602, 2603 (2000).

Convention on the Means of Prohibiting and Preventing the Illicit Import, Export, and Transfer of Ownership of Cultural Property (Convention 1970). Nov. 14, 1970, 823 U.N.T.S. 231, *need international citation*, http://www.unesco.org/culture/laws/1970/html_eng/page3.shtml

Council on Environmental Quality (CoEQ). 1984. *Fifteenth Annual Report*, Washington DC: Council on Environmental Quality.

Coursey, Don. 1992. The Demand for Environmental Quality. *John M. Olin School of Business, Washington University, St. Louis.*

Daniel Pollak. 2006. Regulatory Takings: The Supreme Court Tries to Prune Agins Without Stepping on Nollan and Dolan. *Ecology Law Quarterly* 33 (925, 929).

David B. Fein. 1985. Historic Districts: Preserving City Neighborhoods for the Privileged. *N.Y.U.K. Rev.* 60 (64).

Dolan v. City of Tigard, 512 U.S. 374, (1994).

Echeverria, John D. 2005. Making Sense of Penn Central. *UCLA Journal of Environmental Law & Policy* 23 (n7).

Emmerich, Andre. 2005. Improving the Odds: Preservation through Distribution. In *Who Owns the Past? Cultural Policy, Cultural Property and the Law*, edited by Kate Fitz Gibbon. Piscataway, NJ: Rutgers University Press, 247–254.Epstein, Richard. 1987. Takings: Descent and Resurrection. *Supreme Court Review* 1987: 1–45.

Fee, John E. 1994. Unearthing the Denominator in Regulatory Takings Claims. *University of Chicago Law Review* 61 (4): 1535–1563.

Fienfrock, Don. Commissioners Rip Tribes for Not Funding Circle Deal. *Miami Herald,* October 2, 1999.

Fitz Gibbon, Kate. 2005a. Alternatives to Embargo. In *Who Owns the Past? Cultural Policy, Cultural Property and the Law,* edited by Kate Fitz Gibbon. Piscataway, NJ: Rutgers University Press, 291–304.

———. 2005b. The Elgin Marbles. In *Who Owns the Past? Cultural Policy, Cultural Property and the Law,* edited by Kate Fitz Gibbon. Piscataway, NJ: Rutgers University Press, 109–122.

Garcia-Toledo cited in Martin Merzer and Alfonso Chardy. 1999. Developer Gets Tough: No Further Delays, Officials Are Told. *Miami Herald,* 10 February 1999.

Gaskill, Gordon. They Smuggle History. *Illustrated London News,* 14 June 1969, 21.

General Agreement on Tariffs and Trade (GATT 1947), art. XI, Oct. 30, 1947, 61 Stat A-11, 55 U.N.T.S. 194 [hereinafter GATT].

Gerstenblith, Patty. 2000. Fifth Annual Tribal Sovereignty Symposium: Protection of Cultural Heritage Found on Private Land: The Paradigm of the Miami Circle and Regulatory Takings Doctrine After Lucas. *St. Thomas Law Review* 13 (65): 65–111.

———. 2001. Ownership and Protection of Heritage: Cultural Property Rights for the 21st Century: The Public Interest in Restitution of Cultural Objects. *Connecticut Journal of International Law* 16 (197).

Haddock, David D. 2003. Irrelevant Externality Angst. International Centre for Economic Research Working Paper Series. Working Paper No. 31/2003. Available online at: http://www.icer.it/docs/wp2003/Haddock31-03.pdf.

*Hawaii Housing Authority v. Midkiff,* 467 U.S. 229 (1984).

Historic Preservation Act of 1966, 16 U.S.C. §§ 470–470a-2 (1991).

Historic Sites, Buildings, and Antiquities Act (Historic Sites 1988). 16 U.S.C. §§ 461–467 (1988 & Supp. I 1989).

Hoskins, L. and A.I. Eiras. 2002. Property Rights: The Key to Economic Growth. In *2002 Index of Economic Freedom,* edited by G. P. O'Driscoll Jr., K. R. Holmes, and M. A. O'Grady. Washington, DC: Heritage Foundation, 37–48.

How to Grow Downtown and Respect Past? 1999. *Miami Herald,* February 18.

*Hunziker v. State* (*Hunziker* 1994), 519 N.W.2d 367, 371 (Iowa 1994).

Kaiser, Timothy. 1990. The Antiquities Market. *Journal of Field Archaeology* 17 (2).

Kanner, Gideon. 2005. Making Laws and Sausages: A Quarter-Century Retrospective on *Penn Central Transportation Co. V. City of New York. William and Mary Bill of Rights Journal* 13 (3).

*Kelo v. City of New London,* 545 U.S. 469 (2005).

Kleinberg, Eliot. 2006. Options Narrowing, But Miami Circle's Fate is Still Unclear. *Palm Beach Post,* 13 November 2006.

*Lebanon v. Sotheby's,* 167 A.D.2d 142 (N.Y. App. Div. 1990).

*Lingle v. Chevron U.S.A. Inc.,* 544 U.S. 528 (2005).

*Loretto v. Teleprompter Manhattan CATV Corporation,* 458 U.S. 419 (1982).

*Lucas v. South Carolina Coastal Council,* 505 U.S. 1003, (1992).

Lueck, Dean, and Jeffrey Michael. 2003. Pre-emptive Habitat Destruction under the Endangered Species Act. *Journal of Law & Economics* 43:27–60.

*Marks v. Whitney,* 491 P.2d 374, 380 (Cal. 1971).

Matsuda, David. 2005. Subsistence Diggers. In *Who Owns the Past? Cultural Policy, Cultural Property and the Law,* edited by Kate Fitz Gibbon. Piscataway, NJ: Rutgers University Press, 255–267.Mayo, Margaret Ellen. 2005. Collecting Ancient Art: A Historical Perspective. In *Who Owns the Past? Cultural Policy, Cultural Property and the Law,* edited by Kate Fitz Gibbon. Piscataway, NJ: Rutgers University Press, 133–142.

Merryman, John H. 1986. Two Ways of Thinking about Cultural Property. *American Journal of International Law* 80 A.J.I.L 831, 832.

———. 2005a. Cultural Property Internationalism. *International Journal of Cultural Property* 12: 11–39.

———. 2005b. A Licit International Trade in Cultural Objects. In *Who Owns the Past? Cultural Policy, Cultural Property and the Law,* edited by Kate Fitz Gibbon. Piscataway, NJ: Rutgers University Press, 269–290.

Miami City Code (Miami Code Sec. 23–2). Chapter 23, Sec.23–2.

Miami City Code (Miami Code Sec. 23–5). Chapter 23, Sec 23–5.

Milanich, Jerald T. 1998. *Florida's Indians: From Ancient Times to the Present,* Gainesville, Florida: University Press of Florida.

———. 1999. Much Ado About a Circle. *Archaeology,* September/October 1999.

Nafziger, James. 1985. International Penal Aspects of Protecting Cultural Property. *The International Lawyer* 19 (3): 835–852.

National Environmental Policy Act of 1969 (Environmental Policy Act 1988). 42 U.S.C. §§ 4321–4370a (1988 & Supp. III 1991).

Native American Graves Protection and Repatriation Act of 1990, 25 U.S.C. §§ 3001–3013 (1991).

*Nollan v. California Coastal Commission,* 483 U.S. 825 (1987).

North American Free Trade Agreement (NAFTA 1992). Art. 2101. U.S.-Can.-Mex. Dec. 17, 1992. 32 I.L.M. 289.

Nye, John V.C. 2002. Irreducible Inequality: Library of Economics and Liberty. Retrieved July 10, 2007 from http://www.econlib.org/LIBRARY/Columns/Nyepositional.html.

Olds, Kelly. 1994. Privatizing the Church: Disestablishment in Connecticut and Massachusetts. *Journal of Political Economy* 102 (21).

*Palazzolo, v. Rhode Island,* 533 U.S. 606, (2001).

Pearlstein, William G. 2005. Cultural Property, Congress, the Courts and Customs: The Decline and Fall of the Antiquities Market? In *Who Owns the Past? Cultural Policy, Cultural Property and the Law,* edited by Kate Fitz Gibbon. Piscataway, NJ: Rutgers University Press, 9–23.

*Penn Central Transportation Co. v. New York City,* 438 U.S. 104 (1978).

*Pennsylvania Coal Co. v. Mahon,* 260 U.S. 393 (1922).

*Peru v. Johnson,* 720 F. Supp. 810 (C.D. Cal 1989).

Phelan, Marilyn. 1993. A Synopsis of the Laws Protecting Our Cultural Heritage. *New England Law Review* 28: 63–108.

Posner, Eric A. The International Protection of Cultural Property: Some Skeptical Observation. University of Chicago, Public Law Working Paper No. 141. Available at https://www.law.uchicago.edu/academics/publiclaw/141.pdf.

Public Access Shoreline Hawai'i County Planning Commission, 903 P.2d 1246 (1995), cert. denied, 517 U.S. 1163 (1996).

Rapp, Christopher. 1999. Dung Deal—Brooklyn Museum of Art's "Sensation" exhibition. *National Review* October 25.

Regulation of Importation of Pre-Columbian Monumental or Architectural Sculpture or Murals (Regulation of Importation 1972). 19 U.S.C. §§ 2091–2095 (1972).

*Republic of Turkey v. Metropolitan Museum of Art,* 762 F. Supp. 44 (S.D.N.Y. 1990).

Rock of Ages. 1999. *Archaeology Odyssey* (September/October).

Rodrik, Dani, Arvind Subramanian, and Francesco Trebbi. 2004. Institutions Rule: The Primacy of Institutions over Integration and Geography in Economic Development. *Journal of Economic Growth* 9 (2, June): 131–165.

Rogers, Kristine Olson. 1987. Visigoths Revisited: The Prosecution of Archaeological Resource Thieves, Traffickers, and Vandals. *Journal of Environmental Law and Litigation* 2 (47): 51.

Rose, Carol M. 1984. Mahon Reconstructed: Why the Takings Issue Is Still a Muddle. *Southern California Law Review* 57 (561): 561–602.

S. Rep. No. 97–564, at 27 (S. Rep. 1982) (1982).

Sason, David. 1999. Considering the Perspective of the Victim: The Antiquities of Nepal. In *The Ethics of Collecting Cultural Property,* edited by Phyllis Mauch Messenger. New Mexico: University of New Mexico Press, 69.

Sax, Joseph L. 1990. The Constitution, Property Rights and the Future of Water Law, *University of Colorado Law Review* 61 (257, 269).

Shanks, Hershel. 1999a. Let's Do What We Can! The Impossible Will Take Forever. *Archaeology Odyssey* November/December 1999.

———.1999b. How to Stop Looting: A Modest Proposal. *Archaeology Odyssey* September/October 1999.

———. 1999c. The Great MFA Exposé. *Archaeology Odyssey* May/June 1999.

Solomon, Andrew. 2005. Art in Jeopardy. In *Who Owns the Past? Cultural Policy, Cultural Property and the Law*, edited by Kate Fitz Gibbon. Piscataway, NJ: Rutgers University Press, 239–246. *State v. Lightle*, 944 P.2d 1114 (Wash. Ct. App. 1997).

*Stevens v. City of Cannon Beach*, 114 S. Ct. 1332, 1333 n. (1994).

Stille, Alexander. 2002. *The Future of the Past*. New York, New York: Picador.

Stroup, Richard L. 1995a. The Endangered Species Act: Making Innocent Species the Enemy. *Policy Series Number 3, Political Economy Research Center*. April.

———. 1995b. The Endangered Species Act: Making Innocent Species the Enemy. PERC Policy Series—3. April.

———. 1997. The Economics of Compensating Property Owners. *Contemporary Economic Policy* 15 (October): 55–65.

*Tahoe-Sierra Pres. Council v. Tahoe Reg'l Planning Agency*, 535 U.S. 302 (U.S. 2002).

*Thompson v. City of Red Wing*, 455 N.W.2d 512, 516 (Minn. Ct. App. 1990).

Tierney, John. 2005. Your Land Is My Land. *New York Times*, 5 July.

Treaty of Cooperation between the United States of America and the United Mexican States Providing for the Recovery and Return of Stolen Archeological, Historical, and Cultural Properties (Treaty U.S.-Mexico 1970). U.S-Mex. July 17, 1970. 22 U.S.T. 494.

[Treaty of Rome] Treaty Establishing the European Economic Community, March 25, 1957, Art. 30, 298 U.N.T.S. 11, 1973 Gr. Brit. T.S. No. I (Cmd. 5179-II) [hereinafter EEC Treaty] in *Treaties Establishing the European Communities* (EC Off 'l Pub. Off).

Tullock, Gordon, Arthur Seldon, and Gordon L. Brady. 2002. Government Failure: A Primer in Public Choice. *Cato Institute*.

*Turkey v. OKS Partners*, 757 F. Supp. 64 (D. Mass. 1992).

*United States v. Schultz*, 333 F.3d 393 (2d Cir. 2003).

*United States v. An Antique Platter of Gold*, 991 F. Supp. 222 (S.D.N.Y. 1997).

*United States v. Diaz*, 499 F.2d 113, 115 (9th Cir. 1974).

*United States v. Gettysburg E. R. Co.*, 160 U.S. 668 (U.S. 1896).

*United States v. Hollinshead*, 495 F.2d 1154 (9th Cir. 1974).

*United States v. McClain*, 545 F.2d 988 (5th Cir. 1977); 593 F.2d 658 (5th Cir. 1979).

*United States v. Pre-Columbian Artifacts*, 845 F. Supp. 544, 547 (N.D. Ill. 1993).

Vincent, Steven. 2005. Indian Givers, In *Who Owns the Past? Cultural Policy, Cultural Property and the Law*, edited by Kate Fitz Gibbon. Piscataway, NJ: Rutgers University Press, 33–42.

Warren, Karen J. 1989. A Philosophical Perspective on the Ethics of Collecting Cultural Properties Issues. *The Ethics of Collecting Cultural Property*.

*Whitacre v. State*, 619 N.E.2d 605 (Ind. Ct. App. 1993), *aff'd*, 629 N.W.2d 1236 (Ind. 1994).

White, Nancy Marie. 1999. Cited in Ancient Treasures Lost and Found. *Tampa Tribune*, 14 March.

Whoriskey, Peter. 1999a. The Holes, the Eye, the Axes: Mysteries May Go Unsolved, *Miami Herald*, February 14.

———. 1999b. Price Will Be an Issue if Land Is Seized. *Miami Herald*, February 16.

———. 1999c. County Wins Right to Buy Circle from Developer, *Miami Herald*, 29.

# 12

# BELOW-MARKET HOUSING MANDATES AS TAKINGS

## MEASURING THEIR IMPACT

*Thomas Means, Edward Stringham, and Edward J. López*

## INTRODUCTION

High housing prices in recent years are making it increasingly difficult for many to purchase a home. Prices have been rising all over the United States, especially in cities on the East and West Coasts. In San Francisco, for example, the median home sells for $846,500 (Said 2007, c1), which requires yearly mortgage payments of roughly $63,000 (plus yearly property taxes of $8,500).[1] Not only is the median home unaffordable to most, but there is a dearth of affordable homes on the low end too. In San Francisco, a household making the median income of $86,100 can afford (using traditional lending guidelines) only 6.7 percent of existing homes (National Association of Homebuilders/Wells Fargo 2007). Households making less are all but precluded from the possibility of home ownership (Riches 2004).

As a proposed solution, many cities are adopting a policy often referred to as below-market housing mandates, affordable housing mandates, or inclusionary zoning (California Coalition for Rural Housing and Non-Profit Housing Association of Northern California 2003) The specifics of the policy vary by city, but inclusionary zoning as commonly practiced in California mandates that developers sell 10–20 percent of new homes at prices affordable to low income households. Below-market units typically have been interspersed among market rate units, have similar size and appearance as market price units, and are to retain their below-market status for a period of 55 years.[2] The program is touted as a way to make housing more affordable, and as a way to provide housing for all income levels not just the rich. In contrast to exclusionary zoning, a practice that uses housing laws to keep out the poor, inclusionary zoning is advocated to help the poor. Because of its expressed good intentions the program has gained tremendous popularity. First introduced in Palo Alto, California in 1973, it has increased in popularity in the past decade so now in place in one third of cities in California (Non-Profit Housing Association of Northern California 2007), and it is spreading nationwide having been already adopted in parts of Maryland, New Jersey, and Virginia (Calavita, Grimes, and Mallach 1997).

But the program is not without controversy.[3] In *Home Builders Association of Northern California v. City of Napa* (2001) the Home Builders Association maintained that by requiring developers to sell a percentage of their development for less than market price, the "ordinance violated the takings clauses of the Federal and State Constitutions." A ruling by the Court of Appeal in California stated that affordable housing mandates are legal and not a taking because (1) they benefit developers and (2) they necessarily increase the supply of affordable housing. This chapter investigates these claims by examining the costs of the programs and examining econometrically how they affect the price and quantity of housing.

Our chapter is organized as follows. Section 2 discusses the history of regulatory takings decisions by the courts and relates them to affordable housing mandates. It provides a brief overview of regulatory takings decisions and discusses the arguments about why affordable housing mandates may or may not be considered a taking. When government allows certain buyers to buy at below-market prices, they are making sellers sell their property at price controlled prices. If sellers are not compensated for being forced to sell their property at below-market price it may be considered a taking.

Section 3 investigates how much affordable housing mandates cost developers. By calculating the price controlled level and comparing it to the market price, we can observe the costs to developers each time they sell a price controlled home. After estimating how much the program costs developers, we discuss to what extent they are being compensated. We find that the alleged benefits to developers pale in comparison to the costs.

Section 4 investigates econometrically whether below-market housing mandates actually make housing more affordable. Using panel data for California cities, we investigate how below-market housing mandates affect price and quantity of housing. *We find that cities that adopt below-market housing mandates actually drive housing prices up by 20 percent and end up with 10 percent fewer homes.* These statistically significant findings indicate that the idea that affordable housing necessarily increases the amount of affordable housing can be questioned.

Section 5 concludes by discussing why, contrary to the *Home Builders Association of Northern California v. Napa*, below-market housing mandates should be considered a taking.

## BELOW-MARKET HOUSING MANDATES AND TAKINGS

What are takings and should affordable housing mandates be considered a taking? The most familiar form of taking is when the government acquires title to real property for public use such as common carriage rights of way (roads, rail, power lines). Doctrine for these types of takings is evident in early U.S. jurisprudence, which institutionalized the principle that the government's chief function is to protect private property.[4] As such, the government's takings power was limited in several key respects. Most importantly, the nineteenth century Supreme Court prohibited takings that transferred property from one private owner to another and upheld the fundamental fairness doctrine that no individual property owner should bear too much of the burden in supplying public uses.

But government's taking power has expanded over time. Takings restrictions were gradually eroded beginning in the Progressive Era and accelerating in the

New Deal, as the Court increasingly deferred to legislative bodies and an ever-expanding notion of public use. Starting in the latter half of the twentieth century, the stage was set to green light takings for "public uses" such as urban renewal (*Berman v. Parker* 1954), competition in real estate (*Hawaii Housing v. Midkiff* 1984), expansion of the tax base (*Kelo v. New London* 2005), and other types of "economic development takings" (Somin 2004). By the final decade of the twentieth century, one prominent legal scholar described the public use clause as being of "nearly complete insignificance" (Rubenfeld 1993, 1078).

Regulatory takings differ in that they are generally not subject to just compensation, because they rest on the government's police power, not the power of eminent domain. Regulatory takings differ also in that the owner retains title to the property, but suffers attenuated rights. For example, a government might rezone an area for environmental conservation and thereby prevent a landowner from developing his property. But does an owner still own his property if he is deprived of using it according to his original intent? These were the essential characteristics of the regulation challenged in *Lucas v. South Carolina Coastal Council* (1992).[5] David Lucas owned two plots of land, which he bought for nearly $1 million and he intended to develop, but South Carolina Coastal Council later rezoned his property stating that it would be used for conservation. The Court sided with Lucas saying that if he was deprived of economically valuable use, he must be compensated. Under *Lucas,* current federal law requires compensation if the regulation diminishes the entire value of the property, such that an effective taking exists despite no physical removal.

This so-called "total takings" test is one of several doctrines that could be used to judge regulatory takings. For example, the diminution of value test could support compensation to the extent of the harm done to the property owner. This was the Court's tendency in the 1922 case *Pennsylvania Coal v. Mahon*, which found that a regulatory act can constitute a taking depending on the extent to which the value of a property is lowered.[6] So the *Lucas* Court was not up to something new. As a matter of fact, the concept of regulatory takings was discussed by key figures in the American founding era and became an important topic in nineteenth century legal scholarship as well.[7]

Following in this tradition, the *Lucas* Court addressed several sticking points with regulatory takings law. For example, the majority opinion cites Justice Holmes stating the maxim that when regulation goes too far in diminishing the owner's property rights it becomes a taking. However, as the majority opinion points out, the Court does not have a well-developed standard for determining when a regulation goes too far to become a taking. Finally and most importantly for our purposes, the *Lucas* Court also stresses that the law is necessary to prevent policymakers from using the expediency of the police power to avoid the just compensation required under eminent domain. The *Lucas* Court examines regulators' incentives and voices its discomfort with the "heightened risk that private property is being pressed into some form of public service under the guise of mitigating serious public harm."

Below-market housing mandates seem like they fit into the *Lucas* Court description of what could be considered a taking since they rezone land requiring owners to provide a public service of making low income housing. This specific issue, however, is still being debated in the courts. In 1999, the Homebuilders Association of Northern California brought a case against the City of Napa for mandating that 10 percent of new units to be sold at below-market rates. The

Home Builders Association argued that the affordable housing mandate violated the Fifth Amendment's takings clause that "private property [shall not] be taken for public use without just compensation." The trial court dismissed the complaint, and in 2001 the Court of Appeal decided against the Home Builders Association, arguing that "[a]lthough the ordinance imposed significant burdens on developers, it also provided significant benefits for those who complied."[8] In addition, the California Court argued that because making housing more affordable is a legitimate state interest then below-market housing mandates are legitimate because they advance that goal. Judge Scott Snowden (who was affirmed by Judges J. Stevens and J. Simons) wrote, "Second, it is beyond question that City's inclusionary zoning ordinance will 'substantially advance' the important governmental interest of providing affordable housing for low and moderate-income families. By requiring developers in City to create a modest amount of affordable housing (or to comply with one of the alternatives) the ordinance will *necessarily* increase the supply of affordable housing."[9] The Home Builders Association's subsequent attempts to have the case reheard or reviewed by the Supreme Court were denied.

So the Court's argument rests on two propositions that it considers beyond question: (1) affordable housing mandates provide significant benefits to builders that offset the costs, and (2) affordable housing mandates necessarily increase the supply of affordable housing. Both of these are empirical arguments that can be tested against real-world data. We investigate these propositions in the following two sections.

## ESTIMATING THE COSTS OF BELOW-MARKET HOUSING MANDATES

If one wants to state "Although the ordinance imposed significant burdens on developers, it also provided significant benefits for those who complied" one needs to investigate the costs of below-market housing mandates these programs. Yet when this statement by the Court in 2001 was issued there had been no study of the costs.[10] The first work to estimate theses costs was Powell and Stringham (2004a). Let us here provide some sample calculations, and then present some data for costs in various California cities. Once we present the costs we can consider whether the programs have significant offsetting benefits for developers.

First let us consider a real example from Marin County's drafted Countywide Plan.[11] According to the plan affordable housing mandates would be designated for certain areas of the County (with privately owned property). In these areas, anyone wishing to develop their property would have to sell or lease 50–60 percent of their property at below-market rates.[12] The Plan requires the below-market rate homes to be affordable to households earning 60–80 percent of median income, which means price controlled units must be sold for approximately $180.000–$240,000.[13] How much does such an affordable housing mandate cost developers? New homes are typically sold for more than the median price of housing, but for simplicity let us assume that new homes would have been sold at the median price in Marin, which is $838,750. For each unit sold at $180,002, the revenue is $658,748 less due to the price control. Consider the following sample calculations for a ten-unit project in Marin for how much revenue a developer could get with and without price controls.

## SAMPLE CALCULATIONS FOR A 10-UNIT FOR SALE
## DEVELOPMENT IN MARIN COUNTY

**Scenario 1: Development Without Price Controls** *Revenue from a 10 unit project without price controls* [(10 market rate units) × ($838,750 per unit)] = $8,387,500

**Scenario 2: Development with below-market mandate** *Revenue from a 10 unit project with 50 percent of homes under price controls set for 60 percent of median income households* [(5 market rate units) × ($838,750 per unit)] + [(5 price controlled units) × ($180,002 per unit)]= $5,093,760

As these calculations show, the below-market housing mandate decreases the revenue from a 10 unit project by $3,293,740, which is roughly 40 percent of the value of a project. This is just one example, and there are many more.

Powell and Stringham (2004a and 2004b) estimate the costs of below-market housing mandates in the San Francisco Bay Area and Los Angeles and Orange Counties. By estimating for how much units must be sold below market and comparing this to how much homes could be sold without price controls, one can estimate how much below-market housing mandates make developers forego. Even using conservative estimates (to not overestimate costs), these policies cost developers a substantial amount. Figure 12.1 shows that in the median Bay Area city with a below-market housing mandate, each price controlled unit must be sold for more than $300,000 below-market price. In cities with high housing prices and restrictive price controls, such as Los Altos and Portola Valley, developers must sell below-market rate homes for more than $1 million below the market price.

One can estimate the costs imposed by these programs on developers by looking at the cost per unit times the number of units built. This measure is not what

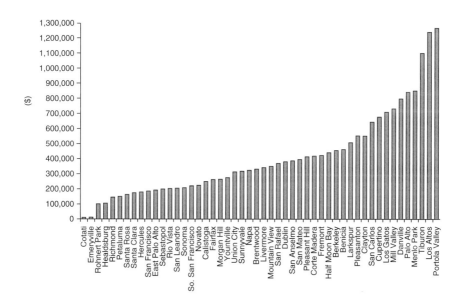

**Figure 12.1** Average Lost Revenue Associated with Selling Each Below-Market Rate Unit in San Francisco Bay Area Cities

*Source:* Powell and Stringham (2004, 15).

economists call deadweight costs (which attempts to measure the lost gains from trade from what is not being built), but just a measure of the lost revenue that developers incur for the units actually built. In many cities no units have been built as a result of the program, but nevertheless the costs (in current prices) are quite high in many cities. The results for the San Francisco Bay Area are displayed in figure 12.2. In the five cities Mill Valley, Petaluma, Palo Alto, San Rafael, and Sunnyvale the amount of the "giveaways" in current prices totals over $1 billion.

The next important question is whether developers are getting anything in return. If Mill Valley, Petaluma, Palo Alto, San Rafael, and Sunnyvale issued checks to developers totally $1 billion, one could say that even though there was a taking, there was a type of compensation. But the interesting aspect about affordable housing mandates as practiced in California and most other places is that government offers no monetary compensation at all. In fact, this is one the reasons advocates of the program and governments have been adopting it. In the words of one prominent advocate, Dietderich (1996:41), "A vast inclusionary program need not spend a public dime." In contrast to government-built housing projects, which require tax revenue to construct and manage, affordable housing mandates impose those costs onto private citizens, namely housing developers. Here we have private parties losing billions of dollars in revenue and getting no monetary compensation in return.

Monetary compensation for developers is not present, but are affordable housing mandates accompanied by non-monetary benefits? The Court in *Home Builders Association v. Napa* stated that "Developments that include affordable housing are eligible for expedited processing, fee deferrals, loans or grants, and density bonuses."[14] According to California Government Code Section 65915 government must provide a density bonus of at least 25 percent to developers who make 20 percent of a project affordable to low income households. The value of these offsetting benefits will vary based on the specifics, but for full compensation to take

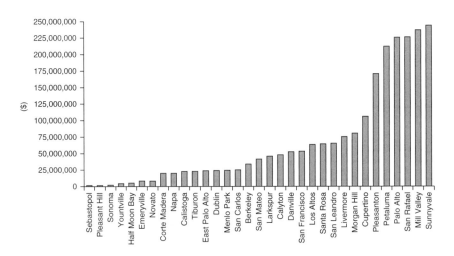

**Figure 12.2**  Average Lost Revenue per Unit Times Number of Units Sold in Below-Market Programs in San Francisco Bay Area Cities

*Source*: Powell and Stringham (2004, 15).

place these benefits would have to be more than $300,000 per home in the median Bay Area city with inclusionary zoning.

One could determine that the offsetting benefits were worth more than the costs in two ways.[15] The first way would be if we observed the building industry actively lobbying for these programs. But in California and most other areas, the building industry is usually the most vocal opponents of these programs. *Home Builders Association of Northern California v. Napa* the Court provided no explanation of why the Home Builders Association would be suing to stop a program if it really did provide "significant benefits for those who complied." If the programs really did benefit developers, there would be no reason developers would oppose them.

Why don't builders want to sell units for hundreds of thousands less than market price for each unit sold? Or why don't California builders want to forgo billions in revenue? All of the builders with whom we have spoken, have stated that the offsetting "benefits" are no benefits at all. For example, a city might grant a density bonus, but the density bonus might be completely unusable because density restrictions are just one of a set of restrictions on how many units will fit on the property. Other constraints such as setbacks, minimum requirements for public and private open space, floor area ratios, and even tree protections make it extremely complicated to get more units on the property. Conventional wisdom suggests that building at 100 percent of allowable density will maximize profits, but in reality developers tend to build out at less than full density. The city of Mountain View recently passed a policy requiring developers to provide an explanation if their project failed to meet 80 percent of the allowable density.[16] Prior projects had averaged around 65 percent of allowable density. So giving builders the opportunity to build at 125 percent of allowable density is often worth nothing when so many other binding regulations exist.

The second and even simpler way to determine whether the affordable housing mandates provide significant benefits to compensate them for their costs would be to make the inclusionary zoning programs voluntary. Developers could weigh the benefits and costs of participating, and if the benefits exceeded the costs, they could voluntarily comply. A few cities in California tried adopting voluntary ordinances, and perhaps unsurprisingly, they did not attract developers. One advocate of affordable housing mandates argues that the problem with voluntary programs is "that most of them, because of their voluntary nature, produce very few units" (Tetreault 2000, 20).

From these simple observations, we can infer that the significant "benefits" of these programs are not as significant as the costs. In this sense the program has the character of a regulatory taking. In addition to observing whether builders would support or voluntarily participate in these programs, we can also analyze data to observe how these programs affect the quantity of housing. If the Court in *Home Builders Association v. Napa* is correct that the benefits are significant, then we would predict that imposing an affordable housing mandate would not affect (or it would encourage) housing production in a jurisdiction. If on the other hand, the program is not compensating for what it takes, we would predict that cities with the program will see less development than otherwise similar cities without the program. Here the program is a taking that will hinder new development.

## TESTING HOW BELOW-MARKET HOUSING MANDATES AFFECT THE PRICE AND QUANTITY OF HOUSING

The Court in *Homebuilders Association v. Napa* puts forth an important proposition, which we can examine statistically. They state, "By requiring developers in City to create a modest amount of affordable housing (or to comply with one of the alternatives) the ordinance will *necessarily* increase the supply of affordable housing" (emphasis added). Although the Court suggests that it is an a priori fact that price controls will increase the supply of affordable housing, the issue may be a bit more complicated than these appellate judges maintain. Before getting to the econometrics let us consider some simple economic theory and simple statistics about the California experience. First, if a price control is so restrictive, developers cannot make any profits and so the price control can easily drive out all development from an area. Cities such as Watsonville adopted overly restrictive price controls and they all but prevented all development in their city until they scaled back the requirements (Powell and Stringham 2005). Over 30 years in the entire San Francisco Bay Area, below-market housing mandates have resulted in the production of only 6,836 affordable units, an average of 228 per year (Powell and Stringham 2004, 5). Controlling for the length of time each program has been in effect, the average jurisdiction has produced only 14.7 units for each year since adopting a below-market housing mandate. Since the programs have been implemented dozens of cities have produced a total of zero units (Powell and Stringham 2004, 4–5). So unless one defines zero as an increase, it might be more accurate to restate "necessarily increase" as "might increase."

Economic theory predicts that price controls on housing lead to a decrease in quantity produced. Since developers must sell a percentage of units at price controlled units in order to get permission to build market rate units, this policy also will affect the supply of market rate units. Powell and Stringham (2005) discuss how the policy may be analyzed as a tax on new housing. If below-market rate housing mandates act as a tax on housing they will reduce quantity and increase housing price. This is the exact opposite of what advocates of below-market housing mandates say they prefer. So we have two competing hypotheses, that of economic theory, and that of the Court in *Home Builders Association v. Napa*. Luckily we can test these two hypotheses by examining data for housing production and housing prices in California.

Our approach is to use panel data, which has a significant advantage over simple cross sectional or time series data. Suppose a city adopts the policy and there is an unrelated statewide decline in demand and housing output falls by 10 percent. A time-series approach would still have to control for other economic factors that might have changed and reduced housing output. One would still need to compare the reduction in output from a city that adopted the policy to a nearby similar city that did not. A cross sectional approach can control overall economics factors at a point in time, but will not control for unobserved city differences. Our approach is to set up a two-period panel data set to control for unobserved city differences and control for changes over time. The tests which we explain in detail below will enable us to see how adopting a below-market-rate housing mandate will affect variables such as output and prices.

## Description of the Data

The first set of data we utilize consists of the 1990 and 2000 census data for the California cities. The 2000 census data is restricted to cities with a population greater than 10,000 while 1990 census data is not. A decrease in population for some cities during the decade resulted in a loss of 15 cities from the sample. We do not include the 1980 census since there were few policies in affect during this decade (Palo Alto passed the first policy in 1972). Focusing on this decade also highlights some economic issues. From 1987 to 1989 housing prices grew very rapidly. Prices for the first half of 1989 grew around 25 percent only to fall by this amount for the second half of the year and continued to slide as the California economy declined. For some areas, prices did not recover to their original level until halfway through the 1990 decade. The California economy grew faster in the second half of the decade due to the dot-com boom in the technology sector. Data from the RAND California Statistics website provided average home sale prices for each city for the 1990 and 2000 period. The Rand data does not report 1990 home sale prices for some cities resulting in a loss of more observations. Summary statistics are provided in table 12.1.

Data on the policy adoption dates came from the California Coalition for Rural Housing and Non-Profit Housing Association of Northern California. Table 12.2

**Table 12.1**  Summary Statistics

| Variable | Observations | Mean | Standard Deviation | Minimum | Maximum |
|---|---|---|---|---|---|
| Population 2000 | N=446 | 65,466 | (197,087) | 10,007 | 3,694,834 |
| Population 1990 | N=431 | 58,468 | (187,014) | 1,520 | 3,485,398 |
| Households 2000 | N=446 | 22,251 | (68,673) | 1,927 | 1,276,609 |
| Households 1990 | N=431 | 20,512 | (66,074) | 522 | 1,219,770 |
| Housing Units 2000 | N=446 | 23,278 | (71,843) | 2,069 | 1,337,668 |
| Housing Units 1990 | N=431 | 21,745 | (70,331) | 597 | 1,299,963 |
| Density 2000 (persons/acre) | N=446 | 7.62 | (6.06) | 0.42 | 37.32 |
| Density 1990 (persons/acre) | N=431 | 6.87 | (5.88) | 0.08 | 37.01 |
| Median House hold Income 2000 | N=446 | 52,582 | (21,873) | 16,151 | 193,157 |
| Median House hold Income 1990 | N=431 | 38,518 | (14,543) | 14,215 | 123,625 |
| Per Capita Income 2000 | N=446 | 23,903 | (13,041) | 7,078 | 98,643 |
| Per Capita Income 1990 | N=431 | 16,696 | (8,070) | 4,784 | 63,302 |
| Rents/Income 2000 | N=446 | 27.60% | (3.1%) | 14.4% | 50.1% |
| Rents/Income 1990 | N=431 | 28.9% | (2.7%) | 14.9% | 35.1% |
| Average Home Price 2000 | N=360 | 300,594 | (235,436) | 49,151 | 2,253,218 |
| Average Home Price 1990 | N=352 | 206,754 | (112,804) | 52,858 | 1,018,106 |

**Table 12.2** Summary Statistics—Policy Variables

| Variable | # of Cities with Inclusionary Zoning (in That Year) | Variable | # of Cities with Inclusionary Zoning (in That Year) | Variable | Change in # of Cities With Inclusionary Zoning (over 10 Years) |
|---|---|---|---|---|---|
| iz1985 | 15 | iz1995 | 50 | iz95delta (which is iz1995–iz1985) | 35 |
| iz1986 | 19 | iz1996 | 52 | iz96delta (which is iz1996–iz1986) | 33 |
| iz1987 | 19 | iz1997 | 54 | iz97delta (which is iz1997–iz1987) | 35 |
| iz1988 | 22 | iz1998 | 54 | iz98delta (which is iz1998–iz1988) | 32 |
| iz1989 | 23 | iz1999 | 59 | iz99delta (which is iz1999–iz1989) | 36 |

describes the summary statistics of the policy variables that we construct. IZyr is a dummy variable defined to equal one if the city passed a below-market-rate housing ordinance that year or in prior years. As noted above, differences in population cutoff points and missing 1990 housing prices reduced the sample of cities that passed (or did not pass) an ordinance. Starting in 1985 our sample contains 15 California cities that had passed an ordinance. The number increased to 59 cities by the end of 1999. The last column reports the difference between decades. In other words, iz95delta reports the number of cities that passed an ordinance between 1985 and 1995. The difference variables are fairly constant and capture a large number of cities that passed ordinances during the decade. Focusing on the 1990–2000 decade should allow us enough observations to capture the impact of the policy.

## Empirical Tests

Wooldridge (2006) provides an excellent discussion of how to test the impact of a policy using two-period panel data. Our approach is to specify a model with unobserved city effects that are assumed constant over the decade (1990–2000) and estimate a first difference model to eliminate the fixed effect. We also specify a semi-log model so that the first difference yields the log of the ratio of the dependent variables over the decade. Estimating the models in logs also simplifies the interpretation of the policy variable coefficient as an approximate percentage change rather then an absolute difference in averages. For the policy variable we define IZyr as a dummy variable equal to one if the policy was in effect during the current and previous years. To see the importance of the first-difference approach, consider a model specified for each decade.

**Level Model:**
$$\ln Y_{it} = \beta_0 + d_0 YR2000_{it} + d_1 IZyr_{it} + \beta_1 X_{it} + a_i + v_{it} \quad \text{(Equation 1)}$$

$i$ = city
$t$ = 1990, 2000

The dependent variable is either housing output or housing prices, YR2000 is a dummy variable allowing the intercept to change over the decade, IZyr is the policy dummy variable and the $X_{it}$ are control variables. The error term contains two terms; the *unobserved* fixed city component ($a_i$) considered fixed for the decade (e.g. location, weather, political tastes), and the usual error component ($v_{it}$). If the unobserved fixed effect is uncorrelated with the exogenous variables, one can estimate the model using ordinary-least-squares for each decade. The coefficient for IZyr measures the impact of the policy for each decade.[17] Unfortunately, estimating the level model may not capture the differences between cities that passed an ordinance and the ones that did not. In other words, suppose cities with higher housing prices are more likely to adopt the policy. The dummy variable may capture the impact of the policy along with the fact that these cities already have higher prices.

The above issues can be addressed by differencing the level models to eliminate the fixed city effect, which yields the first-difference model.[18]

**First-Difference Model:**
$\ln Y_{i,2000} - \ln Y_{i,1990} = d_0 + d_1 IZyr_{i,2000} - d_1 IZyr_{i,1990} + \beta_1 X_{i,2000} - \beta_1 X_{i,1990} + v_{i,2000} - v_{i,1990}$ (Equation 2)i—city
which can be rewritten as:
$\ln(Y_{i,2000}/Y_{i,1990}) = d_0 + d_1 \Delta IZyr_{i,t} + \beta_1 \Delta X_{i,t} + \Delta v_{i,t}$ (Equation 3)i—city

Eliminating the unobserved fixed city effect, which we show below in the last two columns of table 12.3 and 12.4, has an important effect on estimating the impact of the policy variable. Differencing the panel data also yields a dummy variable that represents the change in policy participation over the decade (an example of this is the iz95delta appearing in tables 12.2 through 12.6). When policy participation takes place in both periods (1990 and 2000) the interpretation of the differenced dummy is slightly different from the usual policy treatment approach. The differenced dummy variable predicts the average change in the dependent variable due to an increase (or decrease) in participation.

**Table 12.3** Summary of Policy Coefficients from 15 Regressions on the Price of Housing by Model and by Lag Year

| Level Models for 1990 Data | | Level Models for 2000 Data | | First Difference Models (2000–1990) | |
|---|---|---|---|---|---|
| Policy Variable | Coefficient of Policy Variable | Policy Variable | Coefficient of Policy Variable | Policy Variable | Coefficient of Policy Variable |
| iz1985 | .389 | iz1995 | .627 | iz95delta | .312 |
| iz1986 | .431 | iz1996 | .642 | iz96delta | .298 |
| iz1987 | .431 | iz1997 | .637 | iz97delta | .278 |
| iz1988 | .442 | iz1998 | .637 | iz98delta | .270 |
| iz1989 | .457 | iz1999 | .642 | iz99delta | .265 |

*Note*: Dependent Variable: ln(Price)

**Table 12.4**  Summary of Policy Coefficients from 15 Regressions on the Quantity of Housing by Model and by Lag Year

| Level Models for 1990 Data | | Level Models for 2000 Data | | First Difference Models (2000–1990) | |
|---|---|---|---|---|---|
| Policy Variable | Coefficient of Policy Variable | Policy Variable | Coefficient of Policy Variable | Policy Variable | Coefficient of Policy Variable |
| iz1985 | .777 | iz1995 | .665 | iz95delta | −.045 |
| iz1986 | .751 | iz1996 | .614 | iz96delta | −.024 |
| iz1987 | .751 | iz1997 | .585 | iz97delta | −.027 |
| iz1988 | .679 | iz1998 | .585 | iz98delta | −.038 |
| iz1989 | .653 | iz1999 | .618 | iz99delta | −.051 |

*Note*: Dependent Variable: ln(Housing Units)

**Table 12.5**  Regression Results of How Below-Market Housing Mandates Affect Price of Housing: First Difference Model with Control Variables

| Independent Variable | Coefficients and (Standard Errors) $N = 431$ | Coefficients and (Standard Errors) $N = 431$ |
|---|---|---|
| Constant | 0.001 (0.025) | −0.009 (0.025) |
| iz95delta | 0.228*** (0.038) | |
| iz99delta | | 0.217*** (0.037) |
| median income | 0.173*** (0.0126) | 0.178*** (0.0125) |
| density | −0.007 (0.011) | −0.008 (0.011) |
| population | −0.0017 (0.00661) | −0.00112 (0.00662) |
| rent % | −0.002 (0.005) | −0.003 (0.005) |
| Adj. R-Squared | 0.4332 | 0.4300 |

*Notes*: Dependent Variable: ln(average price 2000/1990)
*, **, *** denotes significance at the .10, .05, .01 levels, two-tailed test.

To see the advantage of the first difference approach we first estimated (without control variables, which we will add in tables 12.5 and 12.6) the un-differenced equations of the log of average housing prices and output ($\ln Y_i = \beta_0 + d_1 IZyr_i$) over various lagged policy dummies. The first four columns in table 12.3 report the estimated coefficients ($d_1$) for each lag year for the level models. The left two columns show the coefficient estimates for the five regressions that look at housing prices in 1990 and have iz1985, iz1986, iz1987, iz1988, or iz1989 as the policy variable. The third and fourth columns in table 12.3 show the coefficient estimates for the five

**Table 12.6** Regression Results of How Below-Market Housing Mandates Affect Quantity of Housing: First Difference Model with Control Variables

| Independent Variable | Coefficients and (Standard Errors) $N = 431$ | Coefficients and (Standard Errors) $N = 431$ |
|---|---|---|
| Constant | −0.056** (0.023) | −0.054** (0.023) |
| iz95delta | −0.104** (0.042) | — |
| iz99delta | — | −0.097** (0.041) |
| median income | 0.0683*** (0.0132) | 0.0660*** (0.0131) |
| density | 0.113* (0.011) | 0.114* (0.011) |
| population | 0.0233* (0.00729) | 0.0230* (0.00729) |
| Adj. R-Squared | 0.2921 | 0.2911 |

Notes: Dependent Variable: ln(units 2000–1990)
*, **, *** denotes significance at the .10, .05, .01 levels, two-tailed test.

regressions that look at housing prices in 2000 and have iz1995, iz1996, iz1997, iz1998, or iz1999 as the policy variable. For example, the .389 in the first row indicates that that cities with inclusionary zoning in 1985 had 47.6 percent (exp(.389)–1) higher than average prices in 1990 and the .627 in the first row indicates that cities with inclusionary zoning in 1995 had 87.2 percent higher than average prices in 2000. For both decades the impact increases slightly as the lag period is decreased though the impact for the 2000 period is much larger than the 1990 period.

The estimated coefficients ($d_1$) for 1990 and 2000 range from 0.389 to 0.642 and indicate that cities with inclusionary zoning have 48–90 percent higher housing prices, but this does not take into consideration the possibility that cities that adopted the policy already had higher prices when they adopted the policy. To account for this potential problem, the First Difference model estimates how changes in the policy variable (adopting a below-market housing ordinance) alone affect housing prices. The last two columns of table 12.3 report the first-difference estimates ($\ln(Y_{i,2000}/Y_{i,1990}) = d_0 + d_1 \Delta IZyr_{it}$). For example, the .312 in the last column of the first row indicates that cities with below-market housing mandates have 36.6 percent higher prices. Each of the estimated coefficients in table 12.3 are significant at the 1 percent level. The results in the last two columns indicate that below-market housing mandates have increased the price of the average home by 30 to 37 percent.

The results for housing output (the number of units) are even more interesting. These results are presented in table 12.4. The estimates of $d_1$ for the Level Models for 1990 and 2000 are positive and statistically significant at the 1 percent level, which indicates that cities with inclusionary zoning have more housing production, but similar to the housing price regressions do not take into consideration the possibility that cities that adopted the policy already were growing when they adopted the policy. Again we need to look at the difference in output based on cities adopting the policy. The last two columns in table 12.4 show how changes in the policy variable (adopting a below-market housing ordinance) alone affect quantity of housing. Eliminating the unobserved fixed effect by differencing the data switches the sign of the policy variable from positive to negative (though most are statistically insignificant without control variables). This switch in sign of $d_1$ provides strong evidence of the importance of eliminating the unobserved fixed city effect. The negative impact increases in size and statistical significance when control variables are added to the First Difference model.

Tables 12.3 and 12.4 indicate the importance of differencing the data and removing the unobserved fixed city effect.[19] The next set of regressions in table 12.5 report first difference estimates for housing prices for the five-year and one year lag while adding other control variables that may change over time.[20] The other models (using lag periods iz96delta, iz97delta, and iz98delta) yielded similar results. Adding income, whether median household income or per capita income, increases the size of the estimated policy effect. All policy estimates of $d_1$ are larger than 0.20, suggesting that *cities that impose an affordable housing mandate drive up prices by more than 20 percent*. Dropping the insignificant variables and adjusting for heteroscedasticity had little impact on the policy and income variables.

The final set of results in table 12.6 report the estimated effects on housing quantity for the same lag periods as the price estimates. The results are nearly identical for the other lag periods (iz96delta, iz97delta, and iz98delta). Adding control variables increases the policy impact and its statistical significance. Substituting the number of households for the number of units as the dependent variable does not alter the main results. Adjusting for heteroscedasticity did increase the statistical significance levels slightly for the policy variable. The negative policy coefficients (−0.104 and −0.097) suggest that cities *that impose an affordable housing mandate reduce housing units by more than 10 percent*.

## CONCLUSION

Our research provides answers to two important questions: How much do below-market housing mandates cost developers, and do below-market housing mandates improve housing affordability? After showing that below-market housing mandates cost developers hundreds of thousands of dollars for each unit sold, we discuss how developers do not receive compensation in this amount. Next we investigate how these policies affect the supply of housing. Using panel data and first difference estimates, we find that below-market housing mandates lead to *decreased* construction and *increased* prices. Over a ten-year period, cities that impose a below-market housing mandate on average end up with 10 percent fewer homes and 20 percent higher prices. These results are highly significant. The assertion by the Court in *Home Builders Association v. Napa* that "the ordinance will *necessarily* increase the supply of affordable housing" is simply untrue.

The justification for the decision that below-market housing mandates are not a taking rests on some extremely questionable *economic* assumptions. We are not sure the amount of knowledge of economics of Judges Scott Snowden, J. Stevens, and J. Simons. Below-market housing mandates are simply a type of a price control, and nearly every economist agrees that price controls on housing lead to a decrease in quantity and quality of housing available (Kearl, Clayne, Whiting, and Winner 1979, 28). Since these price controls apply to a percentage of new housing and builders must comply with them if they want to build market rate housing, it also will affect the supply of market rate housing. By acting as a tax on new housing, we would expect a supply shift leading to less output and higher prices for all remaining units.

New names for price controls like inclusionary zoning make the policy sound innocuous or even beneficial (who can be against a policy of inclusion?), but in reality the program is a mandate that imposes significant costs onto a minority of citizens. The costs of below-market housing mandates are borne by developers and other new homebuyers who receive little or no compensation. From this perspective, below-market housing mandates are a taking no different in substance from an outright taking under eminent domain. Below-market housing mandates represent the sort of abuse the *Lucas* Court forewarned, and it should rightly be considered a taking. In terms of economics, below-market housing mandates only differ from an outright taking in degree—there is not a "total taking" but a partial taking and clearly a diminution of value without any compensation. The amount of harm imposed by below-market housing mandates should inform their status under the law.

## NOTES

Thanks to Jennifer Miller for research assistance and to Ron Cheung and participants at the April 2007 DeVoe Moore Center Symposium on Takings for helpful comments and suggestions. We also thank Elda Pema for comments on testing panel data. Many of the ideas in this chapter stem from research by Benjamin Powell and Edward Stringham, so we gratefully acknowledge Benjamin Powell for his indirect, but extremely valuable input to this chapter.

1. Assuming a 30-year fixed interest rate mortgage with an interest rate of 6.3 percent.
2. For details about the program see California Coalition for Rural Housing and Non-profit Housing Association of Northern California (2003) and Powell and Stringham (2004a).
3. For review of the literature see Powell and Stringham (2005).
4. "The country that became the United States was unique in world history in that it was founded by individuals in quest of private property.... [T]he conviction that the protection of property was the main function of government, and its corollary that a government that did not fulfill this obligation forfeited its mandate, acquired the status of a self-evident truth in the minds of the American colonists." Pipes (1999, 240).
5. *Lucas v. South Carolina Coastal Council*, 505 U.S. 1003 (1992).
6. *Pennsylvania Coal v. Mahon* 260 U.S. 393 (1922).
7. Legal scholar James Ely writes, "In his famous 1792 essay James Madison perceptively warned people against government that '*indirectly* violates their property, in their actual possessions.' Although Madison anticipated the regulatory takings doctrine, the modern doctrine began to take shape in the last decades of the nineteenth century. For example, in a treatise on eminent domain published in 1888, John Lewis declared that when a person was deprived of the possession, use, or disposition of property 'he is to that extent deprived of his property, and, hence ... his property may be taken, in the constitutional sense, though his title and possession remain undisturbed.' Likewise, in 1891 Justice David J. Brewer pointed out that regulation of the use of property might destroy its value and constitute the practical equivalent of outright appropriation. While on the Supreme Judicial Court of Massachusetts, Oliver Wendell Holmes also recognized that regulations might amount to a taking of property. 'It would be open to argument at least,' he stated, 'that an owner might be stripped of his rights so far as to amount to a taking without any physical interference with his land.'" (Ely 2005, 43, footnotes in original omitted)
8. *Home Builders Association of Northern California v. City of Napa* (2001, 188).
9. *Home Builders Association of Northern California v. City of Napa* (2001, 195–196).

10. The California Coalition for Rural Housing and Non-Profit Housing Association of Northern California (2003, 3) stated, "These debates, though fierce, remain largely theoretical due to the lack of empirical research."
11. Marin County is one of the highest-income and most costly areas in the San Francisco Bay Area.
12. http://www.co.marin.ca.us/EFiles/Docs/CD/PlanUpdate /07_0430_IT_070430091111. pdf (accessed August 19, 2007). To simplify a the specifics, developers have the choice of selling 60 of homes to low income households or 50 percent of homes to very low income households, which calculates the roughly the same loss of revenue so for simplicity we will focus on the latter scenario.
13. Median income for a household of four is $91,200 so a household earning 80 percent of median income earns $73,696 and a household earning 60 percent of median income earns $55,272. The specific affordability price control formula will depend on certain assumptions (for example the level of the interest rate in the formula) but using some standard assumptions we can create an estimate (assuming homes will be financed with 0 percent down, a 30-year fixed-rate mortgage, and an interest rate of 7 percent, and assuming that 26 percent of income will pay mortgage payments and 4 percent of income will pay for real estate taxes and other homeowner costs).

    This formula gives us how much a household in each income level could afford and the level of the price controls. In Marin County a home sold to a four person household earning 80 percent of median income could be sold for no more than $240,003, and a home sold to a four person household earning 60 of median income could be sold for no more than $180,002.

    The price controls may be set at stricter levels depending on the city ordinance. For example, Tiburon sets price controls for "affordability" much more strictly than the above formula. Its ordinance assumes an interest rate of 9.5 percent, assumes 25 percent of income can be devoted to mortgage. According to Tiburon's ordinance, a "moderate" price-controlled home can be sold for no more than $109,800.
14. *Home Builders Association of Northern California v. City of Napa* (2001, 194).
15. Powell and Stringham (2005) discuss this issue in depth.
16. Policy On Achieving Higher Residential Densities in Multiple-Family Zones. Adopted by Mountain View City Council, September 13, 2005.
17. For those readers unfamiliar with semi-log models, $d_1$ provides an interpretation of the policy variable as a percentage change. The estimate of $d_1$ is interpreted as the approximate percentage change in Y for cities that pass an ordinance. When the estimate of $d_1$ is large (greater then 10%), the more accurate estimate is %$\Delta Y$ = exp($d_1$)—1.
18. The first difference model is the fixed effects model when there are two time periods.
19. Controlling for the endogeneity of the policy variable will have little or no impact. The data reveal that cities that passed an ordinance also have higher housing prices on average. It may be that higher priced cities are more likely to pass an ordinance. Given our results, we have some doubts on whether this will impact our conclusion. First we lagged the policy variable from one to five years and found very little variation in the OLS estimates. A lag of five years (for a potential dependent variable) should reduce or eliminate the potential bias. Second, the first difference approach reduced the price effect and significantly changed the output effect by controlling for unobserved fixed effects. Finally, there are some limits to finding instrumental variables for a first difference model. Clearly it would not be appropriate to use any of the 2000 data to control for policies passed in earlier years. One could use the 1990 census data but even here there are some cities that passed the policy prior to 1990. For these reasons, we believe controlling for endogeneity will not change the basic results.
20. The income and population variables are rescaled in units of 10,000 to simplify the coefficient presentation.

# REFERENCES

Allen, Charlotte. 2005. A Wreck of a Plan; Look at How Renewal Ruined SW. *The Washington Post* July 17, 2005: B01.

Calavita, Nico, Kenneth Grimes, and Alan Mallach. 1997. Inclusionary Housing in California and New Jersey: a Comparative Analysis *Housing Policy Debate* 8 (1): 109–142.

California Coalition for Rural Housing and Non-Profit Housing Association of Northern California. 2003. *Inclusionary Housing in California: 30 Years of Innovation.* Sacramento: California Coalition for Rural Housing and Non-Profit Housing Association of Northern California.

Construction Industry Research Board, Burbank, CA, Building Permit Data 1970–2003, *www.cirbdata.com.*

Dieterich, Andrew G. 1996. An Egalitarian Market: The Economics of Inclusionary Zoning Reclaimed. *Fordham Urban Law Journal* 24: 23–104.

Ely, James W. Jr. 2005. "Poor Relation" Once More: The Supreme Court and the Vanishing Rights of Property Owners. *Cato Supreme Court Review*: 39–69.

Fischel, William A. 2006. Before *Kelo. Regulation,* (Winter 2005–2006): 32–35.

Follain, Jr., James R. 1979. The Price Elasticity of the Long-Run Supply of New Housing Construction. *Land Economics* 55 (2): 190–199.

Gelinas, Nicole. 2005. They're Taking Away Your Property for *What?* The Court's Eminent-Domain Ruling is Useless as Well As Unjust. *City Journal* (Autumn 2005).

Glaeser, Edward L., Joseph Gyourko, and Raven E. Saks. 2005a. Why Have Housing Prices Gone Up? *American Economics Review* 95 (2): 329–333.

———. 2005b. Why Is Manhattan So Expensive? Regulation and the Rise in Housing Prices. *The Journal of Law & Economics* 48 (2): 331–369.

Green, Richard K., Stephen Malpezzi, and Stephen K. Mayo. 2005. Metropolitan-Specific Estimates of the Price Elasticity of Supply of Housing, and Their Sources, *American Economic Review* 95 (2): 334–339.

Kautz, Barbara Erlich. 2002. In Defense of Inclusionary Zoning: Successfully Creating Affordable Housing. *University of San Francisco Law Review* 36 (4): 971–1032.

Kearl, J. R., Clayne L. Pope, Gordon C. Whiting, and Larry T. Wimmer. 1979. A Confusion of Economists? *American Economic Review* 69: 28–37.

Mayer, Christopher J., and Somerville, C. Tsuriel. 2000. Residential Construction: Using the Urban Growth Model to Estimate Housing Supply. *Journal of Urban Economics* 48: 85–109.

National Association of Homebuilders / Wells Fargo. 2007. The NAHB/Wells Fargo Housing Opportunity Index Washington, DC: National Association of Homebuilders.

Non-Profit Housing Association of Northern California. 2007. *Affordable by Choice: Trends in California Inclusionary Housing Programs.* San Francisco: Non-Profit Housing Association of Northern California.

Pipes, Richard. 1999. *Property and Freedom.* New York: Alfred A. Knopf.

Powell, Benjamin and Edward Stringham. 2004a. Housing Supply and Affordability: Do Affordable Housing Mandates Work? *Reason Policy Study* 318.

———. 2004b. Do Affordable Housing Mandates Work? Evidence from Los Angeles County and Orange County. *Reason Policy Study* 320.

———. 2004c. Affordable Housing in Monterey County. Analyzing the General Plan Update and Applied Development Economics Report. *Reason Policy Study* 323.

———. 2005. The Economics of Inclusionary Zoning Reclaimed: How Effective Are Price Controls? *Florida State University Law Review* 33 (2): 472–499.

Quigley, John M. and Steven Raphael. 2004. Is Housing Unaffordable? Why Isn't It More Affordable? *The Journal of Economic Perspectives* 18 (1): 191–214.

———. 2005. Regulation and the High Cost of Housing in California. *American Economic Review* 95(2): 323–328.

Quigley, John M. and Larry A. Rosenthal. 2004. The Effects of Land-Use Regulation on the Price of Housing: What do We Know? What Can We Learn? Berkeley Program on Housing and Urban Policy, Working Paper 1052. Available online: http://ideas.repec.org/p/cdl/bphupl/1052.html.

RAND California Statistics. www.ca.rand.org/cgi-bin/homepage.cgi.

Riches, Erin 2004. *Still Locked Out 2004: California's Affordable Housing Crisis,* Sacramento: California Budget Project.

Richer, Jerrell. 1995. Explaining the Vote of Slow Growth. *Public Choice* 82: 207–223.

Rubenfeld, Jed. 1993. Usings, *Yale Law Review* 102 (5, March): 1077–1163.

Said, Carolyn. 2007. Home Prices Rise in July Even as Sales Fall to 12-Year Low *San Francisco Chronicle* August 16, 2007: C-1.

Somin, Ilya. 2004. Overcoming *Poletown: County of Wayne v. Hathcock*, Economic Development Takings, and the Future of Public Use, *Michigan State Law Review* 4: 1005–40.

Tetreault, Bernard. 2000. Arguments Against Inclusionary Zoning You Can Anticipate Hearing. *New Century Housing*, 1 (2, October): 17–20.

Thorson, James A. 1997. The Effect of Zoning on Housing Construction, *Journal of Housing Construction* 6: 81–91.

Westray, Laura L. 1988. Are Landlords Being Taken by the Good Cause Eviction Requirement? *Southern California Law Review*, 62: 321.

Wooldridge, Jeffrey M. 2006. *Introductory Econometrics, a Modern Approach*, 3rd ed. Mason, OH: Thomson South-Western.

## Cases Cited

*Action Apartments Association v. City of Santa Monica*, 123 Cal. A 4th 47 (2007)

*Berman et al. v. Parker et al.*, 348 U.S. 26 (1954).

*Hawaii Housing Authority v. Midkiff*, 467 U.S. 229 (1984).

*Home Builders Association of Northern California v. City of Napa*, 89 Cal. A 4th 897 (modified and republished 90 Cal. A 4th 188) (2001).

*Kelo et al. v. City of New London, Connecticut*, 545 U.S. 469 (2005).

*Lucas v. South Carolina Coastal Council*, 505 U.S. 1003 (1992).

*Poletown Neighborhood Council v. Detroit*, 410 Mich. 616, 304 N.W. 2d 455 (1981).

# 13

## CONCLUSION

### INSTABILITY AND INEFFICIENCY ARE THE INEVITABLE RESULTS OF GOVERNMENT PLANNING AND REGULATORY IMPLEMENTATION

*Bruce L. Benson*

### INTRODUCTION

Somin (this volume) demonstrates that *Kelo v. City of New London* (545 U.S. 469 (2005)) produced a dramatic political backlash as states across the country passed statutes and referenda which appeared to restrict eminent domain powers.[1] Benson and Brown (this volume) explain that the backlash against the *Kelo* decision actually is another in a long chain of backlashes against government efforts to expand the scope and strength of the claim that the state is the actual property owner (i.e., that the population simply serves as stewards for the state). As Mises (1945, 58) emphasizes, all types of "Governments have always looked askance at private property. . . . It is the nature of the man handling the apparatus of compulsion and coercion . . . to strive at subduing all spheres of human life to its immediate influence." As further evidence of both expanding government efforts to strengthen government-ownership claims and of citizen resistance, note that the state-level *Kelo* backlash was not the only effort to restrict government takings. Ramsey (2007, 1) suggests, for instance, the "property rights movement," or what might be called the takings backlash, produced at least two "notable" events within a short period of time: "the reaction to the *Kelo* case in 2005 and the passage of Measure 37 in Oregon in 2004." Measure 37 was a backlash against regulatory takings rather than eminent-domain takings (the history of and reactions to Oregon's land-use regulation efforts are discussed below). As Gieseler et al. (2006, 93), explain, "Oregon's land-use regulation system had become a labyrinth of unreasonably restrictive regulations that made no allowances for the costs and burdens imposed on property owners. The government owned—or exerted regulatory control amounting to ownership upon—most of the state's land."

This takings backlash against both eminent domain and regulations is evident in Arizona, California, Washington, and Idaho where voters considered 2006 ballot measures combining both post-*Kelo* eminent-domain reforms with regulatory-takings reforms similar to those adopted in Oregon in 2004 (Blumm and Grafe 2007, 72–79).[2] Furthermore, while Somin (this volume) details eminent-domain backlash legislation, changes similar to Oregon's Measure 37 were also being considered by other legislatures, including those in Montana, Texas, Wisconsin, and Washington (Gieseler et al. 2006, 103–104). Thus, even though regulatory takings do not have a *Kelo*-like action to serve as a focus for a widespread backlash, a similar process is at work.

Bullock (this volume) criticizes the *Kelo* ruling, arguing against the Court's conclusion that an eminent-domain taking is justified if it is part of a government's development plan (and see Staley (this volume) for complementary analysis). That argument is extended here to encompass regulatory takings. The fact is that planning inevitably fails to do much of what its supporters claim it will do, so it should not serve as an unquestioned justification for any sort of takings. For instance, planning is presumably supposed to reduce uncertainty. Indeed, Sullivan (2006, 131) contends that land-use planning and regulations in Oregon resulted in "uniformity and relative predictability in land-use decision making." In reality, however, as Hunnicutt (2006, 45–46) explains, "the most ardent defenders of Oregon's land-use planning system seem to forget that Senate Bill 100 (1973) [which set up a system of mandatory state-wide planning], amended countless times over the years due to vagaries in the original language, has spawned endless litigation, and has resulted in the creation of two separate state agencies, costing taxpayers millions of dollars annually to staff and operate." The fact is that planning and subsequent efforts to implement plans through land-use regulations and eminent domain, inevitably is destabilizing as rules are constantly changing. It also is tremendously costly, but not just in terms of government expenditures. A more significant cost is the resources diverted into a never-ending competition to avoid and/or alter the plans and regulations, competition that plays out in markets, legislatures, bureaucracies, and courts. Many of the most significant costs are not even measurable. Regulation prevents many resources from being used efficiently, for instance. Regulation also diverts the market's discovery process to a new evolutionary path that is likely to involve innovations driven by regulation avoidance incentives rather than by welfare enhancement (Boettke et al. this volume). The uncertainty that characterizes a constantly changing regulatory environment also shortens time horizons, altering investment and resource-use decisions in ways that reduce the long-run productive potential of resources. Section II offers a discussion of the underlying "theoretical" reasons for the inevitability of these and other results that contradict the alleged justifications for planning, before turning to supporting evidence provided through an examination of Oregon's experience.

## THE INEVITABLE FAILURE OF STATE AND LOCAL PLANNING[3]

The typical justification for government planning and regulation suggests that markets are imperfect as they fail to internalize various externalities, and therefore, that government must step in to pursue and protect the "public interest" (e.g., see Nelson and Duncan 1995, 1). Mises (1949, 692) explains, however, that market-failure justifications for government actions such as planning "ascribe to the state not only the best intentions but also omniscience." He then points out that neither assumption is valid: government is not benevolent since both those who are employed by the state and those who demand state actions generally pursue their own subjectively evaluated objectives, and government is (or more accurately, government officials are) not all knowing since knowledge is widely dispersed and the cost of coordination is prohibitive.

## Special Interest Regulation

An alternative to the "public interest" theory of government assumes that government actions are driven by the demands of special interest groups pursuing wealth transfers (Stigler 1971). This can be somewhat misleading, however, if it is interpreted to imply that individuals become involved in interest group activities only if they can gain (or avoid losing) material wealth. Clearly this is not the case. In fact, while "material" self-interest motives can often be identified for groups demanding various laws and regulations, many members of the relevant groups firmly believe that the regulations they demand are in the "public interest." Of course, the "public interest" is totally a normative concept—it is what each individual subjectively believes it to be—and an individual's perception of the public interest is often colored by (rationalized in light of) underlying personal self interests. Indeed, beliefs may well be endogenous as individuals rationalize their self interests (Ikeda 1997, 110–117; Benson 2008). Nevertheless, use of terms like "wealth-transfer" and even "interest group" should not imply negative judgments about members of such groups.[4]

## Regulatory Transfers

As an alternative, let us define the objects of interest group demand, and the functions of government regulation as (Benson 1984): (a) the assignment of property rights and (b) enforcement of property rights assignments. This is complete-ly consistent with the objectives of members of groups like the Sierra Club and local homeowners associations who may not believe that they obtain any personal gain (defined as material wealth) from their political successes (even though they do gain, given their subjective values). Moreover, property rights "convey the right to benefit or harm oneself or others" (Demsetz 1967, 348), as they dictate the distribution of both material and non-material wealth. Therefore, changes in property rights transfer wealth (destroy wealth for some and create wealth for others). Whenever an interest group is successful in altering the assignment of property rights, whether the group is pursuing material interests or their subjective view of public interests, other individuals lose: wealth is in fact taken. Thus, political competition is likely, because their successes impose costs on others, creating incentives for those who lose to try to regain at least some of their previous level of well-being (Benson 1984; Ikeda 1997, 108).

This property-rights perspective helps illustrate the relationship between theft and political transfers that Tullock (1967) emphasizes. Theft is an attempt to claim assets or resources that are not perfectly protected—that is, property rights are not complete-ly secure. Thus, thieves invest in efforts to claim these assets, and potential victims invest to deter or prevent theft. Tullock points out that precisely the same analysis applies to the political process. Individuals and groups invest time, effort and money as they pursue desired regulations, which result in property rights transfers, while those who may be harmed invest in an effort to avoid the regulations and transfers.

## Regulation Avoidance and More Regulation

Both the "public interest" and various versions of "special interest" theories of government (e.g., Stigler 1971, Tullock 1967) generally focus on the "order" (equilibrium) that should emerge after regulations are imposed, assuming that resulting conditions will remain stable. In reality, however, regulation results in an inherently destabilizing evolutionary process (Benson 2002, 2005). Planning and regulatory authorities clearly attempt to deliberately "design" or engineer stable orders, but their designed rules disrupt spontaneous orders, as Hayek (1973, 51) explains:

> It is impossible, not only to replace the spontaneous order by organization and at the same time to utilize as much of the dispersed knowledge of all its members as possible, but also to improve or correct this order by interfering in it by direct commands....it can never be advantageous to supplement the rules governing a spontaneous order by isolated and subsidiary commands concerning those activities where the actions are guided by the general rules of conduct...the reason why such isolated commands requiring specific actions by members of the spontaneous order can never improve but must disrupt that order is that they will refer to a part of a system of interdependent actions determined by information and guided by purposes known only to the several acting persons but not to the directing authority. The spontaneous order arises from each element balancing all the various factors operating on it and by adjusting all its various actions to each other, a balance which will be destroyed if some of the actions are determined by another agency on the basis of different knowledge and in the service of different ends.

While balance created by a spontaneous order is destroyed by efforts to deliberately implement "isolated and subsidiary commands," these designed or planned rules are not able to comple-ly dictate a targeted behavior because knowledge is incomplete for the rule maker (Hayek 1973; Kirzner 1985, 145; Ikeda 1997, 50–52), and policing is imperfect (Benson 1999, 2001).[5]

The knowledge problem suggests, among other things, that there are too many uncontrolled margins and unanticipated responses for a rule designer to recognize and anticipate, in part because the changes generally create a new set of opportunities that have not previously been available. After all, as Kirzner (1985, 135) stresses, "In the face of these controls, regulations, and interventions there remains, nonetheless, a genuine market...Government controls constrain and constrict; they rearrange and repattern the structure of incentives; they redistribute incomes and wealth and sharply modify both the process of production and the composition of consumption. Yet within the limits that such controls impose, buying and selling continue, and the constant effort to capture pure entrepreneurial gain keeps the market in perpetual motion." Regulations are likely to have a significant impact on the discovery process, however. Deliberate efforts to impose rules create incentives to find and exploit the uncontrolled margins in order to avoid the full consequences of the rules. Thus, the discovery process tends to be redirected along a new path. This means, as Kirzner (1985, 141–144) explains, that discoveries which probably would have been made in the absence of the regulation are never made. A substantial cost of regulation will never be observed because there is no way to know what might have been discovered in the absence of the regulations (Benson 2004). In addition, regulation creates a "superfluous" discovery process as "entirely new and not necessarily desirable [either from the perspective of the interest groups involved or from an efficiency perspective] opportunities for entrepreneurial discovery" (Kirzner 1985, 144).[6]

The transactions costs of defining the new property rights and enforcing the assignments, mean that enforcement also will be imperfect.[7] Therefore, as Cheung (1974, 58) notes, when the right to capture benefits from a resource are "partly or fully taken away" the diverted benefits "will tend to be dissipated unless the right to it is exclusively assigned to another individual." The property rights to those benefits are valuable, so when delineation or enforcement are incomplete, anyone who sees a chance to establish a "politically legitimate" claim to them has incentives to try to establish such a claim. Thus, Mises (1949, 758–776 and elsewhere), Kirzner (1985, 133–145) Ikeda (1997, 94–99 and elsewhere), Benson (1984, 2002, 2004, 2005) and Boettke et al. (this volume) explain that new regulations lead to spontaneous responses, many of which are not anticipated by members of the interest groups, the legislature, or the planning/regulatory bureau.

Mises (1949, 859) stresses that "As soon as something happens in the economy that any of the various bureaucratic institutions does not like or that arouses the anger of a pressure group, people clamor for new interventions, controls, and restrictions." As individuals pursue opportunities, many of which involve ways to avoid or mitigate the intended transfer consequences of the regulations, the intended benefits of the regulation for interest groups fall, they pressure the rule makers (legislators, planners) to do something about it, and the likely response is new rules and enforcement efforts intended to block such maneuvers. Those subject to the new rules react again, however, leading to more "clamor," new blocking efforts, and so on. Therefore, deliberately designed rules and institutions are inherently unstable. The evolution of intentionally created rules is path dependent, however, as such rules are influenced by what has come before and they in turn influence the path of the evolution that follows, but the result is not likely to be equilibrating.

## Political Backlash, Intensified Political Competition, and the Potential for Partial Deregulation

In a political planning and regulatory process those who lose property rights have incentives to exploit errors and uncontrolled margins, but they also have incentives to organize and become politically active in an attempt to regain their property claims and wealth. Therefore, more resources are diverted into the political arena, raising the resource cost described above. The result is a spiraling process of more and more resources being diverted from productive to political activities (Benson 1984).[8]

This political competition to influence the allocation of property rights is not just targeted at legislators. Interest groups will attempt to achieve their objectives through the courts and administrative agencies as well, if they feel that investments in these processes are worthwhile. Furthermore, if they cannot obtain their desired objectives from these "representative" institutions, they may take their case directly to voters through the referenda process. They also may attempt to influence decisions at different levels of government, in hopes of gaining support at one level that may be more difficult to obtain at another.

Wealth is dissipated as resources are diverted into political campaigns, lobbying, and litigation, and bureaucratic enforcement cost will rise as the regulatory apparatus expands to apply new regulations arising from court rulings, legislation, administrative rule making, or ballot measures. If these additional regulations fail to allocate the demanded benefits to the targeted group, more regulations will be demanded. Ultimately, partial deregulation may occur as the regulation effort fails to produce the anticipated benefits and political support for the regulations wanes, and/or as those who discover that they are worse off because of the regulations become effectively organized and demand change (Benson 2002, 2005). Of course, many regulatory regimes persist by continually evolving in the face of market and political changes. Enforcement and compliance costs rise, both to implement the new regulations and to control illegal activities, while political competition (and resource costs) rise, and the path of superfluous adjustments continues.

## Bureaucratic Interests, Entrenchment, and Growth[9]

Bureaucrats also have a large stake in the planning/regulatory process. In this context, however, Tullock (1965, 193) notes that when a bureaucracy is set up to accomplish some political goal, it inevitably fails, and

> The continuous failures of bureaucracies are met in part by continuing reorganizations, the reasoning being that the failure has resulted from organizational details. In part, the failures are met by concealed shifts in the objectives for the organization. As an experiment, if one examines the original arguments for establishment of almost any government bureau and compares these arguments with those that may be currently offered for the retention of the bureau, one is likely to find that a considerable shift has occurred in the specification of the objectives that the bureau is supposed to attain. The governmental bureau becomes a permanent fixture, with the objective continually changing. Over time the vested interests of the bureaucrats themselves become more and more important in justifying the organization, although this can never be the sole argument in discussions with outsiders.

Bureaucracies fail because of the knowledge problem and the superfluous market and political discovery process. Once a regulatory regime is in place, however, the bureaucratic enforcers have incentives to make sure that the bureaucracy (and their jobs) survives whether it accomplishes its objectives or not, so they have incentives to add more regulations, seek new objectives that might be achieved, and so on. Mueller (1989: 248) explained that "Uncertainty creates the potential to exercise power; information provides the capacity to do so."[10]

Importantly, in this context, bureaucrats have very strong incentives to divert blame for failures and for politically unpopular actions. Thus, divisions of inter-related duties across multiple-bureau arrangements (e.g., up and down federalist hierarchies, across several bureaus at one level of government), and things like "public-private" partnerships can actually be attractive to bureaucrats. That way, each can claim that some other bureaucratic or private component of the total effort was at fault when an effort fails. Uncertainty is key to this aspect of bureaucratic behavior, as there is a strong preference for unclear divisions of responsibility.

The bureaucracy is an evolving institution. Even when the demand for regulation declines because the process continually fails to provide many of the anticipated benefits, and the demands for deregulation grow as losers organize, the bureaucracy is not likely to disappear. It will have to supervise the deregulation process, after all, and it inevitably will retain some regulations to enforce as well. Furthermore, any deregulation means wealth is again transferred (from those who have captured some wealth due to the regulation) and some property rights temporarily move back into the public domain, waiting to be captured. Reregulation, perhaps in some new form, becomes attractive to some interest groups, and the cycle starts over. A bureaucracy is likely to survive and prosper for a long time in such a dynamic environment even if it is not achieving the politically mandated objectives that it was intended to provide.

## Legislative Externalities

The possibility of using the state's legal system to take property rights produces a significant "legislative externality," as it shortens time horizons for decision makers.[11] Individual who hold recognized claims to private property see the claims as tenuous, creating incentives to consume the benefits quickly before they are taken away through more legislation. The effect is much like the tragedy of the commons. When many individuals have free access to a common pool they rush in to capture benefits quickly before they are complete-ly dissipated, and the resource is used up or destroyed very quickly. Similarly, no one has incentives to invest in maintenance or improvements because they cannot prevent others from capturing the benefits. When private property rights are insecure due to constantly changing regulations, the result is similar in that the current owner attempts to capture benefits quickly before new regulations take them away. While the potential benefits of future uses of the property might be considerable, leading to conservation when rights are secure, such future benefits are discounted when time horizons are shortened. See Alder (this volume) and Brown and Stroup (this volume) for examples. Furthermore, the costs of trying to make investments in or improve property, or to move property into higher valued uses, rises dramatically, as so-called owners must obtain "permission" from regulators, courts or legislators to proceed, and as other politically active individuals attempt to influence the decision in ways that will benefit them (e.g., increase their material wealth or achieve their subjective perception of the "public interest"). As a consequence, economic growth and development slows, and the hidden costs of insecure property rights grow. Let us consider an example.

## 35 YEARS OF LAND USE PLANNING AND REGULATION IN OREGON

Oregon has been at the forefront of the land-use planning movement since at least the late 1960s and early 1970s. This is exemplified by the Oregon legislature's creation of a new state agency in 1973, the Department of Land Conservation and Development (DLCD) headed by the Land Conservation and Development Commission (LCDC). This agency was vested with the power to establish statewide land-use policy.[12] The DLCD established 19 goals over a three year period (Or. Admin. R. 666–015–000, 2006).[13] Local governments in all cities, counties, special districts, or any other government bodies making land use decisions, including state agencies, were ordered to develop comprehensive land-use plans that conformed with and implemented the 19 LCDC-created statewide policy goals. A comprehensive plan was defined to be a (1973 Or. Laws 80, § 2):

> Generalized, coordinated land use map and policy statement…that interrelates all functional and natural systems and activities relating to the use of lands, including but not limited to sewer and water systems, transportation systems, education systems,

recreation facilities, and natural resources and air and water quality management programs. "Comprehensive" means all-inclusive, both in terms of the geographic area covered and functional and natural activities and systems occurring in the area covered by the plan. . . . A plan is "coordinated" when the needs of all levels of government, semipublic and private agencies and the citizens of Oregon have been considered and accommodated as much as possible. "Land" includes water, both surface and subsurface, and air.

All of Oregon's local governments had to get their plans approved with an acknowledgement of compliance with the statewide goals established by the LCDC (see discussion below). For the next 30 years Oregon engaged in statewide land-use planning efforts that always appeared to be more extensive than anything being undertaken by every other state; in fact, Oregon's land use planning system has served as a model to other states who attempted to follow their lead (Knapp and Nelson 1992, 227; Leonard 1983, 134–137).

The political rhetoric used to justify the statewide comprehensive-planning process stressed citizen involvement (goal 1), preservation of both agricultural and forest resources (goals 3 and 4, as well as 5 dealing with open space in general), management of population growth (primarily goal 14, but also 8, 10, 11, 12, and 13), and promotion of economic growth (goal 9).[14] However, Leonard (1993, 33) explains that limiting the geographic scope of growth through establishment of urban growth boundaries, and preservation of farm lands and forest lands proved to be the dominant foci of the land use planning system that evolved.[15]

Oregon's urban growth boundaries were supposed to encompass enough land so that residential, industrial, commercial, and recreational needs could be met for 20 years. Therefore, local planners had to try to project such needs for 20 years into the future.[16] Land within the boundary can be used for urban development, although such development also has to meet certain requirements. In particular, development decisions for areas within urban growth boundaries must include "orderly and economic provision" of public facilities and services, and encourage development within existing urbanized areas before developing lands that are not yet urbanized, while complying with all LCDC goals and approved local comprehensive plans. The plans and growth boundaries are supposed to insure that sufficient land is available for the various urban land uses to provide choices in the market. Implementation and impacts of this process are discussed below. Initially, less that 1.25 percent of the land in Oregon (as noted below, over half of the land in Oregon is government owned) was placed within urban growth boundaries (O'Toole 2001a, 26).

Land outside the boundary is supposed to remain rural (open). Goal 3 mandates that local governments impose exclusive farm-use zoning on all agricultural land, and defines agricultural land very broadly. It is not simply land being used for agriculture. Instead, it is land outside urban growth boundaries that exhibit certain soil characteristics, as specified in the Soil Capability Classification System of the United States Soil Conservation Service,[17] as well as "other lands" considered to be suitable for farming,[18] and "lands in other classes which are necessary to permit farm practices to be undertaken on adjacent or nearby lands." In 2002, more than 17 million acres or Oregon land was classified as agricultural (over 25 percent of the state), although only 54 percent of this land was operated by full-time farmers (U.S. Department of Agriculture 2004, 6). As Hunnicutt (2006, 29) explains, "In defining agricultural land under Goal 3, LCDC does not take into account parcel sizes, development on the land or on adjacent or nearby parcels, historic activities—or lack thereof—on the parcel or adjoining parcels, or the capability of the parcel to produce any income—much less a net income—from agricultural activities."

Goal 4, forest land preservation, requires that local governments create comprehensive plans that are consistent with a very complex and detailed forest land-use regulation system made up of DLCD regulations as well as state zoning and forest management statutes. LCDC goal 4 limits forest land uses to a specified set of activities.[19] And "like Goal 3, LCDC did not consider parcel size when determining whether land should be defined as forest land, nor did it take into account activities on the land or adjacent lands or the capability of the parcel to produce harvestable timber. In fact, given the broad definition of forest land contained in Goal 4, it is difficult to imagine any land with trees that would not meet the definition of forest land" (Hunnicutt 2006, 29–30).

Gieseler et al. (2006, 91) explain that "the state never adopted a land use program which identifies the farm and forest resource land which truly merits 'conservation,' it simply mandated that almost every rural acre be 'preserved' regardless of productivity, and banned most non-farm and non-forest use of such acreage." Almost 55 percent of the land in Oregon is actually government owned (about 34 million acres), and roughly 90 percent of the remaining privately owned land outside urban growth boundaries was classified as either agricultural or forest land (about 24.8 million acres) in 1995 (Hunnicutt 2006, 33), so over 96 percent of the land in the state is virtually off limits for building homes and businesses (early "illegal" building and remaining limited exceptions for farm and forest lands are discussed below). About 3.5 percent of the private land or 1.6 percent of total acreages (roughly one million acres) in the state was zoned as rural other than farm or forest use in 1995, and about 6.5 percent of private property or 2.9 percent of total acreage (about 1.8 million acres) was zoned for urban uses.

## Special Interest Regulation

Oregon's 100-mile-long Willamette Valley runs from south of Eugene north through Salem to Portland and the Columbia River. It contains most of the state's largest cities, and it attracted 80 percent of the state's population growth between 1950 and 1970. The Valley's population reached about 1.5 million (about 70 percent of the state's total population) in the early 1970s (Little 1974, 6, 13). As Leonard (1983, 5) explains the valley's "mild climate, gently rolling countryside bounded by mountain ranges, proximity to water and land transportation and major marketing centers" made the area extremely attractive, particularly for immigrants from California trying to escape the rapid urbanization of the California coastal valleys. After they moved into the valley and obtained their homes and businesses, "These residents provided the core of the constituency committed" to preservation of the remaining rural lands in the valley (Leonard 1983, 5). Since the valley's characteristics also make it one of the "most productive specialty crop farming" areas in the country (Leonard 1983, 5), the non-urbanized areas of the valley floor were dominated by agriculture, and the demand for preservation of open space in the valley translated into a demand to protect agricultural land form urban development. The valley is divided into 9 counties, however, with more than 80 municipalities, so "political pressures for state action rose" (Leonard 1983, 6). One of the early responses by the state, in 1961, was to authorize lower tax assessments on lands used exclusively for farming. Nonetheless, by the end of the 1960s an estimated 10,000 acres of farmland were being converted to urban uses each year as population continued to increase. Over two million acres of the valley was still devoted to agricultural uses in 1975, however (Leonard 1983, 6), while over 5 million acres (over 70 percent of the "valley proper") were "forested slopes—not primary targets for developers" in 1974 (Little 1974, 13).

Pressure to restrict urban growth in the valley led to legislation passed in 1969 requiring the governor to impose comprehensive plans on local governments that did not adopt their own plans (1969 Or. Laws 324), making it the second state in the country, after California, to do so (Leonard 1983, 6). Wong (2007, 1) notes that the emergence of this political pressure "coincided with the emergence of the environmental movement. It also tapped into conservatism and a resistance to rapid change." Indeed, as discussed below, early environmental groups were an important source of demand for planning and land–use regulation, but so were groups advocating limiting (or prevention of) growth and change.[20] The 1969 legislation also outlined the goals that local governments were to pursue in their plans, "the most important of these goals—to preserve prime farmland for the production of crops" (Leonard 1983, 9). It did not establish a statewide policy or monitoring process, however, so actual local planning efforts varied considerably.

The Willamette Valley Environmental Protection and Development Council was formed in 1970. The alleged objective was to assess the valley's development trends and resources, and to recommend programs for attaining the goals stated in the 1969 legislation, but "Most significantly, the council campaigned hard to increase public awareness of the consequences of growth trends, primarily by preparing and distributing a book, *The Willamette Valley: Choices for the Future,* and a 35 mm slide show that depicted the physical and environmental conditions of the valley in the year 2002 under alternative scenarios" (Leonard 1983, 7–8). "Project Foresight" was set up to expose people in the valley to the book and slide show, and a nonprofit organization, "Feedback," was established to facilitate the accumulation of responses (Little 1974, 9). As a study by the state's Local Government Relations Department noted, "The scenario approach proved uniquely provocative . . . , The impact of the project did not result in a widespread formulation of the Valley goals, but rather its effect was more immediate: widespread Valley support for statewide land use planning legislation" (quoted in Leonard 1083, 8). This support arose in the state's most populous urban areas. These people already had their homes and work places, and they wanted to preserve the remaining rural areas proximate to their locations, for their use and enjoyment (i.e., they wanted to prevent more urbanization, essentially by preventing others from obtaining what they already had). With this support, a Land-Use Policy Action Group was formed. The group included representatives from environmental organizations, local planning bodies, and volunteers from some established businesses.[21] The organization prepared materials "to dramatize Oregon's land-use problems," set up and led public meetings around the state to advocate increased state influence on land-use planning, and drafted the legislation that would accomplish its goals.

Little (1974, 9) notes that "heated opposition from local home-rulers" had materialized by the early 1970s. In fact, resistance was sufficiently well organized by 1970 to place a measure on the ballot to restrict government powers to establish zoning, subdivision regulations, and building regulations, but it did not pass in the statewide referendum. When the Policy Action Group's proposed legislation was presented to the 1973 legislature, a number of organized groups entered the fray, including the Oregon Environmental Council (representing some 80 environmental and conservation groups around the state), the Association of Oregon Counties, the League of Oregon Cities, the Oregon State Homebuilders Association, and the Oregon Association of Realtors (Leonard 1983, 11). Opposition to land use planning also increased, as people began to recognize the potential for increasing state-level influence on local land-use decisions. The strongest opposition came from rural areas of the state, where individuals saw a growing threat to their property values (O'Toole 2001a, 26). The Oregon Rural Landowners Association had been focused in Washington County, but under the leadership of Jim Allison, it began recruiting a statewide membership in order to fight the bill (Little 1974, 16). In light of the demands of their local-landowning constituents, it also is not surprising that many local government officials, particularly from rural areas, also opposed mandatory state zoning and planning requirements (Leonard, 1983, 6). In light of these developments, when the Policy Action Group began presenting its proposal to various groups in late 1972, they found substantial resistance (Little 1974, 15–16): for instance, "At a presentation at an Oregon League of Cities meeting in Portland on November 15, there was some support, but for the most part the audience was hostile. During a question and answer period, city officials against the bill howled down its proponents. One planning commissioner said the bill was 'like trying to squash a problem bug with a sledgehammer....Outraged local officials and landowners [were] fearful for the 'constitutional rights.' "

When hearings about the bill started in the state Senate, they were "packed with lobbyists, citizens, politicians, [and] businessmen elbowing each other for microphone room" (Little 1974, 17). Environmental groups such as the Oregon Environmental Council and the Sierra Club threw their support behind the bill, but while clearly involved in the hearing and committee process, "the powerful economic interests if the state—developers, industry, loggers, farmers, tourism groups—had not, in any organized way, come out flat-footed against the bill" (Little 1974, 18). An "Opposition Group to the Macpherson Bill" was formed in early January, however, and the Oregon Rural Landowners Association launched a campaign against the bill soon afterward. The Oregon Taxpayers' Protection Association also was allied with the Rural Landowners on this issue. A number of organized interest groups supported creating a state agency to oversee local planning, however, even though there was disagreement about the amount of power that the agency should have. This disagreement, along with vocal opposition, was sufficient to force some compromises into the legislation as it had been written by the Land-use Policy Action Group (Leonard 1983, 9–10). For instance, a section designating "areas of critical state concern" was dropped, as it would have granted actual permitting authority to the state in those areas. Many local governments strongly opposed ceding the power to grant permits in their local areas. Similarly, a section was deleted that would have created 14 regional planning districts to coordinate local government planning, thereby taking power away from county governments who were more responsive to local landowner demands (see discussion below). As Little (1974, 18) explains, the 14 districts were seen as "an unlocal decision-making process undertaken by unelected officials operating through an uneconomical third layer of government. The 'home rule' issue, freighted with emotional overtones of individual liberty, property rights, and citizen participation in government, could [have derailed] the whole concept." In addition, the senate added a provision calling for state funds to be given to local governments to help them cover the cost of developing their comprehensive plans (between 1973 and 1981 roughly $30 million in state and federal funds were spent on land-use planning activities, and approximately 80 percent of this money was transferred to local governments), thereby reducing some of the opposition from local governments.[22] The Oregon Rural Landowners Association continued to oppose the bill, as did the Oregon Taxpayers' Protection Association, many city governments objected to the coordinating role given to county governments, and various environmental groups were disappointed with the deletion of state control over critical areas, but the compromise garnered enough support to pass.

Implementation of the legislation was not immediate. The LCDC was given until January 1, 1975 to create the statewide planning goals. Fourteen of the nineteen goals were adopted and put into effect by January 25 (Hunnicutt 2006, 29), and local governments were ordered to adopt their comprehensive plans in compliance with the goals, and submit them to the LCDC by January 1, 1976. None of the 277 planning jurisdictions in the state met this deadline, however, and planning extensions were given with a new deadline of July 1, 1980 (Leonard 1983, 14). Leonard (1983, 33) explains that "In addition to the complexities of the local level, it took LCDC several years to outline in a coherent fashion the most important features of the new land-use planning program. . . . Not until 1978 had the three cornerstones of the Oregon program . . . emerged clearly enough to serve as guides for local planners." Many plans were also rejected by the LCDC, so as O'Toole (2001a, 26) notes, "Over the next decade, Oregon cities and counties wrote and rewrote their land-use plans to meet the standards set by the LCDC." The LCDC reported that last of the state's 277 local comprehensive plans was finally certified as being in compliance on August 7, 1986 (Oregon Land Conservation and Development Commission 1987, 1), although litigation regarding certification of various other local plans actually continued.[23] This delay reflected both the extreme complexity of local comprehensive plans under the statewide goals, and the uncertainty that local governments faced in trying to develop their plans (see discussion below), which created incentives to wait and see what would be approved by the courts and the LCDC (Leonard 1983, 34).[24]

As the statewide goals were developed and the approval process got under way, individuals began to see how planning was going to be implemented. Indeed, "as local governments continued to delay, it [the LCDC] gradually used more of its enforcement powers. Several times between 1977 and 1980, LCDC issued enforcement orders directing local governments to comply with urban growth, agricultural, and forest land goals before completion of their comprehensive plan" (Leonard 1983, 15). During this process, "tens of thousands of citizens attended countless meetings to argue about their local plans. . . . [And] Land use lawyers in the state were deluged by clients seeking representation before county commissions, city councils, LCDC, the Land Use Board of Appeals (LUBA) [discussed below], and the courts" (Leonard 1983, 34). Furthermore, incentives to organize for both support and opposition increased. The supporters moved first, and did so effectively.

O'Toole (2001a, 27) explains, for example, that once the urban service area boundaries were put in place, the boundaries themselves "created a constituency for not moving them. People who lived near the boundary enjoyed scenic vistas and open space just a short distance away. Urbanites who lived on rural residential lands just outside the boundary enjoyed knowing that their neighbors would not be allowed to subdivide their land." Henry Richmond, a staff attorney for the Oregon Student Public Interest Research Group (a Ralph-Nader style consumer and environmental advocacy group that also took up land-use issues in 1973), founded 1000 Friends of Oregon in 1975, along with outgoing governor, Tom McCall, to represent such interests. Richmond recognized that the courts would play a major role in shaping Oregon's land use system, so he hoped to raise $100 per year from 1000 people in order to hire a full time legal staff and "use the LCDC appeals process and the court system to raise issues [he considered to be] important to the comprehensive planning process" (Leonard 1983, 20). Indeed, a large amount of litigation has occurred in the context of Oregon's land use planning system as local governments, individuals, and organizations such as 1000 Friends of Oregon attempt to use the courts to manipulate the policy process.[25] 1000 Friends have consistently been the most aggressive litigation organization, however, and "the group's appeals and lawsuits quickly developed a case law that made planning much stronger than either the legislature or LCDC intended" (O'Toole 2001a, 26).

1000 Friends also moved beyond its initial litigation focus. Indeed, "The key factor underlying the success of 1000 Friends is that is has operated on so many different levels…petitioning the courts, appealing local decisions and plans before the LCDC, preparing studies and background papers on issues such as housing density and the definition of farmlands, publishing a newsletter on important land-use issues, testifying before the state legislature, forging broad-based coalitions among diverse interest groups, working with the executive staffs of…governors, and even assisting local governments in preparing their comprehensive plans" (Leonard 1983, 30). 1000 Friends has engaged in increasing levels of lobbying and coalition building efforts through the 1980s, 1990s, and 2000s, while maintaining its litigation activities.[26] As the influence of the organization has increased its staff has moved into powerful jobs in state and local government. Robert Stacey, a 1000 Friends attorney, was chosen to be Portland's chief planner, for instance, and as noted below, another staff attorney became the director of the DLCD in 1991. The organization has become the most powerful non-profit group in the state, with most funding now coming from out-of-state foundations (O'Toole 2006a, 25, 29–28).[27]

Oregonians in Action was founded in the early 1980s by Frank Nims, a former landowner and farmer from Eastern Oregon, to pursue various measures intended to limit the size and power of government. In 1989 this organization decided to focus exclusively on private property rights issues in order to resist the efforts of 1000 Friends of Oregon. In 1991 Oregonians in Action established a legal arm, offering to represent land owners in land-use cases. Their most spectacular success in the litigation venue arose with their representation of John and Florence Dolan in challenging a conditional building permit issued by the planning commission of the city of Tigard. The Dolans had a plumbing store in Tigard, and they applied for a land-use variance to expand the store and pave the parking lot. The city planning commission agreed to approve the application, but only if the Dolans dedicated some of their land to a public greenway along an adjacent creek and to develop a pedestrian and bicycle pathway. The Dolans appealed to the Land Use Board of Appeals (LUBA),[28] arguing that the land dedication requirements were not related to the development, so this constituted a taking and required compensation under the Fifth Amendment to the U.S. Constitution. LUBA ruled that the conditions had a reasonable relationship to the development because the larger building and paved lot would increase runoff into the creek, and the expected increase in traffic justified the pathway. The LUBA decision was subsequently affirmed by the Oregon State Court of Appeals and the Oregon Supreme Court. The case was then appealed to the U.S. Supreme Court on constitutional grounds. The Supreme Court over-turned the LUBA and Oregon court decisions, ruling that the city's requirements amounted to an uncompensated taking.[29] Nonetheless, the city continued to resist complying with the U.S. Supreme Court ruling, and the Dolans initiated a suit seeking compensation: "After long, costly city proceedings and protracted court litigation the City of Tigard agreed to settle the case by paying the Dolan family $1,500,000 for a bikepath" (Huffman and Howard 2001, 65, note 72).[30] *Dolan* is not the typical outcome of a regulatory takings case in Oregon (or elsewhere), how-ever. Regulations that take some property rights and wealth, but still allow some private use of the property are regularly allowed. Therefore, before continuing the story of the struggle over land-use regulation in Oregon, let us consider the nature of the takings and transfers that occur.

## Regulatory Transfers

Some landowners' rights were significantly attenuated through Oregon's state-wide planning and land-use regulation process, while others gained considerably. Indeed, the takings implications were clearly recognized at the time, as the statute mandating comprehensive planning also created a Joint Legislative Committee on Land use to oversee the DLCD, and mandated that the Joint Committee develop recommendations for the "implementation of a program for the compensation by the public to owners of land...for the value of any loss of use of such lands result-ing directly from the imposition of any zoning, subdivision or other ordinance or regulation regulating or restricting the use of land" (1973 Or. Laws 80, § 24 (4)). This provision was deleted in 1981 (1981 Or. Laws 724, § 24), but the takings did not disappear. As Gieseler et al. (2006, 92) explain, Oregon's land use regulations "deprived many landowners of the right even to build homes on their properties, in the name of preserving 'natural areas' and wildlife habitat. The effects on prop-erty values were harsh. Owners of residential lots found their values diminished by ninety percent." These reduced property values were widespread in rural areas (i.e., outside urban growth boundaries).

One well-documented example of attenuated rights, and resulting reduction in property value involves a 40 acre parcel of land zoned for forest use in Hood River County.[31] When the owners purchased the land in 1983 for $33,000, the land-use regulations applying to the property allowed construction of a single-family dwell-ing. Following the purchase, Hood River County adopted new regulations in order to bring its comprehensive plan into compliance with statewide goal 4. Under these new regulations, construction of a dwelling on the property was prohibited. The owners then submitted applications for a number of permits and changes (land-use permit, condition use permit, zoning and comprehensive plan changes) in order to allow them to build the home they had planned. In support of their application, the owners provided a report from a forestry expert estimating that the value of the 40 acres without the ability to build a home was $691. The county's own forester countered that there was $10,000 worth of timber on the property. The owners filed suit against the country challenging the regulation as a takings. The Oregon Supreme court ruled for the defendant (the county) because the regulation did not result in loss of all economic benefits from using the property. In particular, they noted that the ability to generate $10,000 in revenues from the timber on the land "certainly constitutes some substantial beneficial use" (*Dodd v Hood River County* (Or. 1993) at 616). The implication is that if the taking allows some beneficial use of property, then the landowner has not been deprived of property. Property has not been taken. The loss is "*damnum absque injuria.*"[32]

The transfer results of regulation are evident because other owners saw increased land values due to the regulatory process. As noted above, for instance, placement of the urban growth boundaries created a constituency that did not want to boundaries to move. Individuals who owned residents near the boundary saw their land values escalate because of the resulting secure "rights" to views of and easy access to open spaces; rights transferred to them because of the rights taken away from landowners outside the boundaries. Many landowners outside the boundaries wanted the boundaries to be moved outward as demands for housing, retail sites, and other urban uses expanded. However, "they were vastly outnumbered by the [existing] urban residents who wanted to see the boundary fixed in perpetuity" (O'Toole 2001a, 27).

The early 1990s also saw the consequences of stringent rural land use controls (see below for discussion) materializing within the urban growth boundaries. The original urban growth boundaries were drawn to include a substantial amount of vacant land to accommodate urban growth. In fact, the mandate was to estimate and include enough land to accommodate 20 years of growth. Thus, urban development was relatively unconstrained for quite a long time, particularly relative to rural development. The cities had to accommodate most of the development in the state, of course, as rural development became more difficult and costly.

By the late 1980s the urban boundaries were becoming binding, particularly in the western part of the Portland area (the Beaverton, Tualatin, Hillsboro area). When the concept of urban growth boundaries was proposed they were described as a flexible tool for planners that would be expanded to allow for orderly development while preventing "leapfrogging" subdivisions. 1000 Friends of Oregon represented the constituency demanding fixed boundaries, however, and "inspired by the need to protect the boundary 1000 Friends conceived and developed an entirely new view of growth management. Instead of moving the boundary to accommodate growth, vacant lands and existing neighborhoods inside the boundary should be built and rebuilt to much higher densities" (O'Toole 2006a, 27).[33] In 1992 a regional government called Metro was given substantial new powers to coordinate planning for the 24 cities and three counties in the Portland area, and within a few months, this government published a draft plan to implement the 1000 Friends urban-growth policies.[34] As these new policies were implemented land prices within the boundary "started rising at double digit rates" (O'Toole 2006a, 29). Developers began pressing for expansions of the growth boundaries, but 1000 Friends helped form a new coalition, the Zero Option Committee, to oppose any expansions. Metro applied new minimum density zoning ordinances to existing neighborhoods to prevent construction of single family homes on lots zoned for higher density (for instance, an owner of a lot zoned for up to, say 24-unit-per-acre apartments, is not allowed to build a single-family home, or even a duplex on the lot; instead a minimum of perhaps a six-unit-per-acre complex might be allowed). While some single-family units continued to be allowed, they were restricted to very small lots.[35] As a result, Portland has turned

from one of the nation's most affordable market for single-family housing in 1989 to one of the least affordable since 1996. Since 1990, the cost of an acre of land available for housing has risen from $20,000 to $200,000. Clearly, those who own any land that is still available for development are reaping huge benefits. Similarly, anyone who owns a previously constructed single family home, particularly on a reasonably large lot (and especially if it is near the urban growth boundary) has seen a dramatic increase in wealth, as long as the home is not destroyed (in some zones, if a single-family home burns down it must be replaced with a multi-family unit). A reduction in supply of desirable housing benefits those who sell such housing, but harms those who want to buy. For instance, according to the National Association of Homebuilders, in 1989 more than two-thirds of Portland households could afford to buy a median priced house. Today it is around 30 percent. (O'Toole, 2006b, 23)

Indeed, the average price of a residence in the Portland metropolitan area rose by $72,300 over the seven year period between 1992 and 1999 (Huffman and Howard 2001, 57). The Portland Metro planners' "response to the lack of affordable housing has been the implementation of more regulation" (O'Toole 2006b, 23) by mandating that developers provide some "affordable housing" units in each new development.[36] As Means et al. (this volume) show, of course, such mandates lead to much higher prices for the rest of the housing in the development.

Changes in land values due to restrictions are the most obvious examples of transfers arising from Oregon's land-use planning process, but there are many other transfer consequences. For instance, Huffman and Howard (2001) explain that land-use regulation has significant negative impacts on small and emerging businesses, thereby creating competitive advantages for, and even entry barriers to protect, large establishes businesses (note that this may explain why some businesses have supported 1000 Friends). Land-use regulations tend to reduce the availability of land for development, and therefore drive up the price, whether the development is residential or commercial, for instance, thus raising the cost of entry for a new business.[37] Furthermore, given the extensive zoning that exists in Oregon, individual who want to start or expand businesses generally will "need to request variances, conditional use permits, and comprehensive plan amendments to develop such land. Any one of these application processes will cost the applicant significant preparation and legal fees with no guarantee of ultimate success" (Huffman and Howard 2001, 57).

Even if the applications are successful, anyone who feels aggrieved by a local government's land-use decision can appeal it to LUBA. If LUBA affirms the local government decision, the aggrieved party can appeal to the Oregon Court of Appeals. Opposition "almost always occurs" either due to objections from local planning officials or the "inevitable not-in-my-back yard objections of neighborhoods" (Huffman and Howard 2001 62). After all, Goal 1 requires local planning processes to "adopt and publicize a program for citizen involvement" (Or. Admin R. 660–015–0000 (1)). People located within specified distances of proposed changes also are suppose to be notified about any proposed land use decision, and they are allowed to participate in making the decision; if they do not agree with the result they (or their representative, e.g., 1000 Friends) can appeal any decision (Or. Rev. Stat. §§ 215.416 (11), 277.175 (10)). This has led to the creation of numerous "grassroots" neighborhood groups that monitor applications, attend hearings, and routinely object to land-use changes (Huffman and Howard 2001, 64). Furthermore, even citizens who do not receive notices because they are not considered to be proximate enough to the location to be directly impacted, still are likely to have legal standing to claim that they are somehow aggrieved by a decision.[38] As Huffman and Howard (2001, 64–65) note, "This reflects a much broader acceptance of the idea of stakeholder than is required in other government processes. Citizens with no more than a generalized interest, which is shared by all citizens, participate and influence the land use decision process."[39] Thus, groups like 1000 Friends can play a major role in shaping local land-use decisions, just as they do in shaping statewide policy.

In an effort to reduce the probability of denial of their applications, individuals generally must hire lawyers and experts (Huffman and Howard 2001, 59–60):

> While the costs can vary significantly from one case to another, most applicants will spend $5,000 to $20,000 to gain approval for a basic conditional use permit [permission to engage in a special use in a particular zone]. This estimate does not include fees which might be incurred for transportation engineers who add $5,000 to $10,000 or for wetland consultants or fish biologists who add around $5,000 each to the small business owner's application costs. The cost estimate also does not include the expense of educating neighbors or the local government's staff who oppose the small business owner's application. Small business owners can expect to pay at least another $10,000 per objection. As these figures demonstrate, costs incurred to obtain permit approvals generally far exceed the statutorily-imposed processing fee. However, the most difficult issue concerning application fees is that the considerable discretion of land use officials and the difficulty of anticipating challenges from third parties make the ultimate cost of the application hard to anticipate with any degree of accuracy. The uncertain cost of permit applications causes them to be a significant budgetary challenge in the development of a business plan.

In addition to the costs of simply getting permission to locate a new business or expand an existing business, state and local governments continue to impose exactions on property owners in exchange for permission to develop their business activities. These include efforts to require dedication of property to some public use (e.g., as in the *Dolan* case). Indeed, as Gieseler et al. (2006, 92) observe, the extraction of exactions in exchange for permits has actually allowed local governments to avoid state law by using land-use regulation to obtain public use of private property without paying for it, rather than by "purchase, agreement, or legislative authorization of eminent domain" as the law requires (Or. Rev. Stat. 271.725 (2003)).[40] Exactions also can involve monetary payments in lieu of property dedications. One form of exaction that has particularly significant impacts on small and emerging businesses is the so-called system development charge or impact fee, allegedly as a payment for the use of infrastructure. Local governments in Oregon will only approve permits if the applicants pay these impact fees,[41] and the fees have been increasing in recent years (Huffman and Howard 2001, 66).

All businesses in Oregon, large or small, face similar costs of entry or expansion, of course (and therefore, economic growth is clearly reduced, as noted below), but these costs still have distributional impacts. First, a "large developer or other business has the benefit of experience as well as the economies inherent in recurrent regulatory compliance. This is not to say that the costs of regulation are not significant for large businesses, only that they are likely to be even more significant for small businesses" (Huffman and Howard 2001, 68). Furthermore, most of the compliance costs occur up front, before a new location or expansion is created. For large businesses, these costs are smaller portions of the total cost of the enterprise. Thus, "large companies are often advocates for regulation, presumably because of both their competitive advantage [under regulation] relative to small business and because of public relations benefits associated with a perception of corporate responsibility" (Huffman and Howard 2001, 69).[42] Second, they limit entry by or expansion of small businesses, and therefore, reduce the level of competition that existing businesses, large or small, expect to face. Not surprisingly, if individuals subject to the negative consequences of takings, such as small businesses or individuals who want to build or live in single family homes, can find a way to avoid those consequences, they have strong incentives to do so.

## Regulation Avoidance and More Regulation

As an illustration of the incentives regulations create to exploit the uncontrolled margins that arise because of the knowledge problem facing regulators and limitations on enforcement, let us consider some of the reactions to Goal 3's agricultural-land preservation regulations.[43] While the legislation enabling statewide planning and exclusive farm zoning passed in 1973, the LCDC did not actually issue its goals until January of 1975. Local governments were then supposed to develop their plans to conform to the goals, but they did not do so immediately, as noted above. Leonard (1983, 77) describes the resulting "rush to subdivide and develop" during the mid-to-late 1970s as local governments throughout the state were "inundated with proposals for land partition, subdivision, and building permits, many apparently from landowners wanting to avoid the effects of goal 3." These proposals were generally made after the LCDC issued its goals in January 1975, but before a county's plan was acknowledged to be in compliance with the statewide goals, often a span of several years, as explained above. Leonard (1983, 78) also notes that many of the partitions produced "paper lots" in that the owners did not sell them. Owners simply were obtaining partitions in order to "create lots of record in hopes that the LCDC would not apply the provisions of EFU zones to lots that already existed, or that the state legislature or county would pass 'grandfather' legislation exempting preexisting lots from Goal 3 provisions" (Leonard 1983, 78).[44] In other words, they were trying to keep their options open to pursue political methods of reestablishing their property rights in the future.

As threats to property were perceived to increase responses were often immediate. As an example, when the LCDC announced, in December 1978, that it was going to issue an enforcement order against Jackson County and hold hearings on the order in late January, because it was not meeting the Goal 3 requirements, 106 new land partition requests were filed by county residents before the end of the month, "far exceeding previous monthly totals" (Leonard 1983, 77). The first seven working days of January saw an addition 96 requests filed. By the time the LCDC hearing was held on January 25, a total of 246 new requests had been filed.

The LCDC responded to the widespread pre-acknowledgement granting of land division and building permits (and other regulation-avoidance activities noted below) by requiring minimum lot size standards for lots formed before EFU zoning, stating that "New dwellings on all preexisting lots cannot be allowed outright since this would, in effect, change a conditional use (nonfarm dwelling) into a permitted use (farm dwelling). Such an act would render the local EFU zone less restrictive than the state statute. Such a zone would not meet the requirements of Goal 3 or ORS Ch. 215" (Quoted in Leonard (1983, 78) from a DLCD publication on "Common Questions About Goal # 3"). While the LCDC (and the state leg-islature[45]) resisted pressure to grandfather the lots, various counties also resisted the LCDC mandates for some time, and continued to issue building permits for small rural lots. Leonard (1983, 77–79) discusses large numbers of permits issued in Washington, Columbia, and Coos Counties, for instance. In fact, many counties apparently were frequently violating the Goal 3 criteria. Leonard (1983, 79) cites the 1980 study by 1000 Friends of Oregon mentioned above which claimed that counties were approving about 75 percent of the proposals for rural land division, and that 75 percent of the county approvals of farm parcels and 97 percent of the approved non-farm parcels "would have been overturned on procedural grounds alone" if they had been appealed to the state.

As noted above, the LCDC imposed minimum lot sizes in rural areas, in part because of the widespread property divisions that were being approved. This was done despite the fact that it was generally recognized that this should not be done, even within counties, since land varied significantly, and because different types of agriculture require different sized parcels to operate efficiently (Leonard 1983, 73). There was another reason for the imposition of lot-sized minimums. The lack of a minimum was quickly seen as a loophole that could be exploited by individuals who wanted to build residential dwellings in EFU zones (Leonard 1983, 74). One way for individuals to circumvent the limitations on rural residency was to become "part-time farmers,"[46] or hobby farmers.[47] The LCDC tried to close this loophole by mandating that counties distinguish between farm and non-farm parcels, with farm parcel designation requiring that the parcel be a commercially viable farm. Construction on non-farm parcels was not allowed unless it met "elaborate jus-tification and compatibility requirements" and subdividing farm parcels was not allowed if any part of the farm parcel would no longer be commercially viable. The LCDC's imposition of minimum lots sizes was also intended to prevent this regulation-avoidance method.

Richard Brenner, one of the first lawyers hired 1000 Friends of Oregon, was chosen as the director of the DLCD in 1991. "Brenner worried that wealthy people might try to escape to the rural areas" (O'Toole 2001a, 29). As O'Toole (2001a, 29) explains, despite earlier recognition that different areas and different farm prod-ucts require various sized parcels, "LCDC had already passed a rule saying that it was not enough to limit rural lot sizes to 160 acres [raised from an earlier minimum of 40 acres. Brenner decided that] Owners of such parcels must prove they are genuine farmers by planting crops on the land for three years" before they can get permission to build.

In order to deal with this three-year requirement, individuals who wanted to build on rural lots began planting blueberries. They did this because blueberries do not mature for four years, so they could claim that they were farmers with planted crops, and build their homes before they actually had to harvest (O'Toole 2001a, 29). When one individual requested permits to build a 40,000-square foot home on his blueberry farm Brenner pushed for a new restriction. Goal 3 was amended in 1992 in order to categorize agricultural land. For one of these categories, "high-valued farmland," the LCDC established much stricter standards than the enabling statute allowed.[48] Individuals had to generate farm revenues of $80,000 per year on such land in order to get permission to build a new house. Only one out of six farmers in Oregon earned that much at the time, so building was virtually halted on rural farmlands. Only 322 new homes were approved in farm areas during the next three years, a period during which Oregon's population grew by roughly 140,000 (O'Toole 2001a, 29). Brenner was pleased with the result, noting that "Before we started using this test, lawyers, doctors, and others not really farming were building houses in farm zones" (O'Toole 2001a, 29).

The state legislature reacted to political pressure to reign in at least some DLCD excesses in 1993 with legislation that explicitly repealed all LCDC amendments to goal 3 (1993 Or. Laws 792 § 28). Nonetheless, this legislation also adopted a "high value farmland" category with strict restrictions on building. For instance, if someone wants to put a dwelling on "high-value farmland" he/she must demonstrate that at least $80,000 in gross annual farm income was generated by the parcel during two consecutive years, or during three of the previous five years.[49] By comparison, owners of other land zoned as agricultural must demonstrate that $40,000 was generated during the same time periods, or must own a parcel of at least 160 acres in size. These requirements are now so strict that even individuals who actually want to enter some agricultural markets as their primary business cannot build homes on their farms for several years. These individuals are forced to live in town and commute to their farms (Huffman and Howard 2001, 67). This is a particularly strong barrier to entry for markets in which entrants do not start to earn profits for several years.

One market of particular interest in this context is the winery industry, given the discussion of political activities below. Profits do not begin to appear for several years after vines are planted, and "It is difficult for a farmer to efficiently operate or develop a farm, no matter its size, when forced to live in town and commute to the farm for the first several years of operation" (Huffman and Howard 2001, 67). Thus, existing Oregon vintners benefit significantly from land-use regulations (Wong 2007, 2; Oregon's Outdoor Report 2007).

As increasingly stringent restrictions on rural land use are being imposed, the transaction costs of trying to build homes outside urban service boundaries has become extremely, and for many, prohibitively high. This might suggest that the LCDC and its supporters, such as 1000 Friends of Oregon have finally won. Perhaps the rules will stabilize? Unfortunately, for the planning advocates at least, when adjustments along one margin are finally contained, some people can still look for other margins to try to achieve what they desire. And one margin that is always available to those who can organize is political action.

### Political Backlash, Intensified Political Competition, and the Potential for Partial Deregulation

While political pressure on the state legislature led to a number of amendments to the LCDC goals and processes, the legislature was not willing to make the major changes that opposition groups demanded (Sullivan 1998, 819).[50] Therefore, opposition efforts also focused on both litigation (e.g., recall discussion of the *Dolan* case above) and ballot referenda. A 1976 ballot initiative sought to repeal the statewide land-use planning statutes, for instance, but it failed to pass by a 57 to 43 percent margin.[51] Another ballot measure followed in 1978. It proposed a constitutional amendment that would have eliminated all LCDC goals, required legislative approval of any new goals, mandated compensation for reductions in property values that resulted from land-use regulations, and in general, shifted state planning from the LCDC to the legislature.[52] This referendum also did not pass, as only 39 percent of the voters supported it. 1982 saw yet another referendum, however, which again attempted to shut down the LCDC, change the statewide goals from their status as requirements to recommendations, and repeal the land-use planning statute.[53] This ballot initiative passed in 21 of the state's 36 counties but still lost by a 55–45 percent margin.

Even as these statewide efforts were failing, ad hoc organizations were springing up in many counties to oppose local planning efforts. Local officials in a number of counties who supported land-use planning were facing recall campaigns and a substantial number lost their jobs (Leonard 1983, 37). These ad hoc groups were successful in bringing the planning process to a standstill in some counties for several months. The situation was ripe for a well organized state-wide interest group to take up the cause, and Oregonians in Action filled this niche.

Oregonians in Action was a primary actor in getting two reform measures on the 1998 ballot. One, which passed with 80 percent of the voters supporting it, required both state and local governments to mail notices to landowners describing any proposed changes in land use regulations and laws.[54] The second, a proposed amendment to the state constitution to allow citizens to petition to the state legislature for review of administrative rules, failed with 48 percent of the voters supporting it.[55] These ballot measures were quickly followed, in 2000, with an initiative to amend the takings clause in the Oregon Constitution in order to require state and local governments to compensate landowners for reduced property values arising from any law or regulation that restricted the owners' use of their land.[56] Opponents to the amendment, such as 1000 Friends of Oregon, contented that passage would cost the state an estimated $5.4 billion a year.[57] If this was true, of course, it would suggest that annual land use planning was imposing huge losses on Oregon property owners. Over 54 percent of Oregon's voters cast ballots in favor of this amendment, with majorities for approval in 30 of the state's 36 counties.

Compensation was specified to be the entire difference between the market value of the land before and after the regulation is applied, including the "net cost to the landowner of an affirmative obligation to protect, provide, or preserve wildlife habitat, natural areas, wetlands, ecosystems, scenery, open space, historical, archeological or cultural resources, or low income housing."[58] Compensation was mandated for any regulation restricting land use that was adopted, enforced or applied after the property was purchased and that was still being applied 90 days after an owner applied for compensation. It was widely assumed that this 90-day condition meant that the relevant government entity could avoid paying compensation by waiving the land use regulation.[59] However, before the amendment could be implemented opposition groups challenged its constitutionality. The Marion County Circuit Court declared the amendment unconstitutional in February 2001 in a summary judgment, concluding that it violated two clauses of the Oregon Constitution.[60] The Circuit court decision was appealed, but the Court of Appeals upheld the decision, and the State Supreme Court agreed.[61]

Oregonians in Action did not give up after the court loss. The amendment was modified and reintroduced as an amendment to state statutes rather than the state constitution. The result, Ballot Measure 37,[62] went before Oregon voters in 2004 after a heated and expensive campaign by both supporters and opponents. Supporters raised about $1.2 million, primarily through a political action committee, Family Farm Preservation PAC, as well as through Oregonians in Action (Blumm and Grafe 2007, 27). The timber industry apparently was the primary source of the PAC's funds, along with real estate and development firms. Individual landowners provided funding to Oregonians in Action.

Opponents raised much more money, roughly $2.7 million, primarily through the No on 37 Take a Closer Look Committee. 1000 Friends of Oregon contributed about $100,000, while Eric Lemelson and his mother contributed a total of $585,500. Recall that existing members of the wine industry are protected by Oregon's land-use regulations. In this context, it is interesting to note that two members of 1000 Friends of Oregon's 13-person board of directors are vintners, and that one of them, Eric Lemelson, has been the largest single contributor to pro-planning political campaigns for the last several years. No doubt, Lemelson's contributions are driven by strong beliefs (and deep pockets) but those beliefs are certainly complementary to his passionate pursuit of wine making. He "is the son of a prolific inventor with a family and personal fortune to spend and makes no apologies about putting it to use in Oregon's land use fights. He arrived in Oregon in 1979, attended Reed College and Northwestern School of Law of Lewis & Clark College and stayed to become a successful producer of the state's signature pinot noir wine" (BlueOregon 2007, 1). Tremendously wealthy, as an heir to one of the nation's largest fortunes, he decided to plant several acres of Pinot noir and Pinot gris on his small farm in 1995, apparently as a hobby farmer. He did not become a "full time winegrower and winemaker [until] several years later" ((1000 Friends of Oregon, 2007 3). Lemelson stresses that deregulation to allow more development would make it more difficult for him to expand his operations (land prices would clearly rise), and would also limit his access to ground water (BlueOregon 2007. 1), suggesting that water he is currently using is available only because those who would have water rights in a deregulated environment are not currently using the water. He also notes that he only pays $800 in property taxes on 200 acres of land he owns in Glendale, arguing that it is "growth management's insurance that even the lowest-income farm and rural landowners don't go broke keeping their land undeveloped" (Cogswell 2007, 3).

Organized opponents outspent supporter organizations by over two to one, but even so, 61 percent of the voters approved the measure. Furthermore, a majority of voters supported the measure in 35 of the state's 36 counties. Not surprisingly, supporters of land-use planning (opposition to measure 37) moved quickly in an effort to prevent the measure's application, and to limit its application if it could not be prevented. 1000 Friends of Oregon was joined by several Farm Bureaus and various individuals, including Senator Hector Macpherson, who sponsored the bill that established comprehensive planning in 1973, in filing a challenge in the Marion County Circuit court in January 2005, alleging violations of both the U.S. and Oregon Constitutions.[63] The Circuit court ruled for the plaintiffs in October of 2005, stating that Measure 37 violated the fourteenth amendment of the U.S. Constitution,[64] several provisions of the Oregon Constitution,[65] and also inappropriately limited the plenary power of the legislature to regulate. The decision was appealed to the Oregon Supreme Court, however, and the lower court ruling was reversed by unanimous judgment in February 2006.[66]

While litigation was in progress, opposition groups were also lobbying the state legislature, as were supporters. A number of bills were introduced in the 2005 legislature that would have altered various aspects and implications of Measure 37 in one way or the other, including bills to: (1) establish procedures for local government processing of claims, (2) establish application requirements, (3) require public hearings as local governments process claims, (4) allow denial of claims if the reduced value due to the regulation is less than the reduced value of neighboring land if the regulation is waived, (5) prevent suits against local governments for losses arising as a result of a waiver on neighboring land, (6) allow only prospective but not retrospective claims under Measure 37 and then only if the land value fell by at least 25 percent, (7) establish uniform application and court appeals procedures and specify which government entities have authority to waive regulations, (8) require claimants whose waivers allowed them to develop land to pay the government for tax breaks received in the past, (9) specify land use regulations that are exempt from Measure 37, and (10) allow property owners who obtained waivers to transfer the waivers when they sell the property. Most of the bills never left their committees, however, and none of them were enacted, perhaps because legislators hoped that the court would overturn the Measure. The legislature did create a task force to evaluate the state's land use planning system as a whole. The ten-member board was ordered to provide an initial report to the 2007 legislature and a final report in 2009.

Before the 2007 legislature could take any action roughly 7,560 Measure 37 claims were filed in Oregon (i.e., as of April 2007). Estimates of the monetary value of these claims range from $10.4 billion to over $19 billion (Blumm and Grafe 2007, 80, n. 452), and more than 750,000 acres of land were estimated to have been involved. Most of these claims were due to Goals 3 and 4 and their implementation (Hunnicutt 2006, 30).

Critics of Measure 37 contend that determining the amount of compensations is highly speculative (Blumm and Grafe 2007, 32; Sullivan 2006, 141–142). These criticisms are quite valid. After all, while Niemann and Shapiro (this volume) demonstrate that, in theory, compensation that is both equitable and efficient is possible, Kaufman (this volume) illustrates that in reality, compensation determination is highly politicized and subjective. It is not clear that the criticisms are actually very relevant in this context, however, since virtually all of the claims that have been processed resulted in waivers rather than payments (Blumm and Grafe 2007, 81). The important consequence of the Measure may not be that compensation actually arises, then, but that planners and regulators can be forced to consider the costs they impose on private parties, and if those costs are greater than the perceived public benefits, they may choose not to impose the costs (i.e., they may deregulate). As Huffman and Howard (2001, 69) note, "If the government is not willing to pay the costs imposed on...businesses and landowners by land use regulation, one can only conclude that the cost of regulations will be greater than the benefits resulting from the land use regulation." Since regulation is driven by political pressure from interest groups, rather than consideration of costs and benefits, the only way that the cost-benefit analysis that Huffman and Howard advocate is likely to even come close to arising is by imposing constraints on the planners/regulators that force them to consider the costs they impose.[67] Attempts to impose such constraints are themselves likely to be unsuccessful in a political environment, of course since actions such as Measure 37 need not survive in the face of political backlash from those who have been benefiting from planning without facing the costs.

The 2007 legislature faced considerable pressure to act on land-use regulation and/or amend Measure 37 (Blumm and Grafe 2007, 82). The first action taken was to give government entities more time to adjudicate claims. Measure 37 had allowed 180 days, but the legislature extended this to 540 days for any claims filed after

November 1, 2006.[68] This bill was signed by the governor on May 10, 2007, just a few days before the 180 day deadline would have hit for a large number of claims that had been field in November and early December of 2006 (the large number of claims in this period reflected the fact that landowners had two years after Measure 37 went into effect on December 4, 2004 to file claims for losses from regulations imposed before that date[69]). More importantly, the legislature also drafted a 21 page revision to Measure 37 to be referred to the voters in November 2007, as a ballot measure—Measure 49.[70] The proposal to put the measure on the ballot passed both houses along strict party-line votes (Democrats supported it).

Both sides once again accumulated large amounts of money for the campaign to follow. Three PACs were established to oppose the measure: "Fix Measure 49," "Oregonians in Action PAC," and "Stop Taking Our Property." Wetherson (2007, 1) reports that the total amount raised to campaign against the measures was almost $2.26 million, with about 61 percent coming from timber related interests. Two timber firms, Stimson Lumber and Seneca Jones Timber Co., contributed $375,000 and $332,000 respectively. Supporters of the measure raised about twice as much money, however, accumulating over $4.69 million. Eric Lemelson, the vintner who was the largest contributor to the anti-37 campaign, contributed $1,025,000 himself, and the Dorothy Lemelson Trust Account contributed another $126,000. Lemelson noted that "Measure 37 development claims border his Carlton-area vineyards, threatening his ability to farm, to expand his operations and his access to ground water" (BlueOregon 2007. 1).[71] The Nature Conservancy contributed $1,212,583, 1000 Friends of Oregon contributed $105,445, and Environmental Oregon, Inc. provided $135,510. This time the pro-planning side won as Measure 48 was affirmed by 61 percent of the voters. Strong support in the urbanized counties in northwestern Oregon was sufficient to offset strong opposition in most rural counties in eastern and southern sections of the state (Mortenson 2007, 1).

This massive ballot measure substantially altered several aspects of Measure 37, but recognizing that it would have to be acceptable to a majority of Oregon voters, legislative advocates realized that they had to leave some aspects of Measure 37 in place. Thus, for instance, it retained the ability of landowners to make Measure 37 claims against land-use regulations that "restrict the residential use of private real property or a farming or forest practice and that reduce the fair market value of the property" but it withdrew the ability to make such claims for regulations limiting commercial or industrial uses of land. It also imposed a variety of limits on residential use claims, as explained below.

Measure 49 created two different processes for adjudicating claims, one for regulations enacted before January 1, 2007 and one for regulations enacted after this date. Claims regarding any pre-2007 enactments had to be filed by the end of the 2007 legislative session, June 28, 2007.[72] Waivers for all these pre-2007 claims, including those already approved under Measure 37, were limited by imposition of restrictions on the number of residential dwellings that claimants could be permitted to build. Landowners receiving waivers (after showing a regulation prevented establishing a lot, parcel or dwelling and that the reduction in land value using a formula specified in the Measure[73]) within urban growth boundaries could build up to ten dwellings, as could landowners with waivers outside the growth boundaries but on "non-high value" land. Successful claimants with high-value farm or forest lands (where claims did not require showing a reduction in land value, but only that the regulation prevented establishing a lot, parcel or dwelling) could only receive waivers to build up to three dwellings. In addition, no single land owner could obtain waivers for more than 20 home sites, no matter how many pieces of property the individual owned. Claims arising because of land use regulations enacted after January 1, 2007 face different restrictions. In particular, the three and ten home site limits do not apply, although the overall limit of 20 home sites does hold. Thus, Measure 49 prevents waivers that would allow large residential developments, in addition to industrial and commercial developments (Mortenson 2007, 1).

Measure 49 imposes a number of other important changes in Oregon land-use regulation,[74] but as with previous legislation and successful ballot measures, it is likely that the new arrangements will not last. Given the tumultuous and every changing history of Oregon planning and land use regulation, there surely is no reason to expect that interest groups like 1000 Friends of Oregon or Oregonians In Action will be satisfied with every aspect of the system produced by Measure 49. Court challenges are bound to arise, lobbyists will be hard at work in future legislative sessions, attempting to revise the law in their favor, and ballot initiatives will provide a focus for more expensive political campaigns. Uncertainty about what property rights really are will persist, as long as the planning process' entrenched bureaucracies and easily manipulated politicians (and voters) facing interest group pressures have the power to make and impose decisions on how property can be used.

## Bureaucratic Interests, Entrenchment, and Growth

The operating assumption during the early years of Oregon's statewide planning was that once the acknowledgement process was completed, all control over land use would revert back to local governments, and at least some observers, including some legislators who supported the legislation creating the bureaucracy, assumed that the LCDC and DLCD would "go out of business" (Leonard 1983, 25). In fact, however, the LCDC is still in operation, as illustrated above, and the DLCD budget has grown substantially. For instance, the department's actual 1995–97 budget was $10,744,392 (Legislative Fiscal Office 1999, B7), but it reached $14,455,567 for 2001–03 (Legislative Fiscal Office 2006, B9), the legislature adopted and approved an $18,171,843 budget for 2005–07 (Legislative Fiscal Office 2006, B9), and the legislature (governor) adopted (recommended) a 2007–09 budget of $23,124,377 ($23,138,069) (Legislative Fiscal Office 2007, E9). Furthermore, a second state agency was created to take over some of the LCDC's activities, as explained below.

Leonard (1983, 25) uses the "Nirvana of Acknowledgement" to describe the belief that the LCDC would disappear once local government plans were acknowledged to be in compliance with the statewide goals. He notes that two issues were not recognized in this context. One was the issue of enforcement: who would make sure that the local governments actually followed their plans? Obviously, those who believed that the LCDC would go out of business assumed that landowners and local governments would willingly comply with the statewide rules, but as explained above, that has certainly not been the case. The second issue was the question of change: how would plans be altered and updated? Clearly, those who saw the LCDC as a temporary agency must have assumed that planning actually involves a permanence or stability that does not in fact exist. But there also are other reasons for the permanence of the LCDC. After all, those who work for and run the bureaucracy do not want it to shut down. Thus, they have created a process that requires its continuation. For instance, recall that it took several years for the LCDC to develop a coherent set of policies to guide local governments in their efforts to develop their comprehensive plans (Leonard 1983, 34).

Leonard (1983, 33–34) explains that "the gradual and somewhat erratic evolution of LCDC policy for applying statewide goals was intentional. Neal Coenen, Coastal Management Program supervisor for the Department of Land Conservation and Management (DLCD), states LCDC made an explicit decision to develop policy by deciding cases rather than by outlining *a priori* interpretations." The justification for this allegedly was to keep the system "politically sensitive" and prevent "technical capture." The result, as Roger Kircher, who had been the information coordinator for DLCD, noted in March 1981, was that the LCDC still had "no precedent programs to follow as a guide. It was besieged by opponents of land-use planning; it was buffeted by it proponents, each with its own view on how the program ought to proceed" (quoted in Leonard 1983, 34). Perhaps the real reason was unstated? Planning through the courts allowed the creation and imposition of much more stringent rules than the LCDC would have been able to propagate on its own. The LCDC was subject to considerable political monitoring and pressure. Indeed, as explained elsewhere, the legislature was not averse to overturning LCDC rules. On the other hand, 1000 Friends was able to file large numbers of lawsuits "eliciting key court decision on the meaning of Oregon's planning laws....dealing with politically sensitive questions," thereby attracting the animosity of local governments and anti-planning interest groups and diverting the "blame" for controversial actions off of the LCDC (Leonard 1983, 23). Tom McCall, governor of Oregon when the 1973 legislation was passed, explains that he actually was an advocate of federal land-use planning so the LCDC could shift blame on the national planners when they make highly controversial decisions, but that 1000 Friends and the courts have proven to be a "viable substitute for the higher authority that often must be invoked in America to transcend parochial concerns and private interests" (quoted in Leonard 1983, 24).

The result of the case-based policy-determination process was that local governments were suppose to draw up and submit plans that would be judged by standards that were themselves still not coherently established. Thus, local governments had strong incentives to stall their processes in order to see how other local government plans would be treated.[75] The lack of predictability (precedent) also clearly led to demands for changes in the process, as the legislature reduced LCDC duties/powers in 1979 by creating LUBA, a three-member board appointed by the governor, with power to hear virtually all individual and county government appeals of local land use decisions.[76] As Leonard (1983, 19) explains, the creation of LUBA was intended to "simplify and expedite" the appeals process, while reducing demands on LCDC and reducing the level of appeals going to Oregon's courts. Blumm and Grafe (2007, 11) also contend that the legislature hoped to "encourage consistent adjudication." If precedents are being created so that local governments and individuals are increasingly able to predict how disputes are going to be resolved, however, it seems reasonable to expect that LUBA's caseload would decline over time. Yet, Huffman and Howard (2001, 54, note 18) observe that LUBA reviews between 150 and 200 cases each year. For example, LUBA issued final orders on 153 cases in the fiscal year ending July 1, 2005, and published volume 49 of the

LUBA Reports (a reporter containing all final orders issued by LUBA since 1979) in 2006 (Hunnicutt 2006, 45, note 115).

Since LUBA was created to take over some of the LCDC's duties, its budget should be added to the DLCD budget numbers listed above for a more accurate picture of the state-level bureaucratic enforcement outlays (note that many other state agencies, including those dealing with agriculture, forestry, transportation, environmental issues, recreation, etc., also have seen their duties increase as they have had to consider state-wide goals and coordinate their own actions with the LCDC, but the budgetary consequences are not easy to ascertain). Thus, for instance, LUBA's actual budget was $1,262,625 for 1995–97 (Legislative Fiscal Office 1999, B7). This budget was actually lower for 2001–03, at $1,237,232 for 2001–03 (Legislative Fiscal Office 2006, B9) although the DLCD budget rose by almost $4 million over the same period. The legislature adopted and approved a $1,346,875 LUBA budget for 2005–07 (Legislative Fiscal Office 2006, B10), however, and the legislature's (governor's) adopted (recommended) 2007–09 budget for LUBA is $1,478,171 ($1,480,575) (Legislative Fiscal Office 2007, E10).

The tax dollars allocated to budgets for the state-level planning and regulatory agencies are only a portion on total tax-financed planning and enforcement costs, of course. All local governments had to develop comprehensive plans during the 1970s (and into the mid-1980s). Since many local governments, particularly in rural areas, did not engage in very much planning before this (Hunnicutt 2006, 33), many have had create new or substantially expand existing planning departments. Similarly, the Portland area MPO, Metro, was granted the power to oversee the planning and regulation process for the Portland metropolitan area, clearly requiring additional staff and other expenditures. This division of bureaucratic authority is quite consistent with bureaucratic incentives, since when many different agencies are involved in the effort to produce a particular outcome, and the effort fails to achieve most of its targets, as it inevitably does, each agency can claim that the failure was due to some other agency's decisions (Benson 1995). As taxpayer costs for local planning and regulatory agencies mirror and multiply those at the state level, so does the uncertainty about what the rules are, and the resulting bureaucratic power that comes from such uncertainty. Huffman and Howard (2001, 60) explain that the planning and regulatory process creates considerable discretion for local government officials, and while statute law indicates that all land use decision must be made in accordance to their approved plans, the fact is that "local governments make ad hoc decisions which are often inconsistent with prior decisions"; they quote *Brentmar v. Jackson County* (27 Or. Land Use B.A. 453, 463, *aff'd*, 882 P. 2d 1117 (Or. Ct. App. 1994) where the court states that "in the land use arena, subjective standards are the rule rather than the exception."

Huffman and Howard (2001, 62) go on to explain that it is the inherent uncertainty about land use approval decisions that leads applicants "to employ experts— attorneys, engineers, wetland consultants, etc.—to help them prepare and obtain approval of an application." After all, if the rules were well known and predictable, the need for such experts would be substantially reduced, as people could look at past decisions to predict, with considerable certainty, how their application will be treated. It would not make sense to apply if the prediction is that the application will be rejected. The discretion that regulators have gives individuals hopes of success, creating stronger incentives to pursue applications, while the added costs of the process reduce such incentives for others. The net effect regarding the number of applications is probably not determinate, but there clearly is a distributional impact, as noted above. Small and emergent businesses are much less likely to be able to cover the costs than large established businesses that are repeat players who have ongoing relationships with both experts and regulators. In this context, it is also worth noting that the demand for such experts created by the regulatory process creates a natural constituency in support of continuing the regulatory regime and making it even more complex: the attorneys, engineers and consultants whose livelihood depends on complex regulations with many unpredictable implications. The inevitable result, recognized by Governor Kulongoski (quoted in Gieseler et al. 2006, 96–97) in 2005, is that "What began as a visionary program in 1973 has become more and more complex with more regulations, resulting in more controversy."

## Legislative Externalities

The direct tax expenditures going to regulatory and planning agencies are trivial compared to the total costs of the regulatory process, which include the litigation costs and compliance costs imposed on those subject to the regulation, the opportunity cost of the resources engaged in the ongoing political competition as individuals and groups attempt to reduce or increase the power and impact of regulations, and opportunities forgone because of the inefficient allocation of scarce resources. Some of the resource misallocations are obvious.

Recall that limitations on single family housing are driving up prices in the Portland metropolitan area, for instance, and as a result, there is a significant undersupply of affordable housing. Metro planners also have attempted to relieve the shortfall in affordable housing by increasing rental housing. Existing neighborhoods often put up strong resistance to high-density rental zoning, so the planners have chosen to rezone farms and other open space remaining within the urban growth boundary for high-density development. O'Toole (2006b, 22) cites examples of more than 10,000 acres of farmland being targeted for high density development, and one suburban county also rezoned a golf course for a 1,100-unit housing development (along with 200,000 square feet of office space). Similarly, Portland sold city park lands on the condition that the buyer would build high-density developments, and Metro bought land with federal grants and then sold the lands at less than they paid for it for similar developments. When developers showed little interest in building at higher densities along the light rail lines, Portland offered developers 10 years of property tax waivers or direct grants to subsidize construction. This occurred after city council member, Charles Hale, stated, in a 1996 council meeting, that "We are the hottest real estate market in the country [but] most of those sites [along the light rail lines] are still vacant" (Quoted in O'Toole 2006b, 23). These high-density units are not what residential consumers want, however, so the developers were correct in their reluctance to provide them. As O'Toole (2001b, 23) notes, "Portland residents have failed to embrace Metro's high-density developments. In 1999, apartment vacancy rates were at seven percent, the highest in the decade, and reached 11 percent for apartments built in the 1990s. In a market where single-family home prices have nearly doubled, apartment rents have failed to keep up with inflation."

Metro's transportation policy is similarly inefficient. As O'Toole (2001a, 29) notes, "Despite several voter rejections of further light-rail construction, Metro has insisted on putting most of the region's transportation dollars into new rail lines. Saying that 'congestion signals positive urban development,' Metro's official policy has been to let congestion increase to near gridlock…on routes paralleled by existing or planned rail lines." This decision is made despite that fact that "no light-rail line in the nation carries half as many people as a single lane of a typical urban freeway" and the freeway is much more cost effective. Traffic from Vancouver, Washington to Portland is very heavy, for instance (thousands of workers in Portland live in Vancouver to escape Portland taxes and land-use regulations). I-5, which connects the two cities, had three lanes going both directions for most of the distance between them, but a two mile section of the southbound side of the highway only had two lanes, causing a severe congestion problem for commuters. In 2001 the cost of widening that section of I-5 would have been between $10 and $20 million dollars but Metro refused to allow it until a $480 million light-rail line between Portland and Vancouver was fully funded (O'Toole 2001b, 23–24). In an effort to raise the cost of driving, presumably in hopes of gaining support for more light-rail, Metro has also engaged in significant reductions in road capacity on major arterials throughout the metropolitan area. Right-turn lanes have been removed, left-turn lands have been blocked with concrete barriers, former traffic lanes have been designated as bike lanes, and so on. Note that congestion is a negative externality problem that is supposedly a market failure, but in this case planning is intentionally creating congestion in an effort to force people to use a more costly, and clearly in the minds of travelers, a less desirable mode of transportation.

Numerous other examples of allocative inefficiencies are discussed above. For instance, barriers to entry have been created in agriculture, including the requirement that farmers earn $80,000 a year for three years before they can build dwellings on their farms, forcing new farmers to commute to work. And yet, a large portion of rural Oregon currently is not being farmed even though it is zoned exclusively for agriculture. Barriers to entry extend well beyond agriculture, however. Compliance costs, the need for experts to successfully pursue permits, likely challenges and litigation before LUBA and the courts, and exactions all limit competition for existing firms, allowing them to charge more and obtain larger profits. Scale economies are distorted because large firms have advantages over small firms in dealing with the regulatory system. And so on.

Other inefficiencies are harder to observe. The insecurity of property rights resulting from the uncertainty about what the rules are or will be in light of the virtually constant stream of rule changes is amply illustrated above. As noted in Section II, when property rights are perceived to be insecure due to ease with which legislation (broadly defined to include rules created and amended by administrative bureaucracies and by courts), time horizons are shortened.[77] The change in time horizons arising from Oregon's statewide planning efforts became apparently very quickly, resulting in what Leonard (1983, 77) describes as a "rush to subdivide and develop," as discussed above. Individuals have incentives to capture whatever benefits they might be able to from property as quickly as possible, before the rules change again in a way that prevents them from capturing benefits in the future. Indeed, if new rules are not developed quickly and/or enforcement is sufficient incomplete, "economic growth" could appear to be enhanced. If this occurs, it tends to be a short-term phenomenon, however. For instance, development within urban growth boundaries faced relatively few restrictions for many years after the statewide planning process went into effect (O'Toole 2001a, 26), while development became increasingly difficult and costly elsewhere. Under these circumstances, those with development rights, urban-area landowner, also probably saw those rights as relatively insecure in the regulatory environment, so they had incentives to develop their property relatively quickly, before the rules changed for them too. Given the demand for large lot, single family homes, developers were able to "continue to please the market with large-lot subdivision" for several years (O'Toole 2001a, 26). Growth within the Portland area urban growth boundary was becoming binding by 1989, however, particularly in the area west of Portland proper (O'Toole 2001a, 26). Recall that the boundaries were supposed to be drawn to allow 20 years worth of land for urban growth. The implication is that the planners were unable to correctly predict 20 years worth of demand. This clearly is likely, given the amount of information required to make such predictions, but another factor probably is that the regulatory environment shortened time horizons, creating incentives to develop land more quickly than it had been developed before. And of course, as the boundaries became binding, "smart growth" policies were implemented, and rights to produce large-lot single family dwellings began to be taken away, as noted above. High density developments were mandated, and freedom to "please the market" was taken away, with the resulting inefficiencies discussed above. Thus, while growth appeared to be continuing in Oregon even as land-use regulations were imposed, the inevitable result is the opposite. As Gieseler et al (2006, 93), suggest, "Touted as 'smart growth,' the state's land-use regulatory regime has in reality resulted in no growth, which in turn has led to a stifled economy, reduced tax revenues, and skyrocketing housing costs, to list but a few of the unfortunate consequences."

## CONCLUSIONS

Nelson and Duncan (1995, 22) contend that "Despite the lengthy period required for adoption of local plans, and the problems of administering and enforcing state goals, Oregon's planning program is widely considered one of the most comprehensive and effective in the nation." Just what has the effect been? As Benson and Brown (this volume) explain, there are at least five ways in which political transfers of property rights reduce wealth (i.e., are inefficient): (1) involuntary transfers (e.g., through regulations under the police powers) generally produce deadweight losses (e.g., a net reduction in wealth) to society because resources are allocated inefficiently; (2) resources are consumed in the process of seeking property rights changes through the political process (Tullock 1967) and (3) in the face of efforts to achieve property rights changes, potential losers expend resources to defend against such changes, so a never-ending political completion consumes ever-increasing amounts of time and effort; (4) in order to induce compliance with discriminatory transfer rules enforcement bureaucracies will have to be created and courts will be called upon, resulting in resources diverted to compliance, implementation, enforcement and litigation; and (5) takings power undermines the security of private property rights, and importantly, insecure private property rights result in the same kinds of "tragedies" as those which arise in a common pool: rapid use (as suggested above) along with under maintenance of resources relative to the efficient level of conservation. All of these results are clearly evident in Oregon. Furthermore, when it is recognized that the evolution of a regulatory regime is path dependent, and that at least some transactions costs are endogenous (e.g., created through strategic misinformation releases by bureaucrats and political interest groups) it becomes clear that many of the "opportunity costs" of the planning and regulations are not measurable (Benson 2004).

The story of Oregon's tumultuous planning and land-use regulation history is playing out all over the country. Legislation such as Oregon's Measure 37 is being proposed (e.g., Gieseler et al. 2006, 103–104 note that similar legislation was under consideration in Montana, Texas, Wisconsin, and Washington), while other states are combining post-*Kelo* mandates to constrain eminent-domain takings with Measure-37-type mandates to constrain regulatory takings. Arizona, California, Washington, and Idaho voters considered 2006 ballot measures of this kind. Arizona's passed by a substantial margin, with 64.8 percent of the voters favoring it, while the other three failed, although California's was close, with 52.4 percent of the voters against passage and 47.6 favoring the initiative (Washington's voters rejected their initiative by a 59 percent to 41 percent margin, and Idaho's measure was soundly defeated by a margin of 76 to 24 percent). Note that the fact that the ballot measures failed elsewhere clearly does not mean that the issue is settled, as illustrated by the repeated efforts to restrict state regulatory takings in Oregon, many of which failed before Measures 7 and 37 passed.[78]

The totality of the eminent-domain backlash legislation detailed by Somin (this volume), and the anti-regulatory takings legislation illustrates a much larger phenomenon. Indeed, describing this as a backlash is too simplistic. As illustrated here and in Benson and Brown (this volume) what is being observed is a continuous struggle to restrain the powers of the state to take and transfer property. Those who advocate government takings powers, whether it involves compensation under eminent domain or uncompensated regulatory takings, are essentially arguing that the state actually owns all property, and that the private citizens who claim to have property rights to parcels of property are simply stewards for the state.

Measure-37 efforts attempt to make the state treat regulatory takings like they treat eminent domain, by paying compensation. This clearly is appropriate. In fact, the Michigan Supreme Court recognized this in 1874:[79]

> It is a transparent fallacy to say that this is not a taking of his property, because the land itself is not taken, and [the owner] utterly excluded from it, and because the title, nominally, still remains in him, and he is merely deprived of its beneficial use, which is not the property, but simply and incident of property. Such a proposition...cannot be rendered sound, nor even respectable.... Of what does property practically consist, but of the incidents which the law has recognized as attached to the title, or right of property?.... And among the incidents of property in land, or anything else, is not the right to enjoy its beneficial use...the one most real and practicable idea of property, of which it is a much greater wrong to deprive an ownership, except the right to dispose of it; and this latter right or incident would be rendered barren and worthless, stripped of the right to the use. Property does not consist merely of the right to the ultimate particles of matter of which it may be composed,—of which we know nothing,—but of those properties of matter which can be rendered manifest to our senses, and made to contribute to our wants and enjoyments.

Despite this and other court-recognized problems with regulatory takings,[80] the courts have allowed such takings, apparently in large part because actually imposing a fifth-amendment requirement of "just compensation" to regulatory takings "would undoubtedly require changes in numerous practices that have long been considered permissible exercises of the police power.... [and] would render routine government processes prohibitively expensive or encourage hasty decision-making" (*Tahoe-Sierra Pres. Council, Inc. v. Tahoe Reg'l Planning Agency*, 533 U.S. 302, 335 (2002)).[81] But that is precisely the point of Measure-37 and similar efforts in other states. Many citizens want to make impermissible those government practices that reduce the value of their property, even though they have been permissible. The process of taking wealth without compensation should not be "routine" for government. Indeed, the *Kelo* backlash legislation indicates that requiring compensation is not enough for many citizens. The process of takings with compensation should not be routine either. Much more significant limitations on government's taking powers are widely desired. The chapters in this volume illustrate why by detailing many of the inefficient and inequitable consequences of government takings powers, whether through uncompensated regulatory takings, or compensated eminent-domain takings.

## NOTES

1. Somin (this volume) explains that only a portion of the state level legislation is actually likely to impose significant restrictions on eminent domain use, but the widespread political reaction is still reflected in the total amount of legislation, whether superficial or not.
2. Recall that Benson and Brown (this volume) emphasize that restrictions on the use of eminent domain could lead to increased uses of regulatory takings to induce a similar transfer of property rights, but without compensating the losers. This suggests that restrictions on eminent domain powers should be accompanied by restrictions on the use of police powers (e.g., a requirement of compensation for regulatory takings) if takings are actually going to be effectively constrained.
3. Section II draws from Benson (2002). Benson (1984, 1995, 1996, 2004, 2005), and Boettke et al. (this volume) provide more detailed discussion of various aspects of the theoretical foundations for what follows.
4. Of course, if "wealth" is more broadly defined to mean subjective well-being or satisfaction (as Stigler and others who have written on the subject may suggest it should be), there is little cause for confusion, but then the model can lose considerable predictive power as testable hypotheses are not readily apparent. A related alternative, the rent-seeking approach (Tullock 1967), suffers in a similar way. Rents are returns to the use of unique assets (real resources such as fertile land, advantageous locations, personal skills, or artificially created assets such as licenses, franchises, or legally defined markets), but some interest groups do not appear to capture any "economic returns." Again, if these rents are considered more broadly to include gains in subjective well-being or satisfaction then the concept might be applied to such groups, but by focusing on property rights changes, it becomes clear that even if interest groups believe they are pursuing the public interest rather than rents, their success means that others will lose: rents are taken from them. See Benson (2002, 2005) for discussion of the relationships between the rent-seeking, the Chicago-School (i.e., Stigler and others), and the property rights theories of regulation.
5. It is widely recognized today, given the wholesale upheaval in Eastern Europe, that government attempts to complete-ly plan economies (totally eliminate private property rights) are destined to failure, but the fact is that even governments that have done relatively good jobs at supporting free markets can have debilitating impacts on an economy by undermining private property rights through planning and regulation. Indeed, as Staley (2007) explains, the implications of so-called socialist calculation debate between Mises (as well as others such as Hayek) and the socialists such as Lange and Lerner, apply to development planning and land use regulation, just as they do for centralized national planning.
6. Kirzner (1997, 62) explains that discovery of opportunities in a market environment gradually and systematically pushes back the boundaries of ignorance, thereby driving down costs

(both production and transactions) and prices while increasing both the quantity and quality of output. Such opportunities can arise through discovery of a new product that will fulfill consumers' desires more effectively, or of a production technique that lowers the costs of providing an existing product. They can also arise through discovery of an "error" (or a "difference in knowledge") in a market that creates an opportunity for arbitrage, for entry into a profitable niche in an existing market, or entry into an untapped market for an existing product. And they can arise through discovery of an organizational innovation that lowers transactions costs. When a market is subject to planning and regulation, the potential for discovery may actually be enhanced, although importantly, it is also redirected (Kirzner 1985, 141–145). Planning and regulations introduce "errors" into markets, so by finding ways to circumvent regulations or reduce their impact, entrepreneurs gain rewards, just as they do when they discover new products or production techniques.

7. It should be noted, in this context, that private property rights precede the rise of the state (Ellickson 1993, Benson 1999). The state need not be the source of property rights, but the state is a threat to property rights because of its coercive power and ability to reassign or attenuate rights.

8. Individuals might also pursue political offices where they are in a position to make and/or enforce rules in ways that will generate personal benefits [for instance, once in office they may simply have to threaten to reallocate some property rights in order to extract part of the existing rents for themselves (McChesney 1987)].

9. For detailed discussion of models of and empirical evidence about bureaucratic behavior, see Benson (1995).

10. For instance, bureaucrats often has access to and control over a great deal of information, and they can use that control to expand uncertainty through "selective distortion" including: "(i) alterations in the flows of in information . . . ; (ii) variations in the quality or quantity of information leaked to the media, to other bureaus in the organization, to special interest groups, and/or to opposition parties and rival suppliers; and (iii) changes in the speed of implementation of policies as these are put into effect" (Breton and Wintrobe 1982: 37–39).

11. In this regard, it must be recognized that formal channels of legislation are not the only source of legislative externalities. As such legislative activity is legitimized in the minds of the populous who are convinced that it is OK to take property through political action "There is no way to quarantine this contagion against a spread to other parts of the legal system" (Fuller 1964, 153). Decision-makers in other government entities such as administrative bureaucracies and the courts also see themselves as legitimate sources of new rules, and political pressures are directed at all of them. Indeed, as Mises (1944, 16) suggests, the courts also have failed to resist the arbitrariness of centralized, bureaucratic management of legal affairs.

12. 1973 Or. Laws 88 (codified as amended at Or. Rev. Stat. § 197 (2005))—note that subsequent references to specific Oregon laws passed before 2005 are from this same source, so specific citations are not provided. This is certainly not the first land use regulation law passed in Oregon, as explained below.

13. These goals dealt with: (1) citizen involvement, (2) land-use planning processes, (3) agricultural land, (4) forest land, (5) open spaces, scenic and historic areas, and natural resources, (6) air, water and land quality, (7) natural hazards and disasters, (8) recreation, (9) economic development, (10) housing, (11) public facilities and services, (12) transportation, (13) energy conservation, (14) containing urban growth, (15) the Willamette River greenway, (16) estuarine resources, (17) coastal shore lands, (18) beaches and dunes, and (19) ocean resources. The actual goals are fairly detailed, and are available at *http://www.oregon.gov/LCD/goals. html* (also see Leonard 1983, 141–159) and all of the quotes from the goals which appear in the following discussion are from this source.

14. The first goal in the LCDC list is that public bodies be required "to develop a citizen involvement program that insures the opportunity for citizens to be involved in all phases of the planning process." Goals 3 and 4 require preservation of agricultural and forest lands. Management of population growth is represented by Goal 14 which requires local governments to establish urban growth boundaries in order to prevent sprawl, encourage efficient use of land, and promote orderly development. Goal 9 requires that planning "provide adequate opportunities throughout the state for a variety of economic activities vital to the health, welfare, and

prosperity of Oregon's citizens." Issues of citizen involvement and economic growth are discussed below.

15. On the other hand, Gieseler et al. (2006, 92) suggest that "as Oregon's land-use system evolved, it became clear that two of the goals—Goal 5 and Goal 14—trumped all others. Goal 5 requires the preservation of 'open space,' and Goal 14 aimed to 'contain' urbanization. Other goals became more tools to realize the ant-growth aspirations of numbers 5 and 14." These two views are not inconsistent, as forest and farmland preservation translates into open space preservation.

16. As Huffman and Howard (2001, 59) note, of course, estimating urban land use needs for 20 years into the future is an "immense challenge...As planned economies across the globe have learned the hard way, even short term economic planning is very difficult. A slight modification in planning assumptions, including minor changes, can produce dramatically different results."

17. Classes I, II, III, IV, V, and VI.

18. These other lands are "lands which are suitable for farm use taking into consideration soil fertility, suitability for grazing, climatic conditions, existing and future availability of water for farm irrigation purposes, existing land use patterns, technological and energy inputs required, or accepted farming practices."

19. See Or. Admin. R. 660–006–0025 (2007) for a detailed list that includes uses related to forest operations, recreation, agriculture, location dependent uses (e.g., communications towers), and dwellings authorized by law, as well as conservation of soil, water and air quality, and fish and wildlife resources.

20. It is clear that many advocates of the planning process were much more concerned with restricting growth than encouraging it. For instance, considerable negative political and media attention was being given to rapid growth occurring in the Willamette Valley, the coastal area near Lincoln City, and even the rangelands in eastern Oregon (Leonard 1983, 4–7, 64; Knapp and Nelson 1992, 18–19).

21. The organization was created through the initiative of Hector Macpherson, a state senator, farmer, and former local planner, with the help of the Local Government Relations Division of the state government. Macpherson cosponsored the 1973 state-wide comprehensive planning legislation discussed above.

22. Actually, the bill that the Senate sent to the house called for a $3 million biannual budget as startup funding but that was reduced to $1.00 by the House Ways and Means subcommittee due to pressure for the Rural Landowners and the Taxpayer's Protection Associations (Little 1974, 21). A special bill was later passed to provide startup funding, however.

23. *1000 Friends of Oregon v. Land Conservation and Dev. Comm'n.* 724 P.2d 268, 274 n.5 (Or. 1986).

24 The 1977 legislation also mandated that local governments conduct regular review of their comprehensive plans to make sure that they remained consistent with statewide goals, however, and required the LCDC to approve these reviews.

25. For a partial list of examples, see *South of Sunnyside Neighborhood League v. Bd. Of Comm'rs of Carkamas County,* 569 P.2d 1063 (Or. 1977); *Fifth Av. Corp. v. Washington County,* 581 P.2d 50 (Or. 1978); *1000 Friends of Oregon v. Land Conservation & Dev. Comm'n* 724 P. 2d 268 (Or. 1986); *Cope v. City of Cannon Beach,* P.2d 1083 (Or. 1993); *Dodd v. Hood River County,* 855 P 2d. 608 (Or. 1993); *Lane County v. Land Conservation & Dev. Comm'n,* 942 P.2d 278 (Or. 1997); *Volny v. City of Bend,* 523 P.3d 768 (Or. Ct. App. 2000); *League of Oregon Cities v. Oregon,* 56 P.3d 892 (Or. 2002); *Coast Range Conifers, LLC v State ex rel. Or State Bd of Forestry,* 117 P.3d 990 (Or. 2005); *City of West Linn v Land Conservation & Dev. Comm'n,* 119 P.3d 282 (Or. App. 2005); *Cobos v. Marion County,* No. 05C16640 (Marion County Cir. Ct. July 2006); *MacPherson v. Dep't of Admin.Serv,* 130 P. 3d (Or. 2006); *Columbia River Gorge Comm'n v. Hood River County,* 153 P.3d 997 (Or. Ct. App. 2007). A number of other cases are cited above and below.

26. For instance, during the 1990s they revived "a moribund group known as Sensible Transportation Options for People (STOP)" to support their demand for light-rail development in the Portland area, and started the Coalition for a Livable Future, "ostensibly" including numerous environmental and social organizations, but "in practice, the coalition was run as a branch of 1000 Friends" with donations and payments for publications going directly to 1000

Friends (O'Toole 2001a, 28). The organization also helped start "Livable Oregon" which gets funding from the state government to help cities write their local plans, and 1000 Friends members serve as board members for many other organizations, ranging from the Oregon Environmental Council to the Bicycle Transportation Alliance, and as members of government commissions such as the Future Visioning Commission in Portland, the Willamette Valley Livability Forum, and the Governor's Task Force on Growth.

27. O'Toole (2006a, 28) notes that these funders include the Energy Foundation which is a joint project of the Pew Charitable Trust and MacArthur Foundation, Surdna Foundation, Nathan Cummings Foundation, Joyce Foundation, the U.S. Environmental Protection Agency, and the U.S. Department of Transportation.

28. The legislature reallocated some of LCDC's powers in 1979 by creating the Land Use Board of Appeals (LUBA) for reasons discussed below. This three-member board is appointed by the governor, and it has the power to hear virtually all individual and county government appeals of local land use decisions. Both LCDC orders and LUBA decisions can be appealed to the Oregon Court of Appeals.

29. *Dolan v. City of Tigard*, 512 U.S. 374 (1994). The Court ruled that a government agency cannot require a person to surrender constitutional rights in exchange for discretionary benefits, where the property surrendered has little or no relationship to the benefit. There must be an "essential nexus" between the permit conditions and state interest, which the court felt existed, but in addition, the degree of the exactions required by the permit condition must bear the required relationship to the projected impact of the proposed development. The Court held that the City failed to make an individualized determination that the required dedications are related to the proposed impact. The Court also ruled that the City failed to demonstrate that the proposed pathway was necessary to offset increased traffic from the proposed expansion, and that the requirement for a public greenway was excessive (i.e., as opposed to a private greenway in which other rights remained with property owners, including the right to exclude).

30. Other local governments continue to expand the use of exactions and to resist compliance with the *Dolan* ruling, however (Huffman and Howard 2001, 65), leading to more litigation. Oregon cases applying *Dolan* include *Art Piculell Group v. Clackamas County*, 922 P.2d 1227 (Or. Ct. App. 1996), and *Clark v. City of Albany*, 904 P.2d 185 (Or. Ct. App. 1995).

31. The information about this example is from *Dodd v Hood River County*, 855 P.2d 608 (Or. 1993). Also see Hunnicutt (2006, 34–35) for discussion.

32. *Fifth Av. Corp. v. Washington County*, 581 P.2d 50, 60 (Or. 1978). Hunnicutt (2006, 35–37) explains that despite the level of takings that has occurred through Oregon's comprehensive planning process, there have been relatively few takings challenges. This occurs because, (1) the Oregon court's consistently deny regulatory-takings claims when some beneficial use of property remains, (2) the courts have not clarified the factors that might be considered as a justification of a regulatory takings (there is considerable uncertainty about what the rights are), and finally, (3) Oregon regulations require that a property owner must "ripen" a takings claim before it can be pursued in court. Ripening a claim requires "submitting a sufficient land-use application to the public entity to demonstrate that the regulatory scheme results in sufficient deprivation of property use to constitute a taking." Precisely what is "sufficient" also has never been stated by Oregon courts. For instance, see *Larson v. Multnomah County*, 854 P.2d 476, 477 (Or. Ct. App. 1993), aff'd on reh'g 859 P.2d 574 (Or. Ct. App. 1993). Another factor is the high expected cost of litigation, particularly given the uncertainty about what arguments the courts might accept and the inevitable need to deal with appeals in an effort to achieve clarification, let alone compensation. Therefore, as explained below, much of the litigation dealing with Oregon land-use regulation has been financed through interest groups.

33. They also resisted road construction within the boundaries, advocating that transportation needs be served by public rail and bus transit. A large scale study dealing with land use, transportation and air quality (LUTRAQ) was commissioned by 1000 Friends to support this strategy for dealing with population growth. As O'Toole (2001a, 27) explains, LUTRAQ advocated what is now called "smart growth": high-density mixed-use development in the centers of the three communities west of Portland with the centers connected by light rail, along with large numbers of transit-oriented developments within a mile of the light rail or

express-bus routes, and retailers located on sidewalks rather than having parking lots in order to reduce the incentives to drive. 1000 Friends hired "experts" to support their claims that the transit system would reduce automobile ownership and use, and therefore the need for more roads (e.g. an engineering consultant who earned millions of dollars designing and building light rail systems, an architect who was a strong proponent of anti-automobile policy (O'Toole 2001a, 27)). 1000 Friends also advocated "traffic calming devices" such as speed bumps and traffic circles to slow traffic and further discourage driving.

34. The basis for this new regional government was established in the 1960s as a response to a federal government requirement that each metropolitan area in the country form metropolitan planning organizations (MPOs) in order to apply for and distribute federal funds from the Department of Transportation, and the Department of Housing and Urban Development. The organization was not created to "dictate to local governments" on planning and land-use regulation, even though it ultimately obtained the authority to do so (O'Toole 2006b, 21).

35. O'Toole (2006a, 29) gives an example of a development in Orenco where single-family homes do not have back yards, and each home owner has only a 10 foot wide side yard on one side of the house (the 10 foot side yard on the other side belongs to the neighboring homeowner).

36. By 1997 Metro projected a 32,370 dwelling unit housing deficit in the Portland area. The urban growth boundary was finally extended in 1998, and then again in 1999 and 2000 in order to achieve an alleged 100 unit surplus (Huffman and Howard 2001, 58). However, the surplus estimate was made before Metro finalized its Goal 5 (open space) program. With the changes in that program the surplus turned into an estimated 15,000 unit deficit.

37. Metro estimated that they had a 694 acre commercial land deficit in 1997, for instance (Huffman and Howard 2001, 58).

38. *Jefferson Landfill Comm. v. Marion County*, 686 P.2d 310, 316 (Or. 1984).

39. Eagle (this volume) contends that owners of condemned parcels should be given realistic opportunities for planning and equity participation. His argument focuses on the use of eminent domain to assemble land for redevelopment, but the same argument should apply for regulatory takings in order to "assemble land" for "preservation" rather than development. Planning advocates in Oregon would probably argue that all stakeholders, including landowners facing property rights restrictions, already have standing to participate in the process, of course, but the flip side of Eagle's argument is that those whose property rights are not affected have too much influence. The state's very broad designation of stakeholders (Huffman and Howard 2001, 64–65) reduces the relative impact of those who lose property rights. Those who bear costs should have a large influence, not an equal influence.

40. Benson and Brown (this volume) note that regulations can serve as a substitute for eminent domain, to avoid restrictions on eminent domain powers such as those passed since *Kelo*, but in Oregon regulation also substitutes for eminent domain so the government can avoid paying compensation.

41. They do this despite the fact that Oregon statute law explicitly states that impact fees should not include "the cost of complying with requirements or conditions imposed upon a land use decision" (Or. Rev. Stat. §223.299 (4) (b)).

42. This point is quite consistent with Staley's (this volume) observation that eminent domain is usually not necessary to promote redevelopment even in high profile cases such as *Kelo*. Instead, he notes that eminent domain is used to achieve political expediency, often for projects that are characterized by higher risk with few public benefits. Staley also stresses that eminent domain has become sufficiently wide spread so that private developers use it primarily as a way to minimize costs and avoid market transactions. Thus, businesses that have to political clout to get land cheap through eminent domain transfers obviously have incentives to support government transfer powers.

43. An examination of this effort could start even earlier. For instance, the Oregon legislature created a farm tax deferral program in 1961 with legislation to allow counties to create exclusive farm use (EFU) zoning (Leonard 1983, 66). Very few counties implemented EFU zoning, however, and as Leonard (1983, 66) notes, "In many cases the tax breaks did little more than finance rural speculation, as land owners sold out at urban prices after reaping the benefits of farmland tax assessment for many years." Thus, when Oregon became the second state in the country to require local governments to adopt comprehensive planning in 1969, and

outlined 10 broad goals that these governments were to consider, "The most important of these goals [was] to conserve prime farm land for the production of crops" (Leonard 1983, 6). Local opposition prevented significant changes in local decision making processes, however, and this was a primary motivation for the 1973 legislation that established the LCDC and mandatory compliance with statewide goals, along with an accompanying bill on agricultural land use policy.

44. Political pressure actually led to legislative consideration of bills in 1977, 1979 and 1981 to exempt existing lots in rural areas from the restrictions on building in Goals 3 and 4. The 1977 and 1979 efforts failed, and all that passed in 1981 was a compromise providing that a limited portion of these preexisting lots were exempted: "those who would experience a genuine hardship if denied building permits on lots created or acquired between January 1, 1965, and December 1, 1974" (Leonard 1983, 78).

45. See note 44.

46. For instance, a study commissioned by the LCDC found that 75 percent of the farms with new dwellings approved by local governments had annual farm revenues of less than $10,000 (Department of Land Conservation and Development 1991, 1).

47. Goal 3 originally allowed exceptions to agricultural uses for schools, churches, golf courses, power generating facilities, and forestry. Farm residences and related buildings were also allowed, and other single-family dwellings were allowed under certain circumstances. Such dwellings had to be approved by the local government, could not interfere with farming practices, could not alter the overall land use pattern of the area, and had to be located on land that was not suitable for agricultural use because of terrain, soil, drainage, or other factors (Leonard 1983, 68). In addition, all land divisions involving parcels of less than 10 acres had to be reviewed by the county government to make sure that the land use conformed to the state's mandated policies.

48. The LCDC "justified" this by referring to the study cited in note 46 to demonstrate that local governments were not adequately protecting commercial farmland.

49. The legislation also eased the restrictions on dwellings located on "less productive land," however, and it established a process by which local governments would be allowed to permit dwellings on agricultural or forest lands meeting certain conditions, including that it was acquired before January 1, 1985.

50. Virtually every legislative session has amended the land-use planning statute (Blumm and Grafe, 2007, 11). For instance, political pressure to ease the consequences of urban growth boundaries led to 1988, 2000, and 2005 amendments to DLCD goal 14. The 1988 amendment also reduced compliance costs for local governments (and therefore for those seeking development approvals) by allowing them to refer to their approved comprehensive plans rather than to the DLCD goals in justifying their land use decisions. The 2000 amendment indicated that single-family dwellings can be located outside the urban growth boundaries if the area is zoned for residential use or if it is an area not covered by the farm or forest land preservation requirements of goals 3 and 4. Finally, in April 2005 the LCDC amended goal 14 in an effort to streamline and clarify the requirements that local governments had to meet in order to amend their urban growth boundaries, and then in December 2005 another amendment incorporated a legislative requirement that certain kinds of industrial development can be located on rural land despite goal 14. Similarly, exclusive farmland zoning restrictions have attracted considerable opposition. The LCDC first amended Goal 3 in 1983 when the legislature mandated that a marginal land classification program be instituted to allow local governments to relax the exclusive farm-use zoning criteria for lands designated as marginal for agriculture. Similarly, Goal 3 originally allowed exceptions for schools, churches, golf courses, power generating facilities, and forestry, but reactions to the DLCD's inflexible policies have force the Oregon legislature to repeatedly add more non-farm use exceptions for land in the exclusive farm-use zones. The original list of 5 exceptions has grown to 48 (see *www.oregon.gov/LCD/farmprotprog.html* for a complete listing). Simultaneously, however, the LCDC was also amending goal 3 to make it more restrictive, as noted above. Goal 4 has also had a tumultuous history, with numerous amendments since initial establishment. Amendments occurred in 1983, 1990, 1993, and 1994.

51. See Oregon Repeals Land Use Planning Coordination Statutes, Ballot Measure 10 (1976) at http://bluebook.state.or.us/state/elections/elections19.htm

52. See Initiative, Referendum and Recall: 1976–1978 at http://bluebook.state.or.us/state/elections/elections19.htm
53. See Initiative, Referendum and Recall: 1980–1987 at http://bluebook.state.or.us/state/elections/elections20.htm
54. Expands Notice to Landowners Regarding Changes to Oregon Land Use Laws, Ballot Measure 56 (1998).
55. Amends Oregon Constitution: Creates Process for Requiring Legislature to Review Administrative Rules, Measure 65 (1998). This amendment would have applied broadly; the LCDC was the primary target.
56. Amends Oregon Constitution: Require Payment to Landowner if Government Regulation Reduces Property Value, Measure 7 (2000). There were specified exceptions to the compensation requirement, however. Landowners could not obtain compensation if the regulation involved "historically and commonly recognized nuisance laws," regulations to "implement a requirement of a federal law," or for regulations that prohibited using property "for the purpose of selling pornography, performing nude dancing, selling alcoholic beverages or other controlled substances, or opening a casino or gaming parlor."
57. See *Measure 7, Arguments in Opposition*, which offers 30 arguments against the measure, at *http://www.sos.state.or.us/elections/nov72000/guide/mea/m7/70p.htm* .
58. For discussion of the takings that arise through such affirmative obligations, see papers in this volume by Adler, Means et al., and Brown and Stroup.
59. The state Attorney General assumed that this was the case for state regulations (Or. Op. Att'y. Gen. 284 (2001), 2001 Ore. AG LEXIS 11), and a substantial number of local governments adopted ordinances allowing waiver of land use laws rather than compensation to landowners. 1000 Friends of Oregon sued at least 23 cities, however, challenging their authority to waive state land use laws to avoid paying compensation (Nokes 2000, B01).
60. *League of Or. Cities v. Oregon*, No. 00-C-20156 1, 2 (Marion County Cir. Ct., Feb. 22, 2001). First, it was concluded that it violated the "separate vote" provision in that it actually contained two amendments, and the constitution mandated that all amendments must be voted on separately. It clearly amended the taking provision of the constitution which had previously required compensation only when all economically viable uses of property were denied, but opponents also successfully argued that it implicitly amended the free speech clause because governments did not have to pay compensation if the relevant regulation prevented the landowner from engaging in the sale of pornography. The free speech clause stated that "no law shall be passed restraining the free expression of opinion, or restricting the right to speak, write, or print freely on any subject whatsoever" which had been interpreted to mean that local governments cannot treat people who sell so-called expressive material any more strictly than those who sell any other goods. The amendment required different treatment for such sellers, however, so it was seen as an amendment to the free speech clause. The Circuit Court also concluded that the amendment violated the "full text" clause of the constitution which requires that a ballot initiative must contain the full text of the proposed amendment. While the ballot measure did contain the full text of what it proposed to add to the constitution it did give proper notice of all of the other constitutional and statutory provisions that it was changing. One example had to do with the definition of just compensation. The amendment added attorneys fees and expenses required to collect compensation if the landowner was not paid in 90 days, and this, the court concluded, changed compensation provisions in both state and local laws.
61. *League of Or. Cities v. Oregon*, 56 P.3d 892 (Or. 2002).
62. Oregon Governments Must Pay Owners or Forgo Enforcement When Certain Land Use Restrictions Reduce Property Value, ch. 197, Measure 37 (2004); reprinted in *Environmental Law* 36 (Winter 2006): 3–5. Measure 37's actual provisions are very similar to the provisions of the amendment that the courts struck down, except for the fact that it altered statute rather than constitutional law. It also explicitly allows government entities to "modify, remove or not apply" a regulation rather than pay compensation, something that had been inferred from the previous measure. Also, five situations are specified under which compensation is not required. Four are similar to those specified in the previous constitutional amendment: (1) regulations prohibiting activities "commonly and historically recognized as public nuisances

under common law" but "construed narrowly in favor of a finding of compensation under the act," (2) regulations to "comply with federal law," (3) regulations passed before the current owner (or the current owner's family) obtained the property, and (4) somewhat less restrictively, regulations against the use of property to sell pornography or present nude dancing. In addition, "regulations that restrict or prohibit activities in order to protect "public health and safety, such as fire and building codes, health and sanitation regulations, solid or hazardous waste regulations, and pollution control regulations" are designated as exempt from compensation. Blumm and Grafe (2007, 52–71) provide detailed discussion of potential implications of these exemptions, which, in all likelihood, will all be the subject of litigation as landowners attempt to obtain compensation or relief, and as opponents attempt to restrict the application of the new law. A landowner must make a claim for compensation within two years of a regulation's application to his or her land (or two years of the date when Measure 37 went into effect, December 4, 2004, with the potential for retroactive application to deal with regulations imposed on the land before passage), through a written notice to the government entity that either enacted or is enforcing a regulation, and that government body then has 180 days to decide what to do. If the regulation is still in place after 180 days and compensation has not been paid, then the landowner has a recognized cause for action in court.

63. *MacPherson v. Dep't of Admin. Serv.,* No. 05C10444 (Marion County Cir. Ct. Oct. 14, 2005). The first plaintiff listed is Hector Macpherson. The first defendant named is the state Department of Administrative Services, but other defendants include LCDC, the state Department of Justice, Clackamas County, Marion County, and Washington County. Other parties also intervened for the defense, including those who had sponsored Measure 37, represented by Oregonians In Action.

64. Both procedural and substantive due process were allegedly violated. Procedural due process supposedly was violated because the Measure did not provide neighboring landowners affected by a successful petition under Measure 37 with a meaningful right to object, as challenges would not arise until after a decision to waive was made. Substantive due process was seen as an issue because waivers could arbitrarily deprive neighbors of a property interest.

65. These alleged violations involve the provisions regarding: (1) "equal privileges and immunities" because it distinguishes between landowners who acquire their property before and after a regulation is imposed, (2) "suspension of laws" because it violates the equal privileges and immunities clause and suspends laws for some landowners but not others, and (3) "separation of powers" because it allows the legislature to delegate powers to local governments that the legislature did not have, including the power to suspend laws and to distinguish between different types of landowners when doing so.

66. *MacPherson v. Dep't of Admin.Serv,* 130 P. 3d 308 (Or. 2006). The Supreme Court ruled that the measure does not limit the legislature's plenary power, but instead that it is an exercise of that power because it allowed state and local government authorities to decide if they want to pay compensation, modify regulations, remove regulations, or not apply the regulation. The equal privileges and immunities issue was also rejected because the clause only applies to "those individuals or groups whom the law classifies according to characteristics that exist apart from the enactment of that challenge" and this is not the case with Measure 37. Similarly, it is not a suspension of a law, but an amendment allowing government bodies to grant waivers. Given these findings, the Measure also does not violate separation of powers. Finally, the federal Constitution due process issues were rejected because the Measure authorizes local governments to develop their own procedures to administer the Measure and does not prevent those procedures from considering the objections of neighbors. See Blumm and Grafe (2007, 36–39) for much more detailed discussion.

67. Recall the point in note 38, and recognize that Eagle's (this volume) contention that the requirement of compensation is not sufficient, and that owners of condemned parcels should be given realistic opportunities for planning and equity participation. This should also apply when compensation is required for regulatory takings in order to "assemble land" for "preservation" rather than development.

68. H.B. 3546, 74th Leg. Reg. Sess. § 2(2)(a) (Or. 2007).

69. See note 61.

70. H.B. 3540, 74th Leg. Reg. Sess. (Or. 2007).

71. This argument is echoed by other vintners, such as Russell Gladhart, a partner in Winter's Hill Vineyard who says that land-use regulation make it possible for the wine industry to expand. According to a study by Environment Oregon, some 1,273 Measure 37 claims involved "103,282 acres of otherwise protected high-value vineyard land," 98,202 acres of which were in the Willamette Valley (the other 5,031 acres were in the Columbia River Gorge) (Oregon's Outdoor Reports 2007, 2). The report was suppose to be written in support of Measure 49, It also notes, however, that there was only about 10,000 acres planted with wine grapes in the valley, with vineyard acreage expanding by an average of about 770 acres a year during the previous 3 years. At that rate of growth in vineyard acreage, it would take about 135 years to plant the acreage affected by Measure 37 claims, and the study does not report how much potential vineyard land remains unaffected by such claims. Clearly, in the absence of Measure 37, a tremendous supply of potential vineyard land exists, keeping the price of such land low for people like Lemelson who want to remain in the wine business and prevent development on neighboring lands. Of course, with his wealth, he could easily buy all of the Measure 37 lands around his properties and hold them for future expansion if he wanted to.
72. Landowners can only make claims under regulations enacted while they personally own the land, however. This eliminates the ability to make claims under regulations that were imposed before inheriting the land from someone else (H.B. 3540 § 4(3)).
73. The reduction in value was to be calculated by subtracting the fair market price one year after the regulation was enacted from the fair market value one year before enactment (H.B. 3540 § 9(6)).
74. For example, the Measure establishes that: waivers can be transferred when property is sold; specific provisions in the state land-use code, agricultural and forestry regulations, LCDC rules and goals, and local comprehensive plans are defined to constitute "land-use regulations" under the Measure; the government body that enacts a regulation is responsible for compensation if the enforcing and enacting agencies are different; neighbors who allege harm due to a waiver are explicitly allowed to seek judicial review of the decision; an ombudsman must be appointed to "analyze problems of land use planning, real property law and real property valuation and facilitate resolution of complex disputes"; the health and safety exception does not apply for any future agricultural and forestry regulation unless the primary purpose of the regulation is protection of health and safety; the federal-law compliance exception for future regulations does not apply if the government enacting the regulation can decline to comply with the federal law (Blumm and Grafe 2007, 85–86).
75. This delaying strategy apparently backfired on many of the local governments who followed it, however, since the plans faced increasingly stringent scrutiny over time, as the LCDC gradually decided more and more cases. Many of the plans approved early probably would not have been approved later.
76. 1979 Or. Laws 748. The LCDC retained jurisdiction over certification, reviews, and approval of exceptions to comprehensive plans, but LUBA was given "exclusive jurisdiction to review any land use decision or limited land use decision." There were also earlier efforts to alleviate some of the costs imposed on local governments by the LCDC's case-by-case review process. As initially established, local governments had to review every local land use action to make sure that they complied with LCDC goals. County governments and individuals could then petition the LCDC, challenging such local-government land-use decisions when they felt that the decisions were inconsistent with the goals, and the LCDC had the power to enjoin local government decisions. The state legislature attempted to streamline the process somewhat in 1977. This legislation created a process which allowed local governments to petition the LCDC to review its land-use plan and certify that it was consistent with the goals. Once certified, local government land-use decisions could be justified by showing their consistency with the local plan rather than with the DLCD goals.
77. Recall note 11 and the point that legislative externalities arise because government decision-makers in legislatures, administrative bureaucracies and the courts see themselves as legitimate sources of new rules. The beliefs of many officials in Oregon clearly are that individuals should not have rights to do what they want with their own property. Little (1974, 25) quotes the first Vice Chairman of the LCDC, for instance, who, in commenting on the issue of compensation, stated "The lawyer in me says, I'm damned if we have to pay anyone to down-zone, just so long as the landowner still has use of his land. Nobody has an inalienable right to

develop." The same anti-private property beliefs characterize pro-planning activists. O'Toole (2001a, 30) quotes 1000 Friends of Oregon lawyer, Robert Liberty, who stated "I grew up on a 50-by-100 lot, what is good enough for me should be good enough for anyone." This came up as planners proposed to increase the density requirements for a Portland suburb, and one "naïve resident" called 1000 Friends of Oregon for help.

78. See Blumm and Grafe (2007, 72–79) for discussion of the four ballot initiatives and some of the political background.

79. Quoted in Gieseler et al. (2006, 81–82) from *Grand Rapids Booming Co. v. Jarvis*, 30 Mich. 308, 320–321); accord *Pumpelly v. Green Bay Co.*, 80 U.DD. (13 Wall.) 166, 177–78.

80. For instance, the New York Court of Appeals recognized, in *Fred F. French Investing Co. v. City of New York*, N.E.2d 381, 387 (1976), taking the value of a person's property "under the guise of police power [has the effect of] forcing the owner to assume the cost of providing a benefit to the public without recoupment." This same court also noted (at 387) that with regulatory takings "the ultimate economic cost of providing the benefit is hidden from those who in a democratic society are given the power of deciding whether or not they wish to obtain the benefit despite the ultimate economic cost."

81. In writing this opinion, Justice Stevens sites *Pennsylvania Coal v. Mahon*, 260 U.S. 393, 413 (1922) where Justice Holmes wrote "government hardly could go on if to some extent values incident to property could not be diminished without paying for every such change in the general law."

# REFERENCES

1000 Friends of Oregon. 2008. 1000 Friends Board of Directors. *About 1000 Friends.* http://www.frineds.org/about/board/html.

Adler, Jonathan. This Volume. The Adverse Environmental Consequences of Uncompensated Land-Use Controls.

Benson, Bruce L. 1984. Rent Seeking from a Property Rights Perspective. *Southern Economic Journal* 51: 388–400.

———. 1995. Understanding Bureaucratic Behavior: Implications from the Public Choice Literature. *Journal of Public Finance and Public Choice* 8: 89–117.

———. 1996. Uncertainty, the Race for Property Rights, and Rent Dissipation due to Judicial Changes in Product Liability Tort Law. *Cultural Dynamics* 8: 333–351.

———. 1999. An Economic Theory of the Evolution of Governance and the Emergence of the State. *Review of Austrian Economics* 12: 131–160.

———. 2001. Law and Economics. In *The Elgar Companion to Public Choice*, edited by W.F. Shughart II and L. Razzolini. London: Edward Elgar 547–589.

———. 2002. Regulatory Disequilibrium and Inefficiency: The Case of Interstate Trucking. *Review of Austrian Economics* 15: 229–255.

———. 2004. Opportunities Forgone: the Unmeasurable Costs of Regulation. *Journal of Private Enterprise* 19: 1–25.

———. 2005. Regulation, More Regulation, Partial Deregulation, and Reregulation: The Dynamics of a Rent-Seeking Society. *Advances in Austrian Economics* 8: 107–146.

———. 2008. Beliefs as Institution Specific Rationalizcd Self-Interest. In (Eds.) *Ordered Anarchy: Jasay and His Surroundings,* edited by Bouillon, H. and H. Kliemt. London: Ashgate, 103–145.

Benson, Bruce L. and Matthew Brown. This Volume. Eminent Domain for Private Use: Is It Justified by Market Failure or an Example of Government Failure.

Blue Oregon. 2007. The Funding Behind the Measure 49 Campaigns. *BlueOregon*, http://www.blueoregon.com/2007/10/the-funing-beh.html

Blumm, Michael C. and Erik Grafe. 2007. Enacting Libertarian Property: Oregon's Measure 37 and its Implications, *Denver Law Review* 85: 2–90.

Boettke, Peter J., Christopher J. Coyne, and Peter T. Leeson. This Volume. Land Grab: Takings, the Market Process, and Regime Uncertainty.

Breton, Albert and Ronald Wintrobe. 1982. *The Logic of Bureaucratic Control.* Cambridge: Cambridge University Press.

Brown, Matthew and Richard L. Stroup. This Volume. Market versus Takings and Regulation: Deciding the Future of the Past.

Bullock, Scott G. This Volume. The Inadequacy of the Planning Process for Protecting Property Owners from the Abuse of Eminent Domain for Private Development.

Cheung, Steven N. S. 1974. A Theory of Price Control. *Journal of Law and Economics* 17: 53–71.

Cogswell, Grant 2007. Its Timber Companies vs. Enviros in a Battle for Oregon's Future. *Portland Mercury* October 11, http://www.portlandmercury.com/portland/Content?oid=440864&category=34029

Demsetz, Harold. 1967. Toward a Theory of Property Rights. *American Economic Review* 57: 347–359.

Department of Land Conservation and Development. 1991. *Analysis and Recommendations of the Results and Conclusions of the Farm and Forest Research Project.* Portland: Oregon Department of Land Conservation and Development.

Eagle, Steven J. This Volume. Assembling Land for Urban Redevelopment: The Case for Owner Participation.

Ellickson, Robert C. 1993. Property in Land. *Yale Law Journal* 102: 1315–1400.

Fuller, Lon L. 1964. *The Morality of Law.* New Haven, CN: Yale University Press.

Gieseler, Steven G., Leslie M. Lewallen, and Timothy Sandefur. 2006. Measure 37: Paying People for What We Take. *Environmental Law* 36: 79–104.

Hayek, Friedrich A. 1973. *Law, Legislation, and Liberty,* Vol. 1. Chicago: University of Chicago Press.

Huffman, James L. and Elizabeth Howard. 2001. The Impact of Land Use Regulation on Small and Emerging Businesses. *Journal of Small and Emerging Business Law* 5: 49–70.

Hunnicutt, David J. 2006. Oregon Land-Use Regulation and Ballot Measure 37: Newton's Third Law at Work. *Environmental Law* 36: 25–52.

Ikeda, Sanford. 1997. *Dynamics of the Mixed Economy: Toward a Theory of Interventionism.* London: Routledge.

Kaufman, Wallace. This Volume. How Fair is Market Value: An Appraiser's Report of Temptations, Deficiencies and Distortions in the Condemnation Process.

Kirzner, Israel M. 1985. *Discovery and the Capitalist Process.* Chicago: University of Chicago Press.

———. 1997. Entrepreneurial Discovery and the Competitive Market Process: An Austrian Approach. *Journal of Economic Literature* 35: 60–85.

Knaap, Gerrit and Arthur C. Nelson. 1992. *The Regulated Landscape: Lessons on State Land Use Planning from Oregon.* Cambridge, MA: Lincoln Institute of Land Policy.

Legislative Fiscal Office. 1999. *Highlights of the 1999–2001 Legislative Adoptive Budget.* Salem: Oregon State Legislature, *http://www.leg.state.or.us/comm/lfo/budghigh99–01.pdf*

———. 2006. *Highlights of the 2005–07 Legislative Approved Budget UPDATE.* Salem: Oregon State Legislature. http://www.leg.state.or.us/comm/lfo/budghigh0507update.pdf

———. 2007. *Budget Highlights of the 2007–09 Adopted Budget.* Salem: Oregon State Legislature. http://www.leg.state.or.us/comm/lfo/2007–09_budget/2007–09%20Budget%20Highlights.pdf

Leonard, H. Jeffrey. 1983. *Managing Oregon's Growth: The Politics of Development Planning.* Washington, DC: Conservation Foundation.

Little, Charles E. 1974. *The New Oregon Trail: An Account of the Development and Passage of State Land-Use Legislation in Oregon.* Washington, DC: Conservation Foundation.

McChesney, Fred S. 1987. Rent Extraction and Rent Creation in the Economic Theory of Regulation. *Journal of Legal Studies* 16: 101–118.

Means, Thomas., Edward Stringham, and Edward López. This Volume. Below-Market Housing Mandates as Takings: Measuring their Impact.

Mises, Ludwig von. 1944 [1983]. *Bureaucracy.* New Haven: Yale University Press. Reprinting by the Center for Future Studies.

———. 1945 [1985]. *Omnipotent Government: The Rise of the Total State and Total War.* Spring Mills, PA: Libertarian Press.

———. 1949 [1963]. *Human Action: A Treatise on Economics,* 3rd Revised Edition. Chicago: Contemporary Books.

Mortenson, Eric 2007. Voters Keep Cigarette Tax As Is but Roll Back Property Rights. *The Oregonian* (November 7). *http://www.oregonlime.com/printer/printer.ssf?/base/news/119418606131680.xml&coll+7*

Mueller, Dennis C. 1989. *Public Choice II: A Revised Edition of Public Choice.* Cambridge: Cambridge University Press.

Nelson, Arthur C. and James B. Duncan. 1995, *Growth Management Principles & Practices.* Chicago" Planners Press, American Planning Association.

Niemann, Paul and Perry Shapiro. This Volume. Compensation for Taking When Both Equity and Efficiency Matter.

Nokes, R. G. 2000. 1000 Friends of Oregon Sues 23 Cities. *The Oregonian* Dec. 22: B01.

Oregon Land Use and Development Commission. 1987. *1985–87 Biennial Report to the Legislative Assembly of the State of Oregon.*

Oregon's Outdoors Reports. 2007. Measure 49: Protecting Oregon's Wine Country. *Environment Oregon,* September 26: *http://www.environmentoregon.org/reports/preservation/preservation-program-reports/mea*.

O'Toole, Randall. 2001a. Exposé: 1000 Destroyers of Oregon. *Liberty Magazine* (May 1): 25–30.

———. 2001b. The Folly of "Smart Growth." *Regulation* (Fall): 20–25.

Ramsey, Bruce. 2007. Making a Loud Noise for Fair Use of Property. *The Seattle Times,* June 11, *http://seattletimes.nwsource.com/cgi-in/PrintStory.pl?document_id=2003688930&zsection*.

Somin, Ilya. This Volume. The Limits of Backlash: Assessing the Political Response to *Kelo*.

Staley, Samuel R. 2007. Takings for Economic Development: The Calculation Debate—Again. Presented at the Southern Economic Association meetings, November 19, New Orleans.

———. This Volume. The Proper Uses of Eminent Domain for Urban Redevelopment: Is Eminent Domain Necessary?

Stigler, George J. 1971. The Theory of Economic Regulation. *Bell Journal of Economics and Management Science* 2: 3–21.

Sullivan, Edward J. 2006. Year Zero: The Aftermath of Measure 37. *Environmental Law* 36: 131–163.

Tullock, Gordan. 1965. *The Politics of Bureaucracy.* Washington D. C.: Public Affairs Press.

———. 1967. The Welfare Costs of Tariffs, Monopolies and Theft. *Western Economic Journal,* 5: 224–232.

U.S. Department of Agriculture. 2004. *Oregon State and County Data, Geographic Area Series* Vol. 1, Pt. 37.

Wetherson, Sarah E. 2007. Measure Campaigns Near $22 Million Mark; Tobacco Money Accounts for Half; Timber Interests Contribute 61 Percent of Total to No on 49 Effort, *Democracy Reform Oregon,* November 1: www.democracyreform.org.

Wong, Peter. 2007. Measure 49 is New Chapter in Land Use, May Not Last. *Statesman Journal,* October 21, *http://www.statesmanjournal.com/apps/pbcs.dll/article?AID=/20071021/STATE/71021031*.

# About the Contributors

## Editor

BRUCE L. BENSON is a Senior Fellow at the Independent Institute and the Economics Department Chair at Florida State University, where he also is a DeVoe Moore Professor, Distinguished Research Professor, and Courtesy Professor of Law. Recent recognitions include the Liberty in Theory Lifetime Achievement Award in 2007 from the Libertarian Alliance in London, the Association of Private Enterprise Education's 2006 Adam Smith Award, the Freedom Foundation's 2004 Leavey Award for Excellence in Private Enterprise Education, the Property and Environment Research Center's Julian Simon Fellowship in 2004, and a 2003–2004 Fulbright Senior Specialist Grant in the Czech Republic.

## Authors

JONATHAN H. ADLER is Professor of Law and Director of the Center for Business Law and Regulation at the Case Western Reserve University School of Law. He is one of the most widely cited academics in environmental law. His articles have appeared in publications ranging from the *Harvard Environmental Law Review* and *Supreme Court Economic Review* to the *Wall Street Journal* and the *Washington Post*. He also is the author or editor of four books on environmental policy including *Environmentalism at the Crossroads* (1995).

PETER J. BOETTKE is the Deputy Director of the James M. Buchanan Center for Political Economy, a Senior Research Fellow at the Mercatus Center, a professor of economics at George Mason University, and editor of the *Review of Austrian Economics*. He has authored numerous academic journal articles and several books, including *Why Perestroika Failed: The Economics and Politics of Socialism Transformation* (1993), and *Calculation and Coordination: Essays on Socialism and Transitional Political Economy* (2001), and he now is coauthor of Paul Heyne's classic, *The Economic Way of Thinking* (2009).

MATTHEW BROWN is program officer for academic affairs at the Charles G. Koch Charitable Foundation where he directs the foundation's higher education and research programs. He previously taught economics at Santa Clara University and Montana State University.

SCOTT G. BULLOCK joined the Institute for Justice at its founding in 1991 and serves as a senior attorney. He currently focuses on property rights and free speech cases in federal and state courts. He has been involved in a number of cases challenging the use of eminent domain for private development, including *Kelo v. City of New London,* where, as co-counsel, he argued the case before the U.S. Supreme Court, and the first post-*Kelo* state Supreme Court case to address eminent domain abuse when, in July 2006, the Ohio Supreme Court unanimously prevented using eminent domain for private development.

CHRISTOPHER J. COYNE is an Assistant Professor of Economics at West Virginia University. He also is the North American Editor of the *Review of Austrian Economics* and a Research Fellow at the Mercatus Center at George Mason University. He has already published a substantial number of journal articles, and his book, *After War: The Political Economy of Exporting Democracy,* was recently published by Stanford University Press.

STEVEN J. EAGLE is a Professor of Law at George Mason University School of Law. He is the author of the only comprehensive treatise on the relationship between government's regulatory powers and private property owners' rights, *Regulatory Takings,* and of numerous other publications on land use regulation and property rights. He is vice-chair of the Land Use and Environmental Group of the Section of Real Property, Probate and Trust Law and co-chair of the Condemnation Committee of the Section of State and Local Government of the American Bar Association, and an elected member of the American Law Institute.

WALLACE KAUFMAN is a science writer, teacher, and editor, and has a broad hands-on background in land management, small business development, mediation of property issues, property appraisal, and transition processes in the former Soviet Bloc. His honors include the New River Award, a Marshall scholarship to Oxford, and a Science Writing Fellowship at the Marine Biological Laboratory in Woods Hole, MA. He has worked extensively in Latin America, Central Asia, Russia, and Eastern Europe doing economic surveys, training, and as the U.S. resident advisor to the government of Kazakhstan on housing and land reform.

PETER T. LEESON is the BB&T Professor for the Study of Capitalism in the Mercatus Center at George Mason University and associate editor of the *Review of Austrian Economics.* He was a Visiting Fellow in Political Economy and Government at Harvard and the F.A. Hayek Fellow at the London School of Economics, and currently is a visiting professor at the University of Chicago. The author of numerous articles for academic journals such as the *Journal of Political Economy, Journal of Law and Economics, Journal of Legal Studies,* and *Public Choice.* He won the 2007 Fund for the Study of Spontaneous Orders Prize for his work on private property anarchy.

EDWARD J. LÓPEZ is a Research Fellow with the Independent Institute, Associate Professor of Law and Economics at San Jose State University, and Scholar in Residence at Liberty Fund, Inc. He has published numerous articles in the area of Public Choice analysis, and he recently edited a book on *Law without Romance: Public Choice and Legal Institutions* for the Independent Institute.

THOMAS MEANS is a Professor of Economics and the Director of the Center for Economic Education at San Jose State University. He also is directly engaged in local policy development as Mayor of the City of Mountain View, California, after having served as a City Council member, a Parks and Recreation Commissioner, and a member of the Urban Forestry Board.

PAUL NIEMANN was awarded his Ph.D. in economics from the University of California—Santa Barbara, in April 2006. He now works at the Colorado Department of Health in Denver, Colorado.

PERRY SHAPIRO is a Professor of Economics and the University of California—Santa Barbara. His research spans a number of applied and theoretical areas, with numerous articles in the leading economic journals. He probably is most well known for his work on the demand for publicly provided goods, and on the economic analysis of property law. His *Quarterly Journal of Economics* article proposed that efficiency does not require compensation in eminent domain takings. The controversial paper spawned a substantial literature on compensation for public condemnation.

ILYA SOMIN is an Associate Professor at George Mason University School of Law. His research focuses on constitutional law, property law, and the study of pop-ular political participation and its implications for constitutional democracy. He is Co-editor of the *Supreme Court Economic Review*, and his work has appeared in numerous scholarly journals, including the *Yale Law Journal, Stanford Law Review, Northwestern University Law Review, Georgetown Law Journal*, and *Critical Review*. He also authored an *amicus* brief in *Kelo v. City of New London* on behalf of Jane Jacobs, which the Court majority cited in their opinion. In July 2009, he testified on property rights issues at the United States Senate Judiciary Committee confirmation hearings for Supreme Court Justice Sonia Sotomayor. He is currently writing a book on the *Kelo* case and its aftermath.

SAMUEL R. STALEY, Ph.D., is Director of urban and land use policy for Reason Foundation. He has written widely on eminent domain and urban economic development policy, and provided expert testimony and/or contributing to *amicus* briefs on takings cases in Arizona, Ohio, and New Jersey. His research has appeared in the Journal of the American Planning Association, the Journal of Urban Development and Planning, and numerous other professional publications. His also co-edited *Smarter Growth: Market-Based Strategies for Land Use Planning in the 21st Century* among other books.

EDWARD STRINGHAM is an Associate Professor of Economics at San Jose State University, but currently on leave and serving as the Shelby Cullom Davis Associate Professor of American Business and Economic Enterprise at Trinity College. He is a Past President of the Association of Private Enterprise Education, *Journal of Private Enterprise* Editor, and an Independent Institute Research Fellow. He won the Templeton Culture of Enterprise Best Article Award, Paper of the Year Award from the Association of Private Enterprise, Best Article Award from the Society for the Development of Austrian Economics, and Distinguished Young Scholar Award from the Liberalni Institut and the Prague School of Economics.

RICHARD L. STROUP is a Senior Fellow of the Property and Environment Research Center and an Independent Institute Research Fellow. One of the originators of the New Resource Economics, also known as free market environmentalism, he recently retired as Economics Professor at Montana State University and now teaches at North Carolina State University. His book, *Eco-Nomics: What Everyone Should Know about Economics and the Environment*, received the 2004 Sir Anthony Fisher Memorial Award. He is also recognized for coauthoring a leading textbook *Economics: Private and Public Choice*.

# Index

# INDEPENDENT STUDIES IN POLITICAL ECONOMY

## THE INDEPENDENT INSTITUTE
100 Swan Way, Oakland, CA 94621–1428, U.S.A. • 510-632-1366 • Fax 510-568-6040 • info@independent.org • www.independent.org